# JAZZ

## ISSUES

# JAZZ
# ISSUES
## A CRITICAL HISTORY

**David W. Megill**
Mira Costa College

**Paul O. W. Tanner**
University of California, Los Angeles
*(Retired)*

WCB Brown &
Benchmark
PUBLISHERS
Madison, Wisconsin • Dubuque, Iowa

**Book Team**

Editor  *Chris Freitag*
Developmental Editor  *Deborah D. Reinbold*
Production Editor  *Peggy Selle*
Photo Editor  *Robin Storm*
Permissions Coordinator  *LouAnn K. Wilson*
Visuals/Design Freelance Specialist  *Mary L. Christianson*
Marketing Manager  *Elizabeth J. Haefele*
Production Manager  *Beth Kundert*

## WCB Brown & Benchmark

A Division of Wm. C. Brown Communications, Inc.

Executive Vice President/General Manager  *Thomas E. Doran*
Vice President/Editor in Chief  *Edgar J. Laube*
Vice President/Marketing and Sales Systems  *Eric Ziegler*
Vice President/Production  *Vickie Putman*
Director of Custom and Electronic Publishing  *Chris Rogers*
National Sales Manager  *Bob McLaughlin*

## Wm. C. Brown Communications, Inc.

President and Chief Executive Officer  *G. Franklin Lewis*
Senior Vice President, Operations  *James H. Higby*
Corporate Senior Vice President and President of Manufacturing  *Roger Meyer*
Corporate Senior Vice President and Chief Financial Officer  *Robert Chesterman*

Chapter opening photo credits: Chapter 2 © 1993
Ray Avery/Michael Ochs Archives/Venice, CA.
All others: Michael Ochs Archives/Venice, CA.

Cover and interior designs by Kay Fulton

Cover and part opener images © Gary Kelley Illustration

Copyedited by Michelle M. Campbell

Printed in the United States of America by Wm. C. Brown Communications, Inc.,
2460 Kerper Boulevard, Dubuque, IA 52001

10  9  8  7  6  5  4  3  2  1

# Contents

PART 2

*Evolutionary Lines of Development*

# *Preface*

**J**azz Issues offers a comprehensive look at the critical issues that have shaped the jazz tradition. The text offers both a chronological survey of jazz with guided listening examples, as well as more involved topical chapters. The first part of the text is designed to provide readers not familiar with jazz history with an appropriate overview before the following historical topics are explored. Readers who feel the overview is unnecessary may opt to skip to the topics themselves. Because the topics are self-contained historical threads, readers can take them in any order they wish or follow the general chronology presented in the text itself.

The historical topics follow ongoing evolutionary lines that reveal the musical and cultural forces that emerge and recede and the influence they exert on the developing jazz tradition. The text is meant to be provocative. Open-ended questions are posed that encourage the reader to explore the many crosscurrents that have both shaped jazz and placed it firmly in American culture. *Jazz Issues* approaches jazz from the context of historical criticism. The macro-issues of a developing art form are central concerns for this study. It is the intent of this text to present critically the context in which the creators and listeners of jazz operate. Although the history of jazz has not always been predictable, it still has a continuity that is best understood at the largest historical level. The topical chapters in this text are situated at that topmost level.

Jazz is a uniquely American experience. This text explores influences that ushered jazz from its cross-cultural roots to the canonized art form we have today. Jazz was forged from cultural and musical interactions blended in shifting proportions. The topical chapters track these uniquely American interactions from their origins to the final emergent jazz art form they ultimately shaped.

The listening guides in the first part of the text are drawn predominantly from the *Smithsonian Collection of Classic Jazz* which has useful notes on the particular recordings.

---

ACKNOWLEDGMENTS    We would like to thank those who graciously offered their time to review and offer valued comments as this text was developed.

Gene Aitken
University of Northern Colorado

George Bouchard
Nassau Community College

Richard Davis
University of Wisconsin–Madison

David Lee Joyner
University of North Texas

Robert Washut
University of Northern Iowa

Jack W. Wheaton
University of San Diego

M. Daniel Yoder
Penn State University

# JAZZ
## ISSUES

# PART 1

## An Overview of Jazz

# INTRODUCTION

## *Toward a Definition of Jazz*

J azz has a relatively short history. Although its sources are quite old, jazz has only been in existence since the turn of the twentieth century. Its recognition as an art form has had an even shorter life span. A critical study of jazz leads to a series of questions. In the pursuit of answers, a history of interwoven forces is revealed. As we begin our study of jazz as a developing art form, we must ask ourselves questions that will lead us in our study. Not all the questions in this introduction have neat answers, yet their provocative nature will lead us along very interesting and revealing lines of inquiry. The chapters that follow this introduction pursue particular lines of study, which help us better understand the process that shaped jazz into one of America's indigenous art forms.

Art forms in general must have some common attributes; therefore, jazz must share some characteristics with other art forms in our culture, such as literature, theater, visual arts, and classical music. What are those characteristics? How does a musical development become an art form? Must the music first be popular and only later mature into an art form? At what point in a musical form's development does a culture grant it art form status? Must the art form be characterized by a smooth transition in style as it evolves—even before its art form status is recognized? If so, what are the commonalities that keep its development intact?

Jazz, by definition, must rest on some public consensus if it is to operate as an art form in our culture. How large must that consensus remain to sustain further development of the music? What is the relationship of an art form to its culture? Is it a passive reflector of current cultural values and events; is it a predictor of future trends? How much of the culture must it serve? Can there be subcultural art forms? What are the characteristics of mature art forms; are they incomplete without critics, historians, and academic acceptance? How do these accoutrements affect the future evolution of an art form? Must evolving art forms be responsible to their traditions?

**AN EMERGING ART FORM**

Certainly, these are not easy questions to address when looking at a music so close to us in both time and taste. Our knowledge of all our histories seem to expand as they draw near us. Jazz is certainly no exception. The dilemma of finding what will last and what is only fashionable is an artifact common to recent histories. We may know too much to be objective in our review of daily developments. We not only know the music, we also know the many cultural associations that are referenced by it. In fact, the many extramusical associations that travel with it are sometimes louder than the music itself.

In long relatively undocumented histories, these associations tend to be lost. However, it may be these same nonmusical experiences that we see only dimly now that were the most relevant to early listeners. Compare how much we know about the impact of liturgical chant on sixth century listeners to what we know about the fervor created by the Beatles.

The proximity of popular music poses questions now that may eventually fall through the historical cracks. For example, can the indicators of ''good'' country music be found in just the music? What does country music represent? How does it differ from ''good'' heavy metal? Heavy metal and country music certainly sound different, but they also have different musical meanings. If both musical lines were to develop art status, would later historians know how they functioned today? Similarly, how will future historians distinguish ''good'' from ''bad'' jazz as it develops in the culture of the next century?

Rock and roll, one of our most recent popular developments, offers us an insight into emerging musical traditions. Is rock following jazz's compressed evolution toward recognition as an American art form? If so, will historians place the many expressions of rock we know today under a single category and describe it as a single evolutionary line? Will history remember that heavy metal was primarily performed by white musicians and rap by black musicians? Was it important at the time? Will it be important in the future? Was jazz less diverse when it began to take shape at the turn of the century? History is sometimes accurate and sometimes misleading as it attempts to define the multifaceted origins of a new art form.

When jazz first took shape, players did not foresee its acceptance as an art form. If it had been known, perhaps better records would have been kept of how it developed. Jazz coalesced out of the many diverse musical influences present at the turn of the twentieth century. It is music that could only have developed in the United States. It required all the elements present in the nation, good and bad. It needed the rich African oral tradition of the slave culture and the formal schooling practices inherited from the western European musical tradition. It needed the urban and rural folk music, as well as the white and black church music. It needed the songs of Tin Pan Alley, the ''Roaring Twenties,'' the marching bands, the jug bands, the tenderloins, the blues, the religious fervor of the Great Awakening, and the hopelessness of slavery. Without all these elements, the recipe for jazz would have been incomplete and not the American expression it is today.

---

Trying to recreate the actual blend of musical cultures from which jazz emerged leads to a great deal of speculation. The musical examples we have are limited by the recording capabilities of the time, and these examples often are stripped of the cultural associations that they reflected. To describe the music, the written accounts tend to use a theoretical system tailored to European classical music, a written system that is significantly limited when applied to music developed out of an oral tradition. Consequently, we cannot notate the expressive singing style practiced at that time.

HISTORICAL FRAME OF REFERENCE

Without appropriate notation and audio recordings, only written descriptions are available. Like all historical accounts, these documentations tend to reflect the dominant cultural view. The language of the descriptions often reflects a frame of reference outside the musical culture being described. Such a report might overlook potentially important nonmusical associations significant to the participants.

As historians and teachers, we are tempted to focus on things that are easy to describe and to overlook other equally important musical domains. What did the expressive church music mean to the slave? Does a powerful meaning for the slave of the time turn into an intellectual curiosity for the later academic? As we look at the substance of the music, we must also strive to place it in a historical and cultural framework that gives it its meaning.

---

Along with the confusion that surrounds the beginnings of jazz also comes some controversy. Can any one culture claim jazz as its own creation? If so, on what grounds? If it belongs rightfully to one group can it be used by another? Can it be changed at will? Can it be stolen? These are not dead issues. Throughout its history, jazz has been assimilated, claimed, commercialized, and even satirized by various groups. These actions tend to mark the stylistic boundaries of the historically recognized jazz periods. These transitions are usually quite volatile and are accompanied by strong language. On the other hand, the boundaries may not be clear. They may only suggest or

JAZZ AND CONTROVERSY

reinforce already existing distinctions. For example, distinguishing characteristics between bop, hard bop, straight ahead, mainstream, progressive and neoclassical are not always easy to discern. The fact that this line of jazz was continually renamed is important, however. When concomitant jazz styles are brought into the picture, the need for name changes becomes clearer. The simultaneous activities of cool, third stream, early jazz/rock, avant-garde and fusion required renewed definition of these more mainstream activities to set them apart from the tributary styles and signal a return to the revered jazz values. The most recent call to traditional jazz values, neoclassical or ''jazz-renaissance'' sits in juxtaposition to the commercially popular fusion jazz.

Very often the controversy that surfaces at these transitions reappears repeatedly throughout jazz's history. Practitioners of an older style often dislike newer developments. However, these developments might later become a part of the jazz canon and later be heralded as a hallowed tradition style. Clearly this has happened with bop. It was not at all liked by the swing players when it first appeared in the late 1940s but has ultimately become part of, if not the foundation of, the jazz mainstream.

## ORGANIZATION OF THE TEXT

This textbook is organized around questions similar to those already offered. Because the issues raised by these questions are not restricted to specific jazz periods, each chapter will cut across many of the traditional stylistic boundaries that describe jazz periods. The overall layout is chronological. We address issues as they first occurred historically; however, once addressed, we follow the historical thread suggested by each issue to the present. Our reason for doing so is to show the larger unifying forces, both musical and cultural, that have defined jazz as an art form.

Jazz is much more than a stream of loosely related styles that center on the individual accomplishments of players and writers. There is an overlapping continuity that ties it all together. This continuity, uneven at times, is defined as much by cultural associations as by the music itself. For example, the early players in New Orleans belonged to the same tradition as the jazz/pop fusion players of the 1970s to the 1990s. The fact that there is disagreement among jazz participants about their relationship is an important factor shaping our current definition of jazz. Consider also the avant-garde jazz movement, in which the players intentionally moved away from traditional jazz approaches. Ironically, this very denial of inherited jazz practice only reinforces their station within the jazz framework.

To understand the large arches that branch over the jazz styles, a general understanding of the basic jazz periods is necessary. Therefore, in part I, chapters 1–3, we have presented a very brief overview of the stylistic periods commonly referenced in jazz appreciation texts. With a foreknowledge of stylistic developments, you can better appreciate the importance of earlier musical events, as well as how those events will manifest themselves later. A strictly chronological order is followed for this overview. Part I concludes with chapter 4, which offers some analytical tools for listening to jazz.

In part II, we explore the evolutionary lines of development that travel through jazz's history. We present the merging influences that contributed to the prejazz period in chapter 5. It is from this historically incomplete time that the issues addressed in later chapters are set in motion, issues such as the balance struck between improvisation and composition, and fashion and art.

Chapter 6 addresses the requirements of the oral tradition and how those requirements are handled in ensembles of various sizes. This balance proves symptomatic of the larger balance between the oral tradition of the African-American culture and the compositional approach revered by the European musical tradition. While chapter 6 deals with those groups founded most on the principles of the oral tradition, chapter 7 and 8 focus on the compositional forces at work in jazz and how these forces helped launch the jazz art form.

In chapter 9, we deal with the eventual recognition of jazz as an American art form. Because it is most commonly agreed that that recognition appeared during the late 1940s and 1950s, this chapter centers on the events of that time. Questions of popularity, fashion, and art are addressed, as well as the musical transitions that were occurring at that time. Instrumental and vocal legacies that shaped the jazz canon are also presented in this chapter.

Chapter 10 takes a more general look at the controversies generated by the jazz evolution. They are placed in various historical frameworks to demonstrate how they contributed to the shaping of our understanding of the jazz mainstream. This chapter also deals with changes in our historical perspective as jazz continues to evolve. It also describes the delicate balance jazz strikes between notational composition and improvisation as the mainstream continues to be defined. Chapter 11 compares the jazz art form with the classical music tradition to see what might be learned from that relationship.

Chapter 12 deals with the most current issues that confront the continued development of jazz, such as the problems that confront an art form when it is faced with renewed popularity. Like all maturing art forms, jazz risks a hardening of definition which may make it less responsive to cultural shifts. The reaction of traditionalists are placed in the context of jazz's new fusion with the popular music market. In chapter 13 we discuss the controversies that appeared in jazz as it made the transitions from one art period to the next.

## CRITICAL LISTENING

Because we are tracking historical threads, various jazz periods will be dealt with several times through the text. At each recurrence, we present those aspects of the stylistic periods that are pertinent to the historical thread at issue. There are advantages to seeing stylistic periods from different sides. By following topical lines, we can place the individual events of a jazz period in a larger perspective more relevant to a grander understanding and appreciation of how jazz has served the American culture. We will also gain an understanding of how art forms serve culture in general.

Following historical lines also offers an effective way to listen critically. By following the listening guides as they are offered, you are encouraged to draw comparisons across stylistic boundaries to see how they differ, as well as how they reflect the issues under discussion. Listening exercises will continue to crisscross throughout the text. Critical listening requires comparative skills that allow you to distinguish between the individual styles of players within a single period, as well as find commonalities shared by players across stylistic periods. For example, you will hear in one case how big bands emerged from the collective improvisations of early ensembles and, in a later instance, how they grew to become the dominant compositional medium for jazz.

## CENTRAL ISSUES

As you read and listen, we suggest you keep several primary issues in mind that continually surface throughout jazz history:

1. The balance between individual expression and stylistic expectations
2. The balance between the oral and written music traditions, as well as between compositional and improvisational intent
3. The balance between individual and group expressions
4. The growing awareness of a jazz tradition among players and critics
5. The reactions players and writers have to their understanding of that tradition
6. The reactions of players to innovations

7. The balance between the substance of the music and the cultural meaning associated with it
8. The balance between functional, fashionable, and art music and how that is reflected in both the musical substance and the theatrical presentation of a style
9. The musical leadership during transitions between stylistic periods

The musical expression of each stylistic period strikes balances. For example, compare the role of the individual player of the Big Band era with the Early Dixieland player. The former played in large ensembles with carefully composed arrangements. The latter worked in smaller ensembles structured on the more loosely defined compositional guidelines inherited from an oral tradition. Compare the performance attitude and presentation of Louis Armstrong with that of Miles Davis in the 1950s. Armstrong's smiling jazz image was the antithesis of Davis who often stood with his back to the audience. Davis saw jazz and the African-American musician's role quite differently in the 1950s than his predecessors had several decades earlier. The musical and theatrical presentations of both of these musicians are important in developing an understanding of their respective stylistic periods. This comparison also demonstrates how later jazz styles can be influenced by earlier musical and cultural events. Armstrong's improvisational style is still at work in today's players, while the role of the African-American musician has changed significantly because of changing social awareness in America. Similarly, as balances shift from style to style, so do the roles of all the participants responsible for shaping that style.

## THE JAZZ ART WORLD

Howard Becker, in his book *Art Worlds,* offers some insights into the workings of art centered networks.[1] Although an art world centers on the work of the artist who initiates the work, it also has other functional bodies. The art must be distributed. Aestheticians must establish the criteria of the art world. Critics must evaluate how the art work adheres to the criteria established by the aestheticians, and an audience must be available to receive the art. The importance of Becker's sociological model is to alert us to the many agents of an artistic effort. To apply this model rigidly to jazz is not appropriate here, but

[1]Howard Becker, *Art Worlds,* (Berkeley: University of California Press, 1982).

it is useful as a general guideline for addressing the influences that surround the making of jazz.

Because jazz is only now becoming a mature art form, Becker's model is perhaps not suitably tailored to address its earlier unstable evolution. Depending again on the balance between the jazz forces previously mentioned, a single person may be responsible for carrying out several art world functions. Jazz also has a rather difficult art work to define. Is the art work of jazz the improvisational moment? Is it the arrangements, written or not? Is it the even more rare original composition? Who were the critics before bop? Who were the critics after bop? How does the audience of avant-garde differ from that of the big bands of the 1940s? Who was the distribution force behind the development of cool in New York in the late 1940s? How did Gil Evans work in that art world in comparison to Miles Davis? Where did the art lay, in the leadership of Davis or the arrangements of Evans? Again, we have difficult questions to answer if we are to understand how cool and other jazz periods contributed to the jazz legacy. Still, Becker's approach helps us appreciate the complexity of the jazz evolutionary process, a process that has yet to be standardized and, therefore, remains rich with possibilities.

## JAZZ AND THE INDIVIDUAL

Unlike the classical music tradition often held up as a model for art traditions, jazz centers its development primarily on the momentary expression of individual performers. Although composition plays a continuing role in jazz, real-time expression is given center stage. The players who have commanded dominant positions in shaping jazz have all had individual voices that brought to the musical fabric a uniquely personal expression. Lesser figures may have commanded the musical materials but were unable to establish equally powerful voices. The unique voices of jazz continue to serve as historical markers around which stylistic periods fall.

Here lies a seemingly paradoxical aspect of jazz history. It is a history of individuals, yet it is also a continuous evolution in which these individuals participate. Which comes first? Do these expressive voices move and possibly redirect our sensibilities and thereby affect the direction of the jazz mainstream, or do they merely reflect the existing cultural values and give them a voice? It is again another question of balance which is struck anew as the players and times change.

# CHAPTER 1

## *Early Influences, Prejazz, Early Jazz*

| | |
|---|---|
| *1740 – ca1800* | The Great Awakening |
| *1861 – 1865* | Civil War, four million slaves freed |
| *1867* | Fisk Jubilee Singers organized |
| *1890 – 1917* | Basic period for Early New Orleans Dixieland |
| *1906* | Scott Joplin performed ''Maple Leaf Rag'' on a piano roll |
| *1914 – 1918* | World War I |
| *1917* | Storyville closed |
| *1917* | First instrumental jazz recorded |
| *1917 – 1932* | Roaring Twenties, Chicago Style Dixieland |
| *1920* | First vocal recording of blues, Mamie Smith's ''Crazy Blues'' |

A general overview of the periods of jazz and their chronological relationship is quite useful as we follow jazz's historical threads. You may already have a working knowledge of the primary periods of jazz and may not need to spend much time with this overview. We present this overview to help lay the foundation for later references. A short overview also allows us to stress the transitional nature of the historical continuum. How the periods are connected often reveals most about the musical substance of each period.

As the periods are discussed, listening examples will be offered to help focus your attention on the unique characteristics of each period. It is always important to keep an aural perspective of each historical period. After all, sound is the medium of jazz. To lose sight (or sound) of it reduces the history to an expressionless line of sociological and theoretical events. The dominant language of jazz has always been the music; what it expresses is the substance of the history. Because this is only an overview, not all of many important contributors can be discussed at this point. Their contributions will be addressed in more detail in later chapters when the topical lines of study are pursued.

As jazz has evolved, so have the analytical tools used to describe it. Jazz is a tradition of complex balances, balances between the oral and literate traditions, between ensemble and solo improvisation, between the African and European traditions, between compositional and improvisational intent. As such balance points shift, so must how we view and describe the actions of musicians in a particular style.

This overview describes the balance each period strikes between the oral and theoretical components of jazz practice. As we will see, sometimes the balance shifts dramatically to one extreme only to be followed by an equally dramatic reversal. The oral tradition is hardest to document historically because it is rooted in the performance practice rather than notation. A comparison might be made to the use of street language which uses words that never make it into the dictionary but carry great meaning at the time they are used, such words and phrases as *cool, hep, hip, right on, for sure, daddy-O,* and *NOT!* These words work like improvised musical phrases used in jazz which are commonly understood but have not been adopted by the formal theoretical system of jazz. Also like street language, they often fall out of favor and even become corny before they can be fully incorporated as a lasting attribute of jazz performance. Although this musical vernacular of the oral tradition seems more fashion than the foundation for a lasting tradition, it is a very important ingredient of the jazz tradition and appropriate for understanding the forces that shaped jazz.

## INTERPRETATION— THE ORAL TRADITION

Our most prominent set of analytical tools have been inherited from the classical music tradition and describe the elemental substance of music rather well. In addition to the musical substance of jazz, the interpretive nature of jazz must be addressed in order to see the entire picture. Jazz interpretation is a very elusive subject. It does not have a formal descriptive language like that of European music theory.

Like the theory, however, it also shifts with the transition to each new style and may be a primary indicator to the average listener of what style is at work. No formal music training is required to distinguish between popular music styles, such as country and rock. The average listener readily distinguishes between classical and jazz music. Certainly, the musical elements in each style signal a difference, but also the stylistic interpretation of each reinforces the delineation. From within one musical idiom finer distinctions can also be made. Only part of the difference between bop and cool can be found in the music itself. The theatrical differences also set the two styles apart. Our mental picture of each style is generally as different from one another as the two musical styles are different.

Interpretation, as used in this text, embraces even the possible antics some musicians might use to enliven their performances. It includes the unspoken conventions that guide the proper performance of a particular style. Louis Armstrong's stage presence differed greatly from that of Miles Davis. The big bands of the Swing era looked and acted differently from the avant-garde ensembles of the 1960s. The theatrics of a style sometimes helps us understand the musical interpretation applied to the music itself.

The swing feel of Early Dixieland is different from that of bop. In fact, the rhythmic feel differed among the bands of any one era. What does it mean to ''swing hard'' or ''lay back''? These actions might be describable in musical terms, but they also rest in the interpretive realm as well. Perhaps that is why using a phrase like ''jazz feel'' to address shades of interpretation seems to fall short when looking at the notation.

Interpretation of jazz is a very personal issue. Somehow the approach to any instrumental or vocal offering in the history of all musics has established an expected range of appropriate interpretations. Within these guidelines, a performance is judged as either correct or not. Granted, it is possible to be ''more correct'' or ''less correct'' according to any one particular listener. In jazz, if a player does not add individual personality to a performance, the listener feels cheated.

Interpretations accepted as a norm in one style often move out of fashion as new styles emerge. To interpret phrases in a way foreign to a particular style may even be considered bad taste. In fact, if trumpeters in the Cool era interpreted a phrase in a manner suggestive of a Dixieland style, their references would most likely be recognized by their peers as musical jokes.

THE MUSICAL
SUBSTANCE OF
JAZZ—THE
THEORETICAL
BALANCE

The musical evolution of jazz has been as eclectic as the interpretive domain. Musical theory falls along the same two general lines that have always been at work in jazz, the oral tradition and compositional practice. In most instances, the oral tradition led the way through the art form's evolution. In the earliest periods, it was the sole musical glue. It is hard to believe that any theoretical interest or even understanding was at work at all. Only later as we try to recreate that period have we used theoretical systems to define the music. The oral tradition lets music pass from generation to generation by inheritance. It is learned by modeling, not by theoretical discovery. As in other musical evolutions, theory tends to follow practice.

There were periods, however, in which theory played a larger role if not a dominant one. Bop used a much more extended harmonic vocabulary than was used earlier, and players who wished to make the transition were faced with learning the new language. Dizzy Gillespie was known to help fledgling boppers with the new chords. As bop became more mainstreamed, it also became a part of the inheritance for later players.

Other periods were also very compositionally based, for example, the swing arrangements, cool arrangements, some avant-garde, and some fusion. Theoretical understanding was essential to the writing or arranging necessary for these styles. The compositional giants of jazz are testimony to the effectiveness of jazz composition. Morton, Redman, Henderson, Ellington, Evans, Miller, Russell, and Taylor are a few across jazz's history.

The oral tradition has been the dominant stylizing agent for this compositional line of development. The arrangement or composition proved to be the voice of the composer as in other written music traditions, but it was also carried by the individual voices of the players in a way unique to this art form, for example, the voice of Hawkins with Fletcher Henderson, Miles Davis with Gil Evans, and the many voices in the Ellington band. Especially in later years, the history of jazz seems to shift alternately between the two poles of individual expression in highly improvised settings and the more formal, composed approach to jazz. Compare, for example, the big band arrangements to the small group of the same time, the cool arrangements to the return to hard bop, the third stream efforts to mainstream jazz, and the blend of both compositional thought and improvisational freedom in avant-garde jazz. While written arrangements were a more practical way of guiding large ensembles in performance, jazz composers' interest in them seem to fluctuate from period to period.

As we discuss the elements of jazz, we will include those aspects that describe the musical substance as we keep in mind the interpretive domain already described, both of which contribute to the inheritance of the jazz tradition. We recognize that the theoretical language available to us reflects predominantly the classical music practice of western Europe, but so does much of the compositional activity that we find in jazz. The balance between a conscious theoretical system and the actual interpretative expression is most aggravated in the earliest jazz stirrings which were grounded more in the practices of folk music than formal training.

---

## PREJAZZ (1850–1900)

This time before the conscious recognition of jazz as an individual music is perhaps its most important. It was then that the musical and cultural influences merged to create the uniqueness and diversity of jazz. However, because records were not kept and recordings were not available, much of the history of prejazz goes unknown. We can look back and try to recreate it by looking at the writings of the day and by projecting backwards from what we know now of jazz.

The influences seemed to come from all directions. The African musical practices that remained a part of the slave culture were superimposed on the dominant white musical culture of western Europe. The Western tradition spanned music as diverse as the songs of Stephen Foster to the operas of Wagner. The popular music of the day had simple harmonies, simple rhythms, and the form often used was AABA. The black tradition depended more on oral transmission and was represented by spirituals, work songs, field hollers, and later the blues. At this same time, four million slaves became American citizens. The four million, mixing their African background with the popular and church music around them, were to be the nucleus of jazz.

### RELIGIOUS MUSIC

Around 1800, a religious mass movement in this country known as the Great Awakening occurred. Appropriately, a great deal of the musical activity in both rural and urban America was centered in the church. The white hymnody was adopted much as the Christian religion was by the African-American church. The presentations of the Western harmonic musical idiom differed most sharply in the two cultures in the balance between melodic and harmonic interest. The African musical tradition wove highly inflected melodic lines through the harmonies, while the white church singing practice maintained an allegiance to the harmonic regularity. Spirituals and revival hymns with a great deal of emotion were commonly sung at camp meetings during the Great Awakening. Spirituals are a good example of the hybrid nature of that church music. They showed the melodic nuance typical of the African-American singing style but also reflected the harmonic underpinning of the white hymnody. Compare the vocal delivery styles of two well-known religious singers, Roberta Martin and George Beverly Shea, to hear how the two approaches differed. The white vocalist generally respected the accuracy of the pitch as written or taught orally. Their tone quality also tended to be a central concern and was seldom compromised except at very expressive moments. African-American singers used a great deal of variation in both pitch and volume as they sang. Individual notes often changed drastically in tonal quality and pitch for expressive purposes.

Even as late as these recordings were made, the vocal stylizations of African-American and white religious singers were recognizable. Listen particularly to how each of the soloists related their melodic delivery to the harmonic underpinning. Martin's vocal line is heavily inflected and floats above the harmonies, while Shea's vocal lines are rooted more in the harmonic structure of the hymn.

The Fisk Jubilee Singers came from one of the first African-American universities in the South, Fisk University, and went on tour to raise money for that college. In 1867, they introduced arranged spirituals and harmonized versions of early plantation songs, establishing even more balance between the two traditions. The early spiritual and later the gospel sound heard in the church reappears continually in jazz, particularly in the hard bop period. An anonymous saying states that each Sunday Buddy Bolden (the first known jazz band leader) went to church and that's where he got his idea for jazz music. The later gospel singing was much more harmonic than melodically driven and remnants of the quartets that were popular then continued to be visible in later popular music like the do wop groups of Motown. The greatest number of spirituals performed in the 1880s employed handclapping and foot stomping in a set pattern of emphasis on the second and fourth beats. Piano players, recalling this rhythm, executed the accentuation with the left hand and brought it into ragtime music.

The singing style heard in the early spirituals was mostly unison and was highly stylized by the oral tradition of the African slaves. Oral traditions are not bound by the restrictions of a written notation. There is a certain liberty when singing ''by ear.'' Inflections impossible to notate are common to this expressive style. Musical notation implies an exact performance and can limit interpretations. As the balance shifts between a concern for written notes and oral expression, the musical emphasis shifts between the musical influences of

The Roberta Martin Singers
''Yield Not to Temptation''
New World Records NW 224

This hymn has an AAB form with B working as the refrain.

:00   Piano introduction, gospel ornamentation is used which is also heard later in the Hard Bop era

:12   Roberta Martin enters with first verse

:26   Listen for vocal inflections typical of later gospel soloists

:40   Repeat of section A

1:05  Chorus or B section with vocal backup which is precursor of the do wop typical of the 1950s. Notice how the soloist now works like a descant above the responding vocal backup.

1:30  Stanza two, section A, similar vocal inflections. Listen for the relationship of the melody line to the harmonic underpinning, as well as the rhythmic relationship of the melody to the implied meter of the accompaniment.

1:55  Repeat of section A

2:20  Chorus, section B with similar vocal backup. Similar descant style in soloist

2:41  Retard

2:50  End

Africa and Europe. Although both the written and oral traditions can sound alike, the balance between the two practices continues to be a fundamental feature of jazz.

## INSTRUMENTAL MUSIC

There was also instrumental music in this early prejazz period. The rural groups used whatever could be found, washboards, jugs, etc. The music they played was polyphonic like the African-American church musical practice, which stressed the independently invented musical lines and, only secondarily, the resulting harmonies. It was not until these musicians moved to the city that the newer instruments were adopted and the Early Dixieland ensembles appeared.

George Beverly Shea
"The Ninety and Nine"
New World Records NW 224

This hymn has a two part structure to each verse, AB.

:00    Introduction on the reed organ
:07    Shea enters with verse 1, section A. Listen for how the chordal underpinning follows the vocal line closely rather than setting up a meter against which the soloist works.
:24    Second part of verse 1
:46    Verse 2, as in the first verse the delivery is lyric based with the harmonies following the melodic line.
1:05   Second part of verse 2, a little more extended than verse 1
1:33   Stanza 3, slight melodic variation
1:55   Second part of verse 3, section B
2:15   Extension of melody as the ending approaches
2:32   Listen for the harmonic suspension typical of classical liturgical music.
2:37   End

Military bands, important in all French settlements in both the nineteenth and twentieth centuries, also influenced the beginnings of jazz. Every secret society or fraternity had its own band, and there were bands for hire who were not attached to any organization. Most of the early jazz players started their careers in such bands. We are discussing here small, six or seven piece bands. We are not yet concerned at this point with the great concert bands of John Philip Sousa or Patrick Gilmore, who went so far as to produce a concert with a band of one thousand musicians plus a chorus of ten thousand. Rather, we are interested in the small band that marched in off the street (especially on the return from a funeral), sat down in a hall or saloon, and played the same music they had marched to, only now people danced. These marching bands became the first jazz bands. The most common instrumentation used by these bands consisted of cornet, trombone, clarinet, tuba, banjo, and drums. Buddy Bolden is considered one of the first leaders of a jazz marching band. Consequently, he is credited with establishing the set instrumentation for these bands.

## RAGTIME AND STRIDE PIANO

Musical form is another connection between this march music and early jazz. The form originated from the European minuet, which became the quadrille in America, and was then adopted by bands for marches and eventually the rag itself. "Maple Leaf Rag" is a good example: 1st section, repeat, 2nd section, repeat, 1st section, 3rd section, repeat, 4th section, repeat—AABBACCDD.

Because ragtime was primarily piano music, its interpretation took on an approach consistent with the characteristics of that instrument. Many of the ragtime players were schooled and heard their music as an extension of European classical practice, at least as far as the melodic line was concerned. However, the highly syncopated parts seemed to determine accents that were not natural for the classically trained pianist. Although there was a specific form for rags and the music was originally notated, much of the highly interpretative performance of rags might even be considered improvised. Combined with the syncopated time, the interpretive stylizations produced the "ragged" performance that gave the style its name. When Stride, an extension of ragtime, entered the picture, piano playing became louder, faster and more rhythmic. True ragtime was more relaxed by comparison.

Not all histories of jazz include ragtime as a jazz period. One of the arguments for not including it is that it was originally written rather than improvised. If this were a valid criticism, most of the accomplishments of the Basie and Ellington bands (among others) also could not be considered jazz. As we will see later, the balance between composition and improvisation is an ongoing concern among jazz participants. Another objection to including ragtime as a jazz period is that it was primarily a piano style and not an ensemble music. The legacy of jazz pianists works against this line of reasoning. Again, it is a matter of balance. How does the jazz expression of a piano soloist differ from that of a small group player? How does the activity of musicians recording in a studio where they may not even play together compare to the interactive role of a third trumpet player in a big band? The issue of group interaction as a jazz criterion is a continuing one and will be addressed in later chapters.

Ragtime recordings have become more accessible since the style was popularized by the motion picture *The Sting*. Prior to the availability of recordings, the player piano preserved and transmitted the ragtime style.

A very authentic example of ragtime piano playing is "Maple Leaf Rag" performed by the best known of all ragtime pianists, Jelly Roll Morton.

Scott Joplin
''Maple Leaf Rag''
Smithsonian A/1 (cd 1/1)

Entire selection is a piano solo.

:00   Section A: Establishes the main recognizable theme

:22   Section A: Repeat of section A forecasts Joplin's involvement with form.

:45   Section B: New theme demonstrates further attraction to syncopation.

1:07   Section B: Repeat of theme 2

1:29   Section A: Reiteration of section A theme helps the ear to hold the form together.

1:51   Section C: Playing in a higher register causes theme 3 to seem brighter even though the tempo stays firm.

2:12   Section C: Repeat of theme 3

2:33   Section D: Syncopation becomes even more daring.

2:54   Section D: Repeat sounds like improvisation which, of course, it is not.

3:14   End

# Maple Leaf Rag

*continued*

*continued*

*James P. Johnson*

Michael Ochs Archives/
Venice, CA

## James P. Johnson

James P. Johnson became the leader of the Harlem piano players when he was in his twenties. He was a schooled player with great interest in classic and semiclassic music. This interest lead him into many successful composing and arranging situations. His greatest contribution, however, was to recast the rhythms of ragtime into the swinging aggressive style known as stride piano.

*1891*  Johnson was born in New Brunswick, New Jersey, on February 11.

*1904*  He was working professionally in New York City by the age of thirteen.

*1917*  He was a leader of Harlem pianists.

*1921*  Johnson recorded ''Harlem Strut'' on the Black Swan label and ''Carolina Shout'' for Okeh Records.

*1930*  He retired to Jamaica, New York, to devote time to composing.

*1940*  Johnson was paralyzed by a stroke.

*1945*  He worked again in clubs in New York City.

*1949*  He spent time in Los Angeles writing show music.

*1951*  Another stroke left him completely paralyzed.

*1955*  Johnson died in New York City on November 17.

## BLUES

Blues was another musical influence that helped shape early jazz. It grew out of the field holler and work songs used by slaves in the late part of the nineteenth century. Slaves were not allowed to talk to one another in the fields while working, but singing was permitted. The slaves established communication between themselves by field

James P. Johnson
"Carolina Shout"
Smithsonian A/12 (cd 1/12)

Entire selection is a piano solo.

:00   Introduction, four bars
:05   Section A: 1st chorus, sixteen bars
:25   Section A: Repeat of 1st chorus
:45   Section B: Starts out with a sort of vamp type part but
        develops, sixteen bars
1:04  Section C: 3rd type of chorus, sixteen bars
1:24  Section C: Repeat of section C
1:45  Section B: Improvisation on section B theme, sixteen bars
2:01  Section D: New theme, sixteen bars
2:20  Repeat of section D theme
2:39  Coda, four bars
2:44  End

hollers, or cries, that whites did not understand. The outstanding element of the field cry that is constantly used in jazz is the bending of a tone. This is simply the overexaggerated use of a slide or slur. A tone can be bent (slurred) upward or downward to specific or nonspecific tones. The adaption of these inflections offered jazz musicians a freedom of embellishment not used in European music.

When African and European music first began to merge, the slaves sang sad songs concerning their extreme suffering. At this time, the name "blues" was not in popular use. The singing was in unison or solo and no chords or specific form were designated. After the Civil War, however, blacks could perform their music more openly

## Player Piano

The player piano, or the pianola as its predecessor was called, served a considerable service in the spread of not only ragtime, but also stride piano which was to follow. These instruments, both the sixty-five and eighty-eight key versions, were popular in homes at the beginning of the twentieth century. Ragtime, with its intricate syncopation, was a difficult music to master; therefore, player pianos were ideal for carrying this popular syncopated music into the home.

Many ragtime players, and later many stride players, made piano rolls. Because of these mechanical music makers, the compositions and the differing styles of these musicians became more identifiable to the listeners of the day, as well as realistic indicators of historical practice. Piano rolls were made by accomplished players from Fats Waller all the way back to Scott Joplin and his contemporaries; in fact, there are at least thirty-three piano rolls bearing Joplin's name. This is the only clue to his technique because he made no records.

and combined their style with European-influenced song structures. Resulting eight-bar, twelve-bar, and sixteen-bar blues forms developed from this merger. By World War I, the twelve-bar construction had become an accepted form. The chordal progression that accompanied this form was built upon the following scale tones (one measure each): I, I, I, $I_7$, IV, IV, I, I, $V_7$, $V_7$, I, I. As late as the 1960s with the influence of rock and roll, the tenth chord in the progression of harmonies has been changed to $IV_7$. This alteration is now considered standard.

## *INSTRUMENTAL INTERPRETATION AND THE ORAL TRADITION*

In the beginnings of jazz, African Americans adapted their musical interpretations to the European instruments they adopted. The natural way for these early instrumentalists to think of their musical lines was as the lines would be treated vocally. Vocal inflections were adopted as much as possible by instrumentalists. Slurring into and out of tones was an easier task on the trombone than on the clarinet or cornet.

Jelly Roll Morton
''Maple Leaf Rag''
Smithsonian A/2 (cd 1/2)

:00   Introduction: Driving very hard, influencing an era to come (swing)
:11   Section A: Shows Morton to be a master of syncopation
:27   Introduction reenters, helps to hold framework together
:33   Section B: Relief from A section, usually called a bridge
:52   Section A: Repeats but with noticeable additions in both hands
1:13  Section C: Interestingly contrasting section
1:34  Section C: Repeat with new variations
1:53  Section D: New section vacillates between a tango and a swing feeling
2:12  Section D: Repeat, this time in most acceptable stride style
2:32  End

However, both of these executed these feats with adroit fingering and lip skills. The cornet used techniques of ''half-valving.'' The attacks on notes were not as crisp as they became in later practice because these early players played as they sang.

This type of performance practice reflects the oral tradition inherent in the ''jazz voice.'' The nuances of this interpretation are impossible to transcribe using European notation. There are no symbols for notes that are sung or played between the keys on a piano nor are there adequate symbols for the bending of notes. Such microtonal variations can only be transmitted from generation to generation by oral tradition. The performers were not concerned with the notational limitations when they played, only the sonic result and its expressive content.

It might be argued that a knowledge of the notational process may actually restrict the free interpretation by a performer. Does seeing notation first preclude a wide expressive range? From the western European perspective, the improvised playing style of jazz was imprecise and was contrasted with what they viewed as the ''cleaner'' sound typical of composed pieces. Whenever a move was

## "Maple Leaf Rag"—Comparison of Joplin and Morton

**W**hen comparing these two performances from the Smithsonian Collection, the original score to "Maple Leaf Rag" should be followed conscientiously. Joplin meant his to be reproduced from the score with accuracy and precision. Keep in mind that when Joplin recorded his version, his prowess had diminished and he was not in good health. It also should be noted that he was the composer of the piece. He, no doubt, wanted to demonstrate exactly what he had conceived note for note. He was avidly true to the ragtime tradition in that the form was to be exact, and the feeling comparatively relaxed. He avowed that ragtime music was not to be played fast or forcefully.

Morton, on the other hand, displayed his outgoing (or even overwhelming) personality from the very beginning. He was aggressive and there was no hiding it. The first thing Morton did was to disrupt the deified form of the rag. Morton showed his freedom immediately by adding an introduction. He borrowed it from the second half of the A section, but except for the diminished chords, it sounds much more Morton than Joplin. His other assault on the form is his disregard for the repeats of either the A or the B sections.

It could be argued that this, the interpretation itself of "Maple Leaf Rag," demonstrates the dividing line between ragtime music and jazz. As one follows the score, it sometimes seems that all Morton salvaged from the original score was the harmonic progression. His version is much more free and loose than Joplin could ever have sanctioned. It is more rhythmic and complex than Joplin's offering and has infinitely more variety because of his refusal to divide the measures neatly into even eighth notes.

As you follow the score while listening to Morton's rendition, you may question whether these differences are improvisations, variations, or merely embellishments. Whatever the conclusion, a stylistic change is evident. Morton seems to have transformed Joplin's "Maple Leaf Rag" into a New Orleans jazz performance. It is easy to agree with those afficionados who feel Joplin's version is the dividing line between ragtime and the emergent jazz style.

## Blue Note

The blue areas settled between the third and the lowered third, and the seventh and the lowered seventh; eventually, the lowered fifth also became a staple of blue tonalities. They can be found in every type of blues vehicles, as well as in music not normally associated with blues or jazz. Notice the extensive use Joe "King" Oliver makes of the D flat over B flat major chords in his famous solo on "Dippermouth Blues" noted on page 47.

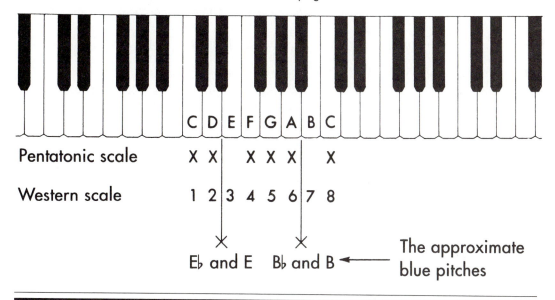

made in jazz to this more controlled type of sound, a parallel move is usually made toward the western European notational practice of preconceived music and away from spontaneous improvisations. Compare the singing practice of the early African-American spiritual with that of the shaped note readers of the Sacred Harp. Does the tradition of using a notation limit the performance style? An oral tradition has no such interpretive restrictions. However, it also does not benefit from the compositional power of notational practice. Compare the harmonic and structural shapes of cool, big band, and third stream with the more loosely woven music of Early Dixieland and bop. Chapters 6, 7, and 10 deal with the balance jazz strikes between the oral and written traditions.

## Bessie Smith
### "Lost Your Head Blues"
### Smithsonian A/4 (cd 1/11)

Bessie Smith singing "Lost Your Head Blues" with Louis Armstrong playing fill-ins on trumpet

:00  Introduction four bars. Open trumpet solo by Louis Armstrong

:11  1st chorus sung by Bessie Smith, backed by muted trumpet

:44  2nd chorus

1:17  3rd chorus

1:50  4th chorus

2:22  5th chorus

2:54  End

# Lost Your Head Blues

*Sidney Bechet*

Micheal Ochs Archives/
Venice, CA

## Sidney Bechet

**B**echet was the first jazz artist to achieve fame through the use of the soprano saxophone. Sidney Bechet's music was Sidney Bechet himself; he lived for it, going wherever it dictated. He played in various parts of the world making his audiences acutely aware of his roots through his playing of the soprano saxophone and the clarinet. His rich tone and heavy vibrato enhanced his forceful melodic creations to the point that he influenced all who followed him on these instruments.

*1897*  Bechet was born in New Orleans, Louisiana, on May 15.

*1903*  He began playing with professional bands.

*1916*  He worked with Joe "King" Oliver.

*1919*  Bechet moved to New York City.

*1920*  He traveled to Europe with Will Marion Cook's Syncopated Orchestra.

*1920*  He moved to Paris.

*1921*  Bechet returned to New York City and recorded with Clarence Williams Blue Five.

*1924*  He worked with Duke Ellington, and then returned to Europe.

*1928*  Bechet joined Noble Sissle in Paris and played with him off and on for ten years.

*1938*  He left the music business and opened a tailor shop in New York City.

*1940*  He found himself in demand again for clubs, concerts, and recordings. He traveled back and forth between New York City and Paris.

*1959*  Bechet died in Paris, a truly celebrated artist, on May 1.

## PREJAZZ SUMMARY

The combination of African and European prejazz music was a very logical phenomenon. Religious music, especially the rhythmic spirituals, was an influential precursor. Early small marching bands dictated the instrumentation, as well as much of the form and repertoire in unfledged jazz. Field hollers showed the possibility of note bending which has become a trademark of the jazz expression. African rhythms, with their steady consistent beats, were heard in the nineteenth century, and the concept of these beats lent itself logically to

Sidney Bechet
"Blue Horizon"
Smithsonian A/11 (cd 1/11)

Entire selection is a clarinet solo.

:00  Chorus 1: Sidney Bechet plays low-register clarinet, all twelve-bar blues choruses.
:42  Chorus 2: A little higher into the chalumeau register
1:27  Chorus 3
2:11  Chorus 4: Into the medium and high register
2:57  Chorus 5
3:42  Chorus 6: Long, sustained, high register
4:27  Clarinet ritards and plays out the twelve bars with a fermata at the end.

a syncopation so important to jazz. The African rhythms were characterized by a layered polyphony similar to the early vocal practice heard in the church where the use of two or more melodies of equal importance was not unusual. The resulting polyrhythms proved to be the foundation of the syncopation at work in jazz. Finally, the blues joins the harmonic substance of the Western tradition with the rich expressive presentation emanating from the slave culture, so much of jazz is still rooted in the blues.

The breadth of early prejazz influences included the many expressions of folk and popular music of the day and cut across all social boundaries. The diversity of its origins has remained as a defining characteristic of jazz and has been reflected time and again in its willingness to fuse with other emergent musical influences. Chapter 5 deals more specifically with the many prejazz influences at work during this seminal period for jazz.

SUGGESTED
LISTENING

Bechet, Sidney. "Blue Horizon." Smithsonian A/11(cd 1/11).

Classic Jazz Piano Styles. RCA Victor Records LPV 543 and 546.

Folkways Jazz Series. *Piano.* Folkways FJ 2809.

History of Classic Jazz. Vol. 2. *Ragtime.* Riverside Records
  SDP 11.

Jackson, Mahalia. "If We Ever Needed the Lord Before." *Come
  On Children, Let's Sing.* Columbia Records CS8225.

*Mahalia Jackson.* Columbia Records CL644.

Jazz Piano Anthology. Columbia Records PG 32355.

Johnson, James P. "Carolina Shout." Smithsonian A/12(cd 1/12).

Joplin, Scott. "Maple Leaf Rag." Smithsonian A/1(cd 1/1).

*Maple Leaf Rag: Ragtime in Rural America.* New World Records
  NW 235.

Morton, Jelly Roll. "Maple Leaf Rag." Smithsonian A/2(cd 1/2).

Olympia Brass Band of New Orleans. *New Orleans Street Parade.*
  BASF Records 20678.

Piano Roll Hall of Fame. Sounds Records LP 1202.

Ragtime Piano Roll. Riverside Records 126.

The Roberta Martin Singers. "Yield Not to Temptation." New
  World Records NW 224.

Shea, George Beverly. "The Ninety and Nine." New World
  Records NW 224.

Smith, Bessie. "Lost Your Head Blues." Smithsonian A/4(cd 1/4).

# CHAPTER 2

## *Early New Orleans Dixieland to Swing*

| | |
|---|---|
| *1895–1920* | Ragtime |
| *1900–1917* | Early New Orleans Dixieland |
| *1903* | Sidney Bechet began playing professionally |
| *1912–1942* | Boogie-Woogie |
| *1917–1932* | Chicago Style Dixieland |
| *1921* | James P. Johnson recorded "Carolina Shout" |
| *1932–1942* | Swing bands |

**EARLY NEW ORLEANS DIXIELAND (1900–1917)**

As rural music moved to the city and adopted new instruments, the polyphony typical of the African-American singing tradition found an expression in the style now identified as Early New Orleans Dixieland. It differed from the later Chicago Dixieland and the even later revival Dixieland in its instrumentation and rhythmic feeling. These first groups used a "front line" of a cornet, clarinet, and a trombone. The rhythm section was made up of a banjo, tuba, and drums. This instrumentation had its origin in the marching bands popular at that time and reflected the need to move while playing. The rhythm section accompanied the front line in a flat-four fashion, a rhythmic feeling that placed equal emphasis on all four beats of the measure. This equal or flat metric feel was later replaced by Chicago groups with a measure that emphasized the second and fourth beats and was referred to as 2/4 time (accents on 2 and 4). (See examples 2.1 and 2.2.)

**EXAMPLE 2.1**   Early New Orleans Dixieland (no accents—flat four or 4/4)

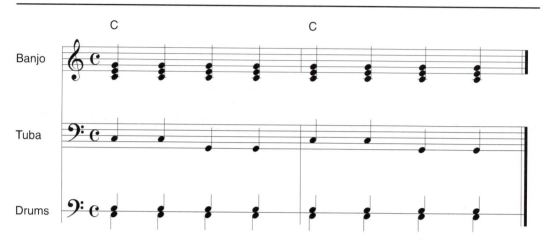

**EXAMPLE 2.2**   Chicago Style Dixieland (accented 2nd and 4th beats—2/4)

***EXAMPLE 2.3***    Early New Orleans scoring sample

The loosely knit interweaving of musical lines established an ensemble standard for group interaction that remains a criterion of jazz to the present (see example 2.3). As we will see later, the roles within the ensembles shift throughout jazz history, but the flexible interaction of players remains an important ingredient of jazz groups. At some times in history, the interaction is significantly reduced in favor of compositional goals, examples being the Big Band era, some third-stream compositions, some cool arrangements, and the recording studio practice in fusion jazz.

## King Oliver's Creole Jazz Band
### "Dippermouth Blues" also called "Sugarfoot Stomp"
### Smithsonian A/5(cd1/5)

———

:00  Introduction—ensemble

:04  Two ensemble choruses: Two cornets, clarinet, trombone. Rhythm played by piano, bass, banjo, and drums—4/4 rhythm. True collective improvisation with Oliver on lead cornet. Trombone slides into each chorus.

:33  Two choruses of clarinet solo (Johnny Dodds). The rest of the band plays what is called "stop time"; it seems to make the solo more predominant.

1:03  Ensemble chorus, same pattern as first chorus.

1:17  Three choruses of cornet solo by Oliver; note his use of the plunger as a mute for his instrument. The clarinet and trombone also play as in an ensemble chorus, except now they are very soft.

1:58  Vocal break ("Oh play that thing!")

2:00  Ensemble chorus similar to the first chorus but a short tag is added on the end.

2:16  End

*King Oliver's Creole Jazz Band*
© 1993 Ray Avery/Michael Ochs Archives/Venice, CA

*King Oliver's Version of "Dippermouth Blues"*

*First two choruses of Oliver's cornet solo on "Dippermouth Blues"*

Of all the jazz styles, Early New Orleans Dixieland recordings are the most difficult to locate. However, repressings by recording companies have eased this problem. The recordings by Joe "King" Oliver have established themselves as the most typical examples of Early New Orleans Dixieland jazz. Oliver's recording of "Dippermouth Blues" offers a good example of this style.

## CHICAGO STYLE DIXIELAND (THE 1920s)

The merger of New Orleans Style Dixieland with ragtime style led to what is now referred to as Chicago Style Dixieland. This style exemplified the Roaring Twenties, or to quote F. Scott Fitzgerald, "the jazz age." Chicago was exciting at this time and so was its music. In 1917 with the closing of Storyville in New Orleans, Chicago became the center of jazz activity. Many workers from the south migrated to Chicago and brought with them a continued interest in the type of entertainment they had left behind.

The New Orleans instrumentation was augmented to include a saxophone and piano and the influence of ragtime added a 2/4 backbeat to the rhythmic feel. The banjo moved to guitar and the tuba moved to string bass. The tempos were generally less relaxed than New Orleans Dixieland, and the music seemed more aggressively performed (see example 2.4).

There was jazz activity in other cities as well, mainly New York and Kansas City. These centers would later claim center stage as they moved toward a definition of swing, but during the 1920s Chicago remained the hub of jazz. Examples of Chicago Style Dixieland follow:

Miff Mole's "Original Dixieland One Step," Folkways Jazz, Vol. 7
New Orleans Rhythm Kings' recording of "Sweet Lovin' Man," Folkways Jazz, Vol. 6
The Wolverine Orchestra recording of "Jazz Me Blues," Folkways Jazz, Vol. 6
Bix Beiderbecke's recording of "Somebody Stole My Gal" and "Margie," Folkways Jazz, Vol. 6

During this time in Chicago, Louis Armstrong's influence as a soloist was influencing the fabric of the otherwise democratic ensemble. His individual style started the trend toward the soloist being the primary spokesperson for jazz. His artistry can be heard in "West End Blues," in the *Smithsonian Collection of Classic Jazz.*

*EXAMPLE 2.4*  Typical scoring for Chicago Style Dixieland

Louis Armstrong
''West End Blues''
Smithsonian B/4(cd 1/17)

:00 Armstrong on solo trumpet cadenza (unaccompanied solo passage) as introduction

:13 Ensemble chorus. Trumpet plays melody, and clarinet and trombone mainly play sustained notes as harmony. Rhythm plays 4/4 with piano, banjo, bass, and drums.

:49 Trombone solo by Fred Robinson. Rhythm section plays 4/4 except drummer who attains special effects by hitting blocks and other items.

1:21 Voice (Armstrong) and low-register clarinet (Johnny Strong) alternate measures, rhythm in 4/4.

1:55 Earl Hines plays a piano solo.

2:07 Hines (on piano) goes into his style of octaves in the right hand, mainly double-time.

2:28 Ensemble chorus: trumpet, clarinet, trombone all play long sustained notes, 4/4 rhythm.

2:40 Trumpet goes into more of a solo, while others continue their sustained notes.

2:52 Hines plays a short solo piano interlude.

3:00 Trumpet, then other ensemble instruments join in

3:10 End

*Armstrong's introductory cadenza to ''West End Blues''*

*Armstrong's version of the melody for ''West End Blues''*

## Chicago Dixieland

It was the Roaring Twenties, what F. Scott Fitzgerald called the jazz age. There were straw hats and arm bands, both Model T and Model A Fords, as well as Stutz Bearcats, raccoon coats, and speakeasies. Gangsters ruled Chicago during this period, and with the musicians playing in the saloons, there is no question that these same racketeers had a great deal to say about the careers of the musicians.

In spite of the fact that Chicago was almost entirely in the hands of gangsters, these were happy times for the general public. Life seemed to be based on having fun. In fact, musicians today call Dixieland music "happy music." World War I was over, and the big stock market crash of 1929 was not even envisaged. Life seemed to be a party.

**THE CHICAGO STYLE**

The theatrical presentation of the music reflected the excitement of the 1920s. A listener has a feeling that these players were on top of the beat, never behind it as in later styles such as cool. Chicago Style Dixieland players approached their musical lines in much the same manner that they approached life.

This is surely a clear case of social outlooks influencing art. Granted, New Orleans trumpet players had become more raucous as time progressed, even to the point of using plungers over the bells of their horns. By comparison, the players in the Chicago area, even those transplanted from elsewhere, approached their melodic lines in a much more aggressive manner. The attacks on notes were more crisp, extreme registers were used more often, and generally everything was played louder and faster.

**BOOGIE-WOOGIE (1920s–1930s)**

Boogie-Woogie is a jazz style that seems quite accessible to the listener. It is a piano style that was occasionally orchestrated successfully. This full-sounding style came into existence when it became necessary to hire a piano player to substitute for an orchestra. The resulting ''barrel-house'' piano which could be found in rural southern juke joints tried to imitate the sound of three guitars: one playing the chords, one the melody, and one the bass.

# Bix Beiderbecke/Frankie Trumbauer
## "Riverboat Shuffle"
### Smithsonian B/9(cd 1/22)

———

:00    Introduction: one bar piano, one bar saxophones, one bar brass, one bar ensemble

:04    Four bars trumpet break (Beiderbecke)

:08    Repeat of eight bar introduction

:16    Chorus 1: Ensemble thirty-two bars, trombone shows the way harmonically.

:51    Chorus 2: First sixteen bars of C melody saxophone solo backed by brass riffs, bars fifteen and sixteen a saxophone break

1:08    Sax solo again with brass riffs in background

1:17    Four bars ensemble

1:21    One bar saxophone break, one bar ensemble, one bar saxophone break, one bar ensemble

1:26    Two bars saxophone section on augmented chord

1:28    Two bars ensemble leading to trumpet solo chorus

1:30    Chorus 3: Trumpet solo (Beiderbecke), bars fifteen and sixteen a break

1:47    Fourteen bars—continuation of trumpet solo

2:03    Two bars piano break

2:05    Interlude—two bars ensemble

2:07    Chorus 4: High clarinets for thirty bars, bars fifteen and sixteen a break

2:41    Two bars trumpet break

2:43    Twelve bars trumpet solo

2:56    Four bars ensemble

3:00    Fourteen bars ensemble similar to 1st chorus

3:16    Two bars break with brass

3:18    End

*Frankie Trumbauer and his Celebrated Recording Orchestra*

Michael Ochs Archives/
Venice, CA

*EXAMPLE 2.5*   Typical Boogie-Woogie bass lines

Most boogie-woogie is played on the blues chord progression with a repeated ostinato. The definite feeling of eight beats to the measure is the signature of this style (see example 2.5).

Listen to Meade Lux Lewis playing "Honky Tonk Train."

Notable among the many boogie-woogie players were Albert Ammons, Pine Top Smith, Jimmy Yancey, Joe Sullivan, Clarence Lofton, and Pete Johnson. The later players included Freddie Slack, Cleo Brown, and Bob Zurke.

## SWING (1932–1942)

There are myriad recordings available of the swing bands. This particular means of expression in jazz became the most listened-to music in the world and nostalgia guarantees its popularity today. The popularity of this style may be in part the engine behind the ultimate acceptance of jazz as a canonized art form.

The swing bands showed a highly organized approach to performing jazz. The fact that the bands were increasing in size presented problems for ensemble performance. This problem was solved in two different ways and in two different geographical locations, New York and Kansas City. The arrangements for the New York bands became an organizing tool for the ensembles. Fletcher Henderson is most

## Meade Lux Lewis
### "Honky Tonk Train"
### Smithsonian C/4(cd 11/6)

:00   Piano solo throughout. Trill for short introduction

:02   Chorus 1: Left hand playing "full moving chords" pattern, right hand playing melodically and very independently

:19   Chorus 2: Lewis shows his control by playing six beats with the right hand, while playing eight beats with the left. This occurs often on this record.

:36   Chorus 3

:53   Chorus 4: Picks up last small idea from previous chorus and expands on it

1:10   Chorus 5: Uses trills and shows extreme independence of hands

1:27   Chorus 6: Shows a small thought then develops a technical display

1:44   Chorus 7: Many full chords and use of the "6 against 8" as in chorus 2

2:02   Chorus 8: Similar to chorus 7

2:19   Chorus 9

2:36   Chorus 10: Getting softer, seems to be tapering down, preparing to stop

2:57   End

*Meade Lux Lewis*

Michael Ochs Archives/
Venice, CA

known for helping this emerging large ensemble take shape in New York. With the help of arrangers like Don Redman, the bands were sectionalized along the same lines first used in the front line of Early Dixieland. The clarinet/saxophone section balanced the trumpet and trombone sections (see example 2.6). These first ensembles were not yet as big as they would become later in the early 1940s.

Even though there were many bands, and though the means of organizing swing arrangements were fairly standard throughout New York, most of the bands developed their own identifying features, which often resided in the arrangements themselves. The bands grew in size to accommodate the large ballrooms that flourished in response to a growing dance craze. The more blues-oriented Kansas City bands generally used less detailed arrangements and used the sectionalization also seen in the New York bands to set up improvised riffs to establish a theme or to back up soloists. The more structured arrangements of the New York bands might be tied to the theater shows for which they sometimes played. Listen to Fletcher Henderson's band play ''The Stampede'' or ''Wrappin' It Up'' for an example of the New York style. Count Basie's recording of ''Taxi War Dance'' is a good example of the riffing style of the southwest bands.

---

## SWING STYLE

The swing players, generally speaking, were more schooled than their predecessors. Playing exactly in tune was often a more important issue than the feeling of the part. In Early New Orleans Dixieland for example, the feeling of the phrase was of much more concern than any other aspect of playing. Some distinction should be drawn between the African-American and white bands in this matter. The white bands tended to avoid inflections that would disturb the ensemble's blend. Because of their size and the nature of the sectionalization, everyone in the ensemble had to conscientiously start and stop each note together. There was a protocol that was silently agreed upon. Some bands played a bit on top of the beat and some played a trifle behind the beat. A newcomer to a band would do well to listen intently to the rhythmic approach of that particular group in order to fit well into the ensemble. The African-American bands generally had a looser ensemble style that reflected more individual inflections. This generalization has, of course, some dramatic exceptions. The late Basie band became an ensemble machine. Its controlled balance among players has seldom been rivaled. However, even that balance was a result of listening more than reading. The musical reading skills of the players were not necessarily their strong point. The notation of the arrangements could not possibly reflect such nuances of performance interpretations.

***EXAMPLE 2.6***  Typical scoring for swing bands

## Count Basie
### "Taxi War Dance"
### Smithsonian D/6(cd 11/21)

:00  Introduction consists of four measures piano solo (Count Basie) in a boogie-woogie pattern followed by four measures brass.

:09  Chorus 1: Tenor sax solo (Lester Young) for sixteen measures (rhythm plays 4/4 except piano)

:27  Eight measures as bridge of chorus, still tenor sax solo

:36  Eight measures to finish up the chorus, same as first eight measures of this first chorus

:48  Chorus 2: Trombone solo (Dickie Wells) for thirty-two measure chorus with the same chords for the bridge that were used in the first chorus

1:24  Chorus 3: Four measures of brass

1:28  Four measures of tenor sax solo (Buddy Tate)

1:33  Repeat of the above eight measures

1:43  Eight measures of piano solo on the bridge chords

1:51  Four measures of brass

1:56  Four measures of tenor sax solo

2:01  Chorus 4: Four measures of full ensemble (piano playing boogie-woogie pattern)

2:06  Four measures of tenor sax solo (Lester Young)

2:10  Repeat of above eight measures

2:19  Eight measures of piano solo on bridge chords

2:28  Four measures full ensemble

2:33  Four measures tenor sax solo

2:38  Two measures brass, two measures tenor sax (Buddy Tate), two measures bass solo (Walter Page), two measures drums (Jo Jones)

2:47  Full ensemble ending

2:50  End

*Count Basie*

Michael Ochs Archives/
Venice, CA

There were some idiosyncrasies that were fairly standard. Triplet eighth notes were played evenly, not so triplet quarter notes. The third note was delayed just a trifle, as shown in example 2.7.

**EXAMPLE 2.7**

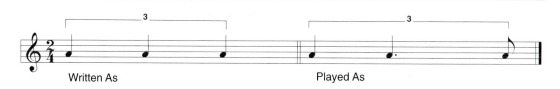

A swing player seldom encountered straight eighth notes, but the dotted eighths and sixteenths were played in a manner always identified as swing style. Notes written as either straight eighths or dotted eighths and sixteenths would normally be played more like triplets as shown in example 2.8.

**EXAMPLE 2.8**

But even here there was room for variation. Consider how the territory band of Lawrence Welk "swung" its eighth notes to that of Count Basie's band (see example 2.9). The second of two eighth notes varied as to how far back it was pushed in the beat and how much accent it received. Welk's style pushed the second eighth far back in the beat, and Basie's style (late band) used more even eighths but strongly accented the second. It became a matter of band style.

*EXAMPLE 2.9*

Welk's Swing Style                                    Basie's Swing Style

Tonguing on the wind instruments was done very hard and aggressively on the loud fast tunes and very soft and delicately on the slow pretty ballads. The players' interpretations no longer imitated the voice as in early jazz, the opposite was now in vogue. To play cleanly was the aim of many of the swing bands, and they even looked the part. They had clean neatly pressed uniforms with middle-of-the-road hair styles and no beards. The audiences wanted them to be neat, controlled, and to appear as if they were having a good time being the entertainers. In general, their playing was neat and controlled.

The later big bands most commonly associated with the Swing era, Goodman, Miller, Ellington and again Basie still reflect the different origins of big band swing. During this later period, the bands became formalized into the ensemble structure we still hear today in groups like the Mel Lewis Orchestra, Tashiko Akiyoshi, and Bob Mintzer and the many school ensembles.

## SMALL GROUP SWING

At the same time that the big bands captured the attention of the American public, there were also small groups that worked in the swing style. Often these groups were subdivisions of the larger bands. One example of such a group is Benny Goodman's Sextet and their recording of "I Found a New Baby."

The smaller group offered soloists the opportunity for more extended solos. Players like Coleman Hawkins flourished both in and out of the big band. His solo on "Body and Soul" is a classic. In this recording, the band takes a back seat to the soloist who is featured throughout.

## Duke Ellington Orchestra
### "In a Mellotone"
### Smithsonian E/3(cd III/17)

:00    Piano solo as introduction: eight measures with unison saxes taking pickups on last measure

:14    Chorus 1: Unison saxes with trombones playing an elaborate backup—thirty measures

1:11    Two measure piano interlude

1:14    Chorus 2: Cootie Williams on trumpet solo with plunger—saxes back up—thirty-two measures with ensemble pickups in the last measure

2:16    Chorus 3: Four measures ensemble

2:24    Alto sax solo by Johnny Hodges, four measures plus next six measures

2:44    Two measure break by Hodges on alto sax

2:47    Eight measure solo by Hodges on alto sax

3:02    Ensemble alternates measures with Hodges on sax for six measures

3:15    Ensemble plays out softly

3:19    End

*Duke Ellington Orchestra*

Michael Ochs Archives/
Venice, CA

# Benny Goodman Sextet (without Goodman)
## "Blues Sequence"
### Smithsonian D/9(cd 11/24)

Featuring Charlie Christian on guitar.

:00  Tenor sax and trumpet with cup mute in unison for the first four measures of the blues chord progression

:05  Solo by Charlie Christian on guitar for the remaining eight measures of the blues plus another twelve measure chorus. This routine continues.

:28  Trumpet and sax unison for four measures

:32  Christian solos eight plus twelve measures

:55  Trumpet and sax unison for four measures

1:00  Christian solos eight plus twelve measures

1:24  Trumpet and sax unison for four measures

1:29  Christian solos eight plus twelve measures

1:52  Trumpet and sax unison for four measures

1:57  Christian solos eight plus twelve measures

2:20  Trumpet and sax unison for four measures with fade

2:24  End

*Benny Goodman and Orchestra*

Michael Ochs Archives/ Venice, CA

## Benny Goodman Septet
### "I Found a New Baby"
### Smithsonian D/8(cd 11/23)

———

Benny Goodman, clarinet; Cootie Williams, trumpet; Count Basie, piano; Georgie Auld, tenor sax; Charlie Christian, guitar; Jo Jones, drums; Artie Bernstein, bass.

:00 Introduction: Two measures brushes

:02 Four measures unison tenor sax and trumpet with cup mute, Goodman on clarinet takes pickups on last measure

:06 Chorus 1: Goodman solos on clarinet backed by trumpet and tenor sax for thirty-two measures. Goodman varies between interpretation and improvisation.

:45 Chorus 2: Charlie Christian guitar solo for thirty-two measures

1:22 Chorus 3: Count Basie piano solo backed by sax and trumpet for sixteen measures

1:41 Bridge of the tune: Basie and Goodman toy with call and response for eight measures

1:49 Basie on piano solo for eight measures

1:58 Chorus 4: Sixteen measures of trumpet solo

2:16 Tenor sax solo with light horn riffs in the background

2:35 Eight measures drum solo

2:44 Ensemble for eight measures, a complete six-way jam session

2:54 End

Coleman Hawkins
"Body and Soul"
Smithsonian C/6(cd 11/8)

———

The entire selection is a tenor sax solo.

:00   Four-bar piano introduction

:09   Chorus 1: Solo starts close to melody in fairly low register and gradually plays a little higher.

1:30  Sixteen bars of sustained brass background, solo becomes more intense.

2:14  Eight-bar bridge, brass tacit

2:35  Six bars—brass sustained back in, solo now becomes very aggressive.

2:51  Ritard—tenor saxophone alone

2:59  Brass sustained on fermata at end

3:03  End

**SUGGESTED LISTENING**

Armstrong, Louis. "West End Blues." Smithsonian B/4(cd 1/17).

Count Basie. "Taxi War Dance." Smithsonian D/6(cd 11/21).

Bechet, Sidney. *Master Musician.* Bluebird Records 2 AXM 5516.

Beiderbecke, Bix and Frankie Trumbauer. "Riverboat Shuffle." Smithsonian B/9(cd 1/22).

*Benny Goodman Carnegie Hall Concert.* Columbia Records OSL 160.

Benny Goodman Sextet. "Blues Sequence" ("Breakfast Feud"). Smithsonian D/9(cd 11/24).

*The Best of Basie.* Columbia Records C3L 33.

*The Best of Dixieland.* RCA Victor Records LSP 2982.

*Big Band Jazz.* Smithsonian DMK 3-0610 cassette edition RC030.

*Big Bands' Greatest Hits.* Columbia Records CG 31212.

*The Bix Beiderbecke Legend.* RCA Victor Records LPM 2323.

*The Bix Beiderbecke Story,* Vols. 1 and 2. Columbia Records CL 8446.

*Boogie Woogie Piano, Original Recordings, 1938–1940.* Columbia Records KC 32708.

*Cuttin' the Boogie.* New World Records NW 259.

Ellington, Duke. "In a Mellotone." Smithsonian E/3(cd III/7).

*The Ellington Era.* Columbia Records C3L 27.

Folkways, Vols. 5–10.

Goodman, Benny. "I Found a New Baby." Smithsonian D/8(cd 11/23).

*The Great Benny Goodman.* Columbia Records CL 826.

Hawkins, Coleman. "Body and Soul." Smithsonian C/6(cd 11/8).

Henderson, Fletcher. *Developing An American Orchestra, 1927–1947.* Smithsonian R 006.

*Jammin' For the Jackpot.* New World Records NW 217.

*Jazz at Preservation Hall.* Atlantic Records S 1409–1 and 1410.

Jazz in Revolution. *The Big Bands in the 1940s.* New World Records NW 284.

*Jive at Five.* New World Records NW 274.

King Oliver's Creole Jazz Band. "Dippermouth Blues." Smithsonian A/5(cd 1/5).

Lewis, Meade Lux. "Honky Tonk Train." Smithsonian C/4 (cd 11/6).

*Little Club Jazz.* New World Records NW 250.

*Louis Armstrong.* RCA Victor Records VPM 6044.

*Louis Armstrong and Earl Hines.* Columbia Records CL 853.

*Louis Armstrong and His Hot Five.* Columbia Records CL 851.

Original Dixieland Jazz Band. *Jazz Odyssey,* Vol. 1. Columbia Records C3L 30.

*The Original Dixieland Jazz Band.* RCA Victor Records LPV 547.

*This Is Benny Goodman.* RCA Victor Records VPM 6040.

Turner, Joe and Pete Johnson. "Roll 'Em Pete." Columbia Records 35959.

*The World of Swing.* Columbia Records F6 32945.

# CHAPTER 3

## *Bop to the Present*

| | |
|---|---|
| *1940–1950* | Bop emerged |
| *1949* | Cool |
| *1954* | Hard bop/funky gained prominence |
| *1960* | Free form, third stream |
| *1969* | Miles Davis records *Bitches Brew* |
| *1970s* | Early fusion, Weather Report and Return to Forever |
| *1980–1990* | Jazz/rock/pop fusion and neoclassical |

Although the swing style may have launched the art status of jazz by placing it in the ears and minds of the world, it was its successor, bop, which claimed mainstream status. More significant changes, both musical and nonmusical, occurred in jazz with the advent of bop than at any other time in jazz history. The military service draft of World War II brought about the dissolution of the big bands and the rise of small combos. The country was nervous, and the music was nervous and agitated. Because many well-known players were in the military, new, young players and their ideas were able to get exposure.

There were considerable changes in techniques and attitudes toward performances. There also were changes of attitude toward audiences. Bop became the first jazz style that was not used for dancing. Consequently, there were great changes in the repertoire. There was also a shift away from the popularity that swing enjoyed to a more elite listening audience. The elitism also expanded to the players. If you were an accomplished swing player, there was no guarantee that you would be able to survive the expectations of the bop musical world. The music's complexity required players to extend their

**BOP (1940–1950)**

former playing knowledge and technique. A theoretical underpinning began to emerge as players stretched the harmonic boundaries of early jazz styles. Players had to have a greater and more immediate sense of chord recognition, as well as their extensions and possible substitutions. The music was generally fast, demanding execution on individual instruments seldom required by previous styles. It is interesting that bop is today considered the mainstream of jazz style, yet it was not enthusiastically accepted by the jazz community at the time of its emergence.

The two most notable players of this style were Dizzy Gillespie and Charlie Parker. Their playing on ''Shaw 'Nuff'' is a good example of what this style expected of its players.

## BOP STYLE

Bop playing mirrored the frenzy of its times. The playing reflected the frantic world in turmoil because of World War II. At this time, interpretation of jazz was aggressive. Dizzy Gillespie and Roy Eldridge both played very high, very fast, and quite loudly. Charlie Parker played in a driving manner with his sure attacks of unusually creative phrases. Jimmy Blanton moved his bass lines higher and played them faster than had been considered logical on such a large instrument. Charlie Christian proved, with the invention of the amplifier, that the guitar could be just as impressive as the wind instruments. It is generally conceded that Eldridge, Blanton, and Christian must be considered precursors of the bop movement. Their great distinctions during the Swing era proved a strong forecast of future possibilities. Perfect unison was not as much the issue as how unusual the unison line that was being performed. Straight eighth notes were more logical on such fast lines and helped to distinguish bop interpretation from swing. However, on the straight eighths (especially noticeable on slower tunes) every other note was emphasized as shown in example 3.1.

*EXAMPLE 3.1*

Although there were good tones (by European standards) being used, such as Parker's, the main issue was the accomplishment of such difficult melodic lines rather than the interpretation of individual notes.

Dizzy Gillespie and Charlie Parker
"Shaw 'Nuff"
Smithsonian E7(cd 111/11)

Charlie Parker, alto sax; Dizzy Gillespie, trumpet; Al Haig, piano;
Curley Russell, bass; Sidney Catlett, drums.

:00   Eight measures—drums, bass, and bass of piano
:06   Trumpet and alto sax in thirds for eight measures
:13   Six measures of unison ending with famous "Salt Peanuts"
       phrase
:17   Piano break for two measures
:18   Unison main theme (head) for thirty-two measures
:47   Alto sax solo by Charlie Parker for thirty-two measures
1:14  Trumpet solo by Dizzy Gillespie for thirty-two measures
1:41  Piano solo for thirty-two measures
2:08  Original theme in unison as chorus 1
2:36  Same as top of record—drums, bass, and bass of piano—
       for eight measures
2:43  Trumpet and sax in thirds again
2:50  Eight bars of unison as in the earlier part of the record
2:56  End

*Charlie Parker and Dizzy
Gillespie*

© 1994 Herman Leonard/
Michael Ochs Archives/
Venice, CA

## Charlie Parker's Re-Boppers
### "KoKo"
### Smithsonian E/8(cd 111/12)

:00  Introduction: Unison alto sax (Charlie Parker) and muted trumpet (Dizzy Gillespie), drums with brushes using many accents (Max Roach)

:06  Muted trumpet solo, drums continue as before.

:12  Alto sax solo, drums the same

:19  Alto sax and muted trumpet in parallel harmony, drums the same

:25  Chorus 1: Alto sax solo, drums on a fast 4/4 rhythm plus accents, bass playing a very fast walking style (Curley Russell), piano enters with his own chordal punctuations. If the piano seems a trifle late, that is because that is also Gillespie. He had to put his trumpet down.

:50  Bridge of first chorus—change of chords

1:04  Last part of first chorus

1:15  Chorus 2: Still Parker on alto sax

1:40  Bridge of second chorus

1:54  Last part of second chorus

2:07  Drum solo—very intricate as far as the pulse is concerned (this gives Gillespie time to go from piano to the trumpet).

2:27  Alto sax and muted trumpet in unison, drums now on cymbals

2:34  Muted trumpet solo, drums the same

2:40  Alto sax solo, drummer a bit lighter on cymbals now

2:45  Alto sax and muted trumpet in parallel harmony (a reminder of the introduction for the sake of continuity)

2:49  End

*Charlie Parker*

Michael Ochs Archives/
Venice, CA

"KO-KO" By Charles Parker, Jr. © 1946 Renewed 1974 SCREEN GEMS-EMI MUSIC INC./ATLANTIC MUSIC CORP. All Rights for the U.S.A. controlled and administered by ATLANTIC MUSIC CORP. All rights for the World excluding the U.S.A. controlled and administered by SCREEN GEMS-EMI MUSIC INC. All Rights Reserved. International Copyright Secured. Used by Permission.

## COOL (1949–1955)

Cool jazz followed bop but was entirely different in mood, in its approach to arranging, and even in its choices of instruments. World War II was over—the country was relaxed and jazz relaxed.

In this era many instruments were used in jazz for the first time. Softer-sounding instruments, unamplified, created a different mood from that expressed earlier. The G.I. Bill made schooling possible for many jazz players, which encouraged experimentations in jazz that had been previously ignored: new meters, longer forms, and explorations in orchestration. Longer forms were also made possible by the introduction of long-playing records.

Although Lester Young came primarily out of the swing style and Miles Davis out of the bop style, they are two of the players associated with the development of the cool style. Young's contribution was the relaxed sound and style of his playing. Davis's work with Gil Evans that led to the recording of the "Birth of the Cool" signaled the beginning of that period. Although these first recordings appeared in New York, many of the later cool groups worked out of Los Angeles and were former members of the Stan Kenton band. Players like Gerry Mulligan, Shelly Manne, and Stan Getz were often associated with this "West Coast" style. Listen to Young's style on "Lester Leaps In" and Davis's "Boplicity" to hear examples of the cool sound. Also listen to Miles Davis on "Summertime" to hear the sonorous sounds typical of Gil Evans's arrangements.

The cool sound was exemplified by players like Paul Desmond on alto saxophone, Chet Baker on trumpet, and George Shearing on piano. These players all typified the relaxed sound and manner of performance associated with cool.

## COOL STYLE

The cool players approached their music in an extremely "laid back" fashion. They had a tendency to play behind the beat, which seldom became very fast. These players stayed in the middle or lower registers of their instruments. It was another case of the feeling prevalent in the world being expressed through the art form. World War II was over. Relaxation was the new manner of expression. If a musician played at all aggressively, he or she was surely out of the style of cool. Many of these players were conservatory trained and knew that a sense of balance in their polyphony was of utmost importance. Aided by improved recording techniques, new instruments (to jazz) entered the scene: flute, oboe, cello, and flugelhorn to mention a few. These are softer sounding instruments and usually, even though in a jazz setting, meant to be played in a legitimate manner. Harsh attacks or aggressive phrasing were out of keeping. The sound was serious, yet relaxed.

## Lester Young and Count Basie
### "Lester Leaps In"
### Smithsonian D/7(cd 11/22)

:00  Four measure piano introduction

:08  Eight measures then repeated—tenor sax, trombone, and trumpet in cup mute in three-part harmony

:19  Bass and piano—eight measure bridge

:27  First theme repeated

:35  Chorus 2: Lester Young solos on tenor sax for thirty-two measures

1:08  Chorus 3: Piano and sax interplay for eight measures.

1:16  Sax solos alone for eight measures.

1:24  Eight measure bridge—sax solo

1:32  Sax alone for six measures, rhythm comes in on next two measures

1:40  On fourth chorus, piano and sax trade fours, first the piano for four measures

1:44  Sax for four measures

1:48  Piano for four measures

1:52  Sax for four measures

1:56  Piano for four measures

2:00  Sax for four measures

2:04  Piano for four measures

2:08  Sax for four measures

2:12  Fifth chorus is still different, ensemble for four measures.

2:16  Sax for four measures

2:20  Ensemble for four measures                    ***continued***

*continued*

*Lester Young*

Michael Ochs Archives/
Venice, CA

2:24   Piano for four measures
2:28   Piano for the eight measure bridge
2:36   Ensemble for four measures
2:40   Sax for four measures
2:45   Sixth chorus starts with ensemble for four measures.
2:49   Bass solo for four measures
2:53   Ensemble for four measures
2:57   Bass for four measures
3:01   Bass and piano for eight measures
3:09   Ensemble for four measures
3:13   Ensemble plays the last four measures out in jam session style.

## Miles Davis
### "Boplicity"
### Smithsonian F/8(cd IV/1)

:00  Chorus 1 (no introduction): Trumpet lead (Miles Davis), bass and drums play a relaxed 4/4 rhythm throughout, piano plays gentle chordal punctuations.

:27  Bridge—change of melody and chords

:42  Last part of first chorus

:56  Chorus 2: Baritone sax solo (Gerry Mulligan), rhythm section continues as before.

1:24  Bridge—sax unison with French horn, trombone, and tuba

1:35  Trumpet solo

1:42  Last part of second chorus, slight variation on the original eight measures of the tune, ensemble

1:58  Chorus 3: Trumpet solo, sustained harmonic background

2:25  Bridge—piano solo (John Lewis) sustained harmonic background for half of solo (saxes, trombone, French horn, tuba)

2:40  Ensemble with the original melody

2:57  End

*Miles Davis*

Michael Ochs Archives/
Venice, CA

## HARD BOP—FUNKY (CIRCA 1954–     )

When introduced, bop was as unpopular as swing had been popular. The complexity of the style often left the audience behind. The funky players were interested in recapturing that audience and reestablishing the "hot" jazz expression that had been abandoned by the cool style. This return was enthusiastic and reached back to the most communicative music in their past—church music. Another motive, less defined and certainly debatable, was the need to reclaim jazz as a predominantly African-American expression. Cool, and particularly West Coast jazz, was predominantly white even though Davis and Young were the forerunners. The structured, soft-spoken arrangements were certainly more typical of the European tradition than the expressive African-American voice first heard in the early blues.

The public accepted this moving music joyfully and appreciated the opportunity to participate once again in jazz performances. Funky jazz uses simpler harmonies, an emphasis on rhythm, easily recognizable tunes, and anything else that players like Horace Silver could invent to increase the audience's involvement and pleasure. Gospel jazz is an extension of funky jazz. Funky jazz can be heard in the performances of Bobby Timmons with Art Blakey, as well as with Cannonball Adderly. The adoption of gospel idioms by Les McCann could place his performances in the church as easily as on stage or in the night club.

## HARD BOP STYLE

Funky piano players imitated the church music they had heard earlier. Their approach was more aggressive but quite simple. It was a step back to a previous catalog of sounds—gospel. The wind players played more driving than cool but never to the extreme of bop. They bent and slurred notes more than cool, and rhythmic church sounds were prevalent.

Although derived from the driving sounds of bop, hard bop had its own characteristics. The dominant saxophone sound was that of the tenor instead of the alto saxophone. The rhythm section dropped some complexity in order to gain a more driving style. The musical repertoire adopted more Latin tunes, as well as the introduction of funky and gospel sounds.

At the same time, some players reverted back to bop. Their attitude was that cool was simply not expressive enough; they missed the explosiveness of bop. This movement also had nonmusical associations based on a retrospective view of jazz. There was a question of whether jazz had changed its voice too much. Perhaps it had lost the expressiveness of the oral tradition from which it was born.

## Les McCann
### "Vacushna"
### Pacific Jazz Records 3075

:00   Eight bars introduction, every other bar is the plagal cadence (IV–I).

:11   Half tone higher, eight bars, again in every other bar is the plagal cadence.

:22   Back to the original key for twelve-bar chorus using the blues chord progression

:40   Chorus 2: Ends with the plagal cadence

:57   Eight bars very similar to the first eight bar introduction

1:08   Half tone higher, similar to the second eight bars of introduction

1:19   Back to the original key for a third twelve-bar chorus using the blues chord progression

1:36   Chorus 4: Locked hands piano style, ends with plagal cadence

1:53   Eight bars made up of alternating between one bar bass solo and one bar plagal cadence

2:04   Half tone higher in same manner

2:14   Original chorus, fifth chorus

2:32   Chorus 6: Ending with plagal cadence

2:49   Eight bars very similar to first eight bars of introduction

3:00   Half tone higher, similar to the second eight bars of introduction, ending with plagal cadence

3:11   End (plagal cadence was used thirty-five times)

*Les McCann*

Michael Ochs Archives/ Venice, CA

Horace Silver Quintet
"Stop Time"
New World Records NW 271

Kenny Dorham, trumpet; Hank Mobley, tenor saxophone; Horace Silver, piano; Doug Watkins, bass; Art Blakey, drums.

- :00    Introductory theme with one repeat at a lower range
- :08    "Head" melody with trumpet and saxophone in unison
- :24    Trumpet solo
- 1:09    Tenor saxophone solo
- 1:54    Piano solo. Listen to the left hand punctuated "comping" patterns as Silver solos with his right hand.
- 2:50    Just as his solo ends listen for the blues (funky) melodic references.
- 2:53    Trumpet solo. The band begins to trade fours at this point. Each player with solo for four measures with four-bar drum solos in between
- 2:56    Four-bar drum solo
- 2:58    Four-bar tenor sax solo
- 3:02    Four-bar drum solo
- 3:06    Four-bar trumpet solo
- 3:09    Four-bar drum solo
- 3:13    Four-bar tenor sax solo
- 3:17    Extended drum solo
- 3:35    Head melody returns with trumpet and saxophone in unison.
- 3:46    Introductory theme restated
- 3:55    End

*Horace Silver*

Michael Ochs Archives/
Venice, CA

As jazz left the 1950s, a fragmentation of style seemed to occur which placed several stylistic lines side by side. Bop had not been abandoned and had found a resurgence in the neoclassical school, and the mainstream was often expressed as a kind of cool-bop. The complexity of harmony and melody had remained a part of the jazz language. As jazz left the dance hall, other music filled the gap. Rock and roll emerged while jazz flirted with the classical music tradition. The first two musical streams at work in America were jazz and classical. Their fusion offered a third stream.

This development arose mainly as a result of the G.I. Bill. This bill made it possible, as early as the Cool era, for many jazz players to attend conservatories and universities. These players continued to develop a greater appreciation and knowledge of classical techniques. Third stream music is now a more fully developed combination of jazz and classical music. As we will see later, some of the avant-garde groups might be viewed as an extension of this type of musical crossover. The Modern Jazz Quartet under the leadership of John Lewis represents a popular expression of this style. Listen to their performance of ''Django'' for an example of third stream jazz.

## CROSSOVER— THIRD STREAM

Free form players have liberated themselves from many of the musical expectations established by jazz tradition. They replaced the traditional protocol with a new one, one that avoids traditional musical idioms but retains the interactive protocol fundamental to jazz performance. It is tempting to compare this musical expression with the similar development in classical music. The two approaches often appear on the surface to be quite similar; at times, it may be only their intent that separates them. If a distinction is to be made, it would fall primarily along the lines of compositional versus improvisation lines. The jazz tradition is one that elevates the improvisatory right of the performer, compared to the classical school, which stresses compositional principles in an improvisational setting. Of all the fusions jazz has effected, this is perhaps the most complete. It is in this area of jazz that performers tend to cross over into each other's arenas, and the theatrical presentation is most similar.

## AVANT-GARDE METHODOLOGY

Jazz, like other art forms, was confronted by the American political and social pressures of the 1960s. The experimentation that was occurring in all art forms also began to be seen in jazz. The university was a major factor in that experimentation process, and jazz was

## FREE FORM— AVANT-GARDE (THE 1960s)

# Modern Jazz Quartet
## "Django"
### Smithsonian H/1(cd IV/14)

John Lewis, piano; Milt Jackson, vibes; Percy Heath, bass; Connie Kay, drums.

:00    Piano and vibes—melody, out of tempo at first then going into tempo

:37    Bass and drums enter rhythmically, vibes solo.

2:59    Piano solo, very delicate (with bass and drums)

4:24    Ritard, bass prominent

4:37    Vibes solo on original melody backed by piano chords.

5:12    Ritard, vibes and piano play arpeggios.

5:33    End

*Modern Jazz Quartet*

Michael Ochs Archives/
Venice, CA

working its way into the university. Its ascendancy to art form status promoted its alliance with the experimental activities in the avant-garde in classical music.

Not all music of the free form genre should be characterized as avant-garde. Not all free form experimentation was carried out as a rejection of former jazz practice, although the avant-garde carries such a connotation by definition. These composer/players, such as Anthony Braxton, worked against jazz tradition and were looking for

*Ornette Coleman*
Michael Ochs Archives/
Venice, CA

a new, more universal music. Other players guided by traditional jazz precepts merely pursued their own interests, which led them into new and freer expressions.

There are two dominant approaches to free playing. One approach leads to freedom out of a seemingly unconscious extension of standard practice. The extension of traditional approaches actually leads to its own breakdown. Players like John Coltrane represent this gradual approach toward freedom. The other approach is to evaluate common practice consciously and decide to leave it as exemplified by members of the AACM. Coleman and Sun Ra sit midway between these two approaches. They are quite likely to begin a performance within the common practice and then move ''outside'' to enhance their delivery. Because they often speak of their theoretical approaches, their performances offer a continuum between common practice and theoretical intent.

If improvisation is a central practice in jazz, it would follow that an environment free of stylistic restrictions would be the ultimate jazz expression. Ornette Coleman is credited with leadership in seeking freer musical environments in which to improvise. His recording of ''Free Jazz'' shows how he extended the melodic and harmonic limits previously at work in jazz.

While Ornette Coleman was pushing the limits of the jazz expression outside the academy, groups like the Art Ensemble were working within the guidelines of the academy. Their efforts are more

## Ornette Coleman
## "Free Jazz"
## Smithsonian J/2(cd V/9)

| | |
|---|---|
| :00 | Introduction |
| :10 | Melody used later for improvisation is played in unison. |
| :22 | Alto sax solo (Ornette Coleman), listen for two basses and the accenting on the drums. |
| 1:10 | Backup horns enter. |
| 3:33 | Horns play independently. |
| 4:10 | Alto sax plays faster, one bass is bowing. |
| 4:45 | Ensemble players now playing very independently |
| 5:05 | Peak |
| 5:30 | Alto sax solos again. |
| 5:40 | Everybody is improvising. |
| 6:10 | Alto sax solos again |
| 6:43 | Everybody is improvising. |
| 7:45 | Everybody plays fast for a moment. |
| 9:46 | Original motive played in unison |
| 10:00 | Fade |
| 10:03 | End |

consistent with the theoretical approaches also taken by classical new music groups. Their performances might just as easily center on the notion of timbre as rhythmic nuances. The interplay among players remains a primary concern, and the improvisational priority reflects a jazz connection. Players like Anthony Braxton and Cecil Taylor represent this more intellectual approach to free jazz.

## JAZZ/ROCK FUSION (1960s–    )

As jazz developed its canon and rock and roll filled its role as America's popular music, a new crossover began between the two musical styles. This musical crossover eventually became known as fusion in the jazz community. Jazz began to import rock's instruments, volume, and stylistic delivery. Like bop, fusion did not occur without controversy. As jazz was establishing its legitimacy, it was taking a risk by fusing with rock. Rock also represented a generational division in the American profile. It accompanied the emergence of the post-World War II baby boom to adolescence. It was first associated exclusively with the young generation and worked as a banner of distinction. Its further association with the social and political polarity of the 1960s tended to reinforce the generational lines. Jazz criticism at that time was founded in the swing and, to a lesser extent, the bop traditions. Rock fusion represented a commercialization of an emerging American art form. As the popularity of rock was carried by the baby boom into the adult listening market, its possible fusion with jazz seemed guaranteed.

The earliest notable fusion experiments happened again under the guidance of Miles Davis in his albums *In a Silent Way* and *Bitches Brew*. This later album included players who later form the most popular fusion groups. Listen to Davis's recording of ''Miles Runs the VooDoo Down'' to hear an early example of jazz/rock fusion.

The most prominent later fusion groups belonged to former Davis players, John McLaughlin, Chick Corea, Joe Zawinul, and Wayne Shorter. At the time, this style offered a new virtuosity which, like earlier technical approaches, has become a part of common practice. Joe Zawinul's recording of ''Fast'' on his *Night Passages* album is a good example of the later fusion groups.

---

## FUSION STYLE

The later fusion players of jazz/rock created another blend of both musical and theatrical performance. Because this musical style is so close to us, it is still unclear which style will prove most dominant. The musical materials, as well as the interpretative style, are quite mixed. The rhythm section is often rock based and the solo lines bop-like. Although the musical materials are blended, the musical theatrics of rock and jazz have remained essentially separate. The early jazz/rock fusion maintained its allegiance to jazz in its dominantly improvisatory nature. The later jazz/pop groups are more difficult to assess. Although the groups support improvisation, the arrangements and the studio protocol limit its interactive expression. The current popularity of their ideas may be reminiscent of the popularity jazz enjoyed in its earliest days. Despite the similarity, the mainstream jazz community is at odds about embracing the new popularity. Commercialism appropriate in earlier styles tends to deny the integrity of the more mature art form. With that maturity comes a more prescribed definition that does not move easily with the winds of fashion. The

# Miles Davis
## "Miles Runs the VooDoo Down"
### Columbia Records GP 26 CS 9995

———

Miles Davis, trumpet; Wayne Shorter, soprano sax; Jack DeJohnette, Lenny White, Charles Alias, drums; Bennie Maupin, bass clarinet; Chick Corea, electronic piano; Harvey Brooks, Dave Holland, basses; John McLaughlin, electric guitar; Jim Riley, percussion.

  :00    Slow rock groove is established. Notice the bass clarinet.

  :36    Trumpet enters with short fragmented phrases that became a trademark of the Davis style. Notice that the harmonic pocket does not change throughout the entire selection. The energy created by the rhythm section continues to build.

2:18    Davis pulls away chromatically from the harmonic center.

2:45    The rhythm section continues to build energy. Notice the comping patterns of the guitar and keyboard.

4:00    Davis drops out. The interplay among the rhythm section players is essentially co-soloing. Notice the short chromatic excursions by the guitar and keyboard players. The guitar emerges as the dominant soloist.

6:25    The soprano saxophone emerges as the dominant soloist but still shares the soloistic stage with the other members of the ensemble.

7:00    Collective improvisation continues.

8:05    Keyboard solo takes the dominant role. Notice the interplay between the keyboard and guitar players.

9:25    The excitement builds as more cross rhythms and soloistic trade-offs occur.

10:26    More chromatic pull aways in the comping instruments.

10:35    The energy begins to subside.

10:43    Davis enters on a much more subdued backup.

11:48    A return to high energy with faster interchanges among players and a faster melodic phrasing by Davis.

12:10    Energy again subsides.

13:00    The energy again increases. Listen for how the rhythm section contributes to that energy.

13:38    Davis drops out as the rhythm section begins to dissolve.

## Joseph Zawinul and Weather Report
### "Fast City"
### 1980 Columbia Records 36793

Joseph Zawinul, keyboards; Wayne Shorter, saxophones; Jaco Pastorius, bass; Peter Erskine, drums; Robert Thomas, Jr., hand drums.

:00   Open, free introduction begins with drums and long tones in the saxophone and bass in unison.

:29   Head begins with very active drums and angular bass fills.

:50   Time begins with jazz/bop feel; notice the complexity of each of the parts. Saxophone solo begins; notice chromatic harmonic shifts in the comping pattern of the keyboards.

1:50   Pedal point in the bass under the sax

2:03   Time returns.

2:10   Syncopated keyboard punches

2:14   Angular cross rhythms among the different players

2:22   Long tones over an active rhythm section followed by stacatto lines over the fast rhythm

2:40   Saxphone and keyboard exchange short patterns that set up a complex cross rhythm.

3:03   Keyboard solo begins over driving rhythm section; notice the apparent independence of the bass part.

3:50   Keyboard change in timbre

4:07   Saxophone joins keyboard to play cross rhythms.

4:23   Keyboard solo continues; listen to bass and drums.

5:03   Saxophone comes back with angular head with complex and fast bass fills.

5:29   Long tone in saxophone and keyboard over fast rhythm

5:42   Cross accents by saxophone and keyboard against the complex bass lines and driving drums

6:05   Quick syncopated ending

expectations generated by the more mature jazz art form is, therefore, more appropriately embodied in the more conservative style of the Marsalises' than the more popular performances of such players as Kenny G or David Sanborn. Listen to later recordings by Chick Corea or Michael Brecker for examples of the more mature fusion style (listening guides in chapter 12).

## STRAIGHT-AHEAD AND NEOCLASSICAL JAZZ (1980s–1990s)

The bop and hard bop styles have become the cornerstones of mainstream jazz, which has two centers of activity, New Orleans and New York. This mainstream can be traced through the activity of player/band leaders like Art Blakey. His playing is rooted in the bop style and his group, the Jazz Messengers, served as a vehicle for launching many jazz players now viewed as straight-ahead players. The self-proclaimed champion of that long list of players is Wynton Marsalis who established himself as a premier player and advocate of traditional jazz in the 1980s.

The line of players that follow in his wake have established a style of jazz often referred to as the neoclassical school. The neoclassical label is borrowed from the other art worlds, such as classical music, and represents a looking back to borrow ideas and material from earlier stylistic periods. The neoclassical school of jazz looks back primarily to the Bop era for its expression and to the New Orleans era for its heritage. With the focus on bop, that era in jazz emerges as the center of gravity for the jazz tradition. The transition from popular to art music is reinforced in the minds of the world listener. Although the movement is a backward looking one, its demeanor presents jazz in a new posture stressing its contributions as America's unique art form.

## NEOCLASSICAL STYLE

Straight-ahead jazz is of the neoclassical school. Players of this style generally consider bop jazz to be the model for all present day jazz interpretations. Although it looks back to traditional performance practice it does not reflect the theatrics of the Bop era. The neoclassical school is quite adamant about its clean living, as well as its respect for tradition. The Bop era was not clean. It was associated with the heaviest use of drugs of any jazz period. It also played to audiences that were looking for an exotic night uptown in the clubs. It was night music that seldom made it to the concert stage. The neoclassical movement has a theatrical image that grants it a "classical" status. It has become an American classical art form and has taken on some of the attributes and theatrics of European classical music. It has entered the university. Its spokesman, Wynton Marsalis, is an accomplished classical musician who paints a jazz image quite different from the giants of the Bop era who were subject to the frailties of street life. The music is perhaps quite similar but the theatrics are not.

## JAZZ/ROCK/POP FUSION (1980s–1990s)

At the same time that the neoclassical movement is making a strong resurgence, jazz continues to fuse with popular musical styles. The popular music scene in the 1970s to the present has become quite technologically advanced and offers some new approaches for the jazz player. Studio recording practices allow small groups to build larger ensemble sounds by stacking recording upon recording. The ensemble interplay is obviously affected. The musical complexity is somewhat reduced to accommodate a wider listening audience. Because of the more "pop" sound of these new groups, cries of commercialism arise from the traditional ranks of jazz.

Groups like the Yellowjackets and Spyro Gyra represent these jazz/pop fusion groups. Because this fusion is so close to us, it is difficult to assess its ultimate impact on the developing jazz tradition. With it, however, has come a new popularity that offers a mixed blessing. It is nice to again have a jazz expression in the limelight, but its commercial intent threatens to compromise jazz's emergent art status.

## JAZZ SINGERS

In spite of their great importance in the history of jazz, we have not discussed many jazz vocalists in this chapter. These talented performers have been prominent in each style but have not often been among the innovators of those styles. However, it was from the oral tradition belonging exclusively to the vocal style that jazz inherited its expressive nature. The earliest prejazz expressions were primarily vocal. Often in the study of jazz, the manner of vocal expression jazz has employed tends to get overlooked, as the attention of historians shifts to a description of the musical materials used by performers. These musical materials, however, only come alive when combined with the jazz expression, an expression rooted in the vocal expression.

The parentage of the jazz expression comes from the early blues singers. Their inflections became the backbone of jazz improvisation. Billie Holiday began to redefine the "blues" singer as a "jazz" singer. Her stylizations were characterized by an individuality and improvisatory nuance expected of the leading instrumentalists.

## Art Blakey and the Jazz Messengers
### "E.T.A."
### Concord Records CCD–4168

Art Blakey, drums; Wynton Marsalis, trumpet; Charles Fambrough, bass; Bobby Watson, alto saxophone; James Williams, piano.

Each chorus of this piece is thirty-two measures long with four eight-bar phrases making an AABA structure, which can be heard most clearly when the theme is played at the beginning and end of the performance.

:00  Drum solo sets up the head.

:26  Section A: Band enters playing the first eight bars of the head in harmony. Section A repeats: Second eight bars of the head.

:37  Section B: Middle eight bars or "bridge"

:42  Section A: Return to first eight bars

:48  Alto sax solo, notice bop phrasing and driving walking bass.

:58  Section B of the chorus

1:04  Section A: Return to the first section

1:10  Second chorus of alto sax solo

1:32  Third chorus of solo

1:54  Trumpet solo, also three choruses

2:15  Second chorus

2:37  Third chorus

2:59  Tenor sax solo, only two choruses

3:19  Second chorus

3:41  Piano solo, again only two choruses

4:25  All the horn players play a single chorus in unison similar to the unison bop heads used in the Bop era.

4:47  Drum solo

5:32  Head returns with the two A sections.

5:43  Section B: Bridge

5:48  Section A: Return to last A section

5:54  Slows down with ending phrases

6:09  End

## Yellowjackets
### "Out of Town"
### MCA Records MCAD 5994

Russell Ferrante, keyboards; Jimmy Haslip, bass; Marc Russo, saxophones; William Kennedy, drums.

:00   Four-beat jazz feel in the bass with slow rock feel backbeat in bass drum and hand claps
:19   Melody enters on saxophone.
:37   Piano/synthesizer enters.
:51   Synthesizer and saxophone unison melody line
1:33   Listen for how the drummer accents (kicks) the melody and synthesizer harmonic accents.
1:38   Return to the melody
1:54   Transition area, backbeat accents in bass and drums (on second and fourth beats)
2:10   Big band ensemble style punches with saxophone, synthesizers, and drum accents
2:22   Extended sax "fill" leading to next chorus
2:32   New chorus with piano solo (possibly MIDI coupled). Listen to how the ensemble "tightens" at the start of the chorus as the bass starts to walk in four and the drums settle in the straight "time."
3:34   Synthesized brass-like punches with drum accents
4:07   Transition with backbeat feel
4:15   Saxophone and synthesizer unison line returns, with straight "time" backup.
4:31   Drum solo
4:38   Melody returns.
5:02   End

*continued*

*continued*

*Yellowjackets*
Courtesy of GRP Records, Inc.

"Out of Town" Written by: Yellowjackets. Administered by: Baracuda Music.

## Billie Holiday
### "All of Me"
### Columbia Jazz Mast./Legacy CK 47031

---

:00   Eight-bar introduction, basically piano solo with subtle saxophone section punctuations

:18   Chorus 1: Vocal with saxophone section background, plenty of piano fills. Listen for the "lay back" which continues to be a feature of jazz stylization.

1:25   Lester Young on tenor saxophone takes the last two bars.

1:30   Tenor saxophone solo for eight bars using the chords from the last eight bars of the tune

1:48   Chorus 2: Holiday sings another chorus with the same saxophone section background except tenor saxophone (Young) takes a break on bars fifteen and sixteen.

2:19   Bars fifteen and sixteen of this chorus (tenor saxophone break)

2:24   Last half of chorus, vocal, goes out in tempo with soft piano punctuation on end.

3:00   End

*Billie Holiday*
Michael Ochs Archives/
Venice, CA

Indeed, the very process of scat singing, which involves the use of nonsense syllables while improvising vocally, seems to reflect the transition jazz has undergone from a vocally defined improvisatory style to an instrumental one. It is ironic that the very jazz ''voice'' based originally on vocal inflections is now defined so much by instrumental techniques. Vocalists now imitate instrumental stylizations with scat singing that mimics instrumental complexity. Although vocal jazz is not often credited with taking the innovative lead in the evolution of jazz, it continues to be an interpretative backbone for jazz phrasing.

## SUGGESTED LISTENING

*Bebop.* New World Records NW 271.

*Best of George Shearing.* Capitol Records S7 2104.

Blakey, Art, and the Jazz Messengers. ''E.T.A.'' *Straight Ahead.* Concord Records CCD–4168.

Blakey, Art, and the Jazz Messengers. ''Straight Ahead.'' Concord Jazz Records CJ 168.

Christian, Charlie. *Solo Flight.* Columbia Records CG 30779.

Coleman, Ornette. *At the Golden Circle.* Blue Note Records 84224 2.

Coleman, Ornette. ''Free Jazz.'' Smithsonian J/2(cd V/9).

Corea, Chick. *Elektric Band.* ''Stretch It.'' GRP Records GRD 9601.

Davis, Miles. *Basic Miles.* Columbia Records C 32025.

Davis, Miles. ''Boplicity.'' Smithsonian F/8(cd IV/1).

Davis, Miles. *Greatest Hits.* Columbia Records CS 9809.

Davis, Miles. *Miles Ahead.* Columbia Records CL 1041.

Davis, Miles. ''Miles Runs the VooDoo Down.'' *Bitches Brew.* Columbia Records GP 26 CS 9995.

Davis, Miles. *Sketches of Spain.* Columbia Records CL 1480.

Herman, Woody. *The Thundering Herds.* Columbia Records C3L 25.

Holiday, Billie. ''All of Me.'' *The Quintessential Billie Holiday.* Vol. 9. 1940–1942. Columbia Jazz Mast./Legacy CK 47031.

*Horace Silver and the Jazz Messengers.* Blue Note Records BLP 1518.

Horace Silver Quintet. ''Stop Time.'' New World Records NW 271.

Jazz in Revolution. *The Big Bands of the 1940s.* New World Records NW 284.

*Les McCann Plays the Truth.* Pacific Jazz Records PJ 2.

McCann, Les. ''Vacushna.'' *Les McCann Plays the Truth.* Pacific Jazz Records 3075.

Modern Jazz Quartet. ''Django.'' Smithsonian H/1(cd IV/14).
Modern Jazz Quartet. *European Concert,* Atlantic Records
    SD 20603.
Mulligan, Gerry, and Chet Baker. *Timeless.* Pacific Jazz Records
    PJ 75.
Parker, Charlie. ''KoKo.'' Smithsonian E/8(cd 111/12).
Parker, Charlie, and Dizzy Gillespie. ''Shaw 'Nuff.'' Smithsonian
    E/7(cd 111/11).
Yellowjackets. ''Out of Town.'' *Four Corners.* MCA Records
    MCAD 5994.
Young, Lester. *Prez.* Mainstream Records 56012.
Young, Lester, and Count Basie. ''Lester Leaps In.'' Smithsonian
    D/7(cd 11/22).
*Young Lester Young.* Columbia Records J 24.
Zawinul, Joseph, and Weather Report. ''Fast City.'' *Night
    Passages, 1980.* Columbia Records 36793.

# CHAPTER 4

## *An Overview of Theoretical Concerns*

| | |
|---|---|
| *1850–1917* | Ragtime popular |
| *1890–1917* | Basic period for Early New Orleans Dixieland |
| *1917–1942* | Boogie-Woogie popular |
| *1932–1942* | Swing bands predominate |
| *1940–1950* | Bop emerges |
| *1949–1955* | Cool emerges |
| *1954* | Funky enters |
| *1954* | Hard bop gains importance |
| *Late 1950s* | Third stream gains importance |
| *1960* | Ornette Coleman recorded *Free Jazz* |
| *1963* | John Coltrane recorded "Alabama" |
| *1965* | Rock and jazz combine as fusion |
| *1969* | Miles Davis recorded *Bitches Brew* |

A s we look for the historical "threads" that weave through jazz's evolution, we will depend on analytical tools that permit us to move across accepted historical boundaries, such as "cool," "bop," and "fusion." These tools, to be effective, must not be specific to any musical style but general enough to work in all styles. Our view of the musical substance of jazz must include more than the normal theoretical labels for the elements of music. It should also embrace the musical processes that make use of these musical elements. The defining characteristics of jazz may not be found alone in such terms as scales, harmony, and rhythm, but in how these traditional elements of music are used. Jazz shares the nomenclature of music with other familiar musical lines of development, yet we are seldom confused, after hearing a style, to which line it belongs. The notation, however, might look quite similar.

Unlike classical music, which traces the history of notated music, jazz traces a line of performance which at times, like classical music, becomes carefully notated. This dialectic between the oral and the notated musical traditions surfaces again as we look for analytical tools for studying jazz. We must move our perspective to a level that helps us focus on this dialectic. Instead of looking only for melodic or harmonic activity, we also will be looking for the *balance* between melodic and harmonic activity. Instead of looking for a metric definition, we will look for how the performer's rhythmic activity relates to a metric underpinning and how that metric underpinning is established. We also will be looking for how the balance among all these larger analytical areas shifts from style to style. As the balance shifts, so does the jazz style. Sometimes the shift is quite dramatic, and at other times, it is quite subtle.

The most difficult analytical areas are those that deal with the intangible and illusive areas of personal interpretation. If personal interpretation were not important, we would have a history of musical composition, not one of individual performers. It is tempting to divorce the individuals from the history and study only those aspects of the music that can be easily described and labeled. Jazz, with its performer centered tradition, refuses to be limited. It becomes the responsibility of the historian to develop the tools required by the medium, rather than redefine the medium in terms of the tools. This type of musical analysis remains relatively uncharted and is somewhat unevenly effective. As we move through the musical lines of development in the later part of this book, we will find that some of the musical styles are tidier than others. Those areas that stress compositional practice and require notational form (usually large-group performance) are normally easier to approach because the notation carries with it a bag of agreed upon tools. These styles are counterbalanced by other open-structured performances that defy notation. We usually approach these styles by first listing what is *not* present rather than what is new, because analytical tools have not yet emerged to address the style.

The following discussion offers an overview of these larger tools and some ways they can be applied to specific jazz styles. These tools are discussed in generic terms so they may be used across all historical periods and styles.

Horizontal music practice

Music can be viewed from two extreme perspectives, as independent horizontal activities in time that inadvertently create simultaneous events (polyphony), or as vertical simultaneous events that follow one another in time (homophony). Polyphony stresses the musical elements of melody and melodic rhythm, while homophony better describes harmony and meter. Jazz works along a continuum that travels between these two poles. The African oral tradition is better understood as a predominantly horizontal practice resulting from the spontaneous creation of music, while the musical tradition of western Europe employs a more vertical activity that helps structure preconceived compositions. To understand jazz practice, we must be able to look at the music from both perspectives. As jazz has evolved, the balance between vertical and horizontal emphasis has shifted to meet stylistic and individual needs.

## VERTICAL AND HORIZONTAL MUSICAL PRACTICE

Rhythm can be defined as a flow of accents in time. If those accents become regular and repeated, a meter is established. Rhythm alone does not establish a meter. The African musical heritage is more typical of a horizontal stacking of rhythmic lines that coincide in very sophisticated ways. The rhythmic groupings of one line may align with those of another line only by accident. The varying interaction of those ongoing lines is more musically significant than their regular alignment. That there may be no apparent meter does not mean that there is no predetermined pulse. The rhythm can still be quite "rhythmic" as the rhythmic melodies interact; there is just no recurring meter, such as 4/4, maintained.

The Western musical tradition has a long history of metrical alignment. For centuries, musical pieces have been described in terms of the meter, particularly dance pieces, such as the minuet, waltz, and cakewalk. Simple metrical dance music is an artifact of Western music. The African tradition brought with it a different type of dance

## RHYTHM—METER

rhythm that was much more free of metrical restrictions. As Western and African music merged, the metrical underpinning of Western dance music was the backdrop against which the free rhythmic lines of the African tradition could work horizontally. This musical merger has continued throughout America's popular music scene, as well as in jazz, through Motown to the rap of the 1990s.

Ragtime is a good example of this two-level approach to rhythm and meter. It is usually accented on beats two and four of the meter and is played by the left hand. Against this metrical rhythm, the right hand plays syncopated melodies that created cross rhythms with the regular meter.

Because early jazz had such a close relationship to dance, meter has always played a dominant role. However, the nature of the accents in the meter have changed to meet stylistic and functional demands of jazz. Early New Orleans Dixieland was almost always played in a flat 4/4, primarily because of its marching background. Chicago Style Dixieland, on the other hand, used four beats to the measure but with the accented second and fourth beats, a combination of ragtime and Early New Orleans Dixieland. Boogie-Woogie was played in 8/8 (eight beats to the bar) to create a fuller sound. This was a situation in which a piano player was hired in place of an orchestra and needed to make up for additional players with rhythmic excitement.

Swing used a 4/4 meter with duplicated efforts in the rhythm section because of large bands and large halls. Because swing functioned primarily as dance music, the beat was predominant and regular. Bop was also played in 4/4, but several changes took place in how it was delivered. The rhythm section abandoned the duplicated efforts of swing and took on individual roles. The accents moved to the second and fourth beats again, the tempos generally increased, and unexpected accents became common. This was not music for dancing but for listening. A particularly complex expression of rhythm and tempos can be found in the compositions of Don Ellis that use compound meters, such as 7/8, 10/8, and 19/4.

Although predominantly played in 4/4, cool used such new meters as 5/4 and 9/4. Funky returned to a more predominant meter with the accents on beats two and four typical of gospel music. Some 3/4 renditions were also successful. The metric clarity of hard bop distinguished it somewhat from bop and the more subtle rhythm section sound of cool. Straight-ahead jazz followed the metrical style of bop and hard bop and is still an influence in the neoclassical school.

When jazz met rock, there were new changes in how jazz approached meter. The sophistication of the bop and later rhythm sections had moved away from the heavy meter associated with earlier

**EXAMPLE 4.1**

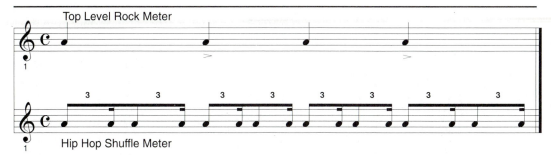

Top Level Rock Meter

Hip Hop Shuffle Meter

**EXAMPLE 4.2**

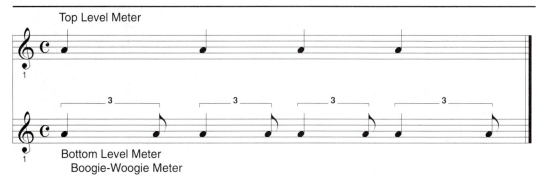

Top Level Meter

Bottom Level Meter
Boogie-Woogie Meter

dance music. With jazz/rock fusion, a predominate dance meter returned and melodic cross accents changed character. The subdivision of each beat moved from three (swing eighths) to four. Later fusion (and also the hip-hop of rap) used a two level meter that used, at the highest level, four beats to the measure with accents on beats two and four. At the lower level, the beat is subdivided into six parts on which the melodic activity above can swing. As the higher level tempo slows, the lower levels can subdivide more successfully (see example 4.1).

Boogie-Woogie is an earlier example of how a 4/4 meter can be subdivided into smaller units, in that case, eighths (see example 4.2).

Fusion, like much of early jazz, often uses a contrasting melodic rhythm to offset the metric regularity at work in the rhythm section. Fusion soloists generally borrow from the bop tradition for their melodic and rhythmic approach.

Third stream and avant-garde are more difficult to generalize, because they often borrow from the more exotic meters of more contemporary classical models. Some expressions of free form jazz would even abandon meter altogether and be left with the interaction of rhythmic lines more typical of the African tradition. Others, like Ornette Coleman, maintained a regular metrical underpinning in most performances.

## MELODY— HARMONY

Much as rhythm has a relationship to meter, melody is related to harmony. Melodies like those used in a round (''Three Blind Mice'') can create harmonies as they are sung, or melodies can be woven through preexisting harmonies. Again, the African and western European traditions represent these two approaches. As jazz styles emerged and receded, the balance between these approaches shifted. It is very difficult to discuss melodic independence without also discussing the rhythmic independence already mentioned. The notes of a melody are only part of the total melodic definition. The rhythm discussed interacts with the meter and the notes with the harmonies, but both are required to describe fully the jazz expression.

The early blues and spirituals often were sung unaccompanied or in unison. As a result, little syncopation was used because there was no steady meter to work against. The blues songs were often slow and sad and defined by the three lyric phrases rather than a harmonic underpinning. Early New Orleans Dixieland developed along the line of melodic independence rather than harmonic integrity. The harmonies were more an accident than a guiding force. The interaction of the melodies, both in terms of pitch and rhythm, was the glue that held the performance together. The inheritance of the more harmonically based Western musical form provided the structural shell in which their musical lines unfolded. The musical performance was easily altered to meet the stylistic needs of each job. The manner in which musicians played in some African-American clubs was considered far too ''rough'' for white dances and the musicians would adjust to a more ''sweet'' style, a smoother handling of the melodies. The ''roughness'' was a combination of the individualization of parts by the players, which seems to create a less precise rendition. The sweet style was more consistent but also more impersonal as the players interacted. These were terms in use at that time, but now we understand that the difference was more one of vertical and horizontal considerations. If a piece is played as a group of individual musical lines, the players feel free to embellish both the pitch and rhythm. On the other hand, if the piece is viewed as basically a stream of harmonies which supported a melody, the players would restrict their individual expressions so the vertical harmonies would sound accurately.

**EXAMPLE 4.3**   Excerpt from Count Basie's ''One O'clock Jump''

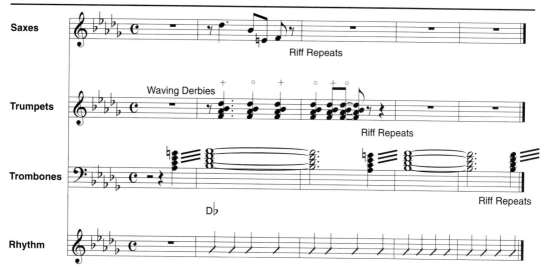

Ragtime melodies, while highly syncopated, were consistent with the predetermined harmonic progression, a process typical of the more precomposed expressions throughout jazz history. The melodies of ragtime are also more instrumental than vocal in nature. As later in bop, they were too disjunct to sing easily. Boogie-woogie melodies were essentially short rhythmic riffs rather than independent melodic lines.

The early swing bands from the Southwest, used repeated refrains or phrases, riffs, that were typical of African melodic phrasing. Sometimes the riffs are used in an ostinato fashion as catalysts that hold the music together by reinforcing or offsetting the meter. Repeated riffs, which cause great momentum and impetus, were used extensively by Kansas City musicians, such as Benny Moten (later Count Basie's band) in the 1920s, and by New York musicians, such as Fletcher Henderson, who was scoring arrangements behind blues singers Bessie Smith, Ma Rainey, and others. The use of riffs became standard in the more jazz-oriented large bands. Sometimes they were used to back up a soloist; sometimes entire sections of a piece were made up of riffs (see example 4.3).

Although known for its up-tempo tunes, swing sported a number of popular songs that did not ''swing.'' A majority of the tunes played by the big bands were jazz interpretations of pretty ballads. The melodies were either pulled from or composed like the popular songs of the day. They were harmonically based melodies played or sung by performers who were jazz oriented. Listen, for example, to Benny Goodman play his theme, ''Good-bye,'' with Harry James playing an obligato in the background.

Bop, with its faster tempos, accented unexpected notes played in unison by the front line instruments. The melodic contour was often quite disjunct and reflected a new complexity in soloistic playing. Although the improvisational lines typical of Charlie Parker's playing floated rhythmically over the driving metric underpinning, the melodic material was closely tied to the harmonic underpinning. A standard format for performing tunes in the bop manner was to play the first chorus in unison (trumpet and saxophone usually), then the improvised choruses, followed by the unison chorus again. Therefore, if a tune had a chorus of thirty-two bars and a form of AABA, the first eight bars (A) would be composed, the second eight would be a repetition of the first eight (A), the third group of eight bars would be improvised (B), and the last eight bars would again be a repetition of the first eight bars (A). All of it added up to thirty-two bars and constituted the first and last chorus. Therefore, all that had to be planned ahead was one eight-bar strain, the A part.

The structural design for many of these tunes was harmonic rather than melodic. In fact, the same harmonic progression might be used for several different tunes, only new melodic material was added. A knowledge of the rhythm changes from the song ''I Got Rhythm'' is still a standard expectation of bop players because this progression appeared in so many songs. Harmonic forms worked for bop in much the same way that it did for blues. The harmonic progression established the form, and the melodic delivery hovered above it in rhythmically individualized lines that also worked consistently with the harmonies. Again, the balance between vertical and horizontal perspectives is a primary performance issue. It was also during this period that players became more conscious of musical theory because more complex harmonies required it. Membership in the bop vanguard was based on a knowledge of and ability to perform the new melodic and harmonic complexity. The balance between melody and harmony established is still a guiding principle in mainstream jazz.

Cool players stepped away from the fast tempos, angular and accented melodic lines, and extended chord structures of bop. They played their melodies smoothly, replacing excitement with subtlety. The relationship between harmonic and melodic independence also shifted with the move from bop to the more modal cool style. Gil Evans also formalized this balance in his arrangements. Fully composed jazz pieces left little room for improvised freedom in melodic

## Charlie Parker and Miles Davis
### ''Klacktoveedsteen''
### Smithsonian E/12(cd 111–16)

:00  Introduction: eight bars, alto sax and trumpet in cup mute in thirds

:08  Eight bars, drum break

:16  Head: eight bars saxophone and trumpet in unison

:23  Repeat

:31  Bridge: eight-bar saxophone solo

:39  Head: eight bars

:47  Chorus 2: Thirty-two bars, saxophone solo

1:18  Chorus 3: Open trumpet solo

1:50  Chorus 4: Sixteen bars, piano solo

2:06  Eight bars bass solo

2:14  Eight bars drum solo

2:22  Chorus 5: Head, trumpet again in cup mute for sixteen bars

2:39  Bridge: saxophone solo

2:46  Head again for eight bars

2:53  Reiteration of the introduction for eight bars

3:01  Two bars, drum solo

3:03  End

Words and Music by Charlie Parker. © Copyright Renewed. DUCHESS MUSIC CORPORATION is an MCA company. International Copyright Secured. All Rights Reserved. Used by Permission.

and rhythmic polyphony. The loose ensemble style heard in New Orleans Dixieland as it evolved through Fletcher Henderson, Benny Goodman, and Gil Evans tightened as it shifted to compositionally rather than improvisationally designed formats.

Later jazz styles have been reflective of the melodic practice of bop, even when the rhythmic feel in the rest of the ensemble has changed drastically as in fusion. This style places a "steady state" rhythmic foundation under a melody line that is individualized with accents and varying degrees of rhythmic independence. This feature may be one of the most consistent attributes that separates jazz from other musical activities since the beginning of this century. The one exception to this statement is avant-garde jazz, which can theoretically redefine any of the traditional underpinnings of jazz. They must, however, retain some relationship to the tradition or risk losing the support of that tradition. Generally, even in very free groups like The Art Ensemble, jazz idioms appear frequently as reference points to the tradition from which they were launched.

---

## INTERRELATIONSHIPS BETWEEN HARMONY, SCALES, AND MELODY

Jazz harmonies have generally increased in complexity and dissonance since their early use in New Orleans Dixieland. The harmonies of the early ensembles were usually triadic with very little use of extended chords. The dissonance heard in the early ensembles was more a result of how the melodic lines of the ensembles interacted than a result of complex chord spellings. The basic musical sound was consonant and restricted to the primary chords, I, IV, and V. These chords are members of the western European tonal structure, but they were changed in practice to meet the expressive and melodic needs more typical of the African music tradition.

The earliest melodies sung for spirituals, hollers, and work songs were unison and not defined by harmonies now common to jazz. The African harmonic tradition was defined by pentatonic relationships (C, D, F, G, A) with some use of the leading tone (B). It is important to note that the tonal implications the western European scales carried were not necessarily at work in the African music tradition. Although their scale was similar to that of western Europe, it served melodic rather than harmonic functions. African music tended to revolve around a central pitch (C) and any harmonization usually involved parallel melody lines a fourth or fifth below the melody. To keep the intervals perfect when heard against the melody, it is necessary to introduce a flatted third and seventh (E♭ and B♭). Such an argument is made by historians to account for the additional E♭ and B♭ in the blues scale. With these notes added to the diatonic scale, all the notes we associate with the blues scale are present (C, D, E, E♭, F, G, A, B♭, B, C); however, the tonal expectations are not the same.[1] It is important to note that the resultant harmonic vocabulary grew out of the melodic activity because the harmony line was essentially nothing more than a doubling of the melody itself, not a counterpoint that independently established moving harmonies. The full blues scale, without clear tonal expectations, allowed the expressive use of blue notes that would sit in between the tonal and modal worlds, as did the early slaves. Their melodic nontonal heritage was thrust into the tonal harmonic language typically used in the white church and folk music. The result was a hybrid of these melodic and harmonic worlds. This dialectic between vertical and horizontal performance expectations has remained active throughout most of jazz's history.

Early blues singing usually divided the blues scale into two parts (A, C, D, E♭) and (E, G, A, B♭). The singer often selected one of these two tetrachords for the melodic material for their blues renditions. Depending on the key of a blues song, Bessie Smith would move to the tetrachord that was best suited to her vocal range and center her melodic activity there.

Jazz soloing continued to be melodically and harmonically balanced up until bop when the complex chord changes and loss of an identifying melody encouraged a more scalar approach. Bop melodies seldom remained in one key and required the performer to shift continually throughout the tune. The rhythm changes mentioned previously are typical of such harmonies. The performer shifts keys as the chords progress. The easiest way to ensure a key change is to change scales as the chords move. Melodies took on a scalar contour as performers focused their attention from a known melody to the shifting harmonic keys. This stylistic shift in melodic activity can be heard when players of the Swing era are contrasted with those of the bop tradition.

The dissonance level in bop was also greatly increased. The use of sevenths, ninths, elevenths, and thirteenths on chords were commonplace. Also, the flatted fifth of the chord was an expected alteration typical of bop harmonies and has become a new blue note. As players worked their solos, they often played predominantly on these extended notes of the chords and even avoided the more consonant lower chord tones.

---

[1]Gunther Schuller, *Early Jazz, Its Roots and Musical Development,* (New York: Oxford University Press, 1968), 43. The argument Schuller offers in this account is informative but still tends to imply that a tonal order was at work in the scale.

*EXAMPLE 4.4*    Harmonic extension for a G chord

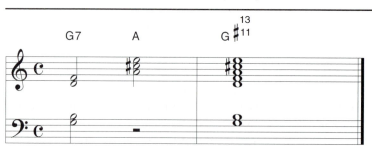

*EXAMPLE 4.5*    ''I Got Rhythm''

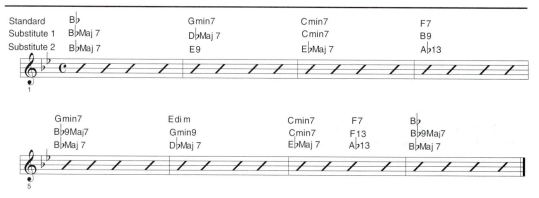

Harmonic sonorities complex enough to be called polychords were used extensively. This harmonic construction can be best understood as a combination of two conventional chords. As long as these chords have a close relationship, such as common tones, they are perceived as one chord in the same key instead of in two separate keys. For example, an A-major chord is placed directly over a G seventh chord to create an augmented eleventh chord (example 4.4).

This type of sound was common to bop. Since the tones of the A-major chord are all contained in the higher harmonics of the G seventh chord, the players considered these extended harmonies and did not think of the sound as being in two different keys.

## SUBSTITUTE CHORDS

Substitute chords became important during the Bop era as well. For example, C to C7 to F could just as well be played C to G♭7 to F (flat V substitution) to create a more interesting progression. The players were stimulated by fresh chords inside old progressions, such as those from ''I Got Rhythm'' (example 4.5).

This shift to the chord extensions created a significant obstacle for players of the Swing era when they wanted to play in the new style. Melodies of the Swing era were basically consonant, and when the solos followed the melody as they did then, the solos were also quite consonant. Bop not only increased the tempo but extended the harmonies. The result was a clear break from former practice and an apparent redirection of the jazz tradition. Jazz had a new kind of elitism that could be seen in both the theatrics of the performance and the substance of the music.

Original chord progressions were often altered to support the more dissonant scale tones the soloist used. These new chords were substituted in the place of the previous more simple ones. New chords were also used to quicken the harmonic rhythm of the original tune. The one chord that usually carried for two measures was now replaced or substituted with four more complex chords. These substitute chords were viewed as enhancements to the original chord, not as a reharmonization. For example, a single G7 chord might be replaced by a Abm7 to Db7b5 progression. The basic tonal function of the progression remained the same, but the substitute chords worked as extensions to the previous harmonies.

Sometimes the soloist would initiate the new chord without any opportunity to notify the chording instruments. The reverse also occurred; the comping instruments would supply substitute chords as the soloist centered on the original chords. Because the tonal function was basically the same, the result of any disagreement was to extend the level of dissonance at which the soloist worked. Melodies now centered on the extensions of the chords instead of the notes that made up the primary triad. This new dissonance level became a trademark of the bop style. When added to the increased harmonic rhythm created by the additional substitute chords on every two beats instead of the slower harmonic movement of the original tunes, bop became the driving, high-energy style playable by only the elite in jazz.

This new approach to playing created a dramatic change in how soloists approached their improvisation. A knowledge of the scale that worked through a variety of fast moving chords allowed the soloist to create longer lines than would otherwise be likely over a fast harmonic rhythm. For example, the chords, Dm7 to G7 to Cmaj7 could all be grouped in the key of C. Soloists did not need to think of each chord as they passed through them but only of a single scale, C major. The melodies often became more scalar, and the sound of the non-chord tones that occurred during the solo actually became the chord extensions expected of bop solos. Some debate exists over how much reasoning actually occurred during a bop solo. The players were certainly in a more complicated harmonic area than previous styles demanded. Some thinking no doubt went into a players practice.

Dizzy Gillespie was known to take young players aside and teach them the new chords. However, by the time the top players were actually improvising, their ears rather than their minds were their guides. There is a sound of bop that can only be maintained by remaining on the chord extensions. To remain there and, at the same time, craft musical phrases like those of Parker and Gillespie requires a freedom from the conscious effort a theory bound approach might offer. Many young players of bop often have a lightning facility but are not yet free of the harmonic patterns used to develop their style. The patterns, although quite impressive technically, do not speak with the same artistic authority of the leading bop soloists.

## MODAL IMPROVISATION

Although the scalar improvisation associated with bop has become the mainstream expression for jazz, this line of development did not stop there. The work of Miles Davis and John Coltrane pushed the concept even further. Davis is considered the progenitor in modal improvisation, which can be heard on his landmark album *Bitches Brew* in 1969.

The melodic improvisations of the Dixieland and swing musicians held no appeal for Davis during his bop period as he joined others in the harmonic/scalar approach. He often stated that he functioned more aptly in slower-moving music and proved that statement true in his work with Gil Evans and the cool movement. His next logical movement was to freeze the harmonies in time to allow expansive solo flights. Chords now moved very slowly and changed only at major articulation points in the song. ''Spanish Key'' from the *Bitches Brew* album is a good example.

This avenue allowed him the freedom of using scales or modes to express himself in improvisations. The players on *Bitches Brew* seem to avoid these static harmonies only to return and reaffirm the tonal centers, establishing the home key by insistence. The relationship of the chords used in a modal approach are not related to one another in the traditional sense. Rather than having tonic and dominant relationships, the basic chords often move by steps, for example, G down to F rather than C to G. Above these chords scalar and modal melodies worked quite well.

By 1954, Davis had set himself apart from the rhythm section by playing scale-oriented rather than chord-oriented long notes. By 1958, he was freed further by the modal scales and slower-moving harmonies. He suspended his melodies, based on early modes, above the harmony. The lack of harmonic movement and the scalar concept of improvisation disassociated the melody from whatever rhythmic underpinning there might be. His *Milestones* recording demonstrates this modal and almost arhythmic melodic approach. This means of improvising fit the Davis personality, which had become quite introspective by this time.

Davis had successfully carried music through the transition from bop to cool and on to a modal jazz that would launch players like John Coltrane (listen to ''So What'' on Davis' album *Kind of Blue*). Coltrane used the modal jazz approach as a springboard for his characteristic melodic extensions. The slow-moving harmonies of modal jazz allowed Coltrane to explore these more complex harmonic extensions. He used this approach on ''Alabama.'' He was able to consistently maintain an extended distance from the basic harmony. The opening and closing statements use only one chord over which Coltrane plays a modal melodic line. His solo on ''My Favorite Things'' shows how he applied his modal and extended harmonic technique to the more traditional song form. As his solo develops, it becomes so extended harmonically that it seems only vaguely related to the ongoing and apparently frozen harmonic center below it.

> There is a fascinating correlation between the quality of jazz solos and the 'feeding capacity' of the chord changes, especially in earlier jazz. In any event, solutions for playing on little-varied 'changes' or in minor keys were not developed consistently until the late thirties and in the 'extended' improvisations of Miles Davis in the late fifties.[2]

Modal jazz begins to breakdown the tonal structures that have served as its backbone since its beginnings. However, the term ''modal'' is actually a reference to very early classical music which had not yet coalesced into the tonal structures that dominate music since the baroque period. The chord progressions of modal music were meant for the color they created rather than to satisfy tonal expectations. Modal jazz works much the same way, although the sounds themselves are quite different from those of early music. This shift from one harmonic area to another creates a colorful shift that adds structural definition to the music. Above these frozen harmonies, the melodic lines of the soloists can spin out unfettered by the expected chordal progressions typical of such earlier tonal styles as bop.

---

[2]Gunther Schuller, *Early Jazz* (New York: Oxford University Press, 1968), p. 130.

ROLES OF THE
RHYTHM
SECTION—A
CONSTANTLY
CHANGING
BALANCE

At first, the three-instrument rhythm section consisted of tuba, banjo, and drums and played as one unit with one job—to keep a steady moving beat. Four even beats to the measure, known as flat 4/4, were played. Ragtime piano players had a different approach. The left hand played both the bass and chords so the right hand could accomplish the syncopated melodies. This caused a rhythmic feeling of accented second and fourth beats. Chicago Style Dixieland included piano players who were ragtime oriented. This influenced how their rhythm sections performed.

The swing bands were large and played in large ballrooms for hundreds of dancers. These dancers needed a definite, unfettered beat. There were no amplifiers at that time for the individual musicians, just microphones for singers and occasional soloists. This situation relegated the rhythm section into a unison performance of a flat 4/4. The swing bass player did not ''walk'' as is common in later four beat styles. The bass player most often repeated notes on the root and the fifth of the chords to accent all four beats rather than walking through the harmonies. The drummer also accents all four beats usually on the bass and snare drums. Although the rhythm section overlapped duties a great deal, their job was extremely important because it was usually the determining factor as to how well the band swung. The Count Basie band was often considered the band who swung the most, and its rhythm section was called a ''swing machine.''

The bop rhythm section changed all this because they were usually small bands playing in small clubs. The assigned parts played by individual members of the rhythm section underwent radical changes. Instead of the regular 4/4 steady rhythm heard in swing music, the drummer now used the bass and snare drums mainly for accents and punctuations. He usually maintained an overall sound by playing swing eighth-note rhythms on the top or ''ride'' cymbal. If the accents were not spontaneous, they were played on either the fourth beat of the bar or the fourth beat of every other bar. The drummer's left foot maintained a back-beat on two and four with the hi-hat or ''sock'' cymbal. The more spontaneous and often surprising accents played by the drummer were called ''bombs'' and were intended to lend impetus and excitement to the performance. The piano player changed from playing a steady 4/4 rhythm to accented and syncopated chord punctuations. With the advent of the amplifier, the guitar was able to move functionally between the rhythm section and the other melody instruments. This left the responsibility for the steady pulse of the beat to the string bass. Although the string bass part now had a more interesting line, the line seldom compromised its responsibility to making good time. Because the bass carried the main responsibility for time, the drummer often worked as a cosoloist with the other instrumentalists. The time keeping role of the string bass was also wedded to the task of signalling chord changes and outlining the harmonies. The resulting walking pattern used by most bass players has become a trademark of mainstream jazz. Because the roles of the various instruments were individualized, they had to be coordinated to create an integrated whole. The composite unity achieved by these rhythm sections was a fitting backdrop for the equally complex and lively solos above them. From this point on in jazz, the rhythm section players were liberated from the purely supportive roles typical of previous styles. They began to interact in the ensemble much like the other soloists. Their work now involved constant improvisation rather than simple timekeeping.

Cool saw a softening of the intensity of the various players, but their functions changed little from bop. The playing was more conservative and the drummer again assumed responsibility for keeping time. Hard bop returned not only to a more basic chord vocabulary but also to a more basic beat. However, once liberated, the rhythm section would no longer merely keep time.

Jazz/rock fusion saw another shift in the function of the rhythm section. The move involved an adoption of the steady rock underpinning at work in the popular music of the 1970s. The dance related rock feel was augmented by a new virtuosity in jazz. Players like Jaco Pastorius on bass and Peter Erskine on drums opened the door for a soloistic display previously unheard of in jazz or rock. Extended performance techniques, such as fast improvisatory flights on bass and complex subdivisions on drums, became common expectations of groups like Weather Report or Return to Forever. Along with the new virtuosity came new disjunct melodic ensemble passages presaged in the unison heads of the Bop era, only now, the rhythm section joined the unison line. Zawinul's ''Birdland'' or Corea's ''Got a Match'' are examples of the expectations of the fusion rhythm section. In many ways, this transition gave the rhythm section players full membership in the improvisational activities of the jazz ensemble.

The later jazz/pop/fusion presented a new twist. The rock feel centered the rhythm around the drummer who held the primary timekeeping role. A role often characterized by virtuosic displays of technique. Because much of this music was created in the recording studio, it required a new relationship between all members of the ensemble. The rhythm section had to be more planned because it would probably be recorded before the soloists or auxiliary tracks were added. Their participation in the real-time improvisation of the developing solo was now impossible. Because of this limitation, groups often recorded albums after they had toured with the music so ensemble tightness resulting from simultaneous playing, as well as the nuances that develop only through repeated performances, could be anticipated in the studio. Also because of the new technology, the roles of the players were sometimes replaced or traded with sequenced synthesizer lines. For example, a harmonic ostinato can be sequenced and played back to establish both a harmonic and rhythmic environment normally supplied by the basic rhythm section. The final solos added to the recording may operate similarly to a previous style with the exception that it will get little feedback from the prerecorded rhythm tracks. The studio, in its own way, restricts the role of the rhythm section in much the same way the dancers did for the earlier bands.

## SUGGESTED LISTENING

*The Best of Count Basie.* Columbia Records C31 33.
Coltrane, John. ''Alabama.'' Smithsonian I/3(cd V/6).
Coltrane, John. *My Favorite Things.* Atlantic Records 1361.
Corea, Chick. ''Got a Match?'' Elektric Band, GRP Records, GRPA-1026.
Davis, Miles. *Bitches Brew.* Columbia Records GP 26 CS 9995.
Davis, Miles. *Kind of Blue.* Columbia Records PC 8163.
Davis, Miles. *Milestones.* Columbia Records PC 9428E.
*Jammin' for the Jackpot.* New World Records NW 217.
*Kansas City Jazz.* Decca Records 8044.
Parker, Charlie, and Miles Davis. ''Klacktoveedsteen.'' Smithsonian E/12(cd 111/16).
Zawinul, Joe, and Weather Report. ''Birdland.'' *Heavy Weather.* Columbia Records 34418.

# PART 2

## Evolutionary Lines of Development

# CHAPTER 5

## *An Art Form in Its Infancy*

| | |
|---|---|
| *1800* | The Great Awakening |
| *1843–1900s* | Minstrel shows |
| *1861–1865* | Civil War, four million Americans freed |
| *1920* | First vocal recording of blues—Mamie Smith's "Crazy Blues" |
| *1928* | Bessie Tucker recorded "Penitentiary Blues" |
| *circa 1933* | Huddie Ledbetter—work songs |
| *circa 1934* | Bessie Jones recorded "Beggin' the Blues" |
| *1934* | Omer Simeon and James P. Johnson recorded "Blues for Lorenzo" |

J azz emerged from the folk music of America. The contributions to the development of the art form went undocumented because their importance was not recognized. The country had recently finished a revolution that freed part of the population to practice religion independently of the mother country, while the other part of the population was brought into the excitement of the Great Awakening that signaled a revival of the religious music of America. These two populations, one white and the other African American, put in place the balance of forces that were to shape the jazz expression. Their separate traditions, both musical and cultural, established a musical genre that would be unique in the world. However, the disparity between the two also set up a constantly shifting balance between the dominant expressions of each culture, one from western Europe the other from Africa. They both brought different values and needs to the musical fusion that continues to define jazz. One tradition is predominantly precomposed and reflects concerns and performance practice of such an approach, while the other carried its tradition through the expressive language of the oral tradition. As these traditions met in jazz expression, a balance of compositional concern and theatrical expression was established that would continue to define jazz.

---

## INTERPRETATION AND SUBSTANCE

All musical styles and traditions have an interpretive system of presentation that cannot always be described fully in terms of the musical elements that make up a performance. Consider the theatrical nature of a classical music concert and compare it to those of a rock concert. The manner in which each presents their musical substance, harmony, rhythm, and melody, is quite different. The musical elements of both are certainly arrayed differently but remain essentially the same. The musical parts alone do not describe the musical meaning inherent in each, just as describing the parts of a butterfly fails to reveal the beauty of the creature.

Jazz, as a hybrid of musical traditions, reflects both a blend of musical interpretations, as well as a blend of musical elements. When looking at musical style, you are tempted to deal with the describable elements of the music and overlook the more elusive but essential expressive delivery. The problem of finding the beauty in a jazz statement is compounded by the tools we use to describe this beauty. These tools are inherited from the western European musical tradition and best describe music from that tradition. The European notation system does not allow for the microtonal variations employed by jazz performers nor does it address the polymetrical delivery typical of jazz. Outside the musical elements themselves, there is also the theatrical context in which the elements are presented. There is currently no real language for describing the theatrical meaning of any music let alone that of jazz. To make matters worse, the theatrical context rather than the musical substance may carry the most meaning to the average listener. The majority of listeners do not know the complex musical jargon wielded by afficionados, but their interest in the music is still genuine. We must keep this context in mind as we look for the influences that shaped early jazz expression.

We will also see that the balance of musical substance and interpretive expression did not remain static during jazz's development. It is common in jazz for the meaningful content to reside more in the expressive nature of the music rather than the describable substance of the music. The majority of jazz's music is borrowed from other musical streams, such as the standard melodies of musical theater. Interpretive expressions shift constantly as jazz responds to current social and cultural needs. It is this shifting balance between the various social and cultural attitudes and their relationship to the musical substance that generates the continuing evolution of jazz. The fact that several cultural groups are working with the jazz expression also means that concomitant interpretive voices may be at work in any jazz period. Compare, for instance, the white and African-American bands working in the Swing era or the cool and hard bop styles existing together under the same umbrella of the jazz definition.

The scattered origins of jazz with their companion oral and notated traditions tend to obscure any clear lines of development toward a jazz definition, because that definition is of a shifting balance that cannot be frozen. Oral traditions leave no notated record of their development making them more difficult for historians to track but a definite advantage for a growing and evolving art form because they are not bound by an established notational practice. They have no guiding force or conscious theoretical systems to keep them historically neat. They develop through practice not theoretical planning. To impose, in retrospect, a neat historical explanation on the development of early folk music in America would be misleading. Oral traditions by their very nature stress the expressive delivery of musical substance rather than the compositional integrity on which they are based. Fascination with the theoretical underpinnings of jazz expression was a much later development.

## CHURCH MUSIC OF THE GREAT AWAKENING

Among the many places from which jazz expression can be traced, the church is a central contributor. The expressive voices heard there were certainly reflective of those heard in the field, but the subject and much of the substance is taken from the white spiritual tradition. After the American Revolution, a religious fervor spread throughout this country which expressed itself in revival services and camp meetings. The services offered a wedding of preaching and singing. Most of these meetings were shared but segregated by race. The religious expressions commonly associated with the black church today grew out of that interaction. The hymns used in these services were of Scottish and English origins, as was much of the singing practice. Although much of the musical material was shared, a distinct manner of singing was maintained. The call and response technique of African musical groups had a counterpart in the "lining out" typical of the Scottish singing tradition. The leader sings a line of the hymn and is then joined by the congregation. The resultant sound is not a harmonically based polyphony but a monophonic "heterophony" composed of the individual expressions within the congregation. Listen to Mount Olivet Regular Baptist Church of Kentucky sing "Guide Me, O Thou Great Jehovah" for the heterophony that results from lining out.

## Mount Olivet Regular Baptist Congregation
### "Guide Me O Thou Great Jehovah"
### New World Records NW 294

:00   Leader lines out the first line of text for the congregation to follow.

:09   The congregation begins to sing the same line behind the leader.

:21   Leader sings the second line.

:24   Congregation joins in.

:42   This process continues to the end of the hymn. Listen for harmonies that occur as the leader and congregation overlap, as well as the heterophony that results within the congregation as the individual variations of the melody interweave.

5:28  Fades out

This monophonic singing style is quite similar to that of the African tradition. It is not controlled by the vertical musical structures, meter and harmony, most often associated with western European music. The rhythm used is freely generated and whatever harmony results is a by-product of the melodic singing style. Such a singing style was accessible to the blacks who shared the camp meetings. However, the theatrical delivery of the whites and blacks differed. Listen to Rev. J. M. Gates's sermon "Dry Bones" for both the type of inflections he uses and how the congregation interacts with him. The call and response used here is spontaneous, and the vocalizations suggestive of later singing styles.

Compare the presentation of Rev. Gates to the presentation of the testimony of George Spangler of the Thorton Regular Baptist Church in Kentucky. Spangler's intonation reflects the white singing style. His testimony (a short personalized sermon) is followed by a lined out hymn with the congregation.

George Pullen Jackson, who authored a great deal of research on the folk music in America after the revolution, suggests that the later and better-known African-American spirituals must be attributed

### Rev. J. M. Gates
"Dry Bones" sermon
Folk Ways FJ 2801

:00   Sermon begins.

:09   Spoken responses from the congregation

:32   Short sung phrases from the congregation

:45   Hymnlike sung lines in the congregation. This continues off and on throughout the sermon.

:59   Shouted responses to the short phrases in the sermon

1:06   Gates begins to intone the sermon as the energy of the sermon mounts.

1:27   Shouts from the congregation

1:33   Gates begins to sing some of the phrases.

1:50   Shouted call and response

2:13   Gates sings a phrase.

2:32   The sermon's intonation here is very similar to that of a holler.

2:40   Gates begins the main point of the sermon as he continues to sing the sermon. The vocalizations are similar to those also heard in early blues. The congregation continues to respond spontaneously.

3:29   End of the recording

completely to the white spirituals typically used in the Great Awakening. This is certainly an extreme point of view not generally supported by other musicologists (see Eileen Southern's *History of Black Music in America*). However, the reciprocal relationship between the two musical expressions and their shared musical substance in a common arena is significant.

African Americans and whites shared the same hymnody but placed their own interpretation on it. The dominant body of hymns were written by the English poet Isaac Watts (1674–1748) whose compositions continued to be adapted by African Americans for over two

**SPIRITUALS AND GOSPEL**

George Spangler
"Testimony"
New World Records NW 294

---

:00 Testimony begins.

:16 Spangler's intonation increases slightly.

26 Claps

:34 He sings a short phrase.

:39 Response from congregation

:56 Begins to intone some lines

1:02 Very heightened speech

1:25 Energy drops as he sets up the hymn to follow.

1:35 Congregation begins to sing.

1:42 Lining out of the first line of text for the hymn

1:58 Second line of text is presented by the leader. This
continues to the end of the hymn. Listen to the type of
slurred ornamentation used by both the leader and the
congregation. Notice that there is no clear metric
underpinning.

4:44 Fades out

---

centuries. It was not until the turn of the century that African-American composers like Charles Albert began to contribute to the pool of gospel songs. The "Dr. Watts" singing style became the dominant expression for the African-American spiritual. It involved interplay between a lead singer who sets out the lyric and the rest of the vocal group. The repeated response to the leader was characterized by ornaments and variations appropriate to the intensity of the moment. Listen to the Dr. Watts vocal style as performed by The Kings of Harmony on "God Shall Wipe All Tears Away." Although the harmonic language now used is more vertically aligned than in earlier spirituals, listen for the freely expressive lines sung by the various singers in their call and response style.

The white tradition, especially in the South became more vertical in its performance with notated hymns that outlined specific four-part harmonies. One popular white spiritual singing style of the rural

## The Kings of Harmony
### "God Shall Wipe All Tears Away"
### New World Records NW 224

:00  Leader begins and is immediately joined by the rest of the group.

:08  Harmonies slide with the individual inflections of the singers.

:26  Leader begins next phrase.

:42  Descant by leader over a single harmony then ensemble phrase in harmony

:59  Descant returns

1:06  Quick call and response section

1:18  Notice the juxtaposition between a leader descant style over a frozen harmony and ensemble phrases sung in harmony. Listen for how the "chords" are improvised into focus. There is no clearly tonal progression underlying the choice of harmonies. Also notice the lack of any fixed meter.

1:31  Leader again leads in a new phrase.

2:22  Quick call and response section

2:45  End

South was the fuging hymns of the Sacred Harp, a collection of 573 four-part hymns sung from notation. This rugged singing style reflects the vertical musical language still at work today in the church.

Spirituals later became associated most with the African-American singing style but could be found in both the white and African-American churches. White sacred music was distinguished originally by the term *gospel,* while African-American church songs were called spirituals. Gospel later became a musical genre performed by African-American professionals, and its influence worked its way through much of the popular music through the twentieth century.

In the earliest forms of church music, the white and African-American churches voiced different concerns in their spirituals and

### Reba Dell Lacy conducts
### "Milford"
### New World Records NW 205

:00    Intonation set for the group

:04    First staggered phrase entrance called fuging

:13    Homophonic phrase extension

:17    New staggered phrase entrance. Notice how each of the phrases end homophonically even though they begin each time in the fuging style.

:24    New phrase, notice that there is a generally understood meter at work, holding the group together as they make their entrances.

:32    New phrase

:40    New phrase

:49    New text as the first half of the piece is repeated musically

:59    Homophonic phrase extension as in the first phrase

1:03    New phrase, continued fuging entrances

1:10    New phrase

1:19    New phrase

1:26    New phrase

1:36    End

gospels. The African-American church and music centered on their daily humanness and the suffering associated with daily life. The music carried the blue notes and "moaning" typical of their other singing styles outside the church. The white gospel tradition was more one of revival and the "good news" associated with the next life. Their music was typically major and used the simple primary chords. Their music was also much more text based with a stanza-chorus format. The purpose of the hymn focused on the transmission of the text than the more expressive emotional release more typical of the repetitive musical style of the African-American church. For contrast, listen to the African-American quartet, the Famous Blue Jay Singers,

## The Famous Blue Jay Singers
''Canaan Land''
New World Records NW 224

:00   Solo with chordal backup, no clear meter
:10   Listen for sliding harmonies that move with individual ornamentation.
:36   Call and response begins, hint of meter.
:52   Listen for individual expression by the descant singer and how the chords take shape beneath him.
1:23   Call and response as the tempo picks up and meter comes into focus
1:45   Meter clearly established
1:57   New verse takes on more energy
2:13   Listen for backup improvisation.
2:29   Call and response continues.
3:00   Slows to ending
3:06   End

sing ''Canaan Land'' for the famous quartet style that developed out of the spiritual style. This is delivered in the Dr. Watts singing style and still allows for individual embellishments in the group expression.

Compare this delivery to that of the congregation of Ridgecrest Baptist Church singing an Issac Watts hymn, ''We're Marching to Zion'' in a more typically white style. The vertical alignment of the harmonies is constant as is the swinging 6/8 meter underpinning the performance.

Most agree that the clearest line to the African heritage could be found in the walk-around or ring shout which was as much a circular dance as a musical custom. This was very charismatic and only later assimilated into the white services during the Great Awakening. The religious fervor of this time drove the expressive voice of American music. The shout was the counterbalance to the mournful spiritual and offered a release for intense religious energy.

## Ridgecrest Baptist congregation
### "We're Marching to Zion"
New World Records NW 224

:00   Organ introduction

:12   Verse 1: Piano improvising over the organ accompaniment

:36   Chorus: Notice the controlled use of harmonies, little use of individual vocal embellishments; chord progressions are clearly tonal.

:53   Verse 2

1:17  Chorus

1:35  Verse 3: Sung a cappella, homophonic structure can be clearly heard here.

2:03  Chorus: Still a cappella

2:23  Verse 4: With organ and piano

2:48  Chorus

3:08  End

"Walk Around" by the Soul Stirrers shows how the later male quartets began to develop into the do-wop style known in the popular music of the 1950s. The harmonies, as well as the call response technique, had become much more standardized.

The harmonizing that developed out of this tradition is still at work today inside and outside of jazz. A current notable example is the vocal group Take 6. Their music is consistent with the quartet tradition, as well as the more recent advents in jazz history. Popular music has a large number of groups that reflect the quartet style, particularly the do wop groups associated with Motown records, such as the Pips, Platters, and others. Gospel is still sung in the church and can be heard on the records of such groups as Andraé Crouch and the Disciples.[1]

---

[1] Andraé Crouch and the Disciples, *"Live" at Carnegie Hall,* Light Records, a division of Lexicon Music LS-5602-LP. This recording is organized like a church service and shows the integration of a popular gospel style in the service itself.

## The Soul Stirrers
### "Walk Around"
### New World Records NW 224

:00   Descant sung over a rhythmic backup supplies the harmonies and meter against which the descant can work.

:17   Chord change

:22   Next chord change, listen for how liquid the chords seem as they resolve (V–IV) back to the home harmony.

:26   Return to tonic harmony

:43   Verse 2: Continue to listen to the liberties taken by the backup singers as they shape the harmonies. Even though the chords are standardized verse to verse, they are still subject to individual improvisations that create constant, small variations in the chords which are perceived more as shifts in intonation than actual chord changes.

1:23   Verse 3

2:01   Verse 4

2:42   End

## BLUES—THE STYLE

Blues has such a singular identity that it cannot be claimed exclusively by any musical tradition. Its influence is as real today as it was at the turn of the twentieth century. In addition to influencing other American music idioms, such as jazz, blues has a tradition all its own. As is typical of most jazz styles, it reflects both the western European and African traditions. The European sources are the Spanish *copla* and the Italian *stornello,* which both have a rhymed couplet set to a strophic melody. The African sources reside in the expressive melodic style. The use of descending lines, blue notes, and melismatic melodies are characteristic of African singing. Add to these ingredients the repressed life of plantation slavery and penitentiary farms, and the spirit of the blues is complete. The blues became more formalized and fully established as it moved from the rural setting to the industrialized urban centers.

*Take 6*

Courtesy of © Warner Bros. Records

The roots of blues can be heard in the solo holler or cry used by African-American workers as they worked in the open fields. These hollers were both communication between workers, as well as an expression of anger about their situation. The hollers were not always sung to words. When they were, they often spoke of things not allowed in normal situations. Because no recorded examples exist before the 1930s, the vocal connection between these hollers and the later blues expression is based on written accounts made by earlier observations. Listen to "Ol' Hannah" by Doc Reese for an example of a solo holler.

It is not easy to distinguish between the various musical expressions of the African-American culture. Although the activity may be different, such as worship or work, the musical expression may be quite similar in expression. The same use of ornamentation and heterophony appears in much of their music. For example, work songs were often religious in nature and considered spirituals, yet their function was clearly different. Consequently, work songs also influenced the developing blues tradition. They certainly reflected one of the reasons the blues were sung. "Julianna and Johnson" sung by Ledbetter is a good example of a work song.

This work song is obviously a later version of an earlier functional music because it is accompanied and tends to speed up for

# Take 6
## "Get Away, Jordan"
### Reprise 9 25670–2

---

This arrangement is reflective of much of the gospel tradition, as well as of other jazz styles, particularly the later big band use of a shout chorus as a climax. The members of the group actually introduce themselves as traditional jazz instrumentalists, e.g., horns, bass, lead, etc.

:00   Introduction: Sound of the surf, do wop-like bass figures

:19   Verse anticipated in descant line

:28   Verse with bass fills

:46   Verse repeats, bass begins phrase with a walking bass pattern

1:05  Harmonized do wop-like figures over bass solo

1:23  Bass continues to work like a descant in a call and response with the rest of the group.

1:42  Short solo phrases between harmonized phrases

2:01  Precise ensemble with tight harmonies

2:21  Brass-like punches by top voices

2:34  Musical joke contrasts their own expressive singing with this stiff over sung vocal phrase.

2:40  Short solo phrases

2:58  Top voices start using brass "shout" figures typical of big bands.

3:12  Phrase extension

3:21  Ritard: "Shout" section with walking bass

3:38  Vocal sound effects

3:41  Continued shout phrases

3:55  Musical joke again

4:01  Extended ending

4:14  Extended harmony as last chord with a cliché trumpet-like tag in top voice

4:23  End

Doc Reese
"Ol' Hannah"
Folkways FJ 2801

This prison holler shows many of the characteristics later incorporated in the blues. The melody is strophic (repeated verses) with a two-part structure, the second phrase responding to the first. Notice the conclusion of the second phrase is shorter than the first phrase, creating an elision that sets up the new verse. Listen for the descending melodic phrases that will become a trademark of the blues, as well as the note bending.

:00   Verse 1: First phrase, notice the descending phrases.

:11   Second phrase: Notice the shorter phrase setting up the next phrase.

:21   Verse 2: Same two phrases

:40   Verse 3

:58   Verse 4

1:17   Verse 5

1:34   Verse 6

1:52   Verse 7

2:10   Verse 8

2:23   Verse 9

2:40   Verse 10

2:57   Verse 11

3:18   Verse 12: A new melody is used still with a two-part phrase structure. Each of the two phrases have two smaller parts. Notice the more rhythmic feel suggested by the melody.

3:24   Second phrase of verse 12

3:30   Verse 13: Continues to use new melody to end

3:43   Verse 14

3:55   Verse 15

4:07   Verse 16: Doc Reese begins to sing in falsetto, a high range above his full voice singing range.

4:21   Verse 17: Second phrase in falsetto

4:26   Verse 18: Phrase structure is compromised as he approaches the end.

4:40   End

## Huddie Ledbetter (Lead Belly)
''Juliana Johnson''
Folkways FJ 2801

---

This work song (axe-cutting song) has a two-part phrase structure for each verse. Listen for the accent vocalization on the third beat of each measure. This accent signals when the coordinated work activity would take place, here the swinging of the axe.

:00   Verse 1: Juliana Johnson, oh Lord
:06   Second responding phrase, Juliana Johnson, oh may
:11   Juliana Johnson, oh Lord
:17   Juliana Johnson, oh may
:23   Gonna leave you, oh may
:28   Gonna leave you, oh may
:33   Look out Juli, oh may
:38   Look out Juli, oh may
:43   What's a matter with Juli, oh may
:48   What's a matter with Juli, oh may
:52   Gonna leave you, oh may
:57   Gonna leave you, oh may
1:02   End

*Lead Belly*

Michael Ochs Archives/
Venice, CA

Bessie Tucker
"Penitentiary Blues"
Folkways FJ 2801

:00    Piano introduction

:19    Vocal enters with first phrase of AAB blues form.

:33    Second phrase (A)

:46    Third phrase (B)

1:00   Second chorus, listen to the relationship of the melody to
       the harmonies and meter. Notice particularly the transitions
       between phrases to hear the polyrhythmic relationship to
       the meter typical of blues melodies. This relationship makes
       the transitions difficult to pinpoint.

1:16   Second phrase (A)

1:30   Third phrase (B)

1:43   Third chorus (A)

1:58   A

2:12   B

2:25   Fourth Chorus (A)

2:38   A

2:53   B

3:05   End

increased excitement. However, its work song derivation is clear, as
well as its relationship to the early blues. Listen to Bessie Jones sing
"Beggin' the Blues" to hear an unaccompanied version of the early
blues (*Roots of the Blues,* New World Records NW 252, Side 2, band
5). Its connection to the field holler is clear. Also listen to Bessie
Tucker sing "Penitentiary Blues."

Even in the early predecessors of the blues uses of vocal inflections used in later blues can be heard, as well as the melodic and
rhythmic activity used by later jazz styles which were borrowed from
the blues. The strophic phrase structure is shared with the blues and
the introduction of the flatted third and seventh notes of the scale are
the most direct attributes used by later styles. More subtle is the relationship of the melodic rhythm to the steady rhythm in the accompaniment. The independence of the melodic rhythm varies with each

## Minstrels

The minstrel shows were very important in the dissemination of jazz around the turn of the century and originated on the plantations. The slaves would perform minstrels for the entertainment of the whites; often, these shows incorporated true slave songs. The slaves acted in such a way as to mock the whites by "putting on airs." The whites enjoyed the shows to the point where they themselves put on these same minstrels. The whites would don black makeup and imitate the slaves mocking the whites. The epitome of this situation came about when the African Americans would put on burnt cork black makeup and imitate the whites imitating the African Americans who were mocking the whites.

Around the turn of the century, traveling minstrel shows were the main form of entertainment for both races. The shows featured the top blues singers of the day, such as Bessie Smith, Ma Rainey, and others. The performances were accompanied by small jazz bands, thus helping to spread the popularity of the new music.

The syncopated rhythms of the cakewalk were part of every minstrel show. There were contests popular for cakewalking and ragtime playing. It is easy to discern how, through the minstrel shows, instrumental jazz, blues singing, ragtime playing, and the highly rhythmic cakewalk demonstrations began to be accepted throughout the country.

verse and establishes a subtle polymetric feeling that becomes a cornerstone of later jazz styles, as well as the trademark of particular performers. It portends the melodic lines of Billie Holiday, Lester Young, and Charlie Parker among others.

The last part of the nineteenth century brought much of the rural and urban music into sharper focus because of the polarizing effects of the post-Reconstruction. The segregation laws triggered a similar need to separate the African-American identity in music. The gospel songs of the church replaced spirituals, the instrumental jazz idiom emerged from New Orleans parade music, and ragtime grew out of the plantation dances and walk-arounds. At the same time, the whites ridiculed African-American idioms in their own version of African-American music called "coon" songs. These were ragtime-based songs borrowed from the developing folk music of African Americans.

Omer Simeon (with James P. Johnson)
"Blues for Lorenzo"
Folkways FJ 2801

:00 Piano introduction (Johnson) that replaces the first A section of the first chorus.

:09 Second A section as clarinet enters

:18 B section to close the blues form

:27 Second chorus, (A)

:38 Second A

:48 B section

:58 Third chorus, same as second chorus with new improvisation. Listen for how phrases begin with the clarinet and finish with piano response.

1:27 Third chorus, piano solo, listen for the use of a stride-like left-hand accompaniment.

1:55 Fourth chorus, clarinet solo

2:25 End

Blues has undergone its own evolution. What began as field hollers became identified as rural or country blues and identified by performers like Robert Johnson. As the singers moved to the city, more contemporary instrumentation was adopted, and the stylized blues began to unfold. City blues adhered to a strict twelve-bar structure and grew out of the minstrel and vaudeville shows. Unlike the intimate, freer, rural blues usually sung by men, city blues was sung mostly by women like Bessie Smith in a performance setting. This urban blues, in turn, was the predecessor of what we now know as the classic blues sung by the female singers of the 1920s. Classic blues continued its legacy in the work of performers like Muddy Waters, B. B. King, Stevie Ray Vaughn, and Eric Clapton.

## THE BLUES FORM

The development of the blues as a formal structure is more than a rhymed couplet in iambic pentameter and a soulful stylistic expression. In addition to this earlier singing tradition, it acquired a formal structure (AAB) defined harmonically. This development is probably a result of a fusion with European song forms popular at the time. The vocal style heard in the hollers and work songs was soon adapted by the instrumentalists and carried into the standardized structural form. The blues form followed the lyric structure of three phrases, AAB, giving each phrase four measures. As you listen to Omer Simeon play ''Blues for Lorenzo'' notice the phrase structure and how the vocal inflections mentioned are a part of his clarinet style. Imagine how difficult it would be to notate the nuances he uses to stylize the melody.

---

**SUMMARY**

Although jazz has imported much from the emerging blues tradition, the blues continued as its own tradition. Just as jazz was to make its move away from the popular audience during the Bop era, blues again exerts its influence on American popular music in the form of rhythm and blues (R & B) and eventually rock and roll. The early quartet music already discussed was centered in the church and also mingled with the early R & B music to form the do wop groups of the 1950s. Although the blues seemed to lay dormant after rock took on its own definition, it made its way across the Atlantic and inspired groups like the Rolling Stones and the Who, who brought it back to the United States fused with rock. The blues tradition still continues today in the work of such players as the late Stevie Ray Vaughn and Eric Clapton. R & B has been able to resist being absorbed completely by jazz and rock as it continues to influence America's popular music.

---

**SUGGESTED LISTENING**

Bechet, Sidney. ''Blue Horizon.'' Smithsonian A/11(cd 1/11).
*Classic Jazz Piano Styles*. RCA Victor Records LPV 543 and 546.
The Famous Blue Jay Singers. ''Canaan Land.'' *Brighten the Corner Where You Are*. New World Records NW 224.
Folkways Jazz Series. *Piano*. Folkways FJ 2809.
Gates, J. M. Rev. ''Dry Bones,'' sermon. Folkways FJ 2801.
History of Classic Jazz. Vol. 2. *Ragtime*. Riverside Records SDP 11.
Jackson, Mahalia. ''If We Ever Needed the Lord Before.'' *Come On Children, Let's Sing*. Columbia Records CS8225.
Jazz Piano Anthology, (4 sides). Columbia Records PG 32355.
Johnson, James P. ''Carolina Shout.'' Smithsonian A/12(cd 1/12).
Joplin, Scott. ''Maple Leaf Rag.'' Smithsonian A/1(cd 1/1).
The Kings of Harmony. ''God Shall Wipe All Tears Away.'' *Brighten the Corner Where You Are*. New World Records NW 224.

Ledbetter, Huddie. ''Juliana Johnson.'' Folkways FJ 2801.
*Mahalia Jackson.* Columbia Records CL644.
*Maple Leaf Rag: Ragtime in Rural America.* New World Records
   NW 235.
Morton, Jelly Roll. ''Maple Leaf Rag.'' Smithsonian A/2(cd 1/2).
Mount Olivet Regular Baptist congregation. ''Guide Me, O Thou
   Great Jehovah.'' *The Gospel Ship.* New World Records
   NW 294.
Olympia Brass Band of New Orleans. *New Orleans Street Parade.*
   BASF Records 20678.
*Piano Roll Hall of Fame.* Sounds Records LP 1202.
*Ragtime Piano Roll.* Riverside Records 126.
Reese, Doc. ''Ol' Hannah.'' Folkways FJ 2801.
Ridgecrest Baptist congregation. ''We're Marching to Zion.''
   *Brighten the Corner Where You Are.* New World Records
   NW 224.
Simeon, Omer. ''Blues for Lorenzo.'' Folkways FJ 2801.
Smith, Bessie. ''Lost Your Head Blues.'' Smithsonian A/4(cd 1/4).
The Soul Stirrers. ''Walk Around.'' *Brighten the Corner Where
   You Are.* New World Records NW 224.
Spangler, George. ''Testimony.'' *The Gospel Ship.* New World
   Records NW 294.
Take 6. ''Get Away Jordan.'' *Take 6.* Reprise 9 25670–2.
Tucker, Bessie. ''Penitentiary Blues.'' Folkways FJ 2801.

# CHAPTER 6

## *Extemporized Ensembles*

| | |
|---|---|
| *1861–1865* | Civil War |
| *1890–1917* | Basic period for Early New Orleans Dixieland |
| *1894* | Code 111 forced Creoles uptown in New Orleans |
| *1914–1918* | World War I |
| *1917–1932* | Chicago Style Dixieland—The Roaring Twenties |
| *1917* | First instrumental jazz recorded—Original Dixieland Jazz Band |
| *1919* | First jazz band to go to Europe—Original Dixieland Jazz Band |
| *1923* | Morton recorded with his Red Hot Peppers, etc. |
| *1923* | Oliver recorded "Dippermouth Blues" |
| *1925–1929* | Armstrong organized and recorded his Hot Five and Hot Seven |
| *Late 1920s* | Bix Beiderbecke recorded with Frankie Trumbauer |
| *1932–1942* | Swing bands predominate jazz format |
| *1940s* | Early New Orleans Dixieland revival |
| *1960s* | Ornette Coleman recorded "Free Jazz" |
| *1960s* | Chicago school of free jazz gains importance |
| *1970s* | Extensive electronic advancements in recording |
| *1980s–1990s* | Jazz/Rock/Pop/Fusion |

———

T o improvise is to perform music created at the moment, not from memory or from written music. Collective improvisation is a concept that is inseparable from the definition of jazz and can be traced to its origins. Simply defined it means that the individual members making up an ensemble are improvising rather than playing precomposed parts. The resulting arrangement created at the moment of performance defines a truly extemporized ensemble. The balance between improvised and pre-composed duties for players in an ensemble has not always remained static. The balance between these two musical deliveries is discussed in detail in chapter 10. The focus of this chapter is the nature of extemporized ensembles and how they have changed throughout the history of jazz.

Each of the players in an ensemble represent a musical line or voice that contributes to the whole. The way these lines are performed changed as stylistic demands changed. In fact, some historical periods, such as the Swing era which is characterized by larger ensembles, deemphasized group improvisation. Large groups prove the most difficult medium for group improvisation. Formal arrangements or compositions are generally used to coordinate the performance of a large number of players. There are, however, such exceptions as Sun Ra in the 1960s that strived to balance individual expressions with group expression. The many historical faces of jazz have successfully balanced these two performance requirements. The ultimate expression of collective improvisation may very well be the music of the 1960s Chicago school of free jazz. Such a carefully struck balance between the voice of the individual and the composite musical expression is a defining characteristic of jazz.

Improvisation should not be equated with total freedom for the player. Even in the earliest ensembles, the role of each of the participants is fairly well-defined. As we will see, the notion of collective improvisation may remain constant, but the responsibilities of the performers in each style does not. The Early Dixieland players had different stylistic responsibilities than those of later free jazz ensembles.

Players have responsibilities to one another. If a single performer overplays, no sonic room is left for the other players. Even today, bands that use both guitars and keyboards face a similar conflict of roles. Which of the two players determines the chords to be used? Who is to be the dominant comping agent (the one who supplies the harmonies in a rhythmic setting)? Must one take the lead at the expense of the other? Herbie Mann prefers to use only one comping player because he feels if he used two strong players neither would have room to operate effectively.[1] As the musical lines become more independent, they must also show a respect for all the other lines around them. The protocol of each musical style determines how these musical lines will operate.

[1]From a conversation with Herbie Mann, August 1990.

New Orleans Dixieland inherited its ensemble approach from the early prejazz activities of the oral tradition which was characterized by a woven texture of individual musical lines. Such music could be heard in the church where the musical lines of soloists and the responding congregation were extemporized. Such improvisation was also at work in the post-Civil War bands, small bands playing for the traveling minstrel shows.

Dixieland was not the only music played in New Orleans. There were performances of French and American folk songs, society dances, parades, church music of varying types, and a great plethora of blues singing and playing. In this chapter, we are concerned with the emerging Dixieland ensembles that reflected many of these ongoing musical influences. French culture was more predominant in the New Orleans area than it seemed to be in any other part of the country. With French culture came the European musical influences heard throughout the territory. In fact, Jelly Roll Morton added his own jazz flavor to much music from the French culture, such as operatic excerpts and French quadrilles, one of which he claimed to have transformed into ''Tiger Rag.''

## MERGING CULTURES

Social discrimination, as it was practiced in post-Civil War segregation, placed the educated Creoles of French-African heritage into the African-American slave society. In 1894, Code 111 forced the Creole uptown, which was not considered a desirable place to live. In 1896, ''separate-but-equal'' status resulted in a closer association of musicians with different backgrounds. Code 111 essentially recognized the distinction between the Creole and African American but legally declared them equal. This intra-ethnic cohesion reduced status anxiety and helped fuse the disparate cultural influences into a single jazz expression. The Creoles, with the French background, contributed harmonic and formal structures to this early music. It would have been impossible for the loosely organized blues or slave music to have jelled enough for Dixieland ensembles to have performed with the great success that was the beginning of this art without directions from the more educated musicians. A blend of the oral tradition and the European musical tradition was also necessary for a successful assimilation by the cross-cultural listening audience of the New Orleans urban society.

## SOCIOLOGICAL INFLUENCES

But the repressive segregation laws passed at the turn of the century forced the ''light people'' into a closer social and economic relationship with the black culture. And it was the connections engendered by this forced merger that produced jazz. The black rhythmic and vocal tradition was translated into an instrumental music which utilized some of the formal techniques of European dance and march music.[2]

Dixieland jazz could only have developed if all the current influences of the day were in place, including the unfortunate circumstances of segregation.

## RAGTIME AND DIXIELAND

Ragtime and Dixieland jazz coexisted and shared some common pre-jazz origins and are often associated with one another. Although they share some characteristics, they offered two different jazz expressions. Ragtime was predominately a solo piano music, whereas Dixieland was an ensemble music. Both have syncopated textures, but they use the syncopation in different ways. Ragtime uses the left hand to alternate between the bass and chord punctuations. Together these two elements create the steady harmonic rhythm against which the right hand can play syncopations. Dixieland syncopation occurs within a polyphonic texture. The front line instruments weave syncopated lines against the steady flat four rhythm created by the rhythm section.

Ragtime was also based on a specific form and represented the notated musical tradition in its harmonic and formal structures. As we saw earlier in the Jelly Roll Morton version of "Maple Leaf Rag," a great deal of freedom was taken by players as they performed a written rag. The variations on the original notation were improvised rather than planned in advance. Even with the improvised variations, rags were still predominantly a written form. In contrast, Dixieland was a predominantly improvised activity. The melody was the only fixed musical element. All the rest were improvised during the performance.

The developing Dixieland ensembles in the territory were based on the interactive interplay more typical of the oral tradition. They also shared different musical functions. Ragtime was most prevalent at social gatherings, theaters, and bars. Dixieland was used for dancing, parades, and funerals.

[2]LeRoi Jones, *Blues People* (New York: William Morrow and Co., 1963), 139.

## INSTRUMENTAL OBLIGATIONS

It may seem unusual to discuss obligations in an area devoted to improvisation. However, the most successful leaders of this ''primitive'' style of jazz did have fairly rigid restrictions concerning the ensemble portions of their selections. The front line of these bands (cornet, clarinet, and trombone) had specific roles to carry out, specific instrumental obligations, in the collective improvisation of the ensemble sections. It should be kept in mind that even though there were solos during most of the selections, the ensemble playing was truly the most important aspect during the first stage of Dixieland jazz, the Early New Orleans Dixieland. Later, the emphasis shifted to the soloists, due to the virtuosity of Louis Armstrong in the 1920s. Compare Oliver's ''Sweet Lovin' Man,'' which opens with the ensemble, goes next into solos, then returns to ensemble, with Louis Armstrong's ''Sweethearts on Parade,'' which starts with a trumpet solo, then Armstrong sings a chorus, then a trumpet solo for the third chorus showing that Armstrong was the main attraction. On his record of ''I Gotta Right to Sing the Blues,'' Armstrong sings the first chorus, the ensemble plays the second, then he plays the third chorus as a solo.

Since by usual standards, the cornet (or later the trumpet) was the loudest instrument in the band, its role was to play the melody. The trumpet player could add his or her own personal interpretation to the original line, but he or she was not to stray so far from the original tune that the listeners could not recognize what piece was being played. Occasionally in more contemporary settings, the trumpet players would venture so far from their assigned duty that it appeared as if they were actually playing an improvised solo. The early players guarded against what, at that time, would have been considered a display of vanity.

The clarinet being a more facile instrument with easier access to a higher register had two definite obligations, a dual role. The primary function was to fashion a countermelody above the trumpet. The clarinet also added fills between the phrases of the melody to add momentum to the performance. Wails and squeals were better relegated to solo opportunities.

The trombone, of course, is a lower pitched instrument and generally not as capable of fast passages as the other two members of the front line. The trombone player's role was also quite specific. The trombone was to play important notes in each of the chord changes (granted the changes were simple by today's standards).

The first chord is an F chord (F A C D); the second chord is a D7 (F-sharp A C D). The trombone player would most likely play the

**EXAMPLE 6.1**   Typical front line syncopation

change from the F-natural to the F-sharp. Such a melodic line would indicate that the chord had changed by selecting the two notes that best signal the change.

Notice the trombone part in example 6.1. In the fourth bar, the seventh of the C chord (B-flat) is added; hence, the trombone player pointed this out. The next chord is an F chord (the IV chord in the key of C); this suggests that the trombonist gliss from the B flat down to A (the third in the F chord), then immediately go to the tonic (F) of the chord. Keep in mind that these ensemble parts had not been written, planned, or even discussed. This trombone part was merely logical in this style of playing jazz, a logic that was inherited from previous generations rather than consciously developed. The notation in example 6.1 is actually a transcription of an improvised performance of a tune called ''Blues for Brown'' and not played from the page at all. The theoretical understandings we now have of how this type of music was played were most likely unknown to the performers of the day. The fact that theory follows practice is a characteristic of an oral tradition and a dominant theme in the evolution of jazz.

Because the players had the freedom to improvise, they also had to exercise their ensemble responsibilities rather than indulge in soloistic displays if they were to maintain the delicate balance which characterized this Early Dixieland style.

The standard rhythm section of these early bands consisted of drums, tuba, and banjo. No piano was used at first because these groups evolved from marching bands. For the same reason the tuba rather than the string bass was used. However, changes took place rapidly when the bands' function turned to primarily dance music and saloon entertainment. These players kept the steady rhythm, a flat four beats to the bar. The wonderful polyphony of the front line had to have steady beats beneath it in order to establish its fascinating syncopation.

Example 6.1 shows the involved syncopation by compiling the attack of each note played by the front line. This demonstrates the shifting accents causing the most intriguing aspect of early collective improvisation (see example 6.1, p. 146).

## CONTROL OF POLYPHONY

Precomposed control might seem a natural extension of the unspoken protocol of the Early Dixieland ensembles. As we have seen, the players were not entirely free to play anything they wished. They were restrained by the expectations of the other players and their audience. Their roles were defined to a great extent by an unconscious consensus. However, this protocol still accommodated a wide range of individual expression. Two of the most important leaders of the time, Joe ''King'' Oliver and Jelly Roll Morton, brought a new compositional control to an otherwise freely extemporized ensemble practice. This move toward more compositional control is only the first such shift in the balance between the individual statement of a composer

# Joe "King" Oliver
## "Sweet Lovin' Man" (1923)
### Folkways 2806

Joe "King" Oliver, lead and solo cornet; Louis Armstrong, also on cornet; Jimmy Noone, clarinet; Honore Dutrey, trombone; Jonny St. Cyr, banjo; Warren "Baby" Dodds, drums; Lil Hardin (Armstrong), piano.

:00   Four-bar ensemble introduction

:06   Twelve-bar verse in typical ensemble fashion with the trombone leading into the strain with a gliss

:27   Chorus 1: Sixteen bars plus a two-bar tag, Oliver plays the melody with Armstrong directly beneath him. Clarinet plays his filigree. Trombone is very busy with runs and glisses. Rhythm section plays in a flat 4/4.

:58   Chorus 2: Clarinet solo using the blues chord progression, piano is the only background.

1:20   Chorus 3: Clarinet solo

1:41   Chorus 4: Ensemble plays eight bars (back to the original chord progression)

1:56   Cornet break for four bars, Oliver has a cup mute half way in

2:03   Four bars ensemble plus a two-bar tag

2:14   Chorus 5: Ensemble for eight bars

2:29   Cornet break again for four bars

2:36   Ensemble for four bars plus a two-bar tag

2:47   Coda, two bars of legato ensemble

2:51   End

or arranger and the individual freedom of the player. Chapter 6 deals specifically with how this issue threads its way through jazz's history.

Although the ensemble sounds of Oliver's band may have seemed wild, they were definitely controlled, and each player had a specified function. Through practice the performers developed specific parts that would be nearly the same, chorus to chorus. Oliver played the melody, Armstrong weaved an embellishment or played

## Joe "King" Oliver

**J**oe "King" Oliver is considered by many to be the first successful band leader of Early New Orleans Dixieland. It is logical that there were two really important aspects to Oliver's career. The first being the roster of musicians who worked in his band, the most notable being Louis Armstrong, Johnny Dodds, Warren "Baby" Dodds, George "Pops" Foster, all the way up to Lester Young. The other and truly most important item is the legacy of records he left us. His records exemplify the type of jazz played before, during, and shortly after World War I. His recording output around 1923 (thirty-seven numbers in all) is considered a cornerstone of traditional jazz.

*Joe "King" Oliver and his Creole Jazz Band*

© 1993 Ray Avery/Michael Ochs Archives/Venice, CA

1885   Oliver was born in Abend, Louisiana.
1907   He started working with local New Orleans bands.
1915   Oliver led his own band.
1918   Oliver moved to Chicago.
1920s   He began recording in Chicago.
1923   He recorded "Dippermouth Blues," recorded thirty-seven numbers in all.
1927   Oliver moved to New York.
1930   He experienced several years of unsuccessful one-night stands (dental problems plus poor management).
1935   Oliver disbanded his band.
1938   Oliver died penniless in Savannah, Georgia.

harmony, Dodds (clarinet) played a filigree, Dutrey (trombone) provided either connecting phrases or whole tones suggesting harmonic patterns. Still, with Oliver's band, you listened to the band; not until Armstrong's later band did your attention shift to the soloist.

Armstrong's stylistic dominance signaled a new format for ensemble performance as the musical center of jazz moved to Chicago due to the closing of Storyville in New Orleans. There is essentially a reversal of prominence between the ensemble as a unit and the individual voice of a soloist. As New Orleans Dixieland preferred to

**CHICAGO ENSEMBLES**

feature the ensemble, Chicago Dixieland seems to feature soloists more and use the ensemble to open and close a given number. Nevertheless, the polyphony of the ensembles still remained as the dominant stylistic process for the group when it played as a unit. Except for Armstrong, the soloistic statements within a composition did not create the necessary excitement expected from an ensemble; it had to be created mainly by the ensemble itself.

Beiderbecke never seemed to let his style on the cornet become as dramatic or sensual as Armstrong's. Instead, his cornet music is usually described as poetic, fluid, moving, and sensitive. In Armstrong were combined well-developed technique, rhythmic feel, strong tone, a high register, and an intuitive sense of phrasing. Opposite of Beiderbecke, Armstrong often seemed gregarious and extroverted, traits that obviously exhibited themselves during performance. Perhaps more important than the many phrasing and jazz idioms Armstrong gave to jazz is his defining role as an individual jazz voice. Since his early work, players still look for their own ''voice'' as a central ingredient of their style.

Chicago players first learned the Dixieland style from records of the Original Dixieland Jazz Band and the New Orleans Rhythm Kings, but they soon traveled to the south side of the city to hear the more original sources, the black bands. By sitting in and playing with them, they could better assimilate the traditional Dixieland style. In the twenties, Chicago benefited from easier communication between the races than did New York City, allowing for an easier transfer of stylistic influences between bands.

---

## JAZZ AND THE ''LOST GENERATION''

In the 1920s, there was the anti-idealistic attitude of the ''Lost Generation'' who was disillusioned by the results of World War I. They saw hypocrisy in the older generation, a situation which seems to be common after wars. Life to them was meant to be fun, i.e., the wild life of the ''Roaring 20s.'' In art, it meant Joyce, Pound, O'Neill, and Picasso. Jazz was fun, sexy, and new. Most entertainment was social dancing, and jazz was the music for dancing. At the same time, African Americans were moving out of the rural areas and ghettos to take advantage of the employment opportunities created by World War I. Many African Americans headed north, which meant moving into a different cultural setting. They carried with them their musical heritage, which influenced the development of Chicago jazz. The invention of the phonograph, a patent which Edison filed for in 1877, also helped launch the popularity of jazz.

Much like the characters portrayed by actor James Dean, Chicago Dixieland expressed a voice of rebellion against traditional

## Louis Armstrong

If the most influential musician in the history of jazz had to be chosen, the choice would likely be Daniel Louis Armstrong. By 1926, he was considered the greatest trumpet player who ever lived. His tone, stamina, range, creativeness, and technique were envied by all jazz performers. At that early age, he became the ideal, the model of how to play jazz improvisation. Although he often seemed gregarious and extroverted, Armstrong could play a blues that was lovely and sad at the same time. Armstrong was the leader for all the other players to follow.

*Louis Armstrong*
Michael Ochs Archives/
Venice, CA

1900  Armstrong born in New Orleans, Louisiana, on July 4.
1913  He was placed in the Waif's Home in New Orleans for 1½ years.
1917  He worked for Joe Oliver in New Orleans.
1918  He worked for Kid Ory.
1920  Armstrong joined Fate Marable's band on a Mississippi river steamboat.
1922  He joined Oliver in Chicago.
1924  He joined Fletcher Henderson in New York.
1925  He returned to Chicago to front his own band.
1925  Armstrong started recording Hot Five and Hot Seven records.
1929  He returned to New York City, this time famous.
1930  He traveled to California as a band leader.
1932  Armstrong headlined a show in London's Palladium.
1933  He made an extended European tour.
1936  He traveled to Hollywood to appear in a Bing Crosby movie called *Pennies from Heaven.*
1947  He began fronting his famous all-star combos.
1948  Armstrong successfully toured the entire world.
1950s  Many movies, honors, books were created about Armstrong, and he attained a true "star" status.
1964  His biggest record success, "Hello Dolly," was mostly vocal.
1971  Armstrong died in Corona, Long Island, New York, on July 6.

*Leon Bismark ''Bix''*
*Beiderbecke*

Michael Ochs Archives/
Venice, CA

## Leon Bismark (Bix) Beiderbecke

**B**eiderbecke was appreciated by only a handful of musicians during his lifetime. However, years after his death, he acquired the status of a legend. This was partly due to Dorothy Baker's book *Young Man With a Horn,* inspired by Beiderbecke's life story.

Beiderbecke possessed an exquisite tone and a lyrical style of improvisation that captured the admiration of both white and African-American musicians of the day. He was the symbol of F. Scott Fitzgerald's *Jazz Age.*

*1903*   Beiderbecke was born in Davenport, Iowa, on March 10.

*1923*   He joined the Wolverines.

*1924*   He made his first recordings with the Wolverines for Gennett Recordings.

*1924*   Beiderbecke went to New York City.

*1925*   He joined Charlie Straight's Orchestra and spent much time in Chicago listening to the African-American players there.

*1926*   He joined Frankie Trumbauer's Orchestra in Saint Louis, then the two joined Jean Goldkette in Detroit.

*1928*   Both musicians joined Paul Whiteman where Beiderbecke was featured until 1930.

*1931*   Beiderbecke died in Long Island, New York, on August 7.

norms. At that time, it was a musician's music which was not enthusiastically followed by a large listening audience. The public supporters of Chicago Dixieland did not find themselves at home with the post-World War I values. The mood of the times was typified by the F. Scott Fitzgerald sense of party. This frivolous lifestyle and its music, Chicago Dixieland, was at odds with those who were still tied to the work ethic and postwar patriotism. Chicago Dixieland became associated with those who stood in the center of the more surface values of the Roaring Twenties.

It was increasingly difficult to discriminate between jazz that was well played and the more commercial derivatives heard at society functions. This is a continuing issue for all developing art forms. Popularity is the engine that drives most art forms but is mistrusted

### Bix Beiderbecke and Frankie Trumbauer
### "Singin' the Blues"
### Smithsonian B/8 (cd 1/12)

:00   Four measures introduction with cornet and saxophone in thirds

:06   Trumbauer on C Melody Saxophone playing solo for fourteen measures, a combination of interpretation and improvisation

:31   Two-measure break on saxophone

:35   Saxophone solo continues for fourteen measures.

1:01   Two-measure break on saxophone

1:05   Beiderbecke plays his solo on cornet for fourteen measures.

1:30   Two-measure break, Beiderbecke goes into double-time for the first measure.

1:33   Beiderbecke continues his solo for sixteen measures.

2:03   Third chorus ensemble for eight measures

2:18   Clarinet solo for six measures

2:29   Two measures of clarinet

2:33   Ensemble on the second half of the tune for nine measures

2:50   Guitar takes a one measure break (Eddie Lang).

2:52   Ensemble takes it out to end; Beiderbecke pushes the ensemble.

3:03   End

when it appears later in more mature forms. Popularity tends to discourage far reaching innovation. The popularity of the swing bands certainly must have influenced how big band jazz was written and played. As jazz left the dance hall, more deliberate innovations were possible. Later, the renewed popularity of jazz because of the fusion groups in the 1970s and 1980s triggered claims of commercialism from the mainstream ranks. Is popularity synonymous with artistic compromise? To many it is.

The European-influenced culture of the Chicago Dixieland era valued music they considered cleanly played, even beautiful. Consequently, much of the listening audience admired what they viewed as the ''clean'' style more than the ''natural'' style they attributed to the African-American bands. Followers of the New Orleans Dixieland encouraged an interest in ''primitivism,'' a term which hardly seems appropriate today. The comparison between the clean and natural ways of playing was not one of skilled versus unskilled. The two performance styles were preferred by each of their audiences and reflected artistic values appropriate to each culture. While the New Orleans natural playing style fulfilled the esthetic needs of those who rejected the traditional values of the day, it also began to exert a strong influence on the clean style typical of Tin Pan Alley.

## THE FIRST JAZZ RECORDS

The opportunity to make the first instrumental jazz record was offered to the famous African-American trumpeter, Freddie Keppard, but he refused on the grounds that he did not want to be copied. It, therefore, fell to the Original Dixieland Jazz Band originally fronted by drummer Johnny Stein. After salary disputes caused his ouster, the band became cooperative and fate stepped in. A Chicago nightclub owner named Harry James went to New Orleans to see a prize fight, heard the band, and booked them into his Chicago club in 1916. The show business personnel who patronized the club helped popularize the band. Then it was off to New York's Reisenweber's Cafe in 1917 and the famous recording dates. Their first records were made February 26, 1917, and the most popular numbers were ''Livery Stable Blues'' also known as ''Barnyard Blues'' and ''Dixieland Jass Band One-Step'' which was usually called ''Original Dixieland One-Step.'' A trip to Europe followed in 1919. It is interesting that the barnyard sounds in ''Livery Stable Blues'' were responsible for much of their instant popularity in New York. At that time, barnyard sounds were as ''hip'' as electronic distortions later became among rock fans. The success of the Original Dixieland Jazz Band was launched by the growing recording industry and reflected the commercial jazz expression of the day.

## THE TWO DIXIELAND STYLES

There are several technical differences that distinguish Chicago Style Dixieland from Early New Orleans Dixieland:

1. A saxophone was added to the front line (usually a tenor saxophone).
2. The guitar replaced the banjo.

*The Original Dixieland
Jazz Band*

The Institute of Jazz Studies

*Sidney Bechet*

Michael Ochs Archives/
Venice, CA

3. Fairly elaborate (by comparison) introductions and endings were added.
4. Ease and relaxation in playing style gave way to tension and drive.
5. Individual solos became more important.
6. The rhythm changed from playing a flat 4/4 to accenting the second (2) and fourth (4) beats, hence called 2/4.

Both Dixieland styles used cornet (or trumpet), trombone, clarinet, and drums. The piano eventually became the norm for both styles, and the string bass replaced the tuba. The players of the Chicago era preferred the guitar to the banjo. The addition of the tenor sax gave more body to the ensemble playing and added additional solo color. The role of the saxophone in ensemble playing was comparable to that of the clarinet except that its harmony line (or countermelody) was below the melody. Because of its range, it could also share some of the melodic activity more typical of the trombone. The rhythmic feeling changed as the rhythm section emphasized the second and fourth beats as seen in examples 2.1 and 2.2, page 44. This is one of the first stylistic shifts to occur in the developing rhythm section, which keeps the same instrumentation to the present. The piano later becomes a substitute or partner with the guitar in contemporary rhythm sections. Stylistic definition is often rooted in the playing practices of the rhythm section. As we will see later, the rhythm section again makes substantial stylistic changes in the bop and fusion bands.

The harmonic vocabulary of the Dixieland band was basically triadic. The use of nonchord tones was a result of melodic activity rather than extensions of the harmonic vocabulary itself. The principle performance activity was still horizontal rather than vertical, and whatever resulting dissonance occurred resulted from interacting melodic lines improvised by the musicians. The scales they used reflected their blues heritage with the use of the flatted third and seventh notes. The use of the added sixth as a chord tone became more prominent in Chicago Dixieland. Although the players were apparently melodically motivated, they still were aware of the harmonic underpinning they had inherited from the popular songs of the day. Their interwoven melodic inventions respected the tonal harmonic progressions typical of both the popular song and the church hymn.

## STYLISTIC COMPLETION

Dixieland as a performance concept reached a stylistic end for the same reasons that made it such a blend of ensemble and individual playing. It was primarily based on ensemble antiphony. The front line could hardly go above four players without reaching a cacophony incapable of swinging. The protocol that held the practice together became so defined that it restricted evolutionary development.

Oliver, the epitome of the New Orleans Dixieland style, had recorded in 1924 with a reed section and written arrangements. This is usually considered an attempt at commercialism rather than an expansion of Dixieland practice. Saxophone sections had been used in New Orleans, not in just the society bands or for society affairs but also on the riverboats and in Jelly Roll Morton bands previous to Oliver's 1924 recordings. However, these bands did employ much polyphony. There were times very early when Oliver, Morton, and others saw that Dixieland with its collective improvisation was going to lose its audiences. Popular interest was swinging to arrangements of Tin Pan Alley songs instead of the improvised performances typical of Dixieland. Oddly enough, some people who condemned Dixieland in the 1920s later considered it not merely popular music but art music by the 1930s. The first seeds of the jazz art canon had been planted.

## REVIVALS

The Early New Orleans Dixieland style had a great revival in the 1940s. Prominent in this movement was Lu Waters and his Yerba Buena Jazz Band (based in Oakland, California). This band, like others in the movement, did everything possible to recreate Joe ''King'' Oliver's style. At first this was a small group in Lu Waters's big band. They were devoted to Morton and Oliver, and they liked the two trumpet concept of Oliver and Armstrong. Spin-offs were trombonist Turk Murphy and trumpeter Bob Scobey. A whole movement seemed to get started in the San Francisco area. It was easy to hear tunes from the Hot Five, New Orleans Rhythm Kings, and Original Dixieland Jazz Band libraries.

The advocates of this style refer to their music as the ''real'' or ''pure'' jazz. The ''purist'' jazz school is fairly intolerant, as revivalist schools tend to be. At what point, with all the borrowings that transpired in the original shaping of jazz, could there be any purity? In the early 1960s, there was a tremendous emphasis on ''Trad'' (traditional) bands in England. Here the musicians imitated the Early New Orleans Dixieland style by using both the instrumentation and interpretations of that time. They used a tuba and a banjo, and they played in a flat 4/4 rhythm.

Chicago Style Dixieland music has not lost its appeal, due primarily to its energetic rhythmic concept. When Dixieland is played today, it is almost always Chicago Style. There continue to be clubs

## "Society Bands"

It is not a recent concept for dance band musicians (including jazz performers with large bands) to vary their style of renditions according to the different expectations of various audiences. In the first quarter of the twentieth century, there were thirty quite well-known bands in New Orleans alone. The music played in some African-American clubs was considered far too "rough" for the white dances. Consequently, the musicians would have to adjust to a more "sweet" style.

In the Swing era, there was an entire category of bands called society bands, sometimes derogatorily called Mickey Mouse bands. The only relationship these bands had with such bands as Basie, Ellington, Lunceford, or Goodman was the established number of personnel. Each had a trumpet section, trombone section, saxophone section, rhythm section, and vocalists. The similarities stopped there.

These society bands almost always performed in the more posh hotels, such as New York's Waldorf Astoria, Lexington, Pierre, Taft, Roosevelt, the Central Park Casino, the Rainbow Room atop Radio City, Chicago's Palmer House, and the Coconut Grove in Los Angeles. Obviously, there was excellent pay for performance in a style to which the society of the country could dance. The bands played overly sweet with tempos set by comparatively uninspired rhythm sections established to entice their usually older patrons to the dance floor. There was very little, if any, improvisation. Some of the more successful bands were Guy Lombardo, Lawrence Welk, Sammy Kaye, Eddy Duchin, Dick Jurgens, Wayne King, and Freddy Martin.

and societies dedicated to the preservation of New Orleans style Dixieland music, such as the Preservation Hall in New Orleans and the Dixieland jazz festivals in San Diego and Sacramento. However, much of contemporary Dixieland heard is seldom played exactly as it was in the 1920s. The musicians have lived through other jazz eras, all of which have become part of their musical personalities. Of course, jazz musicians have always been more concerned about playing with good expression than about playing authentically. The movement toward authenticity brought about the comeback of players like Bunk Johnson. Another, Sidney Bechet, who had been working in a tailor shop, started recording again for Blue Note Records in 1939. In the 1940s, he had again become a celebrated jazz figure.

These revivals played up the fact that there were still two schools of appreciation of Dixieland. One school were advocates of the Original Dixieland Jazz Band, New Orleans Rhythm Kings, and Bix Beiderbecke with the Wolverines. Musicians in the Midwest had been performing in these styles right along with little variation. The other school followed Morton, Oliver, and Armstrong's Hot Five and Hot Seven. They were mainly people who studied the compositional development of jazz rather than the developing performance practice. This legacy played itself out in the later work of Fletcher and Horace Henderson, Don Redman, and Benny Carter.

It was never difficult to hear good Dixieland music in New York City after World War II. Nick's in Greenwich Village was one center as was Eddie Condon's club which opened in 1945 another. These players didn't consider themselves revivalists; Dixieland was just the way they preferred to play jazz.

---

## SWING BANDS AND GROUP IMPROVISATION

The trend toward large bands did not necessarily forecast a dearth of exciting small groups. In the late 1930s and into the mid 1940s, almost all large bands had what was termed ''a band within the band.'' Examples within the swing bands would be Benny Goodman's trio, quartet, quintet, sextet, and septet; Tommy Dorsey's Clambake Seven; Artie Shaw's Gramercy Five; Bob Crosby's Bobcats; Woody Herman's Woodchoppers; and Paul Whiteman's Swing Wing. These groups actually gave the fine soloists out of the band more freedom than that offered the Dixieland bands. The only guideline was that each player take his turn soloing. Usually, but not always, these groups resorted to Chicago Style Dixieland, and much of the protocol from that style was evident. The difference was that the players were now deeply into a different rhythmic feeling and swing 4/4 was prevalent. They really did not sound like traditional Dixieland but like small band swing. The final chorus of a tune was often an opportunity for group improvisation, but it differed from the Dixieland concept of the instrumental duties that crafted the complete improvisational image. It was more a case of the players merely soloing together rather than a division of duties more typical of the Dixieland group improvisation protocol.

---

## THE BOP ENSEMBLE

The classic extemporized ensemble came into focus during the Bop era. Like the earlier Dixieland ensembles, these ensembles based much of their playing on standard tunes of the day and improvised everything else. The precomposed material for these ensembles was called a head and was a short melody that was used to begin and end the performance. The rest of the time the players took solos that borrowed motivic material from the head.

Also like Dixieland, there were (and still are today) unspoken guidelines for each of the players that defined their roles in the ensemble. In the bop ensemble, the harmonic responsibilty had centered squarely in the rhythm section as the soloists played above. In contrast, the Early Dixieland ensemble generated its harmonic support from the interweaving lines of the other melody line players. The improvised harmonies were themselves melodies individualized and capable of dialoguing with the soloist or one another. While the bop ensemble still depends on the interaction and dialogue among its players, it does not generate its harmonic support the same way. The comping agents, either the piano or guitar, in conjunction with the bass player, outline the harmonic progression. The speed of most bop tunes would hardly allow the kind of counterpoint more typical of the Dixieland ensemble. A further discussion of the bop ensemble can be found in chapter 9.

## CONTEMPORARY DIRECTIONS

Collective improvisation flowered again with the development of free jazz. Just as in the earliest Dixieland, the ensemble cannot be successful unless each player knows what the other players are doing. Free jazz, like any collective improvisation situation, is based on the old axiom ''the more freedom allowed, the more discipline necessary.'' Without an agreed upon protocol and empathy among the players, free jazz fails. Rather than inheriting the protocol from traditional development like Early Dixieland, free jazz crafts a new protocol to guide each performance situation.

Although the improvisational protocol can differ sharply from one performance to another, players or organized groups tend to develop systems that are recognizable. Ornette Coleman's work on the album, *Free Jazz,* maintains a calculated distance from the harmonic and melodic tradition in jazz. His group, however, still maintains a consistent allegiance to time. Very seldom does the rhythm section interrupt the metric flow. Coleman's freedom is, therefore, selective and recognizable.

Other groups like The Art Ensemble push the freedom into the areas of time, as well as harmony and melody. Their work reflects the shaping of a theoretical space in which they realize their performance. That theoretical space might just as easily be concerned with timbre as pitch. Without such guiding structures and without the benefit of traditional expectations the success of a performance could not be guaranteed. Sun Ra has one of the most successful large but free ensembles. Because of the size of his ensembles, he requires a great deal of rehearsal time, which helps the players develop a system of dialogue that accommodates very free improvised musical structures. See chapter 11 for a further discussion of free music ensembles.

---

The electronic technology introduced in the 1970s offered, and in some ways required, a new approach to group playing. Fusion jazz took the greatest advantage of this new technology and moved into the recording studio to build their performances. Layers of isolated tracks could be built one on top of another to create a high-tech sound and flawless performance. The process required players to perform one at a time listening to previously recorded tracks while they played. The interactive ensemble process common to previous jazz performance became a one-way street. A real-time relationship existed between the performer and the tape. The later performers could react to previous tracks, but a response was impossible.

**IMPROVISATION AND THE RECORDING STUDIO**

Players also had to learn how to play the original tracks to leave room for later players (which might include themselves) in the process. Effective recording required players to look both forward and back, forward to what will be added later and back to what was already recorded. Often, groups that were quite good at studio performance like to break away temporarily to enjoy the real-time interaction more typical of earlier jazz styles. Chick Corea's work with both his Elektric Band and his Acoustik Band generated albums typical of both approaches. The Yellowjackets also moved to an acoustic format for their *Spin* album.

Corea also tends to produce his albums after going on tour to develop the material in a live performance medium before going into the studio to record it. It is often difficult to capture the live spirit of a performing group when the composition is pulled apart for recording purposes. As in all previous performance venues, the studio performance environment created a breed of players that suited its requirements. The studio jazz approach proved most successful for those groups that fused with the popular music streams of the 1980s and 1990s.

---

Over one hundred years ago, a mixture of cultures spawned small jazz bands featuring extemporized ensemble playing. This concept was so exciting, and yet so normal, that it continues today. Collective improvisation in jazz has traveled from the improvisational ornamentation of Early New Orleans Dixieland counterpoint to the freedom

**SUMMARY**

to decide what improvisational glue should be used in a given performance. To the earliest jazz players, polyphony was the logical and "normal" way to conceive of ensemble music. The melodic and rhythmic freedom of the African heritage when superimposed on the harmonic language of the European culture defined a protocol that guided the players in their improvisation. With the abstraction of the improvisational process itself, new protocols could be imagined for use in performance.

Improvisation is analogous to freedom. With its benefits comes responsibilities. Throughout jazz history players have not had total freedom when they improvise. They were free to embellish what they heard and offer new material to the ensemble. The amount of freedom granted or claimed by the players has varied, from the embellishments of Early Dixieland to the compositional efforts of free jazz. Even at times of greatest freedom, the individual expression has always been tethered to the success of the total ensemble.

The lack of popular success of free jazz may rest in the wide range of freedom claimed by its artists. With such a wide range, it is difficult for the listening audience to find the common ground on which to build their expectations. The protocol of early Dixieland was established on such expectations. The listeners could judge the success of a performance on how it addressed the agreed upon protocol. The fact that a majority of the protocol was unconscious did not matter; it still allowed the listener a set of rules that established expectations to be addressed by the players.

No such set of rules is available to the free jazz listener. Free jazz, by definition, can change the rules at will. There is, however, an abstract principle at work in most performances that remains consistent. If the performers assume a certain level of dissonance or a specific melodic motive, it is maintained as a unifying feature. The first job of the performing unit is to establish an improvisational goal (e.g., timbrel shifts, melodic development) and convey it to the listener. It is against this standard that the listener judges the success of the performance.

The varying degrees of freedom sought out by players reflects the artistic concerns of the day. In the 1960s, jazz was moving into the academic institutions, and the type of abstraction that we see in the free jazz of players like Anthony Braxton and The Art Ensemble are similar to concerns in classical music's new music arena. It was a time of abstraction and scientific research, even in the arts. If jazz were not involved in that movement, it would not have lived up to its responsibility as an art form.

Chapter 10 also addresses extemporized ensembles as it deals with the workings of the larger ensembles. Because jazz has improvisation as a cornerstone in its structure, the art form must strike careful balances between sometimes opposing forces. We discussed here the balance between individual and collective expression. In chapter 9, the balance between compositional and improvisational expressions is discussed.

SUGGESTED
LISTENING

Armstrong, Louis. "I Gotta Right to Sing the Blues."
    Folkways 2806.
Armstrong, Louis. "Sweethearts on Parade." Folkways 2806.
Beiderbecke, Bix, and Frankie Trumbauer. "Singin' the Blues."
    Smithsonian B/8 (cd 1/12).
Corea, Chick. *Akoustic Band.* GRD Records 9582.
Corea, Chick. Elektric Band. *Inside Out.* GRP Records GRD 9601.
Corea, Chick. *Musicmagic.* Columbia Records AL 34682.
Goodman, Benny. *The Great Benny Goodman.* Columbia
    Records CS 8643.
Goodman Septet. "I Found a New Baby."
    Smithsonian D/8 (cd 11/23).
Goodman Sextet. "Breakfast Feud" ("Blues Sequence").
    Smithsonian D/9 (cd 11/24).
Mares, Paul. "Maple Leaf Rag." *Folkways Jazz.* Vol. 6.
    Folkways FJ 2806.
New Orleans Feetwarmers. *Folkways Jazz.* Vol. 11.
    Folkways FJ 2811.
New Orleans Rhythm Kings. "Tiger Rag." *Folkways Jazz.* Vol. 3.
    Folkways FJ 2803.
Oliver, Joe "King." "Sweet Lovin' Man." Folkways 2806.
Original Dixieland Jazz Band. *Jazz Odyssey.* Vol. 1. Columbia
    Records C3L-30.
*Original Dixieland Jazz Band.* RCA Victor Records LPV 547.
*Small Groups.* RCA Victor Records LPV 521.
Sun Ra. *The Futuristic Sounds of Sun Ra.* MG 12138.
Sun Ra. *Heleocentric Worlds of Sun Ra.* Vol. 1, ESP 1014,
    Vol. 2, ESP 1017.

# CHAPTER 7

## *Ensemble Composition*

| | |
|---|---|
| *1906* | Morton composed "King Porter Stomp" |
| *1923* | Oliver recorded "Dippermouth Blues" |
| *1923* | Henderson organized his band in New York City |
| *1923* | Ellington moved to New York City |
| *1926* | Morton recorded "King Porter Stomp" as a piano solo |
| *1926–1927* | Morton recorded with his Red Hot Peppers |
| *1928* | Armstrong recorded "West End Blues" |
| *1928* | Henderson recorded "King Porter Stomp" |
| *1932* | Henderson recorded "New King Porter Stomp" |
| *1932–1942* | Swing bands dominate the jazz format |
| *1935* | Goodman recorded "King Porter Stomp" |
| *1935* | Basie organized his band |
| *1937* | Basie recorded "One O'Clock Jump" |
| *1938* | Morton recorded his Library of Congress oral history of jazz |

L ike any art form jazz has a history balanced by a variety of forces that directs its evolution. Many of those forces work in apparent opposition, e.g., individual and group expressions, improvisation and composition, and the marketplace and personal ideology. This chapter focuses on one of these polarities, the balance between group and individual expressions as they are manifested in the larger ensembles of jazz. It would be unwise to isolate these balancing influences in emergent jazz expressions and expect to have an accurate understanding of how jazz works as a signature art form. However, the issue of the individual and the group can be viewed as a microcosm of the inner forces that always have been a part of the larger flow of jazz styles. Even the avant-garde work of later groups, such as those that came out of the AACM, struggled with the same issue.

> The consequences—which are still being worked with and through today—were several. One of the most crucial was the misnamed ''free jazz'' movement— misnamed because, in fact, it dealt with new kinds of interrelations between composition and improvisation, the dialectical engine that powers what we call jazz.[1]

There is seemingly no apparent limit to the number of ways an effective balance between the expression of a collective ensemble and a player within that collective might be struck. One extreme would be a solo performance where only an individual expression is present and any ensemble interaction is impossible. The other extreme is an ensemble comprised of faceless performers who can be replaced at will with no recognizable change to the outcome. The former rests most heavily on the personal aesthetic of the performer, while the latter places the composer in the lead aesthetically. One might argue that the faceless ensemble must fall outside the definition of jazz because of the individuality inherent in the jazz tradition. However, as we shall see, jazz groups have successfully flirted with the notion of tight compositional direction as a guiding principle while striking some balance to accommodate individual expression.

Such groups have been in a minority throughout the developing jazz tradition. Jazz composers are relatively rare, and the history of jazz centers mostly on performers that have influenced or redirected existing jazz styles. This is reflected in jazz textbooks, which tend to be organized according to a chronology of individuals rather than along the evolutionary lines of stylistic change. The dialectic between composition for an ensemble and the extemporaneous ''composition'' by an ensemble is real. It is fueled by jazz's unnotated, streetwise legacy, a legacy separate from, but interactive with, that of the more literature based academy.

An effort to maintain a separate identity for jazz and avoid a Europeanization of their tradition may only be a conscious effort by historians and critics. The composers and players are more concerned with the immediacy of their task than the development of a potential art form. (This may be changing with the work of the neoclassical school.) One of the difficulties of addressing the issue of jazz

---

[1]Gene Santoro, ''Anthony Braxton,'' *The Nation,* 8 May 1989, 643.

composition and performance is deciding when it is appropriate to map the academic's Europeanized notions of compositional viability into a discussion of group jazz expression. The discussion embraces more than just the balance between the real-time expressions of a group and that of an individual but also the western European compositional approach for larger ensembles and the range of possibilities for real-time expression within that approach.

The range of possibilities is certainly large, and many fine examples have been produced by jazz players and composers. An early example, if not the first, can be found in the work of Jelly Roll Morton, who is recognized by most historians as the first jazz player/composer. Because his contribution was so early in jazz's history, he might be viewed as the germinal protagonist in the dialectic between the preconceived and the spontaneous expressions of jazz.

## JELLY ROLL MORTON AND NEW ORLEANS STYLE JAZZ

At this time, jazz, like any emergent, identifiable music tradition, was coalescing out of many divergent influences. The balance of these influences, as well as their nature, is still heavily debated and is discussed more thoroughly in chapters 8 and 11. Two of those influences are germane to this discussion, ragtime and the New Orleans style. Ragtime is a highly stylized and composed form. Although it was important to the initial stirrings of jazz, it lacked improvisation and, therefore, is often referred to as a prejazz style. Ragtime falls in the tradition of nineteenth-century piano music and is undeniably one of the most direct western European influences on the development of jazz. This influence passed through a black rhythmic filter to develop the ''ragged'' time of ragtime.

Morton's influence, aside from his own claim to have created jazz in 1902, liberated the ragtime compositional strictures and opened up the performance for real-time individual expression.

> In Morton we recognize for the first time the decisive fact that the personality of the performing musician is more important in jazz than the material contributed by the composer.[2]

At the same time as Morton's liberation of ragtime for jazz performance, the many musical styles of New Orleans were merging

---

[2]Joachim E. Berendt, *The Jazz Book: From New Orleans to Rock and Free Jazz,* translated by Dan Morgenstern, copyrighted 1975, Lawrence Hill and Co., Westport, Connecticut, 7.

## Jelly Roll Morton (Ferdinand Joseph La Menthe)

Morton as a pianist/composer/arranger established a new balance between the collective improvisation typical of the New Orleans style and a new compositional approach that would evolve into the big bands of the Swing era. His longevity and later recordings make him one of the earliest jazz historians and theorists.

| | |
|---|---|
| *1890* | Morton was born on October 20. |
| *1902* | Morton began working in the bordellos of Storyville playing ragtime, quadrilles, and other popular dances. |
| *1904–1917* | He traveled mostly around the South as a pianist but also played in New York and Los Angeles. In his travels, his music accumulated the many early influences that were shaping the emergent jazz style. |
| *1917–1922* | He settled in Los Angeles for five years and then moved to the new center of jazz, Chicago. |
| *1923* | He made his first recordings. |
| *1926–1927* | He began recording with the Red Hot Peppers, a seven to eight piece group. |
| *1930* | Morton's style was being overshadowed by the newer band styles of Henderson and Redman, but several of his compositions continued as a standard part of the big band format (e.g., "King Porter Stomp," recorded by both Henderson and Goodman). |
| *1938* | Morton made an oral history for the Library of Congress and recreated many of the styles prevalent at the turn of the century. |
| *1939–1940* | Renewed interest in Morton was created by the New Orleans Revival. |
| *1941* | Morton made several new recordings until his death on July 10, 1941. |

to find a single identifiable expression, now called the New Orleans style. Foremost in the process of New Orleans style jazz were the collective extemporizations created by individual players working together for a single ensemble expression. Although many of the melodic lines played by members of these groups may have been repeated from performance to performance, they were always subject to change as the dynamic interplay between players shifted. (See chapter 5).

The difference between Morton's approach and that of a New Orleans style ensemble is the role of the individual player. The extemporaneous dynamic of ragtime gives way to the improvisational intent of New Orleans style, which begins to resemble the compositional practice of structurally planning a piece. Morton's approach was more formal, usually three themes developed in variation. The notion of structural development was probably not even an issue for the New Orleans style ensembles, and to hold those groups accountable for a less varied and looser structure is inappropriate. However, it is in these terms that historians define historical flow. Martin Williams' glowing account of Morton's contribution is certainly an example of mapping western European expectations into jazz's historical consciousness.

> One can find a lot of reasons for finding this man with
> the clown's nickname still important in the jazzman's
> heritage. In him jazz did produce one of its best
> composers, best leaders, and one of its first theorists.
> More important, he first demonstrated the only way jazz
> has ever found to free its larger structures and groups
> from the tyranny and subjectivity of the moment.[3]

Martin's statement is contrary to the quotation by Berendt. Whether Morton brought order to New Orleans jazz or whether the multiplicity of New Orleans' music unraveled the rigid structures of Morton's ragtime background offers interesting academic debate but is of secondary interest to the polarity established by these two forces, a polarity that continues to resurface throughout the history of jazz. It is difficult to accommodate the momentary aspects of an extemporized medium in historical discussions and, as a result, they are often overlooked. It is easier to deal with fixed forms that promote clearer discussions and theoretical analysis. Composers of jazz, even

---

[3]Martin Williams, *The Jazz Tradition,* (New York: Oxford University Press, 1983), 46.

though they are relatively few, tend to be prominently discussed in the history of its development. Their approach to the materials of music also fits most easily into the established frameworks of musicology.

Composition is not, however, the salient feature of what was then and is now described as jazz. The role of the individual performer is still the focal point. The seeds of a codified jazz may have been planted in the work of Morton, but they have always contrasted with the contributing extempore of the players.

The difficulty of fairly comparing the collectively improvised style of New Orleans with Morton's composed pieces is aggravated by a lack of recordings. The earliest recordings in the New Orleans style were made after many of the main players had moved to Chicago and developed a different style. It is also not clear how composed Morton's music really was. Certainly, each note is not written down as is implied by current notions of composition. Morton himself referred to how difficult it was to get Chicago players to play in the authentic style. His compositions might actually be structural plans that were fleshed out by the players who brought to the composition their own individualized voices schooled in the oral tradition of New Orleans.

What we have heard as New Orleans style in the players of both Oliver and Morton may not be truly indicative of the earlier style. Max Harrison suggests that the American Music recordings of the 1940s might be more closely representative of that earlier style. He discusses the divergence of styles of those who stayed in New Orleans and those who moved away.

> Those who remained at home may slowly have grown towards the kind of jazz caught on American Music in the mid 1940s. This meant looser, more open ensemble textures, lighter rhythm, easier swing. Common to both branches of this generation . . . is their abandonment of elaborate, multi-strain rags for simpler material which facilitates a more continuous style of extempore playing. Those in the North, led by Armstrong, perfected solo improvisation and went on to popular ballads which led to the harmonic sophistication of swing and bop. The others appear to have developed a form of jazz whose chief means of expression were contrapuntal subtlety— on both melodic and rhythmic levels—and variety of ensemble texture.[4]

---

[4]Max Harrison, *A Jazz Retrospect,* (Boston, Mass.: Crescendo Publishing Co., 1976), 49.

The New Orleans style of ensemble reflected the individual contributions of the players but did not feature a single player's expression until individual players like Armstrong began to overshadow the ensemble's definition. The irony here is that the New Orleans style ensemble had achieved such a balanced expression without the aid of highly structured arrangements or focus on a single personality. It becomes obvious that ensemble playing does not require any prescribed balance between composed and extemporized material. The New Orleans ensemble was a loose, amorphous, and perhaps experimental interplay of improvised lines. Whether this ensemble style stood alone or supported a featured player seemed more a matter of choice than a stylistic requirement (perhaps these are equivalent). We will see later that bands like Basie's and Ellington's offer two different but successful balances for ensemble structuring, which might be seen as outgrowths of this earlier practice.

The two main cultural and musical heritages of New Orleans can be seen in the ensembles that represent them. The Creole group, with whom Morton associated, was tied strongly to the French European tradition. His compositional approach would certainly have been supported by his association with that ethnic line. The African-American group represented a different line of lesser social status associated with the descendents of slaves. This early cultural distinction is reflective of two balancing forces at work throughout jazz history—formalized and schooled western European compositional attitudes and the unnotated oral tradition of African Americans. When the balance tips toward composition, there is often a cry of Europeanization from those who see the music as with predominantly African-American roots. As a microcosm, these two jazz expressions in New Orleans represent a fundamental struggle within the developing art form, between improvisation and notated jazz forms. Crusaders on each side of this struggle often confound the issue with cultural associations not unlike the cultural distinctions made in New Orleans between the Creoles and the African Americans.

Because of jazz's allegiance to improvisation, we find the larger ensembles of jazz with their collective improvisatory approaches a natural testing ground for defining jazz as a musical tradition distinct from the classical compositional tradition. It is significant that Morton employed formalism that reflected the more improvised ensembles yet allowed him to spin out consistent and perhaps more reasoned variation more typical of fully composed pieces.

Form in jazz can be a musical attribute that signals a composer's individuality, not unlike a performer's inflection and use of tone color. The priority a composer or performer gives to form can be individually assumed. Because the oral tradition has been such a dominant force throughout jazz's development, jazz forms have been most often inherited from previous styles and not granted great significance by performers. At various times, however, such composer/arrangers as Morton, Monk, Mingus, Ellington, and Russell stepped outside that tradition somewhat and garnered compositional identities much like the stylistic identities normally established only by players.

Compositional attitudes do not have to be notated to be at work in a performance. Composition does, however, have strong associations with the notated side of jazz and the formal training it implies. The dichotomy between improvisation and composition is reinforced by the notated/unnotated distinction that accompanies it. As with any dichotomy, there are those who would campaign for one over the other. At the extreme, does formal training dull one's potential for jazz inspiration, or is untrained improvisation naive compositionally? Rather than try to answer such questions, we would only note that these attitudes are at work in a tradition like jazz, which holds improvisation in such high regard while it assimilates the compositional models offered by the western European tradition.

The fact that Morton has successfully claimed a secure place in jazz history indicates that composition is not viewed as the nemesis of the jazz spirit. Morton successfully met the first challenge and found a balance that allowed both jazz approaches to function interdependently. It is the fluid nature of the many possible compositional and improvisational blends that frustrates an attempt to codify the tradition and establish only one approach as aesthetically sound.

> It is just this interpenetration of composing and improvisation, rarely the same in any two pieces, which creates a part of the critic's problem. . . . Indeed, far from improvisation being codified and stereotyped, its impact is heightened in such cases by the context in which the composer has placed it.[5]

## HARLEM BANDS AND THE SOUTHWEST BANDS

Differing balances between ensemble approaches can also be seen in the work of the Harlem bands in the 1920s and 1930s as compared to the Southwest bands of the 1930s and 1940s. Again, the issue is one of compositional control and individual improvisatory expression. The blues oriented Southwest bands used a riff approach to

[5]Max Harrison, *A Jazz Retrospect,* (Boston, Mass.: Crescendo Publishing Co., 1976), 129.

building a composition generated by the players themselves. Each section would contribute a riff as the compositional texture grew. The Harlem bands used more fully composed arrangements that were preconceived and specifically outlined.

The Harlem bands were noted for a ''hot'' jazz characterized by fairly quick tempos and driving stomps. The most prominent band of the late 1920s and 1930s was Fletcher Henderson's, begun in 1924. Henderson's bands showed an evolution that established the path for big bands to follow, both white and African-American.

The Harlem band line can be followed through Cab Calloway, Chick Webb, and Jimmy Lunceford. Each of these bands exhibited differing balances between improvisation and compositional control. The Harlem tradition meets the Southwest Band line in the early Basie ensemble. Prominent among the Kansas City line from which Basie came were the bands of Bennie Moten, Jay McShann, and Harlan Leonard. These bands used a riff technique that repeated short, melodic, blues-based phrases that often juxtaposed the improvisational work of a solo performer. Unlike the Harlem bands, which grew more directly out of the popular song tradition, the fundamental idiom of the riff bands came from the blues and the melodic activity typical of boogie-woogie.

## FLETCHER HENDERSON

Henderson's first ensembles were rooted in the New Orleans style, and like those groups, they were really not big by today's standards. Their bigness is found more in the number of musical voices rather than the number of players. Two trumpets, two or three clarinets, and one or two trombones, each with their own contrapuntal voice, can create a compositional complexity normally associated with larger ensembles. Because there were no doublings, these early groups had fewer performers than the bands that would follow but had as great, or greater, a number of compositional lines. As Henderson's band began to coalesce into the sections we now associate with big bands, the contrapuntal lines became more formalized and less improvised.

The first signs of sectional activity appeared in the clarinet trios in Morton's arrangements and remained popular through the 1920s. It was not until 1931 with Don Redman's band that the more modern grouping of sections were established, including four saxophones, three trumpets, and three trombones. Each of these sections increased by one (and sometimes two) a little later, but by this time their identities were fixed as was the ''classical'' model for later big bands.

## Fletcher Henderson

Henderson led and arranged for a style setting band that signaled the transition from the stylized dance band typical of the day to the jazz voiced big band. His band membership included the solo voices of Louis Armstrong and Coleman Hawkins who helped shape the jazz vocabulary of succeeding generations of players. His band also launched Don Redman and Benny Carter who also contributed to the formalization of the big band medium with their arrangements and compositions.

*1897*   Henderson was born December 12.

*1920*   Henderson moved to New York from Georgia after taking a degree in chemistry and mathematics. Because he was unable to get a job as a chemist, he took up work as a song demonstrator for publishing firms. He began to form groups to back the singers for the early African-American publishing firm, Black Swan, and eventually developed into a bandleader.

*1924*   He began to perform in the Club Alabam on Broadway and later at the famous Roseland Ballroom. He stayed in this club for a decade. His band developed from a dance band into the pioneering jazz band. This move was enhanced by the addition of Louis Armstrong to the band as a jazz specialist. He introduced the band to the new jazz style. Don Redman arranged for the group and began to shape the basic approach to big band arrangement used for years to come.

*1925*   Armstrong left the band in the fall of 1925, leaving his influence on the later jazz soloists. This band was the model for later groups until the 1930s.

*1927*   Redman left the band, and Henderson became the primary arranger with the help of Benny Carter.

*1934*   The band broke up, and Henderson sold some of his best arrangements to Benny Goodman, who used them to establish his own career.

*1939*   Henderson led bands until this date when he joined Goodman as a full-time arranger.

*1941*   He returned to bandleading.

*1952*   Henderson suffered a stroke in 1950 and died on December 29, 1952.

## Fletcher Henderson and his orchestra
### ''Wrappin' It Up''
### Smithsonian B/12 (cd 11/12)

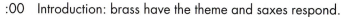

This arrangement is indicative of Henderson's later style and is an arrangement that was passed on to Benny Goodman, which he also recorded later. A comparison of the two performances demonstrates the difference between the early and late swing styles. The later style is generally more polished and exact. The structure for each chorus is ABAC, and the lines between the structural phrases are often reinforced by simultaneous changes in sectional voices.

:00   Introduction: brass have the theme and saxes respond.
:09   Chorus 1: Saxes state the main theme with each phrase being a variation of the previous one, this is structural phrase A.
:19   Structural phrase B
:28   Structural phrase A as the trumpets join the saxes
:37   Structural phrase C
:48   Chorus 2: Hilton Jefferson on alto solo, same ABAC structure for this chorus, backup with muted trumpets
1:25  Chorus 3: Red Allen trumpet solo, backup by saxophones
1:34  Whole brass section plays lead.
1:44  Trumpet solo resumes.
2:03  Chorus 4: The theme is tossed back and forth between the brass and reeds (now on clarinets)
2:13  Clarinet solo
2:22  Saxophones take lead
2:31  Brass join in
2:39  Ending phrase that became a big band cliché
2:42  End

## Benny Carter

**M**usicians have and will always admire Benny Carter—his playing, his writing, and his exemplary personality. It has always been a mystery why Carter never attained the public recognition due him. Possibly there were too many facets to his talent on which the public could center its attention. He was an excellent saxophone, clarinet, and trumpet player. He also arranged music artistically, and was a fine composer. As a saxophonist he displayed a superb tone and wonderful technique. His tone was equally beautiful on the trumpet.

Benny Carter scored television specials, such as "Bob Hope Presents," and "The Sarah Vaughan Special," and such shows as "M Squad," "The Alfred Hitchcock Show," "Name of the Game," "Ironside," and "Chrysler Theater." His film credits include *A Man Called Adam, Buck and the Preacher, Louis Armstrong: Chicago Style, The Five Pennies,* and *The Gene Krupa Story.* Morrie Berger, Edward Patrick, and James Patrick wrote a book about him called *Benny Carter, A Life in American Music* (Scarecrow Press, Metuchen, N.J., 1982). By 1960, Carter was so busy writing and arranging music that he rarely had time to play.

Throughout the development of Henderson's band, we find a very careful balance between the contribution of the individual performers and compositional objectives. Henderson's band consistently attracted players of distinction, particularly saxophonists Don Redman, Benny Carter, and Coleman Hawkins; trumpeters Rex Stewart, Joe Smith, and Roy Eldridge; and trombonists Jimmy Harrison, Benny Morton, and Dickie Wells. The presence of players such as these worked as a counterbalance to the increasing temptation to formalize the contrapuntal activity of a large ensemble with emerging sectional bodies. The lockstep nature of sectional work prevents the contrapuntal freedom enjoyed by the New Orleans style players. However, the presence of signature soloists can set the sectionalization in relief, avoiding a stiff formalized performance.

The band also contained leading players who were arrangers, Don Redman, Benny Carter, and to a lesser extent, Horace Henderson.

| | |
|---|---|
| *1907* | Carter was born in New York City. |
| *Late 1920s* | He studied theology at Wilberforce University. He worked with Horace Henderson, Duke Ellington, and Charlie Johnson at Smalls in New York, and played with Fletcher Henderson, Chick Webb, and McKinney's Cotton Pickers. |
| *1933* | He started his own band. |
| *1935* | Carter joined Willie Lewis' band in Paris. |
| *1936* | He worked as a staff arranger for the BBC in London. |
| *1937* | In Holland, he organized the first truly interracial big band. |
| *1941* | In New York City, Carter organized a sextet which included Dizzy Gillespie and Jimmy Hamilton. |
| *1943* | Carter organized a band in Los Angeles. |
| *1960* | He visited Australia and Japan with his own quartet. |
| *Late 1960s* | He toured Europe with Jazz at the Philharmonic. |
| *1970s* | Carter taught and presented seminars at many universities. |
| *1974* | Carter received an Honorary Doctorate of Humanities at Princeton. There are simply too many albums to list. |

The fact that these arrangers were players may well have influenced the type of arrangement they envisioned, one that left room for the improvisatory freedom they enjoyed as players. It was not until Benny Carter led his own band that the definition of the big band as a primary vehicle for composition began to emerge. The relationship between writers and players is important throughout the history of big band jazz. Henderson himself did not arrange for his own group until about 1931. Up to that time he benefited primarily from the work of Redman and Carter. At this time, the original arrangement was becoming an important signature for big bands. They created an individuality that the stock arrangements of popular songs, available to all bands, could not offer.

Among the other players in the band were two who were particularly important to the development of the Henderson style: Louis

## Don Redman

The first jazz band to play written arrangements in New York City in 1922 was the Billy Paige Band with Don Redman as arranger and lead alto saxophone player. Redman then joined Fletcher Henderson, stayed until 1927, then went to McKinney's Cotton Pickers and eventually organized his own band. Henderson, Redman, and others took parts that generally were written for one trumpet, for example, and harmonized them to be played by three trumpets, eventually dividing the band into choirs of like instruments.

Don Redman played trumpet at three, joined a band at six, and spent his childhood studying every instrument in the band, as well as music theory. He completed his studies in Boston and Detroit Conservatories.

In 1924, Fletcher Henderson had Louis Armstrong, Coleman Hawkins, and Don Redman among his exclusive personnel. Henderson is often given credit for establishing the pattern for swing arrangements along with his brother Horace and saxophonist Don Redman from whom Henderson learned his own skills.

Redman's most successful compositions were "Cherry," "How'm I Doin'," "Gee, Baby, Ain't I Good to You," and the theme song of his own band "Chant of the Weed." (Listen to *Don Redman—Master of the Big Band.* RCA Victor Records RD 7828, RCA Victor Records LPV–520.)

| | |
|---|---|
| *1900* | Redman was born in Piedmont, West Virginia. |
| *1923* | He joined Fletcher Henderson. |
| *1924* | He recorded with Bessie Smith. |
| *1927* | Redman joined McKinney's Cotton Pickers. |
| *1928* | He recorded with Louis Armstrong. |
| *1931–1940* | He led his own band. |
| *1940* | Redman wrote the music for the *Lower Basin Street* show while arranging for numerous orchestras. |
| *1940s* | He led his own band in clubs and on recordings. |
| *1946–1947* | His was the first band to tour Europe after World War II. |
| *1950s* | He led the band for Pearl Bailey. |
| *1964* | Redman died in New York City. |

## Coleman Hawkins

**C**oleman Hawkins was the first jazz musician to attain fame as a tenor saxophonist. He first gained recognition in the Fletcher Henderson Orchestra where he played clarinet, bass, and baritone saxes as well as the tenor sax. He demonstrated a great rhythmic feel while playing a slap-tongue solo (considered strictly a comic approach today). Eventually, his rich tone and long flowing lines became some of the most impressive aspects of his playing. His solo on "Body and Soul" never seems to pause, it just continues on and on. It also seems so logically organized even though it was entirely improvised.

*Coleman Hawkins*

Michael Ochs Archives/
Venice, CA

| | |
|---|---|
| *1904* | Hawkins was born on November 21 in St. Joseph, Missouri. |
| *1922–1923* | He worked with Mamie Smith's Jazz Hounds. |
| *1923–1934* | Hawkins worked with Fletcher Henderson. |
| *1923* | He made his first recordings with Fletcher Henderson. |
| *1934–1938* | He toured England and the Continent. |
| *1939* | Hawkins recorded "Body and Soul" on October 11. |
| *1940s* | He toured with his own band and combos. |
| *1950s* | Hawkins toured Europe. |
| *1940s and 1950s* | He won many awards, proving his dominance in the field. |
| *1969* | Hawkins died in New York City on May 19. |

Armstrong and Coleman Hawkins. Armstrong only played with Henderson for a year at the very beginning of the band's development. However, he planted seeds that would be harvested by both writers and players alike. Don Redman changed his approach to arranging after hearing Armstrong play. This signals the awareness arrangers at that time had of the individual contributions within the band's ensemble structure.

Coleman Hawkins was with the band for much longer than Armstrong and also proved to be an influential force for the arrangers and players around him. It would not be unusual to hear ensemble passages from the Henderson band with Hawkins in a leading role. Because of the nature of the recording process, it is difficult to know, however, if the recordings which tend to feature Hawkins' sound are truly representative of the band's live performance. Balance required in the studio might have been quite different from that actually preferred on stage. If the prominence of Hawkins' sound on recordings is a result of the largeness of his sound and not merely placement in the studio, we can trust that the recording's balance is somewhat indicative of how the band worked in a live situation.

It is unknown how much of a difference in ensemble balance was accepted, or even promoted, during recording compared to a live performance. The absence of any real drums in the early recordings also obscures understanding of how the ensemble functioned in live performance. No doubt, listeners of the day were familiar with the limitations of recording and able to compensate appropriately when listening to recordings. Without a similar exposure, contemporary listeners cannot as easily infer the intended balance from recordings.

If we assume the recordings are representative of the bands in live performance, then leading players like Hawkins were viewed as important if not signature expressions of the ensemble itself. However, Hawkins was not at first the sole reason for the band's popularity. The new arrangements of popular songs offered a new and relevant format for the emerging ensemble. It was from within these arrangements that players like Hawkins were launched as leading soloists. Hawkins was also notable for his development as a player from a slap-tonguing baritone saxophone player to one who was even able to make the later transition to bop groups and set a standard for players to follow. Hawkins was the first popular saxophone soloist.

Although Henderson's arrangements were characterized by sectional work, the performances maintained a looseness reflective of earlier New Orleans style playing. His ''New King Porter Stomp'' of 1932 is typical of what J. R. Taylor describes as ''raggedy technique but intense speed.''[6] Whether this style is a matter of choice or limited technical ability is perhaps debatable. The fact that this band was so popular certainly demonstrates that technical precision was not of central importance. From a later vantage point, technical precision is often a hallmark of big band ensemble, particularly demonstrated by later Lunceford and Basie recordings. Unresolved, however, is whether the imprecision of the Harlem bands was the result of the ensembles' leaving room for individual stylizations on otherwise composed ensemble lines.

---

[6]Smithsonian Collection, *Fletcher Henderson, Developing an American Orchestra 1927–1947.*

## SOUTHWEST BANDS—EARLY BASIE

The Southwest bands offered a different solution to big band improvisational structures. Rather than crafted arrangments realized by individual arrangers, the players themselves contributed to the shaping of the final form. The actual compositional idea would operate like a melodic nucleus around which other player's melodic lines would collect. Basie's signature song, "One O'Clock Jump," is essentially that. Basie's name is attached to the arrangement but, outside of the initial motive, the arrangement belongs as much to the band that developed the final form. See example 4.3, page 103.

Because of the looser compositional structure, the arrangement's focal point shifted away from the arranger and toward the improvising performer. Particular to Basie in the late 1930s were the solo strengths of players like Lester Young and Hershel Evans on tenor sax, Harry Edison and Buck Clayton on trumpet, and Benny Morton and Dickie Wells on trombone. It can be noted that Henderson also had solo voices that helped identify his band; however, it was how these solo voices worked within the ensemble that differentiated the Harlem bands from Southwest bands. The riff style bands depended more heavily on the solo strengths of the players. While the riffing was used to energize the solo work, it was also dependent on it for structural definition. Many of the blues-based riffs were transportable from one piece to another. The soloists were the glue that welded the riff patterns into a structural whole.

The dominant voice of the Basie band was that of Lester Young. Like Coleman Hawkins for Henderson, Young is the signature of the late 1930s Basie band. Besides the difference in the sound of Hawkins and Young was a sense of melody. Hawkins worked more in the hot fashion of Harlem bands, while Young presaged the cool sounds of the late 1940s and 1950s. It is interesting to note that after Hawkins left Henderson's band he was replaced by Young in 1934. His approach was different enough from that of Hawkins that Henderson and the members of the saxophone section did not like his playing.

This incompatibility may have been more than just the lightness of Young's tone when compared to that of Hawkins. In the riff style format, the soloist has more room to expand ideas. In the Harlem bands, the solo areas were more formalized and punctuated by stylized ensemble passages. Young's sense of line may have outranged the solo areas allotted for him in the Henderson style of arrangements. The energy of the riff bands was certainly intended to be as hot as that of the Harlem bands, and Young was more than successful in the most successful Southwest band. In Basie's riff-based band, Young's

*Count Basie*

Michael Ochs Archives/
Venice, CA

## Count Basie

**B**asie became associated with the Southwest Band tradition and continued to lead his band until his death. The band that originally used the riffing style of the Moten band later became known as a tight ensemble capable of the most tailored dynamic control. He was pianist for the group that helped establish the contemporary swing style.

*1904*  Basie was born on August 21.

*1927*  Basie toured on the Keith and TOBA vaudeville circuits as a pianist and accompanist and got stranded in Kansas City where he remained. He played for silent films and joined Walter Page's band in 1928.

*1929*  He joined Bennie Moten's band, Kansas City Orchestra.

*1935*  Shortly after Moten's death he left the band and organized his own nine piece group with several of Moten's players. His new group included Lester Young.

*1936*  His band officially became the Count Basie Orchestra and began to gain international acclaim. After Lester Young left the group, the band began to move toward written arrangements that later characterized the controlled ensemble for which the band is famous.

*1950*  The group disbanded for financial reasons, and Basie worked with a small six to nine piece group.

*1952*  He reorganized the band and traveled internationally.

*1984*  Basie died on April 26.

*1985*  After Basie's death, the band continued under the leadership of Thad Jones and finally under Frank Foster in 1986.

cooler sound had room to shape energetic solo lines not appropriate in the Henderson style. This is not to say that Hawkins was incapable of extended solos (''Body and Soul,'' ''Picasso'') but that his vitality as a soloist was more effective within Henderson's arrangements than was Young's more lyric style.

Even if it were only a matter of personal sound, the fact that the replacement of Hawkins by Young was such an issue supports the notion that the arrangements, to whatever degree they were stylized

## Lester Young

Lester Young was the model for all cool tenor saxophonists. His playing led to a freeing-up of the language of jazz. He matured during the 1930s in Kansas City where jam sessions prepared him for all competition. He first attracted attention with the Count Basie band, but there was some opposition to his playing at first. Compared to Coleman Hawkins, Young's tone seemed light and airy. The younger players, especially Basie, were more than impressed. His linear phrases carried melodic thoughts to their conclusion regardless of bar lines.

He recorded many solos with the Count Basie band that are still available in repressings. Those recordings that are most cherished by his army of admirers are the small combo records, including those backing Billie Holiday. Young's playing naturally matched his personality, soft-spoken and understated.

*Lester Young*
Michael Ochs Archives/
Venice, CA

| | |
|---|---|
| *1909* | Young was born in Woodville, Mississippi, on August 27. |
| *1909–1919* | He lived in New Orleans and was trained by his father. |
| *1929–1930* | Young worked with a touring band called the Bostonians. |
| *1930s* | He played with Joe "King" Oliver and Walter Page's Blue Devils. |
| *1936–1940* | Young worked for Count Basie, recording 105 selections. |
| *1941–1944* | He played with his own combo. |
| *1946–1959* | He played with Norman Granz's *Jazz at the Philharmonic.* |
| *1959* | Young died in New York City. |

were subject to a further stylization by individual performers. Despite the gradual development of sectionally defined ensembles in the Henderson band's arrangements, the role of the improvisor remained a key factor in their successful performance.

The success of the riff approach to band arrangement and performance was even more directly dependent on the personnel in the ensemble. Without outstanding soloists, the energetic riffs might

## Count Basie and his orchestra
## ''Doggin' Around''
## Smithsonian D/5 (cd 11/20)

This selection offers a good example of how riffing can be used to shape an arrangement and give it a varying energy curve. Listen for the contrast in style and sound of the last soloist, Lester Young.

:00    Introduction: Basie on piano

:07    Head of arrangement, saxes have main riff with a responding riff in the brass

:22    Solo: Earle Warren on alto sax, brass punches riffing in background

:30    Head returns

:38    Solo: Herschel Evans on tenor saxophone, his tone is closer to Coleman Hawkins sound, light brass riffs in background

:53    Brass lay out

1:01    Brass back in with riff

1:10    Solo: Harry Edison on trumpet, saxes riff in background

1:24    Solo: Jack Washington on baritone saxophone, no riffing in background

1:39    Solo: Basie on piano

2:10    Solo: Lester Young on tenor saxophone, notice his lighter tone and the way he floats his phrases over the meter, brass and saxes riff in background

2:26    Riffing drops out

2:34    Riffing returns

2:42    Drum solo

2:49    Head returns with sectional riffing

2:57    End

become nothing more than empty structures. Consequently, this de-
pendence did not accommodate a regular change in key personnel.
As we see later, Basie eventually abandoned this approach of performer centered arrangements after he lost Lester Young. Young essentially took with him a significant part of the Basie book. If a
qualified replacement had been found, he potentially might redefine
the arrangements to such an extent that the band's identity might have
changed.

How the sections operated within the ensemble also distinguishes the Kansas City riff approach from the Harlem bands, and
later more compositionally-based bands like Ellington's. Dickey
Wells describes the riff approach with Basie as beginning with Basie's piano and rhythm until the time had been established. The saxes
would then introduce a riff against the rhythm section. After that
settled, the trombones and finally the trumpets would follow. Wells
goes on to say that although it was a big band (expanded for its trip
to New York in late 1930s), Basie "handled it as though it were six
pieces."[7]

This type of ensemble condensation is the most streamlined approach to big band orchestration possible. The Harlem bands arrangements made a much larger use of orchestration in their use of
sectionalization, primarily because the sections themselves were just
developing their classical shape. Because they were not yet as highly
formalized as Basie's approach, the instrumental lines often cut across
the sections to create various instrumental colors. Basie's approach,
like most of the other Southwest bands, viewed the big band as a
higher energy extension of small group polyphony. Because of the
bands' size, the extemporaneous offerings by the sectionalized voices
were more restricted, but the improvisatory structuring more typical
of small groups was still at work. The Southwest riff approach placed
the sections in contrapuntal relationships not typically heard in the
Harlem bands. The riffs used by each section worked much more
horizontally than the more carefully scored tutti ensemble areas we
find in Henderson's arrangements. These ensemble areas, because
they were written out in advance, allowed complex interchanges between sections that were unlikely to develop improvisationally. However, even these juxtapositions were more a tutti ensemble statement
than contrapuntal melodies along sectional lines.

---

[7] *The Best of Count Basie,* Decca DXSB–7170.

## DUKE ELLINGTON

Duke Ellington's Orchestra is a complex configuration of many spiritual and musical elements. To be sure, it was Duke Ellington's music which was created here; but it was just as much the music of each individual member of the band.[8]

Ellington offers perhaps the clearest but most elusive example of the dilemma faced by jazz composers when working with large ensembles. He shares a place in jazz history similar to that of Henderson as a seminal influence for others who followed. On one hand, Henderson added shape to an ongoing development of the modern big band, while Ellington offered a sense of newness and exploration. As Henderson's band developed, so did the standard format for big band ensembles. The sections developed in his arrangements began to act as single voices. Although the playing was loose, the interweaving counterpoint was defined by the arrangement rather than improvised lines offered by the players. Ellington worked in a very loose manner as he developed his compositions. He allowed a great deal of input from his musicians, both in terms of their ideas as well as their manner of playing.

Berendt describes a process Ellington used which led to the transcription of a piece that was actually "improvised into being."[9] Even though Ellington's larger works reflect more of an individual compositional approach, they are characterized by their relationship to the individual players in his band. Harrison considers Ellington a superb miniaturist who was unable to craft large-scale structures successfully.[10] Perhaps it was just Ellington's interest in interweaving his compositional intentions with the individual voices of his band that prevented his large pieces from forming the compositional whole Harrison requires. If the criterion for evaluating a composition's success is its compositional integrity alone, then Ellington did not succeed. However, when viewed in light of the improvisation inherent in jazz big bands, Ellington might have been among the most successful.

---

[8]Joachim E. Berendt, *The Jazz Book: From New Orleans to Rock and Free Jazz,* translated by Dan Morgenstern, copyright 1975, Lawrence Hill and Co., Westport, Connecticut, 59.

[9]Joachim E. Berendt, *The Jazz Book: From New Orleans to Rock and Free Jazz,* translated by Dan Morgenstern, copyright 1975, Lawrence Hill and Co., Westport, Connecticut, 60.

[10]Max Harrison, *A Jazz Retrospect,* (Boston, Mass.: Crescendo Publishing Co., 1976), 128.

## Duke Ellington

**D**uke Ellington, composer, bandleader, and pianist is one of the most significant compositional figures in jazz. His compositions carried the individuality of his own compositional vision, as well as the individual voices of the many great soloists in his band.

| | |
|---|---|
| *1899* | Ellington was born on April 29. |
| *1923* | Ellington made his first visit to New York City. Later that year he moved to stay. |
| *1923–1927* | His small group (quintet) played at the Hollywood and Kentucky clubs on Broadway. His group gradually grew to a ten-piece orchestra. |
| *1927–1931* | At the Cotton Club in Harlem, he became a popular figure in jazz. His group grew to twelve, among the new players, Johnny Hodges. He made about 200 recordings in the "jungle" style he and Bubber Miley made popular. His famous recording of "Mood Indigo" was made in 1930. |
| *1932–1942* | His group now had six brass, four reeds, and four rhythm. He made European tours in 1933 and 1939. Billy Strayhorn joined the band as an additional pianist, arranger, and composer. His association with Strayhorn marked one of his most creative periods. |
| *1946* | His band now had eighteen, and he worked on larger compositions supported by the new long playing record. |
| *1950–1963* | World tours, film music |
| *1964* | Liturgical music, many awards. |
| *1974* | He directed his band until his death on May 24. |

*Duke Ellington*
Michael Ochs Archives/
Venice, CA

In contrast to Ellington's approach, Harrison cites Ornette Coleman's *Free Jazz* as an example of a coherently whole form not needing external aids to define it, claiming that its "shape arises out of its language." A comparison of this kind suggests some interesting inferences. When jazz ensemble compositions are considered (as opposed to small group improvisatory performances), historians may be too quick themselves to import external analytical tools (i.e., western

European compositional models) to evaluate them. Coleman's performance is so clearly of the moment that, from an improvisational stance, it may be praised for its formal and cohesive design, while in compositional terms, it may prove to be structurally naive.

It must be granted that the Morton to Ellington line of development is certainly more European than most other jazz expressions; however, with that same tradition has come an allegiance to improvisation, both collective and individual. It is the balance of those forces, composed and improvised, that is questioned in the work of these band leaders. The band that has developed out of this tradition is one that is characterized not only by the talents of its personnel but by the composer/arranger as well.

It became more and more necessary for band leaders to procure arrangements that would keep their bands competitive. It was advantageous if the leader also arranged or was associated with prominent arrangers. Mary Lou Williams' presence in the Andy Kirk band is cited as a reason for that band's development beyond the riff styled arrangements typical of the other bands in Kansas City.[11] Henderson's early band certainly reflected the work of Redman and Carter. The personality of his band shifted when he began to write for it himself. George E. Lee in Kansas City actually hired Jesse Stone (who also led his own bands) to arrange for and revamp his band to remain competitive with the then popular Bennie Moten.

Ellington, as composer/leader, worked as a guiding force for the musicians in his band as they supplied material to be woven into the arrangement's final shape. The nature of the compositional shape itself reflects an improvisational attitude in the shaping process. His larger works were more collections of the miniatures Harrison speaks of combined with connective improvisations. The looseness of the structure passes improvisatory responsibility back to the performers.

Rather than merely leaving room for improvisational input during performance, Ellington accepted input from performers during the composition process itself. If the performers are active participants in the compositional process, then their solo flights reflect the improvisationally composed ensemble areas. The delineation between solo and compositional areas becomes blurred in the process of collective composition. How much of Hodges' input was at work in the shaping of the compositional ideas in "Passion Flower"? The continuity of compositional and improvisational activity in the

---

[11]Joachim E. Berendt, *The Jazz Book: From New Orleans to Rock and Free Jazz,* translated by Dan Morgenstern, copyright 1975, Lawrence Hill and Co., Westport, Connecticut, 329. Listen to "Dallas Blues," which was probably arranged by Mary Lou Williams, New World Records NW 274.

## Mary Lou Williams

One of the greatest performers to come out of Kansas City was the multitalented Mary Lou Williams. She was the first woman in jazz history to compose and arrange for a large jazz band, and she dominated the performances of the great Andy Kirk band with her skillful piano playing. Her eclecticism held her in great stead, since she became considered one of the great jazz pianists. Her compositions were in the libraries of a dozen leading swing bands. The last years of her life were filled with many honors. There is even a street in Kansas City named after her. Mary Lou Williams was always new—a perennial innovator.

She wrote lengthy scores, such as "St. Martin de Porres" and "Mary Lou's Mass" (Mary Records 102).

Mary Lou Williams was a deeply religious woman. She launched a foundation that helped many musicians.

She received many honorary degrees and taught at the University of Massachusetts. Duke University was privileged to have Mary Lou Williams on its faculty. She was awarded Duke's coveted Trinity Award for her accomplishments at that university.

| | |
|---|---|
| *1910* | Williams was born in Pittsburgh, Pennsylvania. |
| *1925* | She toured with a vaudeville act. |
| *1929* | She joined the Andy Kirk orchestra as arranger. |
| *1931–1942* | Williams became the pianist for Andy Kirk. |
| *1937* | She began writing arrangements for Benny Goodman. |
| *1942* | She worked in clubs in New York City with her own group while arranging for Duke Ellington. |
| *1948* | She played with and wrote for Benny Goodman. |
| *1952* | She lived in England and France. |
| *1958–1965* | Williams played night clubs and concert dates in the United States. |
| *1968–1969* | She toured Europe. |
| *1970s* | She toured the United States performing many concerts. |
| *Later 1970s* | She taught at Duke University. |
| *1981* | Mary Lou Williams died. |

performance suggests a similar continuum in the process that crafted the piece. Ellington taught this arrangement to the band verbally without a written arrangement. Hearing how Hodges' line and sound grow out of the opening voicings in the band shows a continuity seldom, if ever, rivaled in big band arrangements. The instrumental colors selected by Ellington reflect both the color and inflection so typical of Hodges. It is conceivable that instrumental colors were inspired by the player they were meant to support. Such a continuity of style and arrangement would not occur if we were to place either Hawkins or Young as the lead voice in this arrangement. To do so would disrupt the reciprocal compositional and improvisational relationship at work between Ellington and Hodges.

While a riff arrangement typical of the Southwest bands might take on a completely different character with a change in soloist, an Ellington setting might lose its viability. Fortunately, Ellington had one of the most stable bands throughout jazz history. His work for Johnny Hodges lasted because of Hodges' tenure with the band. The loss of Hodges in 1970 was as significant to Ellington's approach to writing as the loss of Lester Young was to Basie's riff style arrangements in 1939.

## BASIE AND ELLINGTON— ENSEMBLES AND SOLO VOICES

Basie solved his dilemma differently than did Ellington. Although Ellington lost Hodges late in the band's history, he did undergo personnel changes from time to time. As players left and were replaced, he would introduce new material centered around the new players. Basie, on the other hand, adopted a new style for the band, one that deemphasized the role of the individual soloist and shifted the focus to the work of the ensemble as a whole. Basie continued to have strong soloists like Thad Jones, Frank Foster, Frank Wess, Eddie ''Lockjaw'' Davis, and Henry Coker, but he was obviously distressed by the loss of Lester Young. To avoid further dramatic shifts like the one caused by Young's departure, Basie settled on a signature ensemble style as the bands new direction. This style actually followed more in the tradition of Henderson than that of the Kansas City heritage. Significantly different, however, was the emphasis on a demanding yet effortless sounding precision. The looseness in ensemble characteristic of Henderson was not adopted, only the shift toward a more dominant, arrangement-based presentation. His ''Blues in Hoss Flat'' from the *Chairman of the Board* album is a good example of Basie's later approach.

Basie's style is also characterized by an economy of sound. His piano playing, although capable of high-energy stride solos is, in his

Johnny Hodges
''Passion Flower''
New World Records NW 274

:00    Piano introduction setting the mood, four measures
       (Ellington)
:13    Alto sax solo in the low register (Hodges) with sustained
       background
:43    Second eight bars, sax goes up an octave
1:08   Bridge, still sax solo ending with long glissando
1:34   Original strain
2:01   Return to the bridge
2:27   Original strain
2:58   Ending retarding with carefully selected piano notes on the
       end
3:01   End

## Johnny Hodges

**J**ohnny Hodges gained renown as a swinging alto saxophonist in the 1930s. He also occasionally played soprano sax. His fame spread through a series of very melodic solos in which he demonstrated an intimate, passionate style. His beautiful tone blended with songs written by Duke Ellington and Billy Strayhorn and the results were lush classics.

| | |
|---|---|
| *1906* | Hodges was born in Cambridge, Massachusetts, on July 25. |
| *1920* | He worked with and learned from Sidney Bechet. |
| *1927* | Hodges played with Chick Webb's orchestra. |
| *1928–1951* | He played with Duke Ellington. |
| *1951–1955* | Hodges had his own combo. |
| *1955* | He rejoined Duke Ellington. |
| *1970* | Hodges died in New York City on May 11. |

*Johnny Hodges*

Michael Ochs Archives/
Venice, CA

later bands, the paradigm of musical economy. Like his own playing, the band arrangements were essentially based on the less-is-more principle. Whether it was Basie's Kansas City background that gave him improvisatory space or a personal aesthetic is unclear. Basie was known to take charts submitted to him and strip them of material he felt was unnecessary.

Basie, in this respect, is at one extreme and Ellington is at the other in orchestral implementation. Basie, not being the original arranger, worked in a subtractive mode to maintain a streamlined vehicle for the band's expression. The charts were essentially independent of specific personnel but in their openness, conducive to the improvising soloist. The lack of customized solo backups allowed the personnel of the band to shift without great impact on the arrangements.

Ellington, as noted above, customized his music to the attributes of individual performers. His compositions are full of new instrumental colors found by cutting across sectional lines and borrowing the voices of individual players. His approach uses paradoxical, detailed arrangements to launch the individual voices within the ensemble. Because the compositions had the improvisers woven into them, a change of soloists would create a musical disjuncture.

It is tempting to streamline the events of the 1920s and 1930s in jazz, creating a cohesive line that signals the development of the classic big band ensemble. The result would be a direct line of evolutionary development from the early New Orleans ensembles with their improvised counterpoint through the improvised/compositional approach of Ellington on to the carefully prescribed compositions of Toshiko Akioshi's ensemble today. Such an attempt to be historically neat presents some problems.

The development of the big band was quite a bit messier. While we focus on the groups of Morton, Henderson, Basie, and Ellington, there are many other bands of various sizes and stylistic leanings at work in this time period that do not fit the historical line set out by these arranger/composers. As historians, we also tend to map our knowledge of the trends that developed from these bands into the intentions of the earlier musicians. It is inappropriate to assume there is a guiding undercurrent supporting the work of these early arrangers. It may be true that a measured amount of innovation was sought by players and composers alike, but their intentions most likely did not include the shaping of this developing tradition into what might one day be called an art form.

The bands of the 1920s were just coming out of the vaudevilles, brothels, and street parades. This music was primarily functional and did not support most musicians full time. Most players were not formally trained. Their playing skills were self-developed with little or no knowledge of music theory. The music they played was shaped primarily by the traditional activities in which they developed their skills. Whatever evolutionary drift occurred was more the result of the immediacy of their own interaction or public fashion.

It was eventually the fashion of dancing that carried the jazz ensemble into the ballroom in the 1930s. Before this could occur, a compromise of the purely oral tradition at work in the early New Orleans ensembles had to take place. The ballrooms used larger bands, which strained the improvisational nature of the early bands. The formalization of the ensemble, begun in the work of Morton, required reading skills of the musicians. Most of the early dance bands, however, did not play the original arrangements of a leader like Morton. The fashion of the day included many popular tunes published as stock arrangements. It was not until the 1920s that a band would begin to be identified by original arrangements.

By this time, the melding of soloistic players into a group expression became a leader's central role.

Dance bands of the day always fed on the work of jazz soloists: their innovations in phrasing and rhythm; their repertoire, including adaptations and assimilations from "classical" music; and, perhaps most tellingly, their own self-popularizations.[12]

How leaders balanced the role of soloists and ensemble identity was a reflection of the leader's own individuality. The possibilities were quite great and not easy to place in neat historical categories. It is here that the classical music models, which trace their lineage through the literature of individual composers, met the oral tradition of jazz, which is much more likely to trace its development through the activities of its performers. This apparent disjuncture in approach presents a dilemma for the historian.

Most historians and critics agree that the jazz tradition began to be recognized as an art form during the Bop era. Assuming this is true, the codification of the art form must have been at work in earlier jazz expressions. The early bands represent, in their tug-of-war between soloist and composer, a microcosm of the forces at work in jazz's struggle for art status. Academic and public institutions tend to see the classical model of art music as the standard against which to measure new music. Such a model leans heavily toward an interest in the literature of the music as an expression of individual composers rather than a continuity of improvisational performers.

If jazz is to move toward the classical model, it is threatened by a loss of identity. To maintain its improvisatory expression puts jazz's codification as an art form at risk. The big band represents the intersection of the two traditions always at work in jazz, the western European and the oral, blues-based traditions. To select one of these models to define the dominant historical line of jazz would be inappropriate. The model must come from the inner workings of jazz as expressed in such groups as those discussed here.

The balance between composition and improvisation was not to any extent universally agreed upon by leaders and arrangers of the 1920s and 1930s. Jesse Stone was a very popular arranger/composer in the 1920s in Kansas who crafted arrangements for himself and others. Although he was working among the riffing bands of the Southwest, he used written arrangements that in some cases even had precomposed solos. This approach can be contrasted to the head arrangements that developed from the collective input of members in the riff band. Stone, like several other arrangers of the time, did not

---

[12]J. R. Taylor, "Jammin' for the Jackpot," New World Records NW 217.

last long as a bandleader because of his interest in overly sophisticated musical ideas that outstepped his public. This attempt to push compositional ideas at the expense of soloistic input was tempered by the marketplace.

The delineation between New York and Southwest bands also is not as clear as historians would like it. Popularity guided much of the development of the bands in both locations. The most popular groups were inspirations and models for less successful groups. The recordings of big bands occurred mostly in Chicago and New York, and the influence of the bands flowed outward to the territory bands. Southwest bands therefore were not limited to loosely composed riffing ensembles. They felt the influence of the East Coast bands and emulated what would work for their own local audiences.

Jesse Stone in Missouri, Walter Page and George E. Lee in Kansas City, and Troy Floyd in Texas all show that their ears were directed to New York and Chicago. Listen to ''Ruff-Scuffling,'' a Jesse Stone arrangement for George E. Lee's band. This arrangement has very tight exchanges among sections of the ensemble. The many duos, trios, short solos, and ensemble breaks are reminiscent of Don Redman's arrangements for Henderson. Although more blues-rooted than the Eastern bands, these territory bands were struggling to find a compositional identity that would capture the public's ear. At the same time Stone was writing for George E. Lee, Bennie Moten's band was the leading competition. That Lee's more arranged band and Moten's riff band both shared a common market shows the type of diversity at work across the Southwest.

The 1920s bands of Chicago and New York also showed a great deal of individuality. Compare the Dixieland-based sound of Jabbo Smith with the lush arrangements of the Leo Reisman orchestra. The two expressions seem worlds apart. Smith employed a more traditional ensemble grouping, and Reisman employed more carefully arranged dance arrangements. Both had, to a greater or lesser extent, room for improvisational solo work.[13]

Another interesting comparison can be seen between the Henderson band and Glen Gray's Casa Loma Orchestra, which sported very popular original arrangements by guitarist Gene Gifford. The Casa Loma Orchestra, like the Henderson band, exerted an influence on other bands because of its popularity. This popularity was

[13]''Jammin' for the Jackpot,'' New World Records NW 217. Listen to Jabbo Smith's ''Till Times Get Better'' and Reisman's arrangement of Cole Porter's ''What Is This Thing Called Love?,'' which features James ''Bubber'' Miley on trumpet.

generated in part by original arrangements. Gifford's arrangements were often purchased or traded for by other band leaders, among whom was Fletcher Henderson himself.

Despite their popularity, the Casa Loma Orchestra has not survived as well as the Henderson band has from an historical perspective. By the time Glen Gray assumed the leadership of the Casa Loma Orchestra, the sectional bodies were already essentially standardized in the arrangements that were already characteristic of the Henderson group. Perhaps unwittingly, Redman, Carter, and Henderson had structured through their arrangements an ensemble that was to be the dominant voice of the Swing era to follow. It would be an era that would continue to serve the ballroom dancer and continue the dialectic inherent in big band jazz.

## STYLISTIC OVERVIEW

Throughout the period discussed several fundamental changes occurred in the way jazz ensembles worked. The formalization of the ensembles through arrangements, although not strictly uniform, offered some compositional options for later writers. As the improvisational counterpoint moved from the player to the composer, the solos became restricted to prescribed areas of a composition. The original ensembles of New Orleans were made up of individuals who improvised constantly, including the members of the rhythm section. The piano player also maintained a steady improvisation in the right hand, while the left hand performed harmonic and rhythmic duties.

As the sections took on more definition, the degree of individual improvisation was reduced. The earliest arrangements often opened with a Dixieland texture and only ended with a more stylized ensemble. Throughout the 1920s the ensemble sections developed into the more complex structures typical of Redman's arrangements. We still hear in the bands of the 1920s and 1930s individual stylizations within ensembles, but the lines themselves are essentially fixed. The Southwest bands with their riff approach sported player generated forms, but even there the sectional breakdown and size of the band narrowed a player's options. Even the piano player's right-hand activity disappeared as the ensembles took on more and more definition.

At the largest structural level, the soloists often work in opposition to the tutti statements of the ensemble. At some times, particularly with the riffing bands, both forces play together at points of high energy. The way the ensemble passages were built separates the riff approach from Henderson's arrangements. The riff tutti sections were built from interacting riff melodies that contrapuntally fell along section lines. Henderson's arrangements were more vertical in their rhythmic structure. Rather than working contrapuntally, the sections were often juxtaposed in tight call-and-response phrases. These ensemble areas were then set apart by short solo areas.

The Southwest bands tended toward a more loosely designed formal structure for the piece because it was likely to take shape during the performance. It would usually begin with an opening head arrangement and then a string of solos, which might have riff backups. High energy riff complexes added structural markers to the piece and ultimately ended it.

It is only in the work of composers like Ellington that the distinction between soloistic statement and the workings of the ensemble are so blurred compositionally. Throughout this seminal period for big bands, a symbiosis existed between soloists and composers. As the literature of these bands has developed, "the transformations of soloistic thought were effected by a composer-orchestrator, usually called an arranger."[14]

---

**SUGGESTED LISTENING**

*The Best of Basie.* Columbia Records C3L 33.
*The Best of Basie.* MCA Records 4050.
*Best of Count Basie.* Decca Records DXSB 7170.
Coleman, Ornette. "Free Jazz." Smithsonian J/2 (cd V/9).
Count Basie. "Doggin' Around." Smithsonian D/5 (cd 11/20).
Don Redman—Master of the Big Band. RCA Victor Records
    RD 7828, RCA Victor Records LPV–520.
*Ellington Era.* Columbia Records C3L 27.
*The Essential Lester Young.* Verve Records U 8398.
Fletcher Henderson and His Orchestra. "Wrappin' It Up."
    Smithsonian B/12 (cd 11/12).
Hawkins, Coleman. "Body and Soul." Smithsonian C/8 (cd 11/8).
Henderson, Fletcher. *A Study in Frustration.* Columbia Records
    C4L 19.
Henderson, Fletcher. *Developing an American Orchestra,*
    *1927–1947.* Smithsonian Collection R 006.
Henderson, Fletcher. "The Stampede." Smithsonian B/11
    (cd 11/1).
Hodges, Johnny. "Passion Flower." *Jive at Five.* New World
    Records NW 274.
*The King of New Orleans.* RCA Victor Records LPM 1649.

---

[14] J. R. Taylor, "Jammin' for the Jackpot," New World Records NW 217.

King Oliver's Creole Jazz Band. ''Dippermouth Blues.''
    Smithsonian A/5 (cd 1/5).
Kirk, Andy. *Instrumentally Speaking*. MCA Records 1308.
Lee, George E. ''Ruff-Scuffling.'' *Sweet and Low Blues*. New
    World Records NW 256.
Morton, Jelly Roll. ''Maple Leaf Rag.'' Smithsonian A/2 (cd 1/2).
Moten, Benny. ''Moten Swing.'' Smithsonian C/2 (cd 11/4).
*New Orleans Jazz*. Decca Records 8283.
Oliver, Joe King. ''Sweet Lovin' Man.'' Folkways 2806.
Smithsonian Collection of Classic Jazz, Vols. 6 and 7.
*Steppin' On the Gas: Rags to Jazz, 1913–1927*. New World
    Records NW 269.
*Stomps and Joys*. RCA Victor Records LPV 508.
Taylor, J. R. ''Jammin' for the Jackpot.'' New World
    Records NW 217.
*This Is Duke Ellington*. RCA Victor Records VPM 6042.
Young, Lester. *Prez*. Mainstream Records 56012.
*Young Lester Young*. Columbia Records J24.

# CHAPTER 8

## *The Engine of Popularity*

| | |
|---|---|
| *1929* | Stock market crash followed by the Great Depression |
| *1932–1942* | Swing bands define the mainstream of jazz |
| *1932* | Tommy Dorsey recorded "I'm Getting Sentimental Over You." In August of 1935 Goodman opened at the Palomar Ballroom in Los Angeles |
| *1936* | First Jazz concert at New York City's Onyx Club |
| *1937* | Count Basie first recorded "One O'Clock Jump" |
| *1938* | First Carnegie Hall jazz concert with Benny Goodman |
| *1939–1945* | World War II |
| *1939* | Glenn Miller recorded "Moonlight Serenade" and "In the Mood" |
| *1941* | Glenn Miller recorded gold record of "Chattanooga Choo Choo" |
| *1941* | Duke Ellington recorded "Take the 'A' Train" |
| *1941* | United States entered World War II on December 7 |
| *1942* | Recording ban by the musicians' union |
| *1942* | Glenn Miller disbanded his orchestra |
| *1944* | Glenn Miller reported missing in action |

E very art form, in order to be canonized, must have a propelling force to gather together the artists, the critics, and the public. The swing bands were this propelling force for jazz. Their overwhelming popularity established jazz as a mainstream American musical expression. Swing became the most listened to music in the entire world. This world popularity was the foundation for the eventual canonization of jazz into the art form we know today. The popularity of jazz during this period helped establish the first stars and the basic style by which later jazz expressions would be measured by the public at large. Only later did the historical perspective of the players, listeners, and critics expand to include the earlier styles on which the swing band tradition was founded. The big bands helped legitimize jazz as a public music and, in turn, open a window through which later jazz enthusiasts could look to rediscover earlier contributions to this developing art form. The Swing era of 1932 to 1942 was a very important period as we trace the emergence of jazz as an American art form.

In general, swing brings to mind large dance bands that played written arrangements with occasional improvised solos. Some jazz terms can become quite confusing, and swing is one of them. Most noteworthy jazz from all stylistic periods is expected to have a rhythmic drive called swing. This generalized notion of swing must be distinguished from the specific Swing era of 1932 to 1942. The confusion between these two uses of the term swing is because jazz began to sense its tradition during this very popular Swing era. It makes sense that a determining criterion for ''good'' jazz of any period is that it swing, a term coined during the zenith of jazz's popularity. However, it is how each period swings that helps define it stylistically.

In spite of this very prominent criterion for ''good'' jazz, some of the most popular swing music did not swing in the same sense the up tempo tunes did. It involved jazz musicians playing jazz interpretations of popular, pretty ballads. One of the unusual aspects of swing jazz is that it is remembered most for its up-tempo tunes. However, the swing bands actually played more ballads than anything else. That we tend to remember the faster tunes may be more a mapping of our own current jazz expectations into the quite different melieu of the Swing era. It should be remembered that those ballads that dominated the swing repertoire were played by very jazz-oriented musicians. The interpretation used by these musicians recast the ballads in a jazz idiom. Listen, for example, to Benny Goodman, dubbed the King of Swing, play his theme, a very pretty ballad called ''Good-Bye''; jazz trumpeter Harry James plays an obligato in the background (example 8.1).

It is seldom easy to find specific dates at which changes in jazz have taken place. The transitions are usually very blurred and seen best in retrospect. There are, however, occasionally some very important events that signal transitions. One such signal was sent when the Benny Goodman band opened in August of 1935 at the Palomar Ballroom in Los Angeles. Although an important date, it is not the official beginning of the Swing era as some might suggest. By the time Goodman became a success, large African-American orchestras

**EXAMPLE 8.1**    Beginning of ''Good-Bye''
World and Music by Gordon Jenkins. © Copyright 1935 MCA MUSIC PUBLISHING, A Division of MCA INC. Copyright Renewed. International Copyright Secured. All Rights Reserved. Used by Permission.

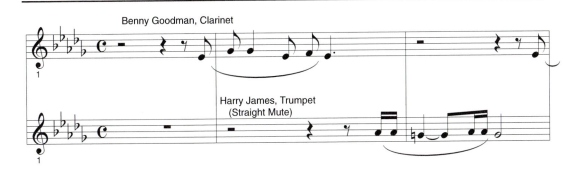

had already established the format for this size of organization. These were the orchestras of Moten, Kirk, and Trent from the Midwest and Henderson, Ellington, McKinney, and Lunceford from the East. As we saw in chapter 7, these bands had already established the sectionalization we see in the later bands, as well as the compositional approach refined by later composer/arrangers. Also remember that much of the success of Goodman's Los Angeles performance has been attributed to his use of Fletcher Henderson arrangements. These were arrangements used almost in desperation at the conclusion of an otherwise unsuccessful tour across the United States. It was actually Goodman's extension of the earlier swing band tradition that nurtured his success in Los Angeles. Henderson continued as Goodman's arranger for several years after the band had claimed a leading role in the developing swing band tradition.

As timing is so crucial to success in most ventures, the timing of the Swing era was perfect. The depression began with the fall of the stock market in 1929. The public, trying to forget this disastrous crash and the ensuing depression, needed a reasonably priced outlet for entertainment—dancing became that outlet. Thousands of people decided they wanted to dance every night. Large ballrooms sprang up over the entire country. Even very small towns would often have huge dance halls. With a minimum of amplification available, large bands were required to fill the large halls. By 1937, there were 18,000 musicians on the road with these bands, and the number continued to increase.

People escaped from daily drudgery by dancing to the hundreds of band leading heroes in cabarets, in ballrooms, or at home on records or on the radio. Only a few of these heroes have survived historical extinction. At that time, they enjoyed the same cultural popularity as the many rock singers do today. Their names were household words.

Musical excellence was only one way of gaining the greatest popularity. Bands also had to align with the cultural mores of the day. Because the primary media channels were catering to white audiences, the white bands enjoyed the greatest national popularity during this period. Bands like Goodman's that compromised the color lines by mixing white and African-American players were taking substantial risks. Only bands of the stature enjoyed by Goodman could even think of taking such risks.

The sentimental music of the depression reflected only one side of the public's profile. The public's optimism was bolstered in the late 1930s by a returning prosperity that demanded a more joyous type of popular music. Records and radio were extremely important in promoting jazz as an expression of this new optimism. As a result, more musicians were working in the jazz field than during any previous period.

Around 1932, there was more employment for musicians in Chicago and New York City than was available in the rest of the country. This was with the exception of Kansas City where the Pendergast Machine (a political regime) also sustained an environment that allowed jazz to flourish. The Machine needed the clubs that hired the musicians for the income they brought in from bootlegging and prostitution. With New York City opening its doors for Duke Ellington's gathering of stellar personalities and Fletcher Henderson's orchestral arranging concept (see chapter 7), such Kansas City bands as Bennie Moten (later to become the seeds of the Count Basie band) were headed in a different direction than large bands in the East. The Kansas City concept used more blues-based music, more riff emphasis, and in general, looser confines for the soloists.

The language of the big band format began to gain widespread public acceptance. This acceptance proved most important for all jazz that followed. More than at any other time in the history of this art form, the jazz idiom was in step with public taste. More specifically, jazz became the dominant musical expression of the media which was becoming more and more influential in establishing public taste.

As the big band style became more and more popular, the composers and arrangers of this music also became popular. Few other periods of jazz placed the arrangers and composers in such high regard. The formalization of the big band ensemble, as well as its size, required a more defined compositional approach. Unlike the smaller ensembles that both preceded and followed the big bands, these larger groups needed predefined arrangements that could coordinate their performance.

As the emphasis shifted from collective improvisation typical of earlier groups to the arrangements of the big bands, the balance between soloists and ensemble playing also shifted. Not only was there less solo improvisation in the big band format than in the earlier Dixieland styles, but there was also less freedom in the ensemble passages for personal interpretation. The control of performance details for ensemble passages had passed from the individual players to the arranger or composer.

The notion of composition in jazz has always been elusive. How specific must the instrumentalists' parts be to be considered composed? The earliest ''compositions'' of Jelly Roll Morton may not have been clearly notated, yet they were compositionally conceived. The individual parts may have been left to the players, but the structural design was outlined by Morton. The Southwest bands also used less defined arrangements. The ensemble sections developed out of the riffing offerings of the players and became fixed over time. The most fully composed arrangements came out of the Fletcher Henderson tradition. It was this tradition that was adopted by the popular white big bands of Goodman, Miller, and Dorsey. Within this more formalized compositional tradition there was little room for the improvisational work of individual players, although each of these bands contained renown solo players.

Most of the big bands were associated with specific arrangers that helped define their sound. Fletcher Henderson's band featured his own arrangements, as well as those of Horace Henderson, Benny Carter, and Don Redman. Carter and Redman went on to have their own bands, which continued to feature them as soloists and writers.

## BIG BAND ARRANGERS AND COMPOSERS

Sy Oliver arranged for Jimmy Lunceford; Billy May arranged for Glenn Miller and Charlie Barnet; Ed Sauter arranged for Benny Goodman; Jerry Gray arranged for Artie Shaw and Glenn Miller; and Billy Strayhorn arranged for Duke Ellington.

A looser compositional approach was maintained by African-American bands, such as Ellington and early Basie. Although soloists tended to carve out longer solo expanses within these bands, the arrangements were still founded on clear compositional structures. Even the late Basie band, sometimes coined ''the ensemble machine'' because of its precise ensemble skills, still held open large solo areas for its outstanding soloists. As we saw in chapter 7, the Ellington band struck perhaps the most unique balance between compositional intent and individual improvisation. The African-American/white line in compositional style is certainly not a universal distinction. Jimmy Lunceford, at his zenith, led a band that was characterized by complex compositions, as well as highly technical ensemble execution by indivdiual players.

The big band format maintains a dialectic balance between the western European reverence for compositional practice and the less definable oral tradition of most other world cultures.

## THE POPULAR BANDS (LATE 1930s–1940s)

The bands of Duke Ellington, Count Basie, Jimmy Lunceford, Benny Goodman, Glenn Miller, and Tommy Dorsey were the most popular among the public as well as the musicians themselves.

### Benny Goodman

The Benny Goodman band played with such drive that it moved all who listened. Somehow sections of the band played with the feeling of a single jazz soloist. In July of 1935, Goodman (the clarinet image of the world) recorded his first record with a trio including Gene Krupa and Teddy Wilson.

The National Biscuit Company sponsored a three hour network radio program every Saturday night for twenty-six weeks. Goodman shared the time with two other entirely different orchestras. This exposure should have boosted his audience appeal. However, as he crossed the nation in 1935, he met with one humiliating experience after another until he arrived in Los Angeles at the Palomar Ballroom in August. Here, the public accepted the band enthusiastically and Goodman became named ''The King of Swing.'' Hit record followed hit record: ''King Porter Stomp,'' ''Don't Be That Way,'' etc. Vocals

## Benny Goodman

**B**esides being dubbed the King of Swing and almost single-handedly cutting through racial barriers in music, Goodman was instrumental in helping jazz musicians earn a decent wage. He was the master of the clarinet, and his playing was a combination of great wit, precise musicianship, beautiful subtleties, and never-ending swing.

| | |
|---|---|
| *1909* | Goodman was born on May 30. |
| *1929* | He joined Ben Pollack Orchestra. |
| *1934* | He organized his first band. |
| *1935* | Goodman first recorded with his trio, Gene Krupa and Teddy Wilson and opened at the Palomar Ballroom in Los Angeles in August. |
| *1936* | Goodman hired Teddy Wilson and Lionel Hampton as regular members of his band. |
| *1955* | Universal-International Studios made a motion picture based on his life. |
| *1960s–1970s* | Goodman continued to tour and appear at jazz festivals. |
| *1986* | Goodman died in June. |

were handled by such talents as Martha Tilton and Peggy Lee. The talented musicians included Harry James, Gene Krupa, Ziggy Elman, and many more.

Goodman often rehearsed his band without the rhythm section. His rightful assumption was that if he could make the music rhythmically stirring without the aid of this aggressive foursome, then when they were added back in, the result would be even more exciting. Goodman's band was exciting.

### Duke Ellington

Duke Ellington, brilliant composer/conductor/pianist gave credit for his success to his famous sidemen who, in turn, gave all the credit to Ellington. His reputation of being a giant in the blending of the jazz spirit and compositional foresight and being one of the truly noble forces of jazz followed him throughout his career.

## "Safe Integration"

**S**ome of the leading white swing band leaders were enthused about the talents of some African-American musicians. They, no doubt, would have hired them, but they feared that a substantial part of a band's following would be lost if it were integrated.

This attitude began to change because of the leadership of Benny Goodman. However, the prevalent separatist attitude cost some talented performers, like Billie Holiday, much of their most lucrative employment. Holiday sang for very short periods with Benny Goodman, Artie Shaw, and Paul Whiteman. Lena Horne also worked for a short time for Charlie Barnet. The public would not accept these African-American singers.

There were occasionally instances of "safe integration," meaning that the light-complected players were acceptable to the public. A good example was Willie Smith, the lead alto saxophone player who worked in the Jimmy Lunceford band from 1930 to 1941. He established himself as one of the best players of that instrument along with Johnny Hodges and Benny Carter. Smith had a very light complexion and caused no furor when he joined the all white Charlie Spivak band in 1942. After he was discharged from the army in 1944, he joined Harry James.

Earle Warren played lead alto saxophone and was the virtual leader for Count Basie from 1937 to 1945. Glenn Miller was intrigued by Warren's talents and, understanding that the public would not question this light-complexioned musician, tried to woo him from the Basie band. However, Warren decided that he was happy where he was, despite the increase in pay offered by Miller.

African-American band leaders also integrated their bands. Drummer Louis Bellson played for Ellington; trumpeter Don Rader played for Basie; and saxophonist Herbie Haymer played for Hampton.

Such instances reflected the feedback loop that existed between the bands and their public. The bands depended on public response and were, on the whole, unwilling to risk breaking the racial lines that had become defined in the music business. Fortunately, some leaders like Goodman, Barnet, and Shaw helped erode this artificial barrier.

**EXAMPLE 8.2**  Beginning of ''Chelsea Bridge''
CHELSEA BRIDGE, Music by Billy Strayhorn. Copyright © 1941 (Renewed) by Tempo Music, Inc. and Music Sales Corporation (ASCAP). All Rights Administered by Music Sales Corporation. International Copyright Secured. All Rights Reserved. Reprinted by Permission.

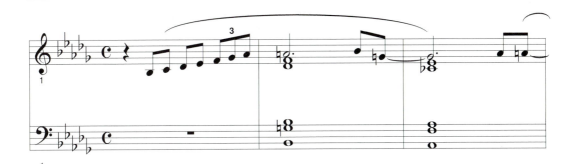

The general public never embraced Ellington as the music world did. Was most of his music too subtle or exotic for them? Was his apparent disregard for the commercial pop tunes to blame? Did he lack the radio exposure so necessary for great popularity? Even though his success was not on the scale of the white bands of the day, he still was responsible for many musical hits, such as ''Perdido,'' ''Take the 'A' Train,'' ''Don't Get Around Much Anymore,'' ''It Don't Mean a Thing If It Ain't Got That Swing,'' ''Sophisticated Lady,'' ''I'm Beginning To See the Light,'' ''Satin Doll,'' and many more. His early commercial success can also be tied to his partnership with publisher and businessman Irving Mills. Leading an African-American band, Ellington seldom was accorded the exposure that many white bands of lesser stature enjoyed. Still, Ellington's name was lauded by enough music people that he was famous and wealthy. (See chapter 7, p. 187 for a brief biography of Ellington.)

## Billy Strayhorn

**W**hen classically trained Billy Strayhorn first met Duke Ellington, Strayhorn hoped to become a lyricist as he auditioned for Ellington with his composition "Lush Life." By 1939, he had become a permanent associate of Ellington. He composed and arranged some of the most significant selections in the Ellington library, including "Chelsea Bridge," "Passion Flower," and the band's theme song "Take the 'A' Train." Strayhorn absorbed Ellington's piano and writing to the point where it was impossible to detect which artist had played or written which work. He was often described as Ellington's "alter ego."

Immediately after Strayhorn's death, Ellington recorded an album of Strayhorn compositions. The album was called *And His Mother Called Him Bill* (RCA Victor Records LSP 3906). Afterward, Ellington concluded every concert by sitting at the piano and playing Strayhorn's "Lotus Blossom."

*1915*  Strayhorn was born in Dayton, Ohio.

*1938*  He first met Duke Ellington in this year and wrote and played for Ellington from then on.

*1950s*  In New York City, he led his own group, which often included Johnny Hodges.

*1960s*  Strayhorn continued to compose/arrange works for Ellington in spite of serious illnesses.

*1967*  Strayhorn died in New York City.

More than any other musician in jazz, Ellington represented a successful blend of the two musical heritages that spawned jazz. While recognized as one of jazz's premier composers, Ellington also never compromised the "voice" of jazz so firmly rooted in the oral tradition. He represents a balance between the western European compositional legacy and the expressive oral tradition of the African heritage.

Billy Strayhorn, often called Ellington's "alter-ego," was a strong arranging and composing force in the band. Both Ellington and Strayhorn were pianists, composers, and arrangers who thought so much alike musically that it was often difficult to tell which musician had written a given work. Strayhorn seemed to nurture influences from the French impressionists as witnessed in his "Chelsea Bridge" (see example 8.2).

It is interesting to note that even with all of his own original compositions, Ellington chose ''Take the 'A' Train,'' a Strayhorn contribution, as his theme song. After Strayhorn died, Ellington finished every concert by sitting at the piano and playing Strayhorn's ''Lotus Blossom'' as a tribute to his colleague's exceptional influence.

### Count Basie

Within the jazz community, Basie had one of the greatest bands of all time that seemed to ''out-swing'' all the rest. The band's tight ensemble and swinging style is often attributed to its rhythm section. Among their most popular records was ''Jumpin' at the Woodside'' and the famous ''One O'Clock Jump.'' Basie's band, however, received even less radio and record exposure than Ellington. (See chapter 7, p. 182 for a brief biography of Count Basie.)

### Jimmy Lunceford

On November 8, 1940, there was a charity affair called a Battle of Bands at New York City's Manhattan Center. There were thirty bands, each scheduled to play fifteen minutes. These bands included Benny Goodman, Glenn Miller, Count Basie, Glen Gray, Les Brown, Guy Lombardo, Will Bradley, Sammy Kaye, and twenty-two others. The show lasted from 8:00 P.M. to 4:00 A.M. with each band playing its alloted fifteen minutes—except for one. The six thousand enthusiastic fans refused to let Jimmy Lunceford's band get off the bandstand. It was as if they had just discovered this talented band.

Musicians knew about the band; it ranked as high as any other swing band. Once again, despite their great talent, their lack of exposure and recording the popular tunes of the day kept the band from reaching the top of the public's popularity polls.

### Tommy Dorsey

Tommy Dorsey had one of the greatest all-around dance bands in history. Testimony to the Tommy Dorsey band's popularity was its continual rating among the top three public favorites. It is easy to say that some other bands swung more consistently and that some may have been more stylistically distinctive, but the Tommy Dorsey band was unusually versatile within the big band venue. With his lush trombone playing and his choice of such singers as Frank Sinatra, Dorsey performed the popular tunes of the day brilliantly. Surprisingly, his best seller in the record field was his ''Boogie Woogie'' written by

## Jimmy Lunceford

**T**he Lunceford band was thrilling to all who were privileged to hear it. It swung with a relaxed 2/4 feeling on most tunes but was also capable of unfathomable fast technical exhibitions.

| | |
|---|---|
| *1902* | Lunceford was born on June 6. |
| *1920s* | He graduated from Fisk University. |
| *1927* | He organized his first band. |
| *1930–1934* | He began extensive recording. |
| *1935–1937* | These were his key years for recording with the best personnel. |
| *1947* | Lunceford died on July 13. |

Eddy Pine-Top Smith. The more rhythmic numbers were guaranteed to swing because of Davey Tough or Buddy Rich on drums, Bunny Berigan or Charlie Shavers on trumpets, and some of the best arrangements the era had to offer, such as ''Well Git It'' and ''Song of India.''

### *Glenn Miller*

The public unquestionably decided that the most popular of the swing bands was one led by trombonist Glenn Miller. It was unusual for the public to find a band's unique signature in its sound, but it was that sound that was most associated with this band. Miller established his individual sound by voicing his saxophone section differently than other bands and using this sound as his identifying feature. The change was simple but effective; he replaced the lead alto sax with a clarinet. See example 8.3, which shows the scoring used for the Miller theme song, ''Moonlight Serenade.''

In 1939, the band played at the Meadowbrook Supper Club in New Jersey, then they played all summer at the Glen Island Casino in New Rochelle, New York, afterward returning to the Meadowbrook. If exposure is a prime issue for gaining popularity, consider that at each of these locations there were nightly network radio programs, as well as some afternoon programs. Miller knew that when those three engagements were over, his band would have gained wide public attention.

## Tommy Dorsey

**T**ommy Dorsey rightfully was considered one of the greatest trombonists of all time. He was definitely the master, if not the originator, of ballad trombone playing. His Dixieland type band-within-a-band was called the Clambake Seven, but it did not register the same significance as that of Goodman's small groups. With the addition of arranger Si Oliver, the full band had the great relaxed 2/4 feeling inherited from the Jimmy Lunceford band. It was a true musical thrill to witness this band play.

*1905*  Dorsey was born on November 19.

*1927*  He recorded several solos on trumpet.

*1932*  He first recorded ''I'm Getting Sentimental Over You'' in September.

*1935*  He left the Dorsey Brothers Orchestra to form his own band.

*1953*  Dorsey reunited with his brother Jimmy.

*1956*  Dorsey died on November 26.

*EXAMPLE 8.3*    ''Moonlight Serenade''
MOONLIGHT SERENADE, Glenn Miller and Mitchell Parish. Copyright © 1939 (Renewed 1967) c/o EMI ROBBINS CATALOG INC. Reprinted by Permission of CPP/Belwin, Inc., Miami, FL. All Rights Reserved.

## Glenn Miller

Glenn Miller, an exceptional trombonist, excellent arranger, and most astute business man put all these attributes together to form this popular band. He had attempted to have a band earlier, but decided that it was not to his specifications in several ways, so he disbanded it. He was truly a patriot and it shocked the entertainment world when he left the music scene to enter the service. The band worked very hard; at times, the demands were almost more than they could physically cope with. They played 140 sessions in two weeks. These included seven shows a day at New York's Paramount Theater, two long sessions a night at the Hotel Pennsylvania, six commercial radio programs a week plus three rehearsals each week. The band's popularity was so great that it saddened the world to learn of his disappearance in 1944.

| | |
|---|---|
| *1904* | Miller was born on March 1. |
| *1926–1927* | He played with Ben Pollack. |
| *1937* | He organized his first band. |
| *1938* | Miller organized the band for which he became best known. |
| *1939* | He recorded "Moonlight Serenade" and "In the Mood." |
| *1941–1942* | He made motion pictures featuring his band. |
| *1941* | Miller recorded "Chattanooga Choo Choo," the first gold record (sold over a million copies since 1927). |
| *1942* | He disbanded the band in order to enlist in the service. |
| *1942* | He organized his very large service orchestra. |
| *1944* | Miller reported missing in action. |

## THE POPULAR MUSICIAN'S IMAGE

Jazz, in its early days, was associated with the activities of the tenderloin, a district of the city largely devoted to vice, prostitution, and other forms of law breaking. Because of this association, the image and morality of the musician was always suspect. Before drugs became a part of the school scene, there was a Daniels Senate Investigating Committee organized to determine exactly who was using drugs. They first headed straight for the musicians (after all, how else, they thought, could one improvise jazz solos) not realizing that if these musicians had a lifestyle equivalent to their reputation, they would find it very difficult to perform in the precise manner usually demanded of them. However, when a person would be arrested for use of a controlled substance and an old delapidated guitar was found in the trunk of his car, the byline would usually read, ''another musician.'' Daniels, however, found that musicians were thirteenth on his list with other reputable professions ranking much higher. The public accepted the fact that drummer Gene Krupa had sampled marijuana. However, this same public would be less forgiving if the solos or the chords used by a band's arranger became too advanced for their acceptance and would sometimes support their reaction with accusations of use of controlled substances or even mental problems.

As jazz began its ascendency to the art form we know today, the image of the musician also began to change. However, before it became the ''clean'' image of the neoclassical school, it suffered some heavy blows during the excesses of the Bop era. As jazz left the tenderloin (and ironically also the church) and moved onto the concert stage and into the universities, the image of the participants (and perhaps their behavior as well) also assumed a new definition. It was during the Swing era and in the big bands in particular that the move towards that newer more ''legitimate'' image began. With this new image, focused by the media, jazz entered middle-class America, a requirement for later assimilation into the country's art community.

## THE BREAKDOWN OF RACIAL LINES

Because of the hybrid nature of jazz, a search for its roots leads in multiple directions. Those directions tend to follow the racial groupings so dominant in the American culture in the first half of this century. Despite the music's hybrid nature, the performance practices of whites and African Americans were separate. As many other aspects of the jazz legacy were undergoing change in the Swing era, so was this separation of African-American and white performance. Unfortunately, the instances of integrated performance are not many; however, they were important changes necessary to keep the hybrid balance of jazz in good working order.

The lines between the African-American and white bands was not always clear. For example, imagine the situation at Savoy Ballroom in the middle of New York's Harlem, the mecca for the most inspiring rhythmic African-American bands, where the attendance record is held by Guy Lombardo, the epitome of the ''society'' band.

Even more notable was the integration within individual bands, in particular, Benny Goodman's band. His small band within the large band included, in various groupings, Gene Krupa, Teddy Wilson, Lionel Hampton, and Charlie Christian.

Although bands have become increasingly integrated, the integration issue, which only began to be addressed in the Swing era, still lingers. As we look back to rediscover ''the'' jazz legacy, it is tempting to stress one source at the expense of others. Because jazz sources often are delineated along racial lines, the hybrid quality of the music is sometimes obscured by the nonmusical social ramifications of America's struggle to resolve questions of race.

## THE BIG BAND LEGACY

The big bands seldom played concerts, they were geared toward dance music. Occasionally, on a two-day visit to a college, an afternoon concert would be included. However, the music played at these concerts was the same as was performed later at the dance. One exception would be some of the larger works performed by the Duke Ellington band. Of course, when the bands would play commercial radio programs from a studio, there would be no dancing. The 1938 Carnegie Hall concert by the Benny Goodman band opened the door for more of a concert approach to jazz. This concert essentially signaled a move from the street into the art community for jazz. Carnegie Hall represented the bastion of classical music, and the presence of Goodman's jazz on its stage signaled an acceptance that would not be fully played out until the 1990s when jazz became part of Lincoln Center's musical season. (See chapter 10 on neoclassical jazz.)

The road tours so prevalent with the swing bands would also include many theater engagements. These were at regular movie houses, and the bands were the answer to a waning vaudeville industry. Still, the musical menu would be directly lifted from the dance repertoire.

Because of the draft for military service and problems of transportation, the Swing era as such came to an abrupt end at the beginning of the United States entry into World War II. Swing bands could not function unless they could play one-night stands. To stay in one location meant a reduced income for a band; however, location jobs were necessary for radio time, a chance to record, and a chance to rest from the rigors of traveling. The bands then went on the road again to recoup their losses, but World War II meant no gasoline and no automobile tires for civilians. All unessential travel came to a halt in the United States. The military draft took 13 million young men (mainly of swing band age). The band leaders simply could not replenish their ranks; however, there were fine bands in the service.

One other event contributed to the shutdown of employment of musicians. The federal government levied a 30 percent cabaret tax on any place musicians worked, and most cabarets simply closed their doors because the public generally refused to pay it. In a single month, December of 1946, eight leaders decided to break up their bands: Woody Herman, Benny Goodman, Les Brown, Jack Teagarden, Benny Carter, Ina Ray Hutton, and Tommy Dorsey. One solution to the problems caused by the draft would have been to form smaller groups.

The 1942 recording ban (a musicians' strike against the record companies) had lasted two years. During that time, there were many records made without using instrumentalists, which pushed singers into the forefront of recorded music. By the time the ban was lifted by the musicians' union, many orchestras had disbanded. It should be noted, however, that the swing bands absolutely had rescued the record companies from financial ruin.

## PROGRESSIVE AND BOP BANDS

The war disrupted a way of life. It disrupted a way of looking at our culture and our art forms. The move jazz was making toward larger and more structured ensembles was redirected by the current events. A historical spiral was played out that took the baton from the composer/arranger and returned it to the individual player. The interest in sectional voicings gave way to a fascination with new chord structures and fast tempos. Some orchestras made the transition to bop elements within their big band formats, notably Stan Kenton, Boyd Raeburn, Woody Herman, and Billy Eckstine. This style was referred to as ''progressive jazz.''

Stan Kenton's band, with Pete Rugolo as chief arranger, used bop harmonic and melodic developments. For a while, Kenton even labeled his band ''Progressive Jazz.'' Great credit should be accorded Stan Kenton for having never compromised what to him was art for the comfort and safety enjoyed by the more commercialized big bands. His arrangers often departed from the traditional voicings used for big bands and helped introduce the extended harmonies that preceded the modal harmonies associated with cool. In fact, many of the players from the Kenton Band were responsible for the West Coast sound of the Cool era.

Billy Eckstine formed a band that had almost every leading bop player at one time. The Earl Hines and Eckstine bands reached their

## Recording Ban

The 1942 recording ban (a strike against the record companies by the American Federation of Musicians) broke off all recording. This ban lasted for thirteen and a half months only to be followed by a second brief strike in 1948. As of April 1, 1942, musicians were not allowed to enter recording studios; however, singers were allowed to record. Singers recorded extensively with no instruments—all voices, including the backgrounds (usually chorales).

The guiding force behind the strike was James C. Petrillo, the head of the vast musician's union; he declared that the musicians should be earning a larger percentage of the profits from recordings. There was a big rush by all the bands to record as much as possible before the April 1 deadline. Recording studios were filled day and night.

The ban on recording did not hurt the established sidemen very much. They had regular incomes, and recording work was considered supplemental. Incidentally, there were many air checks made from location jobs, the primary concern being balance. There were no payments for air checks; however, many of these did make their way into the recording market later, and the musicians then had to be paid.

There were setbacks. Some short-lived bands getting started at that time never were able to record. In fact, this ban nearly

peak during the record ban, which leaves us with little record of their exciting ensembles. Dizzy Gillespie was the musical director of Eckstine's band, which did make some important recordings after April of 1944. Some of the recordings included vocals by Sarah Vaughan.

Dizzy Gillespie, a leader in bop, was enthralled by the big band sounds. His most impressive record, ''Things To Come,'' recorded in 1946, was characteristic of the virtuosic displays of bop musicians, but the frantic tempo proved that most bop was too unwieldy for big bands.

By 1944, Woody Herman had lost all of his Dixieland leanings and some of his Ellington influences as additions in his band began to show heavy bop influences. In the mid-1940s, Herman fronted a succession of bands he called ''Herds'' with his chief arranger being prevented the recording of Miles Davis' and Gil Evans' "Birth of the Cool" sides. Some bands that were attempting to create a name not only ran into the obstacle of a ban on recording but also the wartime draft. Many young musicians no doubt went unnoticed during their peak years because of these two obstacles. Some bands like Earl Hines, were undergoing a stylistic change during these years and no documentation of that change remains.

On the plus side, some bands, like Harry James, had a chance to regroup from changes they were making in personnel and arrangements. There was an odd situation with the bop movement on its way to becoming a force in jazz. Previous styles had a chance to come into the public notice gradually making acceptance more palatable. By the time the ban was lifted, bop was very mature, and recording companies did not pressure groups to water down their approach to increase record sales. The result was a sudden appearance of bop in the marketplace. Added to bop's already sharp contrast to swing, a strong public reaction might well have been anticipated.

Because singers dominated the recordings during the ban, public taste seemed to move away from the instrumentally-based jazz idiom of the swing bands to the more vocal based popular song style.

Ralph Burns. On up-tempo pieces, the bop elements were quite obvious, but on the slower ballads like "Summer Sequence," the band sounded more cool than bop.

The talented young trumpet player Don Ellis, while playing with his big band, carried many of the ensemble practices established in earlier big bands to a very complicated fruition. He expanded non-diatonic possibilities with his quarter-tone trumpet and four-valve flügel horn. The ensemble passages were often characterized by complex meters that required very precise sectional playing. His interest in Indian music greatly influenced his approach to big band writing. He also was one of the first to use electronic effects within the big band format. The Don Ellis rendition of "Open Beauty" from his album *Electric Bath* shows him as a pioneer in electronic effects.

# Woody Herman
## ''Bijou''
### Columbia Jazz Masterpieces CK 44108

―――

| | |
|---|---|
| :00 | Vamp by rhythm section for eight bars, interplay with piano, guitar, and bass |
| :12 | Trumpets play melody for sixteen bars |
| :39 | Saxes in unison, brass in background for two bars |
| :43 | Alto sax improvisation for two bars |
| :47 | Alto sax solo over sax section for four bars |
| :55 | Alto sax solo over ensemble for eight bars |
| 1:08 | Ensemble transition for three bars |
| 1:12 | Trombone solo break by Bill Harris for five bars |
| 1:21 | Trombone solo for thirty-two bars |
| 2:14 | Full ensemble transition with tom-tom type rhythm for sixteen bars (eight bars repeated) |
| 2:41 | Ensemble full with unison trumpets for three bars |
| 2:46 | Trombone enters on solo for one bar |
| 2:47 | Trombone solo for four bars |
| 2:54 | Trombone solo for six bars and one beat |
| 3:06 | Drums diminuendo for two bars |
| 3:09 | Trombones glissando upward with growl for one bar |
| 3:10 | Sax section runs downward for two bars |
| 3:13 | Recapitulation of introduction for four bars |
| 3:20 | Drums diminuendo for two bars |
| 3:24 | End |

## COOL BIG BANDS

Near the end of the 1940s, there were two large bands that, although quite different, were influential in the beginnings of cool jazz: Claude Thornhill's band from about 1946 to 1949 and the Woody Herman band of 1947 to 1949. Both bands moved away from the hot style of bop to the cool feel that elevated instrumental color over the pyrotechnics of complex ensemble passages.

The Claude Thornhill band boasted the membership of such future cool leaders as alto saxophonist Lee Konitz, baritone saxophonist Gerry Mulligan, flutist Paul Horn, saxophonist Med Flory, and arranger Gil Evans. It was this nucleus that made the first Miles Davis/Gil Evans records culminating in the album, *The Birth of the Cool* (1950), a benchmark for later cool recordings. Thornhill's theme song "Snowfall" exemplifies this cool sound.

The Cool era of jazz marked a move toward the more fully composed and formally defined works. It represented a continuation of the compositional legacy begun by Jelly Roll Morton. Emphasis was placed on the compositional scoring and structure of the piece, and individual solos were tailored to meld with the blending cool sound.

## THIRD STREAM ENSEMBLES

This compositional legacy was further developed in some of the Third Stream music (the combination of jazz and classical music). Because Classical music has a history defined by its notation, it places compositional practice (the writing of music) in high regard. Without recordings, we have no record of the performance practice of a musical tradition. Our study of early classical pieces is restricted to the only record we have—the notated compositions themselves. It is, therefore, quite reasonable that blends of classical and jazz music would have a high degree of interest in compositional rather than performance approaches.

Mingus, Sun Ra, and the AACM groups show such a concern for compositional form. Even in the freest expressions, the performances are guided by clearly defined compositional definitions.

## BIG BANDS AND STYLISTIC COMPLETION

Even with later big band experimentation, the big band reached its full flowering in the Swing era. The sectionalization that took shape in the previous periods never was challenged in later periods. More recent bands like Kenton, Evans, Ellis, Raeburn, Eckstine, and Thornhill were the exception rather than the rule. Big bands, like the Toshiko Akiyoshi and Bob Mintzer bands use instrumentation similar to that established in the Swing era. The album *Kogun* shows the swing band structure clothed in modern thoughts and demonstrating a combination of American and Japanese culture. "Slo Funk" from Bob Mintzer's album *Incredible Journey* employs the traditional big band format to play a very contemporary sounding rock-based arrangement. The big band format was also exported to Europe and exemplified by leaders like Ted Heath and Clarke-Boland.

Several of the bands that were once popular and have lost their leaders also operate today as "ghost" bands—Miller, Herman, and Basie. The nostalgia about the big bands is a tribute to the extraordinary popularity enjoyed by these bands. The structure of this ensemble with its trumpet, trombone, saxophone, and rhythm sections essentially became frozen during the Swing era and represents the "classical" jazz ensemble in the minds of many today.

## SUMMARY

The swing big band is possibly the last jazz format that dominated the interest of the American public. It ushered the jazz playing style off the street and onto the concert stage and eventual study in the university. It was able to do this by capturing the white middle class through the ever more powerful media of radio and record. Because these media catered to a predominantly white market, it is no surprise that the most popular bands of this time were the white bands. They received the most attention from the media and, as a result, catapulted this particular jazz expression to a place of prominence both nationally and internationally. With this prominence came a musical legitimacy. With the rise of cultural awareness that grew out of the late 1950s and 1960s, the immeasurable contribution of African-American players to the creation and development of jazz became more fully recognized.

The swing bands, despite their commercial focus, were unwittingly responsible for helping jazz gain a respectability needed for its further development as an American artform. Riding this engine of popularity, the next generation of players were able to strain the commercial link jazz had enjoyed with its public. Without a well-established legacy built on popular support, jazz could very well have been absorbed by, and lost in, the rapidly changing musical culture.

The vestiges of this immensly popular period in jazz are the "ghost" bands, the formalization of the jazz ensemble, and more importantly the rightful place of jazz as an art form that reflects the vitality of the multifaceted American culture, a culture that reflects the activities of the street, the church, the ghetto, and later the university. The International Association of Jazz Educators (IAJE) has been instrumental in helping jazz become a part of music education in America. The dominant jazz format used in most schools is still the big band, which represents schools at competitions and the IAJE conference. Small group jazz, more typical of mainstream jazz, occupies a much smaller part of most music curricula. The big band has become the classical compositional medium for jazz much as the symphonic orchestra is for classical music.

AACM. ''Steppin'.'' Smithsonian J/3 (cd V/10).
Akiyoshi, Toshiko. *Insights*. RCA Records AFL 1 2678.
Akiyoshi, Toshiko. *Kogun*. RCA Records 6246.
*The Best of Basie*. Columbia Records C3L 33.
*The Best of Basie*. MCA Records 4050.
*The Best of Charles Mingus*. Atlantic Records SD 1555.
*Big Bands' Greatest Hits*. Columbia Records CG 31212.
Davis, Miles. *The Birth of the Cool*. Capitol Records DT 1974.
Dorsey, Tommy. *The Great Band Era*. RCA Victor Records
     RD4 25.
*Duke Ellington's Greatest Hits*. Reprise Records S 6234.
Eckstine, Billy. *Big Band Jazz*. Smithsonian.
Ellington, Duke. *And His Mother Called Him Bill*. RCA Victor
     Records LSP 3906.
*Ellington Era*. Columbia Records C3L 24.
Ellis, Don. *Electric Bath*. Columbia Records CL 2785.
*The Futuristic Sounds of Sun Ra*. MG 12138.
Gillespie, Dizzy. *Big Band Jazz*. Smithsonian.
Goodman, Benny. *All Time Greatest Hits*. Columbia Records
     PG 31547.
Goodman, Benny. *Carnegie Hall Concert*. Columbia Records
     OSL 160.
Goodman, Benny. ''Good-Bye.'' *The Great Band Era*. RCA Victor
     Records RD4 25.
Goodman, Benny. *Greatest Hits*. Columbia Records CS 9283.
Goodman, Benny. *Small Groups*. RCA Victor Records LPV 521.
*Heleocentric Worlds of Sun Ra*. ESP 1014, 1017.
Herman, Woody. *Capitol Jazz Classics*, Vol. 9. Capitol Records.
Herman, Woody. *The Thundering Herds*, Vol. 1. Columbia Records
     C3l 25.
Herman, Woody, and Bill Harris. ''Bijou.'' *Thundering Herds,
     1945–1947*. Columbia Jazz Masterpieces CK 44108.
*Kenton in Stereo*. The Creative World of Stan Kenton ST 1004.
*The Memorable Claude Thornhill*. Columbia Records KG 32906.
Miller, Glenn. *The Great Band Era*. RCA Victor Records RD4 25.
Mingus, Charles. ''Eclipse.'' New World Records NW 216.
Mintzer, Bob. *Incredible Journey*. Digital Music Products CD-451.
Modern Jazz Quartet. ''Django.'' Smithsonian H/1 (cd IV/14).
Modern Jazz Quartet. *Third Stream Music*. Atlantic Records 1345.
*This Is Duke Ellington*. RCA Victor Records VPM 6042.
Thornhill, Claude. *The Big Bands of the 1940s*. New World
     Records NW 284.

SUGGESTED
LISTENING

# CHAPTER 9

## *The Developing Mainstream*

In the previous chapters, we have seen the initial stirrings of jazz as a recognizable musical tradition. These stirrings were not preordained to be the birth of the art form we now know as jazz. What were the conditions that shaped it into an American art form rather than let it wash out of control with the tides of fashion? Popular music is an artifact of the Western music tradition. How does a popular music develop a tradition consistent enough to be considered unique, and how does that unique music gain public acceptance as an art form? We certainly see other popular music traditions that have similar developments in their tradition but have not generated a consensus about their art status. Musical lines as unique as country, rock, even blues, have not gained art status yet, but jazz has.

A canon is a historical framework that houses the descriptors of an evolutionary line. Many types of canons exist. There are literary canons, academic canons, visual art canons, etc. Each of these canons

## THE JAZZ, CLASSICAL, AND ROCK CANONS

helps us interpret the historical events that led to the flowering of the art form or discipline it serves. It describes who the heroes of that tradition are and what values are addressed by these heroes. It also offers criteria for judging new work contributed to the tradition by its newest generation of artists. Conscious or not, canons exist for all types of music; however, they only become codified or formalized historically for those that gain a general consensus as being worthy.

To better understand how jazz now works in our culture, it is helpful to compare its developing canon with those of other music canons and see how they may or may not differ. It is agreed upon, that classical music is an art music. It was not always viewed as the art form it is today. Like jazz, it offered the culture of its day a menu of popular music on the leading edge of fashion, much as popular music is today. Only later did the canon become recognized as an art tradition that revered its musical past. Classical music is often described and discussed in terms of its historical canon, and new music must align successfully with it to be included.

Dr. William Weber[1] offers an interesting suggestion that classical music did not develop its canon until about 1850 in France. Prior to that time, only new music was promoted at concerts. Older, previously heard pieces were used only if new music could not be generated by concert time. Since that time, however, the codification of the classical music tradition has narrowed considerably leaving less than fifty valued pieces, most more than one hundred years old, as the main library for concert performance. In fact, most people today who recognize classical music as an art form might find it difficult to name five classical composers living and writing today.

If 1850 is the approximate date for the canonization of classical music, is there a similar date for jazz? The literature of jazz sees a transition of some magnitude occurring in the late 1940s with the advent of bop. What occurred then that was so different? Was its loss of popularity necessary for achieving art status? Bop certainly did not have the same large audience enjoyed by the swing bands. If bop is the turning point in the jazz canon, how does it relate to its predecessors? Despite its own lack of a large audience, how dependent was it on the popularity of the swing period? What role did the earlier Dixieland bands play in the shaping of this canon? How did the players' understanding of jazz as a tradition differ between the early bands and the bop bands? How did it differ later between the bop players and neoclassical players?

---

[1]William Weber, "The Contemporaneity of Eighteenth Century Musical Taste," *Music Quarterly,* 70 (Spring 1984):175–94.

To place such questions in better focus, it helps to look at a musical tradition still in early development like rock and roll. It is undergoing an even more compressed development than jazz did as it has gained public acceptance. Despite its popularity, it is still not viewed as an art form by the general public. Many of the events in rock's development are reminiscent of early jazz activity. It has seen intense popularity, fragmentation of styles, nostalgia for earlier styles, a developing body of critics and historians, and controversy about new styles.

As historians, often we do not notice the events around us that might one day be important to a developing art. If we were twenty-third century music historians, we might find it difficult to resurrect the multifaceted contributions to the rock tradition that are so apparent right now. We find it difficult to decide what present events will really be important as opposed to those that may prove insignificant. Some important ones might be easily forgotten and no record kept of them, while relatively unimportant events are inadvertently preserved (and possibly prove wrongfully important). The jazz and classical canons are more susceptible to this than rock because we now have better recordings and a Library of Congress that throws nothing away, but our understanding of the forces at work forging the rock tradition might still be obscure in the future. What are all the sources of rock? How much should be attributed to blues, or jazz or Western European, or to Latin American influences. What were the social issues at work when rock first appeared? How have they changed since that time? How do we reconcile the many faces of rock and shape them into one cohesive tradition? What style of rock would we consider mainstream—heavy metal, punk, Beatles, rap, underground? Is rock developing a history of past heroes? Why do some survive and others disappear? What is "classic rock"? What stylistic periods does rock have, or is it still too young for any to be recognized?

Perhaps it is not a reasonable goal to expect beginnings such as those we see in rock and jazz to be neat linear lines of development. Time helps us see the forces that shape the canon and drop the less influential developments. However, we also lose the vitality of the times along with many of the details. For example, rock might arguably be as much the countercultural overtones as it is the music. How relevant will the countercultural statements made by many of the rock styles be when reviewed by later generations. Unlike jazz and rock, the classical tradition has a literate foundation that centers most often on the compositional process rather than individual performers. Jazz and rock are based much more on an oral tradition that focuses on the performer. Because the force of the performing personalities dim with time, the historian who focuses on the music may produce an incorrect history.

Only in retrospect do historical leaders emerge. If we look at the music, the heroes are more likely to be the composer/arrangers who offered us a reperformable repertory than the individuals whose interpretation of that repertory gave the music life. It is the job of historians to assure us that these heroes reflect the values of their day rather than those of our time mapped into the circumstances of the past.

Jazz finds itself in the middle of the two contrasting traditions of classical and rock and continues to share attributes with both. It has joined classical music as a functioning art form but is still recent enough historically, like rock, to be confusingly pluralistic. It used to be music of the dance hall, the street, and the church. It now finds itself on concert stages, in universities, and the subject of historical accounts such as this. The players that have been remembered were players that pushed on the developing leading edge of stylistic change. Little of earlier jazz styles was part of their repertoire, yet their repertoire was still a part of the growing mainstream. Their work has weathered several attempts to redirect the mainstream. Today, we have many prominent players who are strong advocates of the traditional voice of jazz, placing a majority of their interest in the past rather than the future. Would a neoclassical school be possible before or without bop? There were attempts at revivals, such as the Dixieland revivals during the 1930s. Today jazz looks back more than it ever has.

As we will see, bop was the era from which a majority of our present canon's jazz giants emerged. The musical changes of that period, although not popular by previous standards, set the framework for the developing jazz mainstream. By this time, the small group medium, which still flourishes today, had been established as the vehicle of mainstream jazz. Through this medium, players could express their personal voices. Improvisation was codified as a valued component of the jazz expression within a dominantly interactive performance medium. The mouth of the mainstream had been found.

## THE ARMSTRONG LEGACY

Louis Armstrong might be considered the one most influential to the developing jazz tradition. His contributions were twofold. He developed a definitive stylization for jazz still felt today and pulled the center of gravity for jazz onto the shoulders of individual players.

By 1926, Armstrong was considered the greatest trumpet player who had ever lived. His tone, stamina, range, creativeness, and technique were envied by all jazz performers. At the early age of twenty-six, he became the ideal, the model of how to play jazz improvisation. He was the first jazz player to achieve international fame.

His fundamental approach is the legacy upon which bop is built. Individual musical prowess is the cornerstone of the bop style and was established as a fundamental precept of jazz as early as Armstrong's first solos. The force of his musicality and technical skill pulled the ensemble approach typical of early New Orleans and Chicago Dixieland into a focus defined by individual performers. Armstrong signals this transition from ensemble improvisation to soloist centered jazz, a change that still defines the mainstream of jazz.

We study Armstrong recordings knowing full well that he probably played each recorded tune many times in live audience situations. Because of the limitations of the recording process at that time, we can never be certain how authentically the solos we hear recorded reflect the level of inspiration typical of a live performance. We are left with these recorded artifacts and hope they are truly reflective of his early playing. Even with the recording limitations, Armstrong's innovations and originality shines through. He is even credited with the first recording of scat singing.

Armstrong's virtuosic genius coincided with the social revolution brought on by the postwar (WWI) industrial boom, and he allowed himself to break the bonds of the established trumpet parts of Early New Orleans Dixieland. Before Armstrong, bands featured mainly ensemble playing with solo spots used as a change of pace. Even with Armstrong's earliest efforts, the listener is drawn to the soloist, and the ensemble offers the change of pace.

Armstrong truly opened the door for a keener acceptance of jazz solos and established himself as the first great jazz soloist. "West End Blues" (recorded in 1928), especially Armstrong's cadenza introduction (example 9.1), became for a time the most imitated of all jazz solos; Armstrong became a household word, and the jazz solo became a defining characteristic of the jazz expression.

In the mid-twenties, Fletcher Henderson's band came to life during Armstrong's solos. He also modified the concepts of how to play lead in a big band's ensemble passages. Armstrong's lead helped define what it meant to swing in jazz. His first solo in a group that used a string bass instead of a tuba was "Mahogany Hall Stomp" in 1929. Probably because of the shift in the sound and feel of the string bass, the recording and Armstrong's solo start to have more of a swing feeling than the previously heard New Orleans spirit. By 1930, every

**EXAMPLE 9.1**   ''West End Blues''

jazz brass player had been affected by Armstrong's innovations in
swing, rhythmic feel, phrasing, and melodic freedom.

> . . . the key to rhythmic freedom lay in a syncopation
> based on a four-to-a-bar beat—not on the two-beat bar,
> in other words. Once a player could detach himself from
> explicitly stating the four beats and thus got 'inside' the
> beats, a vast field of rhythmic emancipation lay ahead.''[2]

Armstrong maintained his reputation as a great innovator and remained immune to the decaying effect of the more commercial
sounding forces at work at that time. His leadership over large bands
truly opened the way for later trumpeters, such as Harry James.

> Armstrong's music has affected all our music, top to
> bottom, concert hall to barroom. No concert composers
> here or abroad write for brass instruments the way they
> used to, simply because Armstrong has shown that brass
> instruments, and the trumpet in particular, are capable of
> things no one thought them capable of before he came
> along. Our symphonists play trumpet with a slight
> usually unconscious vibrato that is inappropriate to
> Beethoven or Schubert because Armstrong has had one.

[2]Gunther Schuller, *Early Jazz,* (New York City, Oxford University Press, 1968),
273.

"Louis changed our whole idea of the band," said Henderson's chief arranger at the time, Don Redman. So did he change everyone's idea of every band, and every soloist's idea of himself. From that, the era and the style took its name: swing. From the Henderson band itself came the Benny Goodman style, and, directly or indirectly, most of the popular bands of the Swing era. American music was not the same after it became swing, and what made it different was the influence of Armstrong.[3]

Historically, jazz has generally been a young person's art. Beiderbecke was dead at the age of 28 and Parker at 34. Lester Young did his best work before he was 30, and Billie Holiday did hers before she was 25. Armstrong who towered over his peers when in his early twenties, has continued to be a recognizable force even after his death. Albert McCarthy quoted Miles Davis in 1958, "You can't play anything on a horn that Louis hasn't played—I mean even modern."[4]

Armstrong's greatest legacy was that he showed the possibilities of turning jazz from a collective music to a soloist's art. For this reason, he is revered as one of the earliest heroes of the jazz tradition. It is his legacy that elevates a balance of virtuosity, melodic innovation, and rhythmic conception as ideals of the jazz expression. His solos had unity and drama, attributes we continue to expect of mainstream players. Great historic solos like Coleman Hawkins' solo on "Body and Soul" are rooted in the Armstrong legacy. The structural curve of that solo extends the improvisational practices initiated by Armstrong.

---

## THE MOVEMENT FROM MELODIC TO HARMONIC IMPROVISATION

For greater freedom of expression, the bop players used extended harmonies in their improvised choruses. The development of new harmonic resources for the jazz musician followed on the heels of experimentations by classical composers. At the turn of the century, harmonies were enriched through the successive inclusion of higher members of the overtone series, resulting in extensive use of ninth, eleventh, and thirteenth chords.

---

[3]Martin T. Williams, "For Louis Armstrong at 70," *Down Beat* 37, no. 13 (July 1970):22.
[4]Albert McCarthy, *Kings of Jazz, Louis Armstrong,* (New York City: A. S. Barnes and Company, Inc., 1959), 27.

**EXAMPLE 9.2**   ''How High the Moon''
By Charlie Parker and Bennie Harris, © 1946 Atlantic Music Corporation. © Renewed and
assigned to Atlantic Music Corporation, 1974. Reprinted by Permission.

It was during the Bop era that much of the mainstream repertoire was established. This repertoire grew from the bop players' use of the chords of a standard tune as the framework on which to compose new melodies. In previous eras, the melody was usually stated in the first chorus, and the improvisation that followed on succeeding choruses was derived from the original melody. The bop innovators, however, often disregarded the initial statement of the melody and began their improvisations at the beginning of the selection.

The above modification led logically to a total disregard for the original melody during improvisation. With that disregard, improvisational interest turned to the harmonic progression instead of the melody. New melodies (or heads) were often written to the chords of standard songs, and the new version would be given a new name. For example, the standard song ''How High the Moon'' offered the chord progression that supports the later jazz standards ''Ornithology'' and ''Bird Lore.'' The bop soloist often did not feel tied to either the original melody or the new head once the head was finished being played. The harmonies served as improvisational guideposts as the melody once had for earlier soloists (see example 9.2).

Jazz is a history of performers, performers who modeled their playing after those who preceded and inspired them. Performers' first understanding of jazz as a continuous history came from their study and modeling of other players they admire. Those that eventually stepped above the others to take their place in jazz history borrowed heavily from the past but added their own voices as a future inspiration for others. The jazz mainstream is comprised of the many instrumental and vocal legacies established and perpetuated by the performers. Just as the players might have followed the line of development for their own instrument through the course of jazz history, we can also trace these historical threads that connect the players to one another.

INSTRUMENTAL
LINES OF
DEVELOPMENT

## THE TRUMPET LEGACY

Among later trumpet players who modeled themselves after Armstrong were Hot Lips Page, Teddy Buckner, and Jonah Jones. Page, who died in 1954, was often mistaken for Armstrong on recordings. Among the white trumpet players who carried the banner of Dixieland, as well as the influences of Armstrong and Beiderbecke, were Muggsy Spanier, Red Nichols, and Phil Napoleon. Nichols' playing was very clean and seemed flawless; however, members of his band still felt that Beiderbecke's music was more sensitive and imaginative.

Members of Nichols' band explained how he would play a solo precisely the same way every time he performed any particular number. The plus side of this approach is that Nichols would hone his solo to a point where it was exactly as he wanted it. The minus side is that imagination would become secondary to perfection of execution. The members complained that this attitude was also demanded of them in their solos and were required to forsake an inspiring idea if the risk of trying to accomplish it were too great.

Beiderbecke's torch was carried on by Bobby Hackett with all the grace and elegance of Beiderbecke himself. Hackett fitted remarkably well in large bands, such as Glenn Miller and Casa Loma, in which he was used strictly as a soloist. The big band required a different kind of soloing from that more typical of Beiderbecke who played solos that could have gone into more contemporary styles like cool. His legacy leads more naturally to players like Miles Davis and Chet Baker. Beiderbecke might easily be considered the first cool soloist in jazz history; his style blossoms in the early Miles Davis work.

Bunny Berigan has often been called a disciple of Beiderbecke. However, if we assume that Beiderbecke and Armstrong were following two different stylistic paths, Berigan's drive, range, and virtuosic bravura reflects the Armstrong legacy. Several trumpet players were avid followers of Berigan until they discovered that the pure stylistic source was Armstrong himself.

Ellington's parade of talented trumpet players included those whose influences were not only Armstrong and Beiderbecke, but also the earliest in Ellington's stable, a player named Bubber Miley. Rex Stewart played rather lightly, reminiscent of Beiderbecke, and added attractive half-valved effects. Cootie Williams, another Ellington trumpeter, used more growls, plunger work, and flutter tonguing than Stewart, thus aligning himself more with Bubber Miley, although he played with the flair and boldness of Armstrong.

Clark Terry, another Ellington alumni, is one of the most talented and versatile jazz instrumentalists. He did not shadow Miles Davis when Davis rose to fame, even though some of Terry's flugelhorn solos are also dark, pensive, and lovely. Although quite capable, he did not follow Gillespie into the bop arena. A record he made with Oscar Peterson on Gillespie's own ''Shaw 'Nuff'' shows his bop potential; however, his own style led him elsewhere. Terry's bravura is directly descended from Armstrong. His approach to swinging a simple melodic line comes from the same source, but what is his alone is his marvelous sense of humor with which he embellishes his solos in a warm and infectious way.

There is a long list of talented swing-oriented trumpeters, such as Buck Clayton, tender Harry ''Sweets'' Edison, Ruby Braff, or high note artist Maynard Ferguson, who all played as they did because of those who preceded them. It was Roy Eldridge, however, who was the logical heir to Armstrong and the precursor to bop's giants. His style and creative solo lines illuminated the paths later soloists would follow. He always sounded like a most impulsive creator. He was fluid and inventive yet still indebted to Armstrong.

Gillespie, more than any other musician, received Armstrong's and Eldridge's legacy. He continued to carry the bop banner straight through all other subsequent styles. Gillespie was sometimes considered Armstrong's antipode. It is not easy to substantiate such an argument when Gillespie's performance persona is so easily traced to the Armstrong legacy.

Gillespie had a host of royal followers, such as Howard McGee, Kenny Dorham, Fats Navarro, and Miles Davis. Yes, Miles Davis at one point was actually an imitator of Gillespie's superb virtuosity, including a high range. Davis said shortly before he died, even after

## Clark Terry

**C**lark Terry is a versatile player of both trumpet and flügelhorn. He makes use of many half-valve effects as did Rex Stewart before him. He also can play double-time passages akin to Dizzy Gillespie. He is one of the most original players in today's jazz. He swings joyfully, is highly creative, and displays an engaging sense of humor. Although the public might know him most for his recording of "Mumbles" with Oscar Peterson, he has recorded many times under his own name, not only on trumpet and flügelhorn, but also as a singer. Terry is in constant demand for jazz festivals and clinics. Suggested albums are *Oscar Peterson Trio Plus One-Clark Terry* (Mercury Records 8559) and *Bobby Brookmeyer Quintet* (Mainstream Records 320).

| | |
|---|---|
| *1920* | Terry was born in Saint Louis, Missouri. |
| *1942–1945* | He performed with the all-star Navy band at Great Lakes, Chicago. |
| *1947* | He joined Charlie Barnet in California. |
| *1948* | He joined Count Basie. |
| *1951–1958* | He joined Duke Ellington. |
| *1959* | He joined Quincy Jones for a European tour. |
| *1960* | He joined the NBC staff in New York City. |
| *1961* | He formed a combo with Bob Brookmeyer. |
| *1964* | He toured Japan with the J. J. Johnson's Sextet. |
| *1994* | Terry currently performs and works as a clinician. |

excursions through different jazz trends such as bop, that nothing is ever played on the trumpet that Armstrong did not play first.

The liquidity and sparceness of Art Farmer's solos attracted attention as cool became accepted. The musicians' trumpet player seemed to be Clifford Brown. His early death cut short an influential career. Brown (along with Sonny Rollins) is sometimes called the "father of hard bop," he had a wealth of brilliant ideas. Also short lived but notable cool players were Chet Baker and Lee Morgan.

With jazz bordering between tonal and atonal, there was need of an important representative among trumpet players. The role was well-filled by the talented Freddie Hubbard. He influenced many contemporary players while still seeming to have one foot in true tradition.

## Roy "Little Jazz" Eldridge

Roy Eldridge is an important precursor of bop jazz. Eldridge was a prominent jazz trumpet player in the Swing era; however, his style of improvisation anticipated the coming bop style. He was a bridge between Louis Armstrong and Dizzy Gillespie, proving to be an important influence for Gillespie himself. His style was constantly described as "creative impulsiveness," "remarkably agile," "saxophone-type lines," "florid," and "risk taking." The most notable solos on records by Eldridge are "After You've Gone," "Rocking Chair," and "Let Me Off Uptown" with Gene Krupa in 1941 (Columbia Records CL753 and Columbia Records C2J-29).

| | |
|---|---|
| *1911* | Eldridge was born in Pittsburgh, Pennsylvania. |
| *1935* | He performed with Teddy Hill's orchestra. |
| *1936* | He played with Fletcher Henderson. |
| *1937* | He led his own trio at the Three Deuces in Chicago. |
| *1938* | He quit music to study radio engineering but later that year joined Mal Hallet. |
| *1939–1940* | He led his own band at the Arcadia Ballroom in New York City. |
| *1941–1943* | He joined Gene Krupa where he also sang. |
| *1943* | He joined the CBS staff in New York City. |
| *1944–1945* | He joined Artie Shaw. |
| *1946* | He led his own quintet at the Spotlite Club in New York City. He later rejoined Gene Krupa. |
| *1950* | He joined Benny Goodman's Sextet. |
| *Early 1950s* | He played in Europe with Charlie Parker, Sidney Bechet, and others. |
| *Late 1950s* | He joined Jazz at the Philharmonic. He co-led a group with Coleman Hawkins. |
| *1960s* | He led his own quintet. |
| *1966* | He joined Count Basie. |
| *1970* | He became the house leader at Jimmy Ryans in New York City. |
| *1979* | Eldridge stopped playing after a heart attack and died in 1989. |

## Dizzy Gillespie

There is no doubt that Gillespie was the most talked about bop musician in the 1940s. Dizzy Gillespie, as talented a trumpet player as he was a showman, combined great technique with fresh thoughts and advanced harmonic knowledge. Along with Charlie Parker, he was a leader in the style of jazz that he and his contemporaries labeled bop. Gillespie's trumpet playing stems from Louis Armstrong by way of Roy Eldridge. He was highly regarded all over the world, and his contributions to modern jazz trends cannot be disputed.

| | |
|---|---|
| *1917* | Gillespie was born in Cheraw, South Carolina on October 21. |
| *1935* | He replaced Roy Eldridge in Teddy Hill's band. |
| *1937* | He toured France and England with Teddy Hill. |
| *1943* | Gillespie played with the Earl Hines band with Charlie Parker and Sarah Vaughan. |
| *1944* | He co-led the first bop band on 52nd Street, New York City with bassist Oscar Pettiford. |
| *1945* | He toured with his first big band—Hepsations of 1945. |
| *1945* | Gillespie recorded classics with Charlie Parker. |
| *1946* | He toured the Middle East. |
| *1968* | Gillespie toured Europe with his "Reunion" band. |
| *1970s and 1990s* | He continued to tour internationally. |
| *1993* | Gillespie died on January 6. |

Of all trumpet players, no one contributed to as many jazz periods as did Miles Davis. Although he began his career in the Bop era and worked with Charlie Parker, he is not recognized as a highly technical player. His contribution to the legacy is one of innovation in general, and a personal voice that transcended all the stylistic periods in which he worked. He found that introspective voice during the Cool era and maintained it even in the high-energy setting of his jazz/rock fusion groups. His sparse style worked effectively in relief to the lush Gil Evans arrangements and hard-driving fusion rhythm sections. Of all trumpet players, his historical shadow is perhaps the longest.

## Chet Baker

Chet Baker had a light and pure sound on the trumpet, stylistically resembling Miles Davis during Davis' cool period. A soft, calm, even mellow approach to melodic improvisation was Baker's signature.

| | |
|---|---|
| *1929* | Baker was born in Yale, Oklahoma. |
| *1946–1948* | He served in the American Army in Berlin. |
| *1950–1952* | He reenlisted in the Presidio Army Band in San Francisco. |
| *1952* | He played dates in California with Charlie Parker, then joined Gerry Mulligan. |
| *1953* | He formed his own group. |
| *1955–1956* | He toured Europe. |
| *1957* | He toured the United States with the Birdland All Stars, then Scandinavia and Italy with his own combo. |
| *1959–1960* | He worked in Italy. |
| *1974* | He recorded a Carnegie Hall Concert with Gerry Mulligan. |
| *1974* | He worked in New York City. |
| *1988* | Baker died tragically in Amsterdam. |

Most well-known contemporary players still work in the bop idiom. There are notable exceptions like Don Cherry who still works in a freer style; however, because free jazz is outside the normal jazz mainstream, he does not command the same kind of attention as contemporary bop players like Tom Harrell and Wynton Marsalis. Of these two Marsalis is certainly the most well-known and emulated. His vocal stance about the importance of the jazz tradition has also worked to tie him to the jazz mainstream. His technical playing is stellar and travels across both the jazz and classical art worlds. Marsalis is a very good example of a performer's tie to the past accomplishments of others. He recognizes that indebtedness and, in turn, promotes a message that performers have a responsibility to the jazz tradition, a tradition currently being connected directly to the bop idiom.

## *THE SAXOPHONE LEGACY*

Because of Armstrong's influence on all jazz instrumentalists, the trumpet legacy is a natural stylistic line with which to begin. However, many consider the saxophone the dominant voice of jazz. Although this position might easily be challenged, the line of jazz shaping saxophonists remains undisputed.

The saxophone legacy begins with a soprano saxophone player known most for his clarinet playing, Sidney Bechet. His stylistic approach included expressive note bending and breath accents characteristic of the single reed family of clarinets and saxophones. The degree to which players throughout jazz history have used the expressive range of the instruments has varied with the stylistic demands of each period, as well as the personal taste of each player. Bechet used a wide range of expression that borrowed heavily from the stylized performances of blues vocalists.

To bring the saxophone to its reigning position as an improvising jazz instrument, one immediately looks to Coleman Hawkins. His full sensuous tone, his never ending ideas, and his ability to craft exciting musical phrases were responsible for his rise to prominence. His performance of ''Body and Soul'' reveals Hawkins as a master of form. He weaves a beautiful tale from beginning to end, starting in an understated manner, building constantly, then letting his listener down calmly at the end just as one's ear hoped he would. He not only does this with creativity and excellent form, but with phrasing that spins a story from gentleness to fury and back. Hawkins had developed into the epitome of tenor saxophonists, a title that rooted him at the beginning of the saxophone legacy. His playing, however, was not developed in a stylistic vacuum. Like all jazz players, he was subject to other stylistic influences, notably that of Armstrong who worked for a year in Henderson's band with Hawkins. (See biographical box in chapter 7.)

The list of Hawkins' pupils includes almost anyone after Hawkins who played the tenor sax well, such as Don Byas, Chu Berry, Hershel Evans, Ben Webster, Frank Wess, Frank Foster, and Paul Gonsalves.

Playing at the same time as Hawkins was Lester Young who also had a host of followers destined for their own prominence. Young was loose, light, and airy, carrying his exotic phrases to their completion regardless of bar lines. Young seemed to free future improvisors by letting the rhythm section take care of their business as he took care of the melodic line. His musical phrasing floats over the meter in a way very similar to the vocal phrasing of Billie Holiday.

It was no wonder that the two worked so effectively together. Lester Young, in his own way, was as creative and important as almost any other jazz improvisor. To hear direct influence of Lester Young listen to Stan Getz or Zoot Sims. Both Hawkins and Young can also be heard in the much later work of John Coltrane.

Alto saxophonist Johnny Hodges recorded many works with Duke Ellington. Hodges was featured so often that he actually became a stamp of identification for the band. His expressive style is reminiscent of the Bechet style. He truly had an individual voice that demanded the listener's attention. It has often been said that ballads are played most meaningfully by instrumentalists who are also talented improvisors. Hodges was always pointed to as proof of this axiom. He performed beautiful, even sad music so skillfully that one would think it his forte (listen to ''Passion Flower,'' ''Warm Valley,'' ''Blood Count,'' or countless others). However, he shows his range of ability as he lifts the rhythm section with driving solos on tunes like ''In a Mello Tone'' or ''I Let a Song Go Out Of My Heart.''

So much has been written about Charlie Parker, his rhythmic sense, his creative genius in general, that it is difficult to add more. Parker specified that his influences were nonjazz players Rudy Wiedoft and Rudy Vallee, jazz alto players Jimmy Dorsey and Frank Teschemacher and tenorist Bud Freeman. It does not make sense to argue with Parker's declaration, but there is no way he could have (even if he had wanted to) avoided listening to the three saxophonists previously discussed. He brought bop to maturity and inspired a legion of followers like Sonny Stitt and Phil Woods. Parker defined mainstream for his instrument. He brought a new complexity to his playing that anchors the bop ideal. His solo lines seemed to be free of the ''patterns'' often heard in later imitators and his phrasing cut long lines across the fast paced rhythmic underpinning. Despite the fast moving melodic lines he played, he still seemed to have time to add expressive inflections to even the shortest-lived note.

Sonny Rollins continues to make recordings of significance. He was associated with all the better bop players in the mid-1940s, absorbing Parker's influence, yet he still has the voluminous sound of Hawkins.

Of the many fine players that followed Rollins and Parker, only a few stand out as a continuation of the bop centered mainstream. Many players that began their careers during the bop period or later were founded in the mainstream tradition but moved off into different stylistic areas. Julian ''Cannonball'' Adderley worked with many of the premier bop groups but was also capable of rock expressions, an example being his recording of ''Mercy, Mercy, Mercy.'' John Coltrane casts a very large stylistic shadow but has come to be known

## Charlie Parker

**P**arker thought that there must be something in jazz improvisation that had not been done before because he thought he could hear things he could not play. He finally found that he could play what he had been hearing by developing melodic lines from higher harmonies of the chords. Parker freed the solo aspects of jazz not only melodically and harmonically but rhythmically. Those who followed him have benefitted from the new freedom.

*1921*  Parker was born in Kansas City, Kansas on August 19.

*1928*  He moved to Kansas City, Missouri.

*1936*  He stood around behind the Reno Club listening and learning.

*1937*  Parker joined the Jay McShann band.

*1939*  Parker first came to New York City and played at Monroe Uptown House. He rejoined Jay McShann band.

*1940*  Parker first recorded solos on transcriptions from a Wichita, Kansas, radio station.

*1942*  He returned to New York City and began playing at Minton's Playhouse with Dizzy Gillespie and others.

*1942*  He joined Earl Hines band.

*1944*  He had his first job as leader at the Spotlite Club in New York City.

*1945*  He made some of his most impressive records.

*1946*  He recorded "Ornithology."

*1946*  He spent seven months in Camarillo State Hospital, California.

*1950*  He recorded with strings.

*1955*  Parker died at the age of 33 on March 12.

more for his work outside the mainstream idiom. (He is discussed in detail in later chapters.) Phil Woods has held true to the bop mainstream and is one of its strongest spokesmen today. He has led many small groups that connect directly to the mainstream as defined by Parker. With Woods, the mainstream was nourished by other saxophonists like Dexter Gordon, Don Menza, Bud Shank, Art Pepper, Harold Land, Tom Scott, and Willie Smith with his "unrestrained immediacy."

## Sonny Rollins

Tenor saxophonist, Sonny Rollins, exercised great influence during the late 1950s. He captured the attention of many of the day's players with his melodic style of improvisation. He often improvised from a melodic line with apparent disregard for chord structure. As previously stated, an improvising player in the Swing era usually had only a few measures in which to express his ideas. Rollins, on the other hand, often improvised for twenty or thirty minutes in order to develop his musical thoughts. He would invent a short phrase and elaborate on it, expanding the idea in every conceivable direction, not unlike Mozart, Haydn, and Beethoven. This expansion and elaboration of theme or phrase is a basic principle of composition.

An interesting aspect of Rollins' career was that after he had become a top nightclub attraction he became dissatisfied with his performance. He retired for two years, from the summer of 1959 to the fall of 1961 (and again in 1969), in order to practice. (It is said that much of this practicing took place on top of the Williamsburg Bridge in New York City.) Such retirement takes great courage and dedication. The consensus seems to be that Rollins' dedication and practice did bring his coordination to a new level of excellence.

The key in Rollins' advancement is thematic improvisation rather than either improvisation on a chord progression or variations on an established melody. Rollins was and is more concerned with fragments of a piece than with the whole melody. He uses these fragments for his own personal expression. Many musicians use this approach, but Rollins has made it his trademark.

Less apparently connected to the mainstream are such players as Branford Marsalis and Michael Brecker. Branford carries the banner of tradition but, unlike his brother, has also flirted with rock (his stay with Sting) and, recently, free jazz. Michael Brecker has a more interesting connection. He is best known for his early work in fusion groups, viewed by many as the antithesis of the mainstream. However, his later albums, for example, *Don't Try This at Home,* contain solos that borrow heavily from the bop tradition. The underpinning rock patterns veil the otherwise bop-like solo lines. His earlier rock/fusion associations come to full bloom as he returned to a

## Dexter Gordon

**D**exter Gordon has been an outstanding player on tenor and soprano saxophones, a composer, and a teacher. He was strongly influenced by Lester Young and was one of the first to transfer bop characteristics to the tenor saxophone. He synthesized the styles of Parker, Young, and Hawkins, and influenced Coltrane and Rollins. He is in constant demand for jazz festivals and recordings and continues to win jazz critics' awards. His albums are too numerous to list, several under his own name; however, one outstanding suggestion would be *Other Side of 'Round Midnight* (Blue Note Records, CDP–7–46397–2), a Grammy winner in 1987.

| | |
|---|---|
| *1923* | Gordon was born in Los Angeles, California. |
| *1940* | He joined Lionel Hampton. |
| *1944* | He joined Louis Armstrong. |
| *Late 1944* | He joined Billy Eckstine. |
| *1945* | He played with Charlie Parker at the Spotlite in New York City. |
| *1947* | He worked in the 52nd Street clubs in New York City. |
| *1960* | He joined the West Coast company of the stage play *The Connection* for which he wrote music, led a quartet, and acted. He recorded an album called *The Resurgence of Dexter Gordon* for Jazzland Records. |
| *1962* | He moved to Copenhagen. |
| *1975* | He toured Japan. |
| *1986* | He played the leading role in the movie *'Round Midnight.* |
| *1987* | He was nominated for the award as the best male actor in 1986. |

## Weldon John (Jack) Teagarden

| | |
|---|---|
| *1905* | Teagarden was born in Vernon, Texas, on August 20. |
| *1927* | He came to New York City. |
| *1928* | He made his first vocal record called "Makin' Friends" with Eddie Condon. |
| *1928–1933* | He played with Ben Pollack. |
| *1934–1938* | He played with Paul Whiteman. |
| *1939–1947* | Teagarden toured with his own large band. |
| *1941* | He made the movie "Birth of the Blues" with Bing Crosby. |
| *1947–1951* | Teagarden played with Louis Armstrong's All Stars. |
| *1951–1963* | He toured with his own small unit, and received many awards. |
| *1964* | Teagarden died in New Orleans on January 15. |

more bop-like idiom. The rhythm section is still rock in flavor, but the extended technique displayed by his band and the architecture of the solos certainly harks back to the bop tradition. He may very well demonstrate one of the most viable jazz/fusion expressions for the future development of the mainstream.

### THE TROMBONE LEGACY

The trombonist's trombone player was, of course, Jack Teagarden. Some call him a blues player. Others call him a blues player with a modern attitude. Of course, he played blues most convincingly, but he played other styles with just as much conviction. An often overlooked example of his stylistic flexibility appeared after some trombonists had joined the bop trend. The standard cliché was to imitate Frank Rosolino's "lip turns." They are tricky and demand a pliable embouchure. Teagarden never used the turns. He felt they were only a showy ploy used when one lacked a fresh invention at the moment. There was a little doubt that Teagarden could accomplish this modern twist. To prove it he recorded one very short record of "Lover" where he did almost nothing but these lip turns; then, he never used them again.

Other jazz trombonists have been impressive and have contributed bop attitudes to the mainstream. J. J. Johnson and Kai Winding showed that bop was possible on a slide instrument. Humor was added refreshingly by Al Grey and Vic Dickenson. The most flexible of the contemporary players include Urbie Green, Bill Watrous, Hal Crook, and Albert Mangelsdorff. Mangelsdorff uses long lines (a rather bop via Tristano element) and seems quite free harmonically.

One of the best jazz trombonists today is Carl Fontana. He is an exciting improvisor who connects directly to the mainstream on his instrument. Fontana was influenced by Teagarden but has all the contemporary nuances derived from the Bop era. He is versatile, flexible, and devises fascinating lines while driving the rhythm section forward.

## THE PIANO LEGACY

When considering the piano, it may be confusing to realize that Art Tatum actually preceded the bop movement to some extent. His work was influential to the leaders of that field. Tatum's advancements in harmonic concepts plus his impressive technique began garnering attention before the Bop era yet could be considered mainstream today. Tatum was overwhelming; he cast such a large historical shadow that mainstream players today must still deal with what he added to the tradition.

Despite the difficulty of following in Tatum's steps, there are two players whose capabilities allow them to play in any style they choose. These players are Oscar Peterson and Paul Smith. There is no desire here to depricate the talent of Bud Powell. Powell fit in perfectly with small bop instrumentations because he seemed to adopt the phrasing of the horns. His style varied from hornlike lines to pure romanticism. Tatum can be heard in Oscar Peterson, especially in his musical vitality. The fact that Peterson's career is ongoing and his performances so impressive puts him in the forefront as far as mainstream is concerned.

Paul Smith's talents are comparable to any pianists in that he can play Tatum-like excursions, romantic ballads, or any other directions, all garnished with a great sense of elegant humor. Thelonious Monk, like Bud Powell, also played horn-type lines. Chronologically, he preceded Powell slightly, but his influence was felt more strongly after the Bop era when he later gained mainstream acceptance.

Since bop, other styles have left their imprints on the mainstream. The very gospel oriented Les McCann was exciting but not intricate enough harmonically to lead a path to mainstream. Horace

## Art Tatum

**A**rt Tatum was possibly the best, surely the most versatile, piano player in the history of jazz. It is impossible (thankfully) to put Tatum in a stylistic category, but stride was certainly one of his favorite styles. Tatum worked occasionally with a small group but felt this was confining, so he usually played alone. He seemed so far ahead of other players technically and harmonically that he was merely listened to in awe. Tatum was very instrumental in bringing advanced harmonies into jazz. He was almost completely blind, but some maintain that his only handicap was his virtuosic technique, that is, Tatum could not possibly harness his rapid flow of thoughts to play with simplicity. However, he often proved this opinion wrong. His closest followers were Bud Powell, Oscar Peterson, and Paul Smith.

Some musicians never have the opportunity to record their achievements for posterity. This cannot be said of Tatum. He was hired by Norman Granz for two days of recording in December 1953, and for two days in April 1954. The result was a set of thirteen long-playing records (twenty-six sides). They were released to the public in 1974. They were called *The Tatum Solo Masterpieces* (Pablo Records 2625703) and are truly a historic event for Tatum followers in particular and jazz fans in general.

Another collection of previously unreleased recordings of Tatum received a Grammy Award from the National Academy of

Silver is an example of a pianist who extended the Powell approach of playing horn-type lines. It appeared that his funk style seemed a trifle commercial but has now become accepted as a part of the mainstream. He had strong church roots which contributed greatly to his jazz/funk idiom.

Bill Evans was one of the few white musicians accepted wholeheartedly by the bop inner circle, yet his style was entirely different from the pianists most closely associated with that idiom. Evans is best known for his beautiful choices of chords and his elegant voicings, and he is considered the first modal pianist. Even though his music was tonal, pianists influenced by Evans seem to play harmonically free. Evans' membership in the mainstream shows that a bop-like style is not a mandated requirement. His acceptance is based more

Recording Arts and Sciences as the best solo album of 1973. The collection was recorded on a portable recording device by a young friend of Tatum. Some of these songs were recorded in an apartment and others in various after-hours clubs. The title of the album, *God Is in the House,* was taken from a remark made by Fats Waller when Tatum entered a club where Waller was working. The remark reveals a respect for Tatum that is quite common among musicians.

| | |
|---|---|
| *1910* | Tatum was born in Toledo, Ohio. |
| *1932* | His first recordings were made in New York City with Adelaide Hall. |
| *1933* | He recorded his first piano solos and worked in the Onyx Club in New York City. |
| *1934* | He led his own group at The Three Deuces in Chicago. |
| *1939* | He recorded "Tea For Two" which was included in the National Academy of Recording Arts and Sciences Hall of Fame. |
| *1953–1954* | He recorded the set of albums called *The Genius of Art Tatum, Volumes 1–13,* also included in the Hall of Fame. |
| *1956* | Tatum died in Los Angeles, California. |

on his influential playing, which emanated from traditional small group settings. He did not join the challenging musical styles of free jazz or jazz/rock fusion.

## THE LEGACY OF RHYTHM SECTIONS

The makeup and role of the rhythm section was established very early in the history of jazz bands. The marching bands, who became the first jazz bands, used a rhythm section composed of snare drum and cymbals, bass drum, tuba, and banjo. Their job was to play a steady and unrelenting pulse. This job never changed until the bop players realized that the duplication of efforts in this situation was unnecessary as jazz was leaving the dance floor. Around 1920, the instrumentation was altered to piano, string bass, guitar, and drums. This arrangement stayed relatively constant for the next twenty years.

## Oscar Peterson

**O**scar Peterson was a disciple of Art Tatum before he developed his own style. He won many awards for his piano work from critics, writers, and fellow musicians. He has also been an accomplished composer, writing among other efforts "Canadiana Suite," "Hallelujah Time," "The Smudge," and "Lover's Promenade." His singing is reminiscent of Nat Cole, and he dedicated an album to that particular jazz great. Peterson presents many college seminars all over the world and published a book entitled *Jazz Exercises and Pieces* (Hansen Publications, 1842 West Avenue, Miami Beach, Florida). A most enjoyable album is his *Trio Plus One with Clark Terry.*

| | |
|---|---|
| *1925* | Peterson was born in Montreal, Quebec, Canada. |
| *1944* | He featured with Johnny Holmes, a popular Canadian band. |
| *1949* | He remained in Canada until he joined Jazz at the Philharmonic at Carnegie Hall. |
| *1952–1954* | He toured Europe with Jazz at the Philharmonic. |
| *1954* | He organized his own trio. |
| *1955* | He traveled Europe with Ella Fitzgerald. |
| *1960s* | He toured internationally. |
| *1971* | He was awarded an Honorary Doctorate of Law from Carleton University. |
| *1973* | He received the Medal of Service of the Order of Canada. |
| *1974* | Peterson had his own award winning television show in Canada called *Oscar Peterson Presents* featuring leading jazz performers. |

His Grammy award winning recordings follow:

| | |
|---|---|
| *1974* | *The Trio* (Pablo Records 2310–701) |
| *1975* | *Oscar Peterson and Dizzy Gillespie* (Pablo Records 2340–740) |
| *1977* | *The Giants* (Pablo Records 2310–796) |
| *1978* | *Montreux '77* (Pablo Records 2308–208) |
| *1979* | *Jousts* (Pablo Records 2310–817) |
| *1990* | *The Legendary Oscar Peterson at the Blue Note* (TELARC CD 83304) |

The art of playing a metronomical underlying pulse, a nonmelodic function, progressed a long way since Dee Dee Chandler, drummer with John Robichaux, made the first foot pedal for the bass drum in 1895. This freed the drummer's hands for stick work on the trap drum set. The first hi-hat was invented by Tony Spargo, the drummer for the Original Dixieland Jazz Band.

There were many situations during the Swing era where drummers seemed to be set apart from the rest of the rhythm section or even from the rest of the band. There were gaudy displays of excess equipment, much of which was only for show. An example of this was Sonny Greer's huge theatrical setup with the Duke Ellington Band. Although he was featured occasionally on tom-toms or some other exotic sounds, his playing was more supportive than his setup indicated. The public began to be more aware of the powerful propulsion generated by the rhythm section when they saw and heard such bands as Chick Webb and later Benny Goodman with his charismatic drummer Gene Krupa.

Two drummers with different approaches to playing appeared to be dominant forces in the stabilization of the jazz drummer's set of traps. Krupa, the crowd pleasing soloist, eventually became a band leader and was on exhibition constantly. Davey Tough, on the other hand, seemed to be driving in a much more subtle and inconspicuous way. Krupa gave the impression visually and audibly that he needed only himself to propel the entire band into a good rhythmic feeling. Tough, however, always seemed to be a cog, a viable cog, in a rhythm section of four excellent players. Sid Catlett, Jimmie Lunceford's drummer Jimmy Crawford, and even Jo Jones from Basie's famous ''rhythm machine'' were from this mold. Some fine swinging drummers never cared to play solos, and others seemed to be soloing constantly as if they alone carried the melodic content of the arrangements. Krupa, with all his histrionics was still an integral part of a fine rhythm section that included Jess Stacy, Teddy Wilson or Johnny Guarnieri on piano, Charlie Christian or Allan Reuss on guitar, and also some excellent bass players.

Goodman sometimes rehearsed the band without the rhythm section. His conception was that if he could make the band swing well without this powerhouse section of rhythm players, then when they were added, the feeling would be truly outstanding.

The Count Basie Band could swing beautifully even without that famous rhythm section, but with them, it was remarkable. The section included Basie on piano, Freddie Green on guitar, Jo Jones on drums, and Walter Page on bass. The feeling of this rhythm section was one of subtlety, of underplaying; but that was only an illusion. They collectively set up a rhythmic context that propelled the music.

## Horace Silver

The funky style of piano playing was brought to public notice by Horace Silver who made many records with his own combo. Critic Don Heckman wrote about the jazz of the 1960s:

> Perhaps the most significant was the music that was called variously, funk, soul, etc. Its roots in modern jazz could be traced to Horace Silver's efforts to translate the Blues-based forms, riffs, and rhythms of the Midwestern and Southwestern bands of the late 20s and early 30s into the idiom of the contemporary small group. Its roots in Negro society were less defined but also important. (Don Heckman, "Ornette and the Sixties," Down Beat, 31, no. 20, July 1964, 59.)

Horace Silver studied piano with a church organist. He also studied saxophone. He was one of the most prolific composers of hard bop, witnessed by "Senor Blues" and "The Preacher." It is often said that musicians go to hear Silver play more for his accompanying prowess than for his solo work. He began his career as a follower of Bud Powell. Later, many pianists began referring to Silver's bluesy figurations. Suggested albums would be

---

They were always compact yet always seemed to stay out of everyone else's way. When Jo Jones left Basie, a succession of fine drummers followed. With players like Buddy Rich and Sonny Payne, the sound of the rhythm section, and consequently the band itself, seemed to get considerably louder. Some critics deplored this change, feeling that the band would forfeit its loose swinging style for one with a drive that was too obvious.

With Buddy Rich's aggressive approach to playing rhythm and his truly extraordinary technique, he dominated the jazz drumming scene for a considerable time. He was a great soloist, and at the same time, one who could push a soloist or an ensemble in dramatic energy curves.

Up to the Bop era, jazz was a music for dancing. There were big bands with usually heavy arrangements. There were large ball-rooms to be filled with generally unamplified sounds. To meet that need, a four-man rhythm section had to duplicate one another's efforts

*A Night in Birdland* with Art Blakey (Blue Note Records, Vol. 1, 1521), *Horace Silver and the Jazz Messengers* (Blue Note Records BLP 1518), *Blowing the Blues Away* (Blue Note Records 4017), *Song For My Father* (Blue Note Records 4185), and *Best of Horace Silver* (Blue Note Records 84325).

| | |
|---|---|
| *1928* | Silver was born in Norwalk, Connecticut. |
| *1950–1951* | He played with the Stan Getz Quintet. |
| *1951–1952* | He played with Art Blakey. |
| *1952* | He played with Terry Gibbs and Coleman Hawkins. |
| *1953* | He played with Oscar Pettiford, Bill Harris, Lester Young, and the Al Cohn Quintet. |
| *1954* | He played with Miles Davis. |
| *1956* | He organized his own quintet. |
| *1961* | He toured Japan. |
| *1962, 1968* | He toured Europe. |
| *1970s* | He composed, wrote lyrics, and recorded a trilogy called *The United States of Mind.* |
| *1975* | Silver came out of retirement and organized a new group. |

to help the band swing, and in some instances even to help hold it together. This was the only way dancers in the rear of the large halls could hear a clear and unencumbered beat.

In the transition from swing to bop, the assigned parts played by individual members of the rhythm section underwent radical changes. Instead of the regular steady 4/4 rhythm heard in swing music, drummers now used the bass and snare drums mainly for accents and punctuations. They usually maintained an overall sound by playing eighth-note rhythms on the top cymbal. If the accents were not spontaneous, then they were played on either the fourth beat of the bar or the fourth beat of every other bar. The more spontaneous punctuations were called bombs and had to be used carefully to add impetus but not be a distraction. The piano player changed from playing a steady 4/4 rhythm to syncopated chordal punctuations. Count Basie had played in this style for some time. These punctuations were played at specific moments to designate the chord changes

## Thelonious Sphere Monk

**E**ver since jazz musicians began hearing Thelonious Monk, they realized that he was an important pianist and jazz composer. After acquiring "Sphere," Monk later stated that he was not a square. Works written by Monk have to be considered "compositions" as opposed to "lines" similar to those written by Charlie Parker, for example. Under some lines, the harmony can be changed, and over some chord progressions new lines can be invented. With Monk's works, it seems necessary to use both his lines and his harmony. When Monk improvised, he did not simply play variations; sometimes he fragmented lines and at other times he elaborated on them. He often started with a basic phrase and, like Sonny Rollins on the tenor saxophone, played the phrase in almost every conceivable manner. However, he received recognition for his composing before he was accepted as an innovative pianist.

An example of Monk's strong influence is the effect he had on John Coltrane. When Coltrane joined Monk's combo, he had to struggle with the repertoire. After his experience in the group, he had the opportunity to become a really great musician and a most important influence himself. It was as if Monk were able to open Coltrane's ears and to point out possible directions as yet unconceived by the saxophonist.

and add to the overall musical excitement. With the advent of the amplifier, the guitar became a melody instrument and took its place with the trumpet and saxophone. This left the sole responsibility for the steady pulse of the beat to the string bass. Although the string bass part now had a more interesting line, the line was secondary to the job of maintaining a rhythmic pulse.

The beauty of the bop rhythm section was that the individual members were freed from duplicating each other's role. As stated before, in the swing style, all four players were forced to keep the pulse because the bands were quite large and the public wanted to feel the pure, unornamented, uncomplicated beat in order to dance. These bop approaches were, in general, not really new, as shown by Basie's piano work, Jimmy Blanton's bass playing with Ellington, and Charlie Christian's guitar work with Benny Goodman's orchestra. The bop players also added rhythm players from Cuba who not only aided the pulse assigned to the bass player, but also brought new rhythmic excitement into jazz through improvised cross rhythms. The

| 1920 | Monk was born in Rocky Mount, North Carolina, on October 10. |
| 1941–1944 | He performed in Monroe's Uptown House and Minton's in New York City. |
| 1942 | He played with the Lucky Millinder Band. |
| 1944 | He worked and recorded with Coleman Hawkins. |
| 1947–1957 | Monk recorded " 'Round Midnight" several times. |
| 1950 | In February he was featured at a concert at Town Hall in New York City. |
| 1951 | His New York work permit was revoked temporarily. |
| 1957 | He was featured performer at the Five Spot Cafe in New York City. |
| 1957 | Monk appeared on CBS TV's *The Sound of Jazz* in December. |
| 1970s | He made many concerts and featured appearances. |
| 1971–1972 | Monk toured with Dizzy Gillespie and Sonny Stitt in a group called The Giants of Jazz. |
| 1982 | Monk died in New York City in February. |

brilliantly accented drumming of Kenny Clarke and Max Roach modified the swing rhythm section into one suitable for bop.

Chico Hamilton's cool approach during the early 1950s required a change in the rhythm section's role. Hamilton had a typically cool group, and he restricted his drumming to brush work in order to blend with his more underspoken type of ensemble. The rhythm section wasn't dominant again until the return to hard bop, which reinstated the driving pulse of the bop period.

Drummers as individuals continued to lead the way in the investigation of unusual and exciting ways to accent. Art Blakey, with his changing personnel in the Jazz Messengers, led, or pushed, many players to realize their abilities as he helped establish what is now considered the mainstream rhythm section.

The rhythm section made its next big change with the advent of fusion jazz. The introduction of a fully electronic instrumentation allowed entirely new balances to be struck between players. Players

## Bill Evans

**B**ill Evans was an intellectual, serious, and skillful musician who always maintained the essential need to swing. He was always original and tasteful. Evans' innovations in chord voicings have become standard practice for modern keyboard players because they were so striking and articulate.

Bill Evans only worked with Miles Davis for nine months, but in that time, he made an indelible imprint on Davis, as is witnessed by the 1959 album *Kind of Blue* (Columbia Records PD–8633E). Evans' piano playing was clearly thoughtful, subtle, and delicate.

Evans published three books of original pieces and transcriptions of solos. He appeared at all major jazz festivals. Besides his Grammy winners, three of his most impressive albums are *Bill Evans Trio with Symphony Orchestra* (Verve Records V6–8640), *Conversations with Myself* (Verve Records (A–68526), and *New Conversations* (Warner Brothers Records BSK 3177).

*1929*  Evans was born in Plainfield, New Jersey.

*1950*  He joined Herbie Fields.

*1953*  He joined the United States Army.

*1958*  He joined Miles Davis.

*1959*  He joined the faculty of the School of Music, Lenox, Massachusetts. He was featured on the sound track of John Lewis' film *Odds against Tomorrow.*

*1960*  He toured not only the United States, but also South America, Japan, and Europe with his trio.

*1971*  *The Bill Evans Album* (Columbia Records 30855) won a Grammy award.

*1980*  *I Will Say Goodbye* (Fantasy Records F–9593) won a Grammy for the most outstanding solo album. *We Will Meet Again* (Warner Brothers Records HS–3411) won a Grammy award for the most outstanding group album.

*1980*  Evans died.

## Art Blakey

**A**rt Blakey's group, established in 1955, can boast some of the most prominent players in this genre: Horace Silver, Freddie Hubbard, Wayne Shorter, Lee Morgan, Hank Mobley, Kenny Dorham, and both Marsalis brothers, Branford and Wynton.

Blakey described his efforts to pass on the jazz tradition by saying, "I look for the new guys, and I just give them a place to hone their art and grow. They do it themselves. I just give them a chance. All they need is a little guidance, a little direction, and they're gone. When they get big enough, I let them go and get their own thing. Then I find some more."[5]

*Art Blakey*
Michael Ochs Archives/
Venice, CA

| | |
|---|---|
| *1919* | Blakey was born in Pittsburgh, Pennsylvania on October 11. |
| *1944* | He recorded with the Billy Eckstine band. |
| *1955* | Blakey formed the Jazz Messengers. |
| *1971–1972* | He toured with Dizzy Gillespie, Thelonious Monk, and others as the "Giants of Jazz." |
| *1980s* | He continued touring with his own group. |
| *1990* | Blakey died in New York City. |

that formerly had supportive roles could step out front in this new balance and establish new ways their instrument could participate in the ensemble. Bass players like Stanley Clark, Jaco Pastorius with Weather Report, and John Patitucci with the Elektric Band have redefined how the bass player is to work in these high energy ensembles. A new virtuosity has accompanied their new found prominence in the ensembles.

The same general process worked for both guitar and keyboard players. Kenny Kirkland, Herbie Hancock, Joe Zawinul, and Chick Corea are a few of the keyboard players that embraced the electronic keyboard and established the new virtuosity. Players like John McLauglin, Mike Stern, and Stanley Clark did the same for guitar. As a result of this new virtuosity, the rhythm section commanded a new image as both a cohesive rhythmic unit and identifiable soloists. The rhythm section often became the centerpiece of the ensemble rather than the support structure for a front line of soloists.

[5]Art Blakey, "Art Blakey in His Prime," *Down Beat* ( July 1985):21.

## MAINSTREAM VOCALISTS

Jazz singing falls logically into three different categories: women, men, and groups. Each grouping has its own history and set of influences.

### FEMALE VOCALISTS

Early women blues singers sang what was termed "urban blues," more sophisticated and controlled than "rural blues." The most obvious examples would be Bessie Smith and Gertrude "Ma" Rainey. Even though Ma Rainey recorded fifty records, her pupil, Bessie Smith, was better known. During her most successful era, 1924–1927, Smith recorded frequently with the great jazz artists of the day including Louis Armstrong, Fletcher Henderson, Sidney Bechet, and numerous others. She started a path that led directly to Ella Fitzgerald and others who continue in the mainstream idiom.

As earlier singers of jazz influenced the instrumentalists, Billie Holiday herself was obviously influenced by instrumentalists. There is no denying the path that leads from Bessie Smith to those who followed, but Billie Holiday was an individualist who has yet to be duplicated in the vocal world. Musicians today enjoy her recordings of blues, lovely ballads, novelty tunes, and even gripping stories of lynching, such as "Strange Fruit." Her recordings lead us straight into the mainstream of vocal jazz. Every singer of the last fifty years who delves into jazz-oriented music owes a debt of gratitude to the intimate personal stylings of Billie Holiday.

The famous Ella Fitzgerald has proven that popular singing and jazz singing can be merged with good taste. She showed bop influences by scat singing that style to "How High the Moon" recorded in 1948, stressing that this was to be the mainstream of the future. She wanted to prove that bop performed with the voice could be comparable to instrumental renditions. Her talented delivery is a brilliant example of the voice imitating an instrument. This attitude was not new; it was shared by Billie Holiday.

Sarah Vaughan played piano with the Earl Hines Orchestra and later became a featured vocalist along with Billy Eckstine. As a pianist, her knowledge of harmony greatly influenced her ability to sing scat, as well as ballads.

Vaughan sang for presidents and toured the world with rhythm sections, a cappella choirs, jazz combos, large jazz bands, and symphony orchestras. Though Vaughan has influenced many singers, she was considerably influenced by those with whom she worked. This most impressive list includes Dizzy Gillespie, Earl "Fatha" Hines,

## Bessie Smith

**B**essie Smith became the best known blues singer of the 1920s. Her recording of "Downhearted Blues" sold 800,000, a remarkable feat. By the end of her first year of recording, she had sold over 2 million records. The Empress of the Blues recorded 160 songs and literally saved the Columbia Record Company from bankruptcy. Public interest began to wane around 1930 and her dipsomania took a considerable toll as employment slackened.

*1894*  Smith was born in Chattanooga, Tennessee on April 15.

*1910*  She joined Ma Rainey's Rabbit Foot Minstrels.

*1917*  She worked for T.O.B.A. (Theater Owner's Booking Agency) and was eventually discovered by promoter Frank Walker.

*1923*  Smith made her first record, "Downhearted Blues" in February.

*1929*  Smith starred in her own show, "Midnight Steppers."

*1933*  In November she made a movie short, "Saint Louis Blues," for Warner Brothers.

*1937*  Smith died in Clarksdale, Mississippi, on September 26 after an automobile accident.

---

Charlie Parker, Miles Davis, Clifford Brown, Herbie Mann, Cannonball Adderley, Count Basie's Band, Thad Jones, Jimmy Rowles, Michel Legrand, and Bob James. This list is included here to show that Vaughan's influences most definitely kept her right in the mainstream of vocal jazz. It is no wonder that her creative vocalizing was so steeped in jazz.

Another straight-ahead jazz vocalist is Betty Carter, formerly with the Lionel Hampton Band. With her rapid execution of nonsense syllables interspersed with actual lyrics, she almost sounds like an instrumentalist playing rapid sixteenth-note patterns.

Betty Carter feels that she is the keeper of a dying flame—the true jazz singer. She agrees that the great jazz singer is linked to the instrumental approach to performing. Carter is profoundly influenced by Charlie Parker and Sonny Rollins. These bop artists are easily detected in her highly creative scat singing. These influences probably

## Billie Holiday

There is a kind of jazz song style that is neither all improvised nor all embellishment but a little of each. Billie Holiday excelled with both paraphrase and invention. Her singing style seemed to stem from her favorite instrumentalist, tenor saxophonist Lester Young. She was undoubtedly also influenced by Bessie Smith and Louis Armstrong. To these wonderful models she added her own feelings, her own lifestyle, and the results were truly intimate and personal. On the other hand, most successful female singers, knowingly or unknowingly, have been influenced by the jazz singing of Billie Holiday.

| | |
|---|---|
| *1915* | Holiday was born in Baltimore, Maryland, on April 7. |
| *1933* | She recorded with Benny Goodman. |
| *1935–1939* | She recorded classics with Teddy Wilson. |
| *1937* | Holiday sang with Count Basie. |
| *1938* | She sang with Artie Shaw. |
| *1939* | She recorded "Strange Fruit" and "Fine and Mellow." |
| *1944* | She recorded "Lover Man." |
| *1954–1958* | She toured Europe. |
| *1959* | Holiday died in New York City of drug abuse on July 17. |

account for her rhythmic daring, her virtuosity, and her leadership in the very center of mainstream vocal jazz. Her favorite singer? Billie Holiday.

Diane Schuur is a contemporary who also follows in the tradition of the great female jazz singers. She has proven herself as both a small group and big band singer. Her work with the Count Basie band demonstrates the influence of singers like Ella Fitzgerald.

## MALE VOCALISTS

It is interesting that many of the better male jazz singers are known primarily for their instrumental prowess. Obvious examples are Louis Armstrong, Jack Teagarden, and Clark Terry with his style of scat

## **Ella Fitzgerald**

| | |
|---|---|
| *1918* | Fitzgerald was born in Newport News, Virginia, on April 25. |
| *1934* | She was discovered by band leader Chick Webb. |
| *1935* | She made her first recording (with Chick Webb), "Love and Kisses." |
| *1938* | She recorded "A-Tisket A-Tasket." |
| *1939* | Fitzgerald took over the leadership of the Chick Webb band on his death. |
| *1946* | She joined the Norman Granz tours. |
| *1955* | She appeared in the movie *Pete Kelly's Blues.* |
| *1958* | She gave a concert at Carnegie Hall with Duke Ellington. |
| *1970s–1990s* | Fitzgerald continued to tour internationally most successfully. |

singing. On the other side of the ledger, there are some excellent instrumentalists who are known primarily for their singing. For example, much of the listening public is not even aware of the talented piano work of Sarah Vaughan or Nat Cole.

The identification of a jazz singer dates back to the late 1920s with Al Jolson, though the jazz community never really accepted the label seriously (*The Jazz Singer* from the movie starring Al Jolson). It is easy to look back and state that Armstrong, Teagarden, Holiday, and Ray Charles were jazz singers; they phrased in the jazz idiom on jazz materials. Today, it is more of a problem to identify jazz singers. We do not yet have the benefit of hindsight. Is a singer a jazz singer if the repertoire is associated with jazz? Is it jazz singing if jazz interpretation is employed? Is improvisation the main dividing line, as is often stated about instrumentalists individually or a band collectively? The rationale has to be that even our best jazz singers do not always sing jazz, any more than our finest instrumentalists always perform in this genre.

Both Armstrong's trumpet and Jack Teagarden's trombone could be heard in their vocalizing. They were premier jazz players, and when they sang what came out was simply their version of how that particular melody line should best be presented. This attitude is obvious in any jazz singer who is first an instrumentalist. Clark Terry's vocals are excellent examples of this approach.

## Ray Charles

| | |
|---|---|
| *1932* | Charles was born in Albany, Georgia, on September 23. |
| *1938* | Charles was blinded by an accident at the age of six. |
| *1954* | He formed his own band. |
| *1957* | His first LP was released. |
| *1960* | He recorded "Georgia on My Mind." |
| *1970s–1990s* | Charles is successfully touring internationally. |

The Count Basie band seemed to need desperately a jazz singer to feature throughout its reign. Mr. Five-By-Five was Jimmy Rushing, known as a blues shouter. Rushing's physique and his rhythmic drive fit the Basie style. Next in line was the wonderfully communicative Joe Williams. Williams also displayed a sense of rhythm that helped the one aspect of that band that did not need help—the drive. As handsome and attractive as Williams was, he was as effective on records as he was in person.

One of the most competent performers in a variety of fields is Ray Charles. His work is ensconced deeply in gospel music, rhythm and blues, country western, pop, and of course, jazz. He is considered a truly convincing singer, authentic in all styles, and he is also an appreciated jazz keyboardist. Charles has had hit records in many musical styles. His combining of jazz and gospel music opened doors for many performers into the jazz field. Whatever he performs, his sounds are some of the most infectious in music. His ability to communicate emotions is seldom rivaled.

A talented ex-drummer who is very knowledgeable as far as harmonies are concerned is Mel Torme. It is true that his variations on ballads are scintillating, but even more daring are his bop-type excursions as he scat sings. He would agree with Gillespie that a knowledge of harmony helps. He would also agree with Gillespie that the bop style of performance is the most exciting way to improvise. Torme represents what has become the mainstream in male vocal jazz.

Bobby McFerrin is a singer of unusual talent. Although his early recordings were offered in the classical music area of extended vocal techniques, he now performs most often in the scat singing tradition of Louis Armstrong, Ella Fitzgerald, Mel Torme, and Clark Terry. His scat ability involves more than improvised syllables with jazz inflections. He also makes percussive sounds as accompaniment to his own improvisations. McFerrin is particularly effective in solo performance. He is able to recreate all the essential parts of a jazz standard by himself. By dividing his time between the melody and the bass line, he is able to give the impression that both are continually present. He complements the performance with percussive sounds created by striking his chest while he sings. His album *Spontaneous Inventions* clearly demonstrates his versatility.[6]

One other male singing soloist to be added to this mainstream galaxy is Harry Connick, Jr. He has been quite successful in the commercial music market and has helped mainstream jazz gain public attention. He is a noted pianist, vocalist, and composer. His piano playing is in the style of classic jazz performers, such as Monk in particular. He received a Grammy award in 1989 at the age of 21 for his musical score for the movie *When Harry Met Sally*. This accomplishment boosted public interest in neoclassical jazz. He sees his advocacy of the hard bop tradition as a return to the essence of jazz.

## *VOCAL GROUPS*

When discussing group singing in this context, there is very little need to go back further than the Mills Brothers. (See chapter 5 for a discussion of early vocal ensembles.) It is true that Connee Boswell is very deserving of mention as she and her sisters opened the door for many other vocal groups. Boswell wrote not only the vocal arrangements, but the instrumental parts as well, making her, along with Mary Lou Williams, one of the first female arrangers/composers in jazz. It is also true that Patty Andrews of the Andrews Sisters used jazz inflections constantly, but this group was more a part of the pop field than jazz. However, the captivating rhythmic feel generated by the Mills Brothers influenced many vocal groups to follow.

From about 1958 to 1963, the vocal jazz group that dominated the field was the Hendricks, Lambert, and Ross Trio. They developed to a high degree the art of taking old jazz records and setting lyrics to just about everything on them—not only the tunes themselves, but also the improvised solos. This technique is labeled ''vocalese art,'' and the records they copied came from mainstream jazz. Annie Ross was replaced by Yolande Bavan, and Jon Hendrick's wife, Judith, and daughter, Michelle join Bruce Scott in the present group. Their work is a contemporary form of onomatopoeia.[7]

---

[6]Bobby McFerrin, *Spontaneous Inventions,* Blue Note Records BT 85110.
[7]*The Best of Lambert, Hendricks and Ross,* Columbia Records KC 32911.

## New York Voices
### "Top Secret"
### GRP Records GRD–9589

Music performed by Peter Eldridge, Kim Nazarian, Sara Krieger, Farmon Meader, and Caprice Fox.

| | |
|---|---|
| :00 | Synthesized ascending melodic motive |
| :09 | Electric bass enters |
| :19 | Vocal enters with melody |
| 1:00 | Repeat of melody, listen for choral "punches" in background. |
| 1:41 | Staccato vocal section |
| 1:52 | Contrasting legato vocal section; listen for synthesizer support. |
| 2:01 | New chorus with more developed vocal background punches |
| 2:43 | Legato interlude |
| 3:03 | "Time" returns in rhythm section |
| 3:14 | "Scat" solo begins (Caprice Fox) |
| 3:54 | Synthesizer doubles scat solo line |
| 4:15 | Synthesized backup becomes more animated |
| 4:34 | Staccato section returns |
| 4:44 | Legato section returns |
| 4:54 | Return to "head" |
| 5:34 | Repeat of final phrase to end |
| 5:55 | Synthesized chords with saxophone solo fade to end |
| 6:19 | End |

Following closely in the tradition of Lambert, Hendricks, and Ross is Manhattan Transfer. They developed from a basically pop-oriented style to a firmly rooted jazz style. They have always employed jazz overtones and used many excellent jazz instrumentalists on their recordings. However, their *Extensions* album[8] came as a revelation with the arrangement of Zawinul's "Birdland" with lyrics by

---

[8]Manhattan Transfer, *Extensions,* Atlantic Records SD 19258.

Jon Hendricks, arranged by the group's own Janis Siegal. The album also included lyricization of ''Body and Soul'' by the great bop singer, Eddie Jefferson. This version was a harmonized transcription of Coleman Hawkins' famous 1939 improvisation.

Manhattan Transfer's 1985 album, *Vocalese,* marshalls impressive jazz forces in the vocalese style.[9] It makes use of such players as McCoy Tyner, Dizzy Gillespie, and the entire Basie band, as well as singers like Jon Hendricks and Bobby McFerrin. ''To You'' on this album demonstrates the vocalese art. The music comes from a Basie and Ellington session, *First Time.*

New York Voices, a group often compared to Manhattan Transfer, produced a 1989 album, *New York Voices,* which boasts of a wide range of styles and developed instrumental accompaniments.[10]

In 1988, a group of six men under the name of Take 6 burst on the music scene and captured the attention of the jazz community. Although they first began singing together in 1980, they did not gain national prominence until 1988; at that time, their success seemed immediate. Their arrangements are a cappella and show a blend of traditional gospel, soul, pop, and jazz. Their arrangements and stylistic delivery reflect influence from earlier groups, such as Lambert, Hendricks and Ross, the Hi-Los, and the Mills Brothers.

---

The jazz tradition is continually changing. At times like those discussed here, particularly hard bop and neoclassical, jazz's mainstream reappears and works to stabilize the more short-lived excursions in new directions. Some of the new influences on jazz will prove more lasting than others, some will lose their identities in the mainstream, while others will work to redefine our understanding of the jazz mainstream itself.

**SUMMARY**

---

Armstrong, Louis. ''West End Blues.'' Smithsonian B/4 (cd I/17).
*Art Blakey and the Jazz Messengers.* ''E.T.A.'' Concord
    Jazz Records CJ 168.
*Art Blakey and the Jazz Messengers.* ''Straight Ahead.'' Concord
    Jazz Records CJ 168.
*The Art of Tatum.* Decca Records DL 8715.
Bechet, Sidney. *Master Musician.* Bluebird Records 2 AXM 5516.
*Best of Ella Fitzgerald.* MCA Records 4047.
*The Best of Lambert, Hendricks and Ross.* Columbia Records
    KC 32911.

**SUGGESTED LISTENING**

---

[9]Manhattan Transfer, *Vocalese,* Atlantic Records 7 81266–1.
[10]New York Voices, *New York Voices,* GRP Records GRD–9589.

*Bix Beiderbecke and the Chicago Cornets.* Milestone Records
M 47019.

The Blues. *Folkways Jazz,* Vol. 2.

Carter, Betty. ''Moonlight in Vermont,'' ''Thou Swell,'' and
''Can't We Be Friends.'' New World Records NW 295.

Casey, Al. ''How High the Moon.'' *The History of Jazz,* Vol. 4.

Charles, Ray. ''America.'' *A Message from the People.* ABC
Records ABCX 755/TRC.

Charlie Parker Story, Vols. 1–3. Verve Records V6 8000 1 2.

Connick, Harry, Jr. *Lofty's Roach Souffle.* Columbia Records
CK 46223.

Connick, Harry, Jr. *When Harry Met Sally.* Columbia Records
CK 45319.

Davis, Miles. *Tutu.* Warner Brothers Records 25490 1.

Davis, Miles, and Charlie Parker. ''Klacktoveedsteen.''
Smithsonian E/12 (cd III/16).

Davis, Miles, and Gil Evans. *Porgy and Bess.* Columbia Records
PC 8085.

Davis, Miles, and Gil Evans. *Sketches of Spain.* Columbia Records
PC 8271.

*Ella Fitzgerald and Count Basie.* Pablo Records 2310772.

*The Essential Jimmy Rushing.* Vanguard Records 65/66.

Evans, Bill. *I Will Say Goodbye.* Fantasy Records F 9593.

Evans, Bill. *We Will Meet Again.* Warner Brothers Records
HS 3411.

Gillespie, Dizzy. *Big Band Jazz.* Smithsonian Collection of
Recordings DMK 3–0610 RC030. *Dizzy Gillespie.* RCA
Victor Records LPV 530.

Gillespie, Dizzy, and Charlie Parker. ''Shaw 'Nuff.'' Smithsonian
E/7 (cd III/11).

Gillespie, Dizzy, and Charlie Parker. ''Wee.'' *Jazz at Massey Hall.*
Fantasy Records 6003.

*The Hackett Horn.* Epic Records EE 22004.

Hawkins, Coleman. ''Body and Soul.'' Smithsonian C/6 (cd II/8).

Hodges, Johnny, and Duke Ellington. ''In a Mellotone.''
Smithsonian E/3 (cdIII/7).

Hodges, Johnny, and Duke Ellington. ''Passion Flower.'' *Jive at
Five.* New World Records NW 273.

Holiday, Billie. ''Fine and Mellow.'' *Billie Holiday.* Mainstream
Records S/6000.

Holiday, Billie. *Singers and Soloists of Swing Bands.* Smithsonian
Collection of Recordings RC 035 IPAT-19881.

Holiday, Billie. *Strange Fruit.* Atlantic Records 1614.

*The Legendary Oscar Peterson Trio at the Blue Note.* TELARC
    CD 83304.
Manhattan Transfer. *Extensions.* Atlantic records SD 19258.
Manhattan Transfer. *Vocalese.* Atlantic records 7 8 1266 1.
*Marsalis Standard Time.* Vol. 1. Columbia/CBS FC 37574.
Marsalis, Wynton, and Art Blakey and the Jazz Messengers. *Album
    of the Year.* Timeless SJP 153.
Marsalis, Wynton, and Art Blakey and the Jazz Messengers, *E.T.A.*
    Concord Jazz Records CJ 168.
McFerrin, Bobby. *Spontaneous Inventions.* Blue Note Records
    BT 85110.
Monk, Thelonious, and Miles Davis. *Bag's Groove.* Prestige
    Records 7109.
*New York Voices.* BRP Records GRD 09589.
Nichols, Red. ''Ida.'' *The Jazz Story,* Vol. 2. Capitol Records
    W 2137 41.
Parker, Charlie. *Smithsonian Collection of Classic Jazz,* Vols. 7
    and 8.
*Ray Charles and Betty Carter.* ABC/Paramount Records 385.
Rollins, Sonny. ''Blue 7.'' Smithsonian H/3 (cd V/1).
Rollins, Sonny. *Saxophone Colossus.* Prestige Records LP 7079.
Schuur, Diane. ''Diane Schuur and the Count Basie Orchestra.''
    GRP Records GRC 1039 C143525.
Smith, Bessie. ''Empty Bed Blues.'' *Empty Bed Blues.* Columbia
    Records G39450.
Smith, Bessie. ''Lost Your Head Blues.'' Smithsonian A/4 (cd I/4).
Smith, Bessie. ''Saint Louis Blues.'' Smithsonian A/3 (cd I/3).
Smith, Paul. *The Art of Tatum,* Vols. 1 and 2. Outstanding Records
    004 and 007.
*Take 6.* Reprise Records 9 25670 2.
Tatum, Art. ''Too Marvelous for Words.'' Smithsonian C/12
    (cd II/14).
Tatum, Art. ''Willow Weep for Me.'' Smithsonian C/11 (cd II/13).
*The Tatum Solo Masterpieces.* Pablo Records 2625 703.
Teagarden, Jack. *Giants of Jazz.* Time-Life Records STL J08.
Teagarden, Jack. *King of the Blues Trombone.* Epic Records JSN
    6044.
Teagarden, Jack, and Paul Whiteman. ''Aunt Hagar's Blues.''
    Decca Records 2145.
Vaughan, Sarah. ''All Alone'' and ''My Funny Valentine.''
    Smithsonian F/11 and 12 (cd IV/4&5).
Vaughan, Sarah. *I Love Brazil.* Pablo Records 2312101.
Vaughan, Sarah. ''Key Largo.'' New World Records NW 295.
Young, Lester and Count Basie. ''Lester Leaps In.'' Smithsonian
    D/7 (cd II/22).

# CHAPTER 10

## Notation and Improvisation—
## A Question of Balance

A s we have seen in previous chapters, jazz is an art form that grows from the interaction of a variety of cultural forces. Two of the dominant forces at work in jazz come from the ethnic groups that have contributed to the developing art form, in particular, the African Americans and the western Europeans. Each of these groups carries with them sensitivities and preferences that play themselves out in the way they each approach the writing and performing of jazz. Depending on which influence is dominant, jazz has changed to reflect that influence. This balance is quite unstable and has shifted dramatically from the inception of jazz to the present.

If forced to reduce the contrast between the artistic approaches of the African-American and western European cultures to a single theme, the African-American influence might be considered an oral tradition that expresses itself in the improvisatory actions of performance in contrast to the notated tradition of western Europe. The exceptions to this very general statement are, of course, many and obvious. However, this distinction is useful for tracing an evolutionary line through jazz that describes the influence between these two cultures.

Beginning with its early stirrings (chapter 5), jazz has been tied to the improvised activities of performers whether this occurred in the church, on the plantation, or in the tenderloin. The extemporaneous ensembles of Early Dixieland extended this early oral tradition into more formalized instrumental settings. It was not until the Jelly Roll

## THE ORAL TRADITION AND NOTATION

Morton arrangements that we see the emergence of a compositional line that indicates the notated tradition reflective of western European practice.

During the late 1930s, as jazz began to move out of the tenderloin and into the spotlight of popular music, it tapped the resources of Tin Pan Alley and the broadcast medium of radio. Both these media were controlled primarily by whites operating in the more formalized art world that featured notated arrangements. Although the original swing bands were African American, the engine behind the popularity of the swing bands was primarily white. The most popular bands during that period were also white and featured well crafted arrangements that placed ensemble execution above individual expression.

Although we are working on an African-American/western European generalization, we must always recognize that the boundaries between the white and African-American musical practices was in no way as clear as the generalization might imply. One of the "tightest" ensembles, directed by Jimmy Lunceford in the 1930s and 1940s, was African American and compositionally based. On the whole, however, the white bands worked for more accurate performance as a unit than did the African-American bands. This is not to imply that the white bands were in any way better performers, only that the accurate execution of their arrangements and instrumental balance among players was a high priority. The African-American bands emphasized other areas. Many of the bands never let go of the individual characteristics of the players who made up the ensemble. The Ellington band is perhaps the most prominent expression of an ensemble that respected the independent "voices" of its membership. Again, such a distinction is vulnerable to many notable examples. Even within Basie's career, we can find bands that exemplified both expressions. His early bands were more typical of the loose style associated with African-American bands, while his later groups were some of the tightest ensembles in the history of the big bands.

Even if this rather vague distinction between playing styles were completely discounted, the fact that big bands worked from notated arrangements reflects this period's predominant interest in larger, more compositionally centered jazz. Small groups were still at work, but they were most often used to "break" the larger group during dances. It is interesting that it was in these small groups that the racial line between players first broke down. Benny Goodman had a "band within a band" that played during the big band's break. In this smaller group, he used Charlie Christian on guitar, Lionel Hampton on vibraphone, and Teddy Wilson on piano to become the first integrated group in jazz. Because the small groups relied on improvisation, it was appropriate that these groups included the leading improvisors of the day who were mostly African American.

The balance shifted again with the emergence of bop. The leaders in this new style were primarily African American and worked in small groups dominated by improvisation. Again, the individual player was the center of the ensemble, and arrangements were created on the spot. Standard popular songs were the only notated compositional element in the performance of bop. A body of these standards was played repeatedly for different performances and changed to meet the requirements of each live performance. With the move to bop, jazz's relationship to its audience shifted drastically. This music was not as popular as swing. Because of its complexity, new harmonic language, and nondance tempos, bop had abandoned the popular music scene and demanded a more elite listening audience. Because the performance of a standard could be so different from performance to performance, the popular listening audience, who expected familiar songs and arrangements, could not easily follow this new direction.

Therefore, with bop, the players claimed an ownership of jazz that was rooted again in improvisation and characterized by the expressive playing style more typical of the early jazz instrumentalists. A possible flaw in this argument that jazz was moving back to a style characterized more by an oral tradition as it shifted from big band composition to small group improvisation is that the musical material used by the players of bop did not get more simple, but more complex. Music based on oral traditions tends to have simpler theoretical and organizational structures than music used by trained composers. With a notated composition, the player is freed from remembering complex details; in an orally based performance details are, instead, created during performance. Large, complex compositions often require notation so that the detail is not lost in performance.

Our argument is strengthened when we realize that the musical complexity of the bop period resided more in the materials used than in the structure of the compositions. The melodies used for improvisation were relatively short and not difficult to hold in memory. However, the harmonic materials used to perform that melody were suddenly more complex than those normally heard in swing. As a result, performers who wished to adopt the new style were required to learn this new harmonic language. This complexity differs from the detail used in large group instrumentation. All the individual parts of a big band were different and had to be played as written for the arrangement to work. The arrangements could also be more complex structurally. Without notation, they would probably be reduced to much simpler expressions capable of being remembered. On the other hand, bop used relatively simple structural designs but pulled from a reservoir of complex harmonies that could be realized during performance.

If jazz favored an oral tradition with bop, it reversed its direction as cool began to emerge. Although we often associate cool with the small group sounds of such players as Miles Davis and Chet Baker, the inspiration for much of early cool came out of the experimentation of a New York group centered around the compositional talents of Gil Evans. This group, mostly white, was interested in finding a new sound that was not as aggressive as the bop expression. Their interest also included a wider range of instruments than was being used in small group jazz. Gerry Mulligan brought the baritone saxophone to prominence in this medium, and the arrangements of Gil Evans used string instruments, as well as other nontraditional jazz instruments.

The experimentations of this group gained more focus when Miles Davis joined the group and was able to get them into a recording studio. The result was the album *The Birth of the Blues*. The sound that accompanied these arrangements was extremely underspoken with an interest in harmonic color outweighing bop's interest in harmonic complexity. The tempos of the style were also relaxed as the music cooled down. Much like bop, the musicians were now making conscious decisions to move in a new direction in response to previous styles.

## COOL AND A RETURN TO COMPOSITION

Unlike the music of Dixieland or bop, the music of cool was as much associated with the arranger, and Gil Evans in particular, as it was with the players themselves. Two of the big bands in the late 1940s, Woody Herman and Claude Thornhill, moved consciously away from the bop sounds to a cool jazz feel. Many of the seminal members of cool in New York came out of the Thornhill band, for example, saxophonist Lee Konitz, Gerry Mulligan, and arranger Gil Evans. Gil Evans continued his relationship with Miles Davis to write other arrangement-based cool recordings, such as, "Sketches of Spain" and the "Porgy and Bess Suite."

It would be misleading to suggest that cool was strictly a compositionally-based style that made use of larger ensembles. As cool moved to the West Coast, many small groups played in the cool style and worked improvisationally off simple musical material. It should be remembered, however, that the style was brought to fruition on the West Coast by players, such as saxophonist Jimmy Giuffre and trumpeter Shorty Rogers and later drummer Shelly Manne. In addition to these players, other cool players, such as Art Pepper, Bud Shank, and Bill Holman were also former members of the Stan Kenton band, which more than any band at that time experimented

## Miles Davis with the Gil Evans Orchestra
### "Summertime" from *Porgy and Bess*
### Smithsonian G/7 (cd IV/12)

0:00   Begins with Davis playing the melody with a very light "cool" backup in the orchestra. Listen for the orchestral colors pulled from the unusual instrumentation, including french horns, tuba, and flutes, as well as saxes, trumpets, and trombones.

0:35   First solo chorus taken by Davis. Motivic response continues in the orchestra.

1:10   Second chorus by Davis. Orchestral colors expand somewhat as the gentle peak of the arrangement is reached.

1:46   Third chorus by Davis

2:22   Davis returns to the melody for the final chorus.

3:03   Slows down

3:16   End

with complex compositional arrangements and instrumentation. The West Coast jazz movement was comprised mostly of white players who had experience in premier big bands like Kenton's.

There was also a relationship between Hollywood and the growing cool jazz stream. In fact, Henry Mancini, a renown Hollywood writer, contributed a great deal of material to this style which is often overlooked by jazz historians. Hollywood's influence carried with it a respect for the musical palette and compositional approach more typical of film scoring. Mancini often used a four-instrument woodwind section that doubled on twenty-seven instruments, offering a wide variety of subtle colorings. His scoring approach emphasized control and cleanliness. For example, even where each note was to end as well as where they started was clearly notated (see example 10.1).

His music often covered (within one selection) a touch of funky and a touch of cool, the obvious example being his "Pink Panther." Mancini said, "The milk of the sacred cows has a way of turning

*EXAMPLE 10.1*

sour. The entire music scene is constantly changing, leaving the narrow-minded and the lazy behind. That which is far out today becomes commonplace tomorrow.''[1]

There were connections between the East and West Coast cool jazz schools, primarily through players like Gerry Mulligan who worked on both coasts. Dave Brubeck's work on the West Coast was somewhat parallel to that of Lennie Tristano on the East Coast. Both of these writers/players infused their performances with musical material that explored compositional ideas.

## HARD BOP, A MUSIC RECLAIMED

In the early 1950s, writers used the rather pretentious name of Funky Hard Bop Regression era for the music that followed cool. The word *funky* referred to the rollicking, rhythmic feeling of the style. The term *hard* meant a performance that was more driving and less relaxed than cool jazz. The phrase *bop regression* implied a return to the elements of the bop style. Because this title combined all these notions, some confusion has developed between the two similar but distinct styles of funky and hard bop. A more appropriate title for this period might have been funky and the hard bop regression or just funky and bop.

This period is important to the historical thread discussed in this chapter. The movement of jazz from New York to the West Coast also signaled the move from the hard driving bop style to the more relaxed cool style. This movement also paralleled a change from predominantly African-American to white players. Hard bop and funky can be viewed as a conscious return to the African-American style which centered on a more theatrical presentation and, in the case of funky, the musical materials found commonly in the African-American church.

---

[1]Henry Mancini, *Sounds and Scores,* (Northridge Music Inc., Northridge, California, 1962), 245.

It may be true that musical styles swing back and forth like a pendulum and that swing is not always smooth. The swing toward complexity is fairly gradual. The players of the Swing era added more musicians; the bop players extended the harmonies and complicated the melodies; and the cool players brought in new instruments, time signatures, and extended forms. The funky style that followed seemed to revert quite suddenly to the most basic of music elements, for example, the "amen chords" from religious services.

With the exception of bop, the complexity of these earlier styles was based on compositional notions rather than performance practice. Bop increased the theoretical expectations of jazz, while it also demanded more extemporaneous skills. The funky style relaxed the harmonic complexity somewhat but returned to the extemporaneous style more typical of Dixieland and bop.

The term *funky* was often used interchangeably with soul during this period. Both the funky and soul styles were associated with the music prevalent in the African-American churches. The term *soul* certainly has a connection to the church, and perhaps it speaks of the intended emotional content of the music. On the other hand, funky has a more earthy association. This blend of earthy and gospel has been a trademark of jazz, originating from a blend of music from the church and the tenderloin. It seems fitting that funky should seek such a balance.

Funky was a rawboned type of playing with a highly rhythmical melody and a less complex harmony than that of the preceding Cool era. This music had a happy sound and lacked tension and the apparent alienation more typical of cool.

Contributing to the development of the funky and gospel styles, no doubt, was the new African-American awareness developing in the United States. During this social development, African Americans found the African-American church, its harmonies and blues inflections, a link to their roots. Some authors suggest that the funky style was an effort among African Americans to recapture jazz as their own expression. The fact that such an effort is conscious represents a new awareness in the jazz legacy. Ever since bop, jazz was becoming a recognized artistic agent in the culture rather than behaving like other popular music styles, which unconsciously followed the winds of fashion. The funky idiom quickly spread throughout the jazz world and was soon played by everyone from school bands to professional ensembles, independent of race.

Perhaps even more than an ethnic reaction, the funky idiom is a reaction to the intellectualism found in music of the cool period. The lively and emotionally exuberant nature of the funky style contrasts strongly with the measured and controlled expression of the

## FUNKY

*EXAMPLE 10.2*

cool players. Unlike the cool style, which looked to European compositional techniques, the funky style adopted the truly American oral idioms found in gospel and blues.

In addition to stylistic differences, the distinction between cool and hard bop was also geographical. The cool style, often called West Coast jazz, was centered in California, while the funky and hard bop styles pulled the jazz focus back to New York. It could even be suggested that a more relaxed lifestyle of California was a factor in the development of the relaxed cool jazz style, contrasted with the more driving bop style typical of New York jazz.

## FUNKY MUSIC

The funky idiom embraces homophonic harmonic construction. Although the lines appear to be invented independently, as can be seen in example 10.2, they are planned homophonically. The lower note is played because of the sound of the specific interval produced when it is played against the melodic note above it. Example 10.2 also illustrates the excessive use of the fourth and fifth intervals. Another identifying feature is the use of many blue notes, the E-flats and B-flats.

Although these blue notes are not the same as the original blue notes produced by church singers, their prevalent use in this style is meant to create the same effect. The original blue notes were slightly mistuned notes (very often the third and seventh of the scale) in a major key. This mistuning created a disagreement between the major key and the almost minor blue notes sung against it. In an effort to recreate the blues sound, many pieces in this period were actually played in a minor key.

## FUNKY PERFORMERS

The homophonic construction of the Swing era and that of the Funky era are compared in examples 10.3 and 10.4. Swing music was harmonized in a closed manner, as shown in example 10.3 by the blocks

*EXAMPLE 10.3*

*EXAMPLE 10.4*

of chords. The funky players, while planning their music homophonically, developed a more open, loose setting, as demonstrated in example 10.4.

This style was introduced by pianists but was quickly adopted by all instrumentalists. The funky style was brought to public notice by pianist Horace Silver and a group led by drummer Art Blakey called the Jazz Messengers.[2] Horace Silver also made many records with his own combo.[3] Most pianists who play funky style music admit that Silver was the progenitor of the style.

The return to jazz roots indicated by the less complex harmonies, excessive use of blue notes, and simpler rhythmic feeling stressed communication between players and listeners and led away from the compositional or technical complexities of cool or bop. It is

[2]Horace Silver (Art Blakey). *A Night at Birdland.* Blue Note Records, Vol. 1, 1521; *Horace Silver and the Jazz Messengers,* Blue Note Records BLP 1518.
[3]Horace Silver, *Blowing the Blues Away,* Blue Note Records 4017; *Song for My Father,* Blue Note Records 4185.

## Horace Silver Quintet
## "Stop Time"
## New World Records NW 271

Trumpet, Kenny Dorham; tenor saxophone, Hank Mobley; piano, Horace Silver; bass, Doug Watkins; and drums, Art Blakey.

| | |
|---|---|
| :00 | Introductory theme with one repeat at a lower range |
| :08 | Head melody with trumpet and saxophone in unison |
| :24 | Trumpet solo |
| 1:09 | Tenor saxophone solo |
| 1:54 | Piano solo. Listen to the left hand punctuated comping patterns as Silver solos with his right hand. |
| 2:50 | Just as his solo ends, listen for the blues ("funky") melodic references. |
| 2:53 | Trumpet solo. The band begins to trade fours at this point. Each player with solo for four measures with four-bar drum solos in between. |
| 2:56 | Drum solo for four bars |
| 2:58 | Tenor solo for four bars |
| 3:02 | Drum solo for four bars |
| 3:06 | Trumpet solo for four bars |
| 3:09 | Drum solo for four bars |
| 3:13 | Tenor solo for four bars |
| 3:17 | Extended drum solo |
| 3:35 | Head melody returns with trumpet and saxophone in unison |
| 3:46 | Introductory theme restated |
| 3:55 | End |

interesting that on early Horace Silver recordings the bop concept is prominent and the afterbeat accent hardly discernible. In the funky style, the bop elements faded gradually as the accented afterbeat developed.

The Hammond organ had been only rarely used before 1951 (by Fats Waller and Count Basie) when Wild Bill Davis surprised everyone by performing real blues-oriented works on it. Later, Jimmy Smith proved the real potential of the instrument. He used a larger variety of organ stops (effects) than any other player in the jazz field—and with incredible technique. The instrument was accepted wholeheartedly in the Funky era. A parallel, if not the root of this style of organ playing, can be found in the African-American church service, a parallel not new to the historical development of jazz. The Hammond organ is to the African-American church what the pipe organ is to the western European cathedral.

At about the time jazz musicians were deciding that they wanted to get back to communicating with the public (about 1953), a reputable critic of symphonic music and opera, Henry Pleasants, wrote a scathing book emphasizing that present-day composers of so-called serious music had lost touch entirely with their dwindling audience.

> He (the contemporary 'serious' composer) finds it difficult to admit that he is simply not producing music that provokes a sympathetic response in his listeners. He forgets that it is the purpose of music to provoke such a response, and that all superior music in the past has provoked it.[4]

Funky players, such as Ray Charles, Cannonball Adderly, and Mose Allison, obviously agreed with Pleasants. Communication at the immediate level was important.

---

## GOSPEL JAZZ

Gospel jazz is an extension of the funky style. If a distinction is to be made between funky and gospel, it can be found in gospel's more triadic use of harmonies, very much like those associated with the improvisational singing of hymns. As the name implies, gospel jazz uses elements from, and has a definite feeling of, early gospel music.[5]

---

[4]Henry Pleasants, *Serious Music and All That Jazz.* Copyright © 1969 by Henry Pleasants. Reprinted by permission of Simon and Schuster, Inc.
[5]Les McCann, *Les McCann Plays the Truth,* Pacific Jazz Records PJ2.

A primary example of these elements is the constant use of the amen chord progression (I, IV, I—the plagal cadence). To hear extensive use of the amen chords, listen to Les McCann's "Fish This Week."[6] Although this style is a return to prejazz music, gospel jazz still reflects the influences of preceding jazz styles, including their harmonies, forms, and advanced musical techniques.[7] However, rhythm and emotional intensity highlight gospel jazz.

Many selections of this form of jazz can just as easily be performed in a church as in a nightclub. One is Les McCann's "A Little ¾ for God and Company."[8] Big gospel bands sometimes perform in a handclapping, "shouting Baptist" manner as they enact a scene of baptism in a work such as "Wade in the Water."[9]

## HARD BOP

Hard bop was a regression, a return to the precepts of the bop style. This regression was also a rejection of the Cool era. Cool jazz was played in a relaxed manner, a much softer style of performance than bop. The term *hard* was used to indicate a move back to the high energy, driving style of bop. The bop players who did not accept cool were labeled hard boppers. The differences between the earlier bop and the later were very slight. Jazz players do not totally disregard what they hear around them as their careers continue, so the later bop players used a few more advanced chord progressions having heard cool. They used more blue notes and plagal cadences having heard funky. They even used more extended choruses having heard Coltrane and others. Despite these additions, hard bop has retained its primary relationship to bop.

## HARD BOP, STRAIGHT-AHEAD, MAINSTREAM, AND NEOCLASSICAL

The hard bop, straight-ahead, mainstream, and neoclassical styles all share the common heritage of bop. Bop remains today the style that defines the classical jazz performance. Each of these labels grew out of circumstances that may have threatened the future of classical jazz in some way. Hard bop was a reaction to the cool intellectualization of West Coast jazz. Straight-ahead was a return to the traditional performance values challenged by the avant-garde practices of Coleman's "Free Jazz." Mainstream and neoclassical were also reactions to the popularization of jazz as it began to fuse with rock. With all of these reactions, the one constant has been the classical bop style.

[6]Les McCann, *Les McCann Plays the Truth,* Pacific Jazz Records PJ2.
[7]The Jazz Brothers, "Something Different," *The Soul of Jazz,* Riverside Records S-5.
[8]Les McCann, *Les McCann Plays the Truth,* Pacific Jazz Records PJ2.
[9]Johnny Griffin, "Wade in the Water," *The Soul of Jazz,* Riverside Records S-5.

During the late 1940s and early 1950s, the jazz tradition came of age. It assumed an artistic role in American culture and established the dominant criteria against which all following jazz styles would be judged. The reverence with which bop has been preserved is a signal that the codification of an art form has taken place. Just as classical music has its center of gravity in the baroque to romantic periods, jazz has centered its artistic balance in the Bop era.

The terms *mainstream* and *neoclassical* also speak to jazz's self-conscious attitudes about its history. Mainstream, by definition, is a historical term that points backward as well as forward. It carries with it an implication that performers and composers of jazz have a historical responsibility. Innovation alone is not enough; that innovation must be tied to the recognized jazz canon. Only then is that innovation a legitimate part of the mainstream. How the mainstream is defined is always subject to change. Not all past jazz styles, despite their popularity, are considered mainstream. Although swing, and the big band style in particular, was the most popular jazz expression in the world at one time, it falls out of the jazz mainstream definition. The most generally accepted chronology leaps from early blues and Dixieland over the Swing era to bop; it leaps again over cool to hard bop and again over avant-garde and fusion to neoclassical. This does not mean these other styles are not considered important. It only means that our current understanding of the mainstream does not include them in the jazz lineage. The irony in such a mainstream definition is that during the Bop era, bop was not popular with the jazz public or with many of the jazz players themselves.

The neoclassical reference attached to mainstream 1990s jazz is an even clearer indicator of a developing historical jazz canon. This term appeared first in classical music history books and referred to contemporary (new or *neo*) music that was based on early (or classical) compositions. Stravinsky's ballet *Pulcinella* is an example of a neoclassical work based on the music of Pergolesi. Jazz critics and historians have borrowed this term and applied it to today's players who look back to the bop tradition for inspiration. The primary spokesperson for this style is Wynton Marsalis.

Today's bop playing is often referred to as neoclassical jazz, more by writers than players. If the classical reference is indeed meant to refer to ''classical jazz,'' there is an unspoken consensus that bop is classical jazz. It is misleading to consider bop the beginning of classical jazz. It certainly is the point at which jazz claimed its artistic role, but that role grew out of a rich tradition that extends backward to the Early Dixieland groups and beyond them to the many musical and cultural sources that converged on New Orleans. The classical line of jazz carries with it a self-preserving skill that precludes elements that were too far from the traditional norms established by the earliest players. The mainstream voice of jazz is an improvisational one. It works in the harmonic and melodic language of western Europe, while it delivers that language in African-American terms. Jazz styles that move too far toward one of these extremes risk being isolated from the mainstream.

## NEOCLASSICISM

As the historical arch from bop to hard bop stretched over the cool period, a similar arch from hard bop spanned later stylistic periods, such as free or fusion, to appear again in the work of players like trumpeter Wynton Marsalis. He speaks quite strongly about the legacy of past jazz styles and is a respected performer of the straight-ahead style. The source of Wynton Marsalis's historical respect for jazz can be attributed to his father, Ellis, a respected player and teacher of traditional jazz. Wynton's brothers, saxophonist Branford and trombonist Delfayeo, are also outspoken heralds of traditional jazz. The neoclassical perspective tends to be exclusive. Excluded are those not properly respectful of the jazz originators according to the neoclassical definition. This perspective jumps from early New Orleans music to the bop period, not seeing the other contributions of the more commercialized jazz periods.

Wynton Marsalis brings the hard bop period full circle. Like so many other strong players in this tradition, Marsalis worked in his youth under the tutelage of Art Blakey in the Jazz Messengers. The straight-ahead legacy can be heard in Art Blakey and the Jazz Messengers, *Album of the Year.*[10]

Wynton Marsalis has created a certain amount of controversy as he speaks out for the acceptance of jazz as America's ''classical music.'' He has effectively worked for jazz's place in such traditional strongholds of western Europe's classical music as the Lincoln Center in New York. However, in his quest to legitimize jazz, he also blasts other jazz styles that do not fit his mainstream definition. His definition of jazz is couched in authenticity but is just another viewpoint crusading for its own reshaping of the jazz legacy. As our interest in jazz shifts from stylistic period to stylistic period, we tend to look back to find new heroes among those that preceded us. The early players cannot change, only our understanding of them changes. It is often tempting to cast their efforts in a light that supports our own views of how jazz took shape.

---

[10]Art Blakey and the Jazz Messengers, *Album of the Year,* Timeless SJP155.

Wynton Marsalis considers fusion jazz, although quite popular and claiming a new jazz audience, to be suspect as a jazz style. The legitimization he seems to offer jazz appears to be welcomed by the traditional classical music audience. Marsalis certainly has helped this legitimization by his stellar classical trumpet playing. However, this victorious entrance into the classical music world may require a compromise in other traditional jazz values, values that have always tolerated musical fusions. A consistent hold to classical jazz values may rob future jazz evolution of its energy. It also may tip bop, which has traditionally been representative of the oral tradition in jazz, toward classical European expectations. Jazz has traditionally been rough, malleable, and open-ended. The move toward classical status works against these characteristics because it is more exclusive than inclusive of new jazz expressions.

---

## POPULAR JAZZ

Harry Connick, Jr. presents another side of the traditional jazz crusade. He is a New Orleans pianist/vocalist/composer who has gained popularity rapidly. His popularity, like Wynton Marsalis's, can frustrate the traditional jazz musician who has struggled to gain recognition during a long career. Connick is well-versed in many of the traditional jazz styles and can perform them quite well. However, his acceptance into the jazz community is not yet confirmed. His performance style is not typical of the jazz mainstream, but the music he plays and sings is. His popularity presents an obstacle to his acceptance as a central jazz figure. As he matured, his interest moved from contemporary rock and jazz more and more to the classic piano players of jazz and the styles associated with them. As a singer, he is often compared to Frank Sinatra. His success with the soundtrack for the movie *When Harry Met Sally* not only launched his career at the age of twenty-one but gave a remarkable boost to the public's interest in neoclassical jazz. The soundtrack album features Connick doing the standard love songs sung by the original artists in the movie.[11] Like the Marsalis family, Connick sees his own role in the revival of traditional jazz. ''But jazz is becoming popular again! Wynton started it, and Branford, and I'm continuing it.''[12] These neoclassical adherents, like those in the hard bop traditions, see their music as a return to the real essence of jazz, revitalized and entertaining. ''In the '40s and '50s, jazz musicians entertained. In the '60s, rock & roll entertained and jazz stopped entertaining. In the '70s, jazz got very

---

[11]Harry Connick, Jr., *When Harry Met Sally,* Columbia CK 45319.
[12]Harry Connick, Jr., *Down Beat* (March 1990):18.

obscure. In the '80s, jazz was dead and rock was #1. Jazz was absolutely nothing until Wynton Marsalis came along and pretty much brought it out of obscurity."[13]

## SUMMARY

The balance between the western European and African-American musical influences continues to be played out today. However, the current consensus that defines the mainstream traces the jazz legacy through the oral rather than the compositional line of performers. This legacy offers new players of jazz a framework in which their own work will be judged. The emergence of a mainstream signals the further maturation of jazz as an art form. Those performers that define the mainstream historically make up the jazz canon that, in turn, guides its future.

It was during the bop period that the crystallization of this jazz canon began to take place. The bop playing style captured the essence of jazz practice as it first emerged from the cultural melting pot of New Orleans. The compositional stirrings of players like Jelly Roll Morton who revered his French heritage and the migration of the African Americans from the plantation to the city first set up the balance between the oral and compositional traditions that shaped jazz's development. In a very grand way, each of the jazz periods can be viewed as shifts in the balance between these two musical heritages.

In the 1990s as jazz has established itself as America's art form, it has begun to take on attributes very similar to other art forms, such as classical music and visual arts. The audience of mainstream jazz is more knowledgeable of the jazz canon than past audiences, which followed the more fashionable and popular expressions of early jazz. With this more educated audience comes a smaller elite support group for the preservation of the art itself. The introduction of jazz into the 1991 Lincoln Center program schedule demonstrates jazz's newfound art status. This assimilation into the art culture of America has put out a call for repertory jazz, that is, historical jazz works that define the jazz canon.

Calls for repertory jazz are certainly signals that the history of the art form has become important to its audience. However, a potential dilemma exists with such an approach for the preservation of jazz. Jazz has been characterized by an oral repertoire, as well as a written one. The written one is certainly easier to recreate for concert purposes, a fact that could restrict many of the performance efforts to notated compositions. If this is the case, the rich oral tradition defined

[13]Harry Connick, Jr., *Down Beat* (March 1990):18.

more by players than compositions and by which the current main-stream of jazz is defined, might be overlooked in favor of the compositions of jazz. Pushed to a hypothetical conclusion, the jazz canon might again shift to reflect predominantly the repertory concert material and, in turn, the mainstream of jazz be redefined. Current historical heroes could recede and new heroes emerge as our historical understanding of jazz shifts from the oral to the compositional traditions. Despite the permanence of history, our understanding of it is fluid. The jazz canon is still young and subject to change. As our cultural values shift, so does our understanding of our history. For now, the jazz mainstream is defined more by the history of performance than the history of composition, although both forces still work as partners in the shaping of our understanding of jazz.

*The Birth of the Cool.* Capitol Records N 16168.

SUGGESTED
LISTENING

Blakey, Art, and Wynton Marsalis and the Jazz Messengers. *Album of the Year.* Timeless SJP 155.

Connick, Harry, Jr. *Lofty's Roach Souffle.* Columbia Records CK 46223.

Connick, Harry, Jr. *When Harry Met Sally.* Columbia Records CK 45319.

Davis, Miles, and Gil Evans. ''Summertime.'' Smithsonian G/7 (cd IV/12).

Griffin, Johnny. ''Wade in the Water.'' *The Soul of Jazz.* Riverside Records S-5.

*Horace Silver and the Jazz Messengers.* Blue Note Records BLP 1518.

Horace Silver Quintet. ''Stop Time.'' *Bebop.* New World Records NW 271.

The Jazz Brothers. ''Something Different.'' *The Soul of Jazz.* Riverside Records S-5.

*Jimmy Smith's Greatest Hits.* Blue Note Records BST 89901.

*Les McCann Plays the Truth.* Pacific Jazz Records PJ 2.

Mancini, Henry. *Pink Panther.* RCA CD 2795-2-R.

Marsalis, Wynton. ''E.T.A.'' *Marsalis Standard Time,* Vol. 1. Columbia/CBS Records FC 37574.

Silver, Horace. *Blowing the Blues Away.* Blue Note Records 4017.

Silver, Horace. *Song For My Father.* Blue Note Records 4185.

Silver, Horace, and Art Blakey. *A Night At Birdland.* Blue Note Records 1521.

# CHAPTER 11

## *Classical/Jazz Distinctions*

| | |
|---|---|
| *1890–1917* | Ragtime very popular |
| *1924* | "Rhapsody in Blue" first performed |
| *1932–1942* | Swing bands predominate |
| *1949* | *Birth of the Cool* album recorded |
| *1949–1955* | Cool jazz emerges |
| *1952–1955* | Sauter-Finegan Orchestra in operation |
| *1959* | Dave Brubeck recorded "Take Five" |
| *1958–1960* | Important Miles Davis/Gil Evans recordings |
| *Late 1950s– Early 1960s* | Third stream emerges |
| *1960* | Modern Jazz Quartet recorded "Django" |
| *1960* | Ornette Coleman recorded *Free Jazz* |
| *1963* | John Coltrane recorded *Alabama* |
| *1965* | John Coltrane recorded *A Love Supreme* |
| *1969* | Ornette Coleman recorded *At the Golden Circle* |

In contrast to the historical thread that traces the developing mainstream of jazz, a counterbalancing thread weaves through many of the jazz art periods, reflecting the cultural milieu in which jazz developed and came to fruition as an art form. As we have seen from chapter 5, the merging of the African-American and western European musical influences created the crucible in which jazz was forged. The mainstream of jazz reflects the oral tradition more typical of the African-American culture, while much of the musical materials and compositional concerns came from the western European culture. At times in the history of jazz, the balance between these forces shifted to create a style that temporarily reflected a dominance of one over the other.

This chapter, in contrast to chapter 10, looks at those times in jazz history that shifted toward the influences of western Europe and the classical music tradition. One part of this historical thread was traced in chapter 7 which dealt with the history of large ensemble composition before and during the Big Band era. That period was a clear expression of jazz's tilt toward the classical compositional model, but it was not the first, nor was it the last.

## RAGTIME AND THE CLASSICAL MODEL

Just as jazz was beginning to appear on the horizon, ragtime music was in full swing. Because this music was notated, it is sometimes considered separately outside of the jazz tradition and considered a participating member of the prejazz style. However, it is one of the first clear expressions of fusion of the two dominant and seminal musical streams of jazz. The ragtime name came from the "ragged" manner in which the music was performed. While the musical structure was fixed and repeated from piece to piece, the stylized performance gave it enough of a new sound that it garnered its own name.

The tradition of notated music belongs mostly to the western European tradition. The formal structure of a rag also signals a compositional priority typical of the classical music tradition. The early jazz influence can be found in the highly syncopated rhythms found in rags and the ragged performance that essentially cheated the strictly notated rhythms. This ragged performance is still prevalent in notated jazz. Jazz standards and even fully-composed arrangements for jazz ensembles when written in a swing 4/4 are meant to be "cheated" to resemble what might be more closely called 12/8. One might argue that classical music also cheats its notation when the final interpretation is placed on a composition; it certainly is a matter of degree. However, jazz certainly seems to take the most liberties, liberties that signal a strong oral tradition at work even though it rides on a classical form.

The later term of *third stream* was used to describe the fusion of the two dominant music streams in America at that time, classical and jazz. Such an argument tends to place jazz as an independently developing music that was originally free from the classical music tradition until it began to fuse with it in the 1950s. Rather than seeing jazz as a balance between western European and African-American music traditions, one would have to consider jazz only an African-American music and overlook such musical influences as ragtime.

Indeed, early orchestras like those led by James Reese Europe demonstrate the early fusion of classical music with the emerging jazz idiom.

The controversy that surrounds ragtime as a jazz expression might be rooted in this one-sided view of jazz's inception. This controversy still is not resolved. We have since had composers that fall into the crack between classical and jazz, an example being George Gershwin with compositions like "Rhapsody in Blue." This piece is not commonly considered a part of the later third stream effort yet has clearly discernable jazz stylizations. Because its compositional structure is so defined, it seems to leave little, if any, room for jazz stylizations. However, the musical material, like that of the rag, borrows jazz idioms like syncopation but is bound to a fixed structural form more typical of classical music.

---

## THE DEVELOPING BIG BANDS

As jazz moved from the small groups of Dixieland to the larger more sectionalized groups that led to the Big Band era, the musical approach again tipped in favor of the western European model. Because that transition was gradual, the role of the soloist was never lost. However, rather than soloing continually to contribute to an ensemble's musical fabric, the soloist became a featured element of an otherwise fully-notated arrangement or composition. Chapter 7 covers this development in depth.

As the bands became more and more formalized, the featured soloist lost ground to the larger ensemble sections in the arrangements. The arrangers themselves became featured members of their musical organizations. We remember the names of Jelly Roll Morton, Fletcher Henderson, Don Redman, Benny Carter, and Duke Ellington for their writing as much as their playing. Notated writing skills began to push hard against the counterbalancing extemporaneous activities that hold the jazz definition together.

During the Swing era, most bands even played some adaptation of classical selections. On Glenn Miller's first important recording session, he recorded Debussy's *Reverie*. Tchaikovsky was listed on the record charts with such beautiful melodies as the theme from *Romeo and Juliet*, a popular selection called "Our Love." Tchaikovsky's *Piano Concerto* became popular as "Tonight We Love." Glenn Miller also recorded Beethoven's "Moonlight Sonata."

The Sauter-Finegan Orchestra was a direct attempt to bridge the gap between jazz and classical music. The group was originally organized strictly as a recording orchestra and was strongly influenced by the impressionistic music of Debussy and Ravel. Eddie Sauter was as well-known an arranger for the Benny Goodman Orchestra as Bill Finegan was for the Glenn Miller Orchestra. Their most ambitious effort was the Lieberman work (Rolph Lieberman's *Concerto for Jazz Band and Symphony Orchestra*). It was extremely well-received when performed and recorded with the Chicago Symphony Orchestra.

These pre-third stream experiments were carried even further by classical composer Igor Stravinsky who scored an original composition, ''Ebony Concerto,'' for the Woody Herman Orchestra. Although these efforts were accepted well by the followers of the bands, they have not claimed a significant role as forerunners of what was to be called third stream.

## COOL

In many ways, cool was a jazz period that reflected the compositional practice of western European art music. Much of the music was arrangement based, and issues of orchestration and musical texture became compositional concerns. This is certainly not a new notion for jazz composers, Ellington being a clear example. During the Cool era, an intellectual and often compositional approach toward jazz was a dominant force. As we saw in chapter 3, cool offered a response to the hot jazz of bop. The energetic performance efforts of bop performers were replaced by subtleties in both the arrangements and the playing style.

André Hodeir outlined three principles that define the cool style:

''First, a sonority very different from the one adopted by earlier schools; second, a special type of phrase; and finally, an orchestral conception that . . . is not its least interesting element.''[1]

The first principle refers to the more classical tone used by the players. A softer attack, a move away from the extreme registers of the instrument, and very little vibrato, all more typical of the classical playing style, characterized the cool sound. The phrasing of cool also did not have the angularity more typical of bop, and the use of syncopation and fast tempos was relaxed. The final principle Hodeir lists is most pertinent to the subject of this chapter. Cool compositions did not restrict their formal structures to the standard twelve-, sixteen-, or thirty-two-bar chorus structure preferred by the bop players. More extended forms were used that reflected a higher level of complexity.

---

[1]André Hodeir, *Jazz: Its Evolution and Essence* (New York: Gove Press, 1956), 118.

## **Gil Evans**

| | |
|---|---|
| *1912* | Evans was born in Toronto, Canada, on May 13. |
| *1943–1946* | He enlisted in the U.S. army. |
| *1941–1948* | He arranged for the Claude Thornhill Orchestra. |
| *1949* | He orchestrated "Boplicity" and "Moondreams" for the *Birth of the Cool* album. |
| *1952* | Evans began playing piano professionally. |
| *1957* | He was reunited with Miles Davis on *Miles Ahead, Porgy and Bess* in 1959, and *Sketches of Spain* in 1960. |
| *1958* | He became a recording bandleader in his own right. |
| *1960s–1980s* | He was involved primarily in composing for recordings and films. |
| *1992* | Evans died in New York City. |

"Boplicity" listening guide can be found in chapter 3.

Cool also included more meters than the standard 2/4 and 4/4 time signatures. 3/4, 5/4, and even 9/4 meters were explored by composer/performers like Dave Brubeck.[2]

During this period, the range of suitable jazz instruments was expanded to include those used more often in the classical music world. The flute became important as a jazz instrument, as did the French horn, oboe, and cello. Notable flute players include Paul Horn, Buddy Collette, Herbie Mann, Bud Shank, and Frank Wess. The French horn players were fewer in number and included Willie Ruff, Johnny Graas, Junior Collins, and Julius Watkins. The double-reed instruments only began to claim jazz status with players like Bob Cooper who played oboe while with the Stan Kenton band. However, it was not until the later third stream and avant-garde periods that the double reeds became more prominent. Although the flügelhorn is not commonly considered a classical instrument, it also gained exposure during the cool period and underscores that style's concern with softer and more mellow sounds.

---

[2]Dave Brubeck Quartet, "Take Five," *Time Out,* Columbia Records CL-1397.

Perhaps the exaggerated movement of bop away from the composition-based music of the big bands triggered an equally dramatic response in the style of cool. Compositional concerns had certainly returned. However, they were to recede temporarily until they again surfaced during the 1960s with third stream jazz.

## THIRD STREAM

There was a period in the late 1950s and early 1960s when a conscious effort was made by many jazz composers to blend the jazz and classical musical streams to form a new third stream. As we have seen, this blend is not new to jazz. In fact, jazz's existence is dependent on that blend. It was only during this period that the fusion of the two music traditions was undertaken as a conscious approach to jazz. The term *third stream* appears almost exclusively in jazz histories rather than histories of Western art music. Third stream is, therefore, a jazz term that describes the importation of classical music models into the working arena of jazz performance rather than an exportation of jazz to the classical model.

Third stream jazz can be seen as an extension of the cool compositional style and linked to Gunther Schuller, who participated with Miles Davis on the *Birth of the Cool* album. The phrase third stream is usually attributed to Schuller, although John S. Wilson is also credited with inventing it. Third stream jazz shares both the instrumental sound and the instrumental variety first employed during the Cool era. The jazz musicians play their instruments in a manner closely resembling the technique used by symphonic players, a technique that employs a precise tonal attack and a minimum of vibrato. Third stream, also like cool, introduces more exotic and typically classical instruments, such as the French horn, oboe, bassoon, and cello.

The harmonies used in third stream music are similar to those associated with contemporary jazz; however, musical forms such as the fugue, canon, theme and variations, and other extended types were borrowed from classical music.[3] The use of these forms by third stream composers resulted in a return to a more polyphonic type of composition. Classical music markedly differs from jazz in its use of meter and rhythmic pulse. Although present in both, jazz has always given it great prominence. Third stream jazz often uses a more classical notion of rhythm, which gives more weight to the melodic and harmonic activity than to a strong rhythmic pulse. For this reason, some contend that third stream music cannot be considered jazz.[4]

[3]Harold Shapero, "On Green Mountain," *Modern Jazz Concert,* Columbia Records WL 127.
[4]Gunther Schuller, "Transformation," *Modern Jazz Concert,* Columbia Records WL 127.

Robert Freedman's "An Interlude" is an example of a third stream composition that uses classical models of polytonal and polymodal techniques.[5] Polytonal and polymodal compositions use more than one tonal center at a time. Polymodal music uses two modes (major and minor) with the same tonic, or two forms of the same chord simultaneously. Such concerns as these are strictly theoretical in nature and certainly more typical of the classical music tradition than that of jazz, even if one considers the harmonic complexity typical of the bop period.

Although third stream was primarily a concern of jazz musicians, there were instances of the classical music world embracing jazz works for performance by symphony orchestras, for example, Brubeck's "Dialogues for Jazz Combo and Symphony Orchestra,"[6] Rolph Lieberman's "Concerto for Jazz Band and Symphony Orchestra," and John Graas's "Jazz Symphony No. 1." Such compositions fall into two groups:

1. Compositions that contain jazz elements intended for performance by large symphonic orchestras using traditional instrumentation
2. Concerto grosso approaches that place a small jazz group of seven or eight players within a large symphony orchestra

The first group offers a better chance to blend jazz and classical approaches with respect to compositional practice but can overlook the extemporaneous contributions of jazz. The second group tends to contrast the two styles. This allows extemporaneous areas but can still fall short of an effective blend of the two approaches. John Lewis's "Sketch" is an example of a third stream composition that combines the Modern Jazz Quartet and the Beaux Arts String Quartet.[7] During this performance, neither of the two groups seems to lose its identities, but an integrated feeling is still created. A more contemporary example that borrows the string quartet format from classical music and combines it with a traditional jazz ensemble is Max Roaches' double quartet which is comprised of a string quartet and a jazz quartet.

---

[5]Robert Freedman, "An Interlude," *Jazz in the Classroom,* Berklee Records BLPIA.
[6]The New York Philharmonic Orchestra with the Dave Brubeck Quartet, conducted by Leonard Bernstein, *Bernstein Plays Brubeck Plays Bernstein,* Columbia Records CL 1466.
[7]The Modern Jazz Quartet, *Third Stream Music,* Atlantic Records 1345.

# The Modern Jazz Quartet
## "Django"
### Prestige Records OJCCD-057-2

Milt Jackson, vibes; John Lewis, piano; Percy Heath, bass; Kenny Clarke, drums. This composition is named in memory of the French gypsy guitarist, Django Reinhardt, who died in 1953. Compare this recording with the one in the Smithsonian Collection (Listening Guide in chapter 3). This song can also be found on the CD collection that accompanies *Jazz*, Tanner, Megill, Gerow, 7 ed., A222296 and A22298.

0:00   Section A: Piano and vibraphone statement of the theme on which the work is based. The first two measures offer the motive that generates the entire theme and piece. See notation below.

0:14   Second four-bar phrase that answers the first. It still uses the same motive.

0:26   Third four-bar phrase extends the second and leads to the second part of the opening theme, which is itself derived from the first part used in these three opening phrases.

0:39   Section B: Second section of the opening theme. The new motive is just three notes shared between bass, piano, and vibes.

0:52   Concluding four bars of this second section, which slows down before solos begin

1:06   Section A: Vibe solo. Two choruses of ABA. Tempo picks up with a light swing feel. Listen for the light comping in the piano behind the solo for twelve bars.

1:33   Section B: Motivic use of the theme in vibe solo as a setup to the next chorus for eight bars

1:50   Section A: Return to swing feel to close the first chorus

1:59   Motivic bass line under the soloist

2:16   Section A: Second chorus follows the same formal design as the first. Return to straight time (first of two six-bar phrases).

2:29   Second six-bar phrase to complete the twelve-bar section

2:42   Section B: Middle phrase of the second chorus for eight bars

2:59   Section A: Return to swing feel for final twelve bars of the second chorus. Motivic bass line reappears.

3:25    A double speed statement (diminution) of the second part of the opening theme is used as an interlude between solos.

3:34    Section A: Piano solo begins. The same formal structure used for the vibe solo is followed for the piano solo—two choruses of ABA.

4:00    Section B: Listen for repeated notes in bass.

4:17    Section A: Same bass motive as used under solo

4:43    Section A: Of second chorus

5:10    Section B: Same repeated notes in bass

5:27    Section A: Last twelve bars with bass motive underneath

5:53    Opening theme is repeated at the same tempo as beginning.

6:30    Second section of opening (now closing) theme

7:00    Slows down and ends

DJANGO by John Lewis. Copyright © 1955, and renewal © 1983, by MJQ Music, Inc. All Rights Reserved. Used by Permission.

The Modern Jazz Quartet during the late 1950s was a pivotal group between cool and third stream. John Lewis's classical training can be seen in the composed nature of the ensemble passages and the formal compositional structures used. His use of Renaissance brass sounds and his own characteristic improvisatory style offers yet another third stream blend in his composition "Piazza Navonna."[8] In a manner similar to Lewis's "Sketch," Chuck Mangione has also merged his jazz quintet with a symphony orchestra as well as a full choir on the album *Land of Make Believe*.[9]

The Stan Kenton orchestra showcased several third stream compositions. William Russo's compositions for this orchestra were often bold and adventuresome in their blend of the classical, avant-garde, and jazz elements.[10]

Yet another approach to third stream music is the actual use of classically composed music in a larger jazz work or the complete statement of a classical work with jazz interpretation. The Swingle Singers used many of Bach's pieces, and Hubert Laws effectively recorded Stravinsky's "Rite of Spring."[11]

Although third stream jazz was not a strong force after the 1960s, the balance toward the classical music model was not over for jazz. A new and very powerful force, rock and roll, was beginning to exert a strong influence on jazz that overshadowed that of the classical model. However, the classical music tradition will again interact with that of jazz as the avant-garde school of jazz emerges.

## AVANT-GARDE AND THE FREE SCHOOL

Jazz has a loosely defined area of activity referred to as "free jazz," originally coined and centered on the seminal work of Ornette Coleman. His activity has spawned a school of players that operate on a short but delineated tradition since the 1960s. Other jazz players contributed to this tradition as well and came more directly out of the conventionalized ranks of jazz players, such as Monk, Mingus, Coltrane, and Taylor.

There is also a consensus that a similar line of music, allied with the "classical" music world, exists. Activity in this line surged during the 1950s–1960s and can be seen in the work of such individuals as John Cage and Pauline Oliveras. Caught in the overlap of these

[8]John Lewis, "Piazza Navonna," New World Records NW 216.
[9]Chuck Mangione, *Land of Make Believe,* Mercury Records SRM 1 684.
[10]William Russo, "Mirage" and "Eldon Heath," New World Records NW 216.
[11]Hubert Laws, "Rite of Spring," CTI Records 6012.

## William Russo
## "Eldon Heath"
## New World Records NW 216

0:00   Brass counterpoint lines in a free-flowing meter; vague tonal area

0:28   Transition melodic figures in brass

0:45   Sax/brass ostinato, more metric

1:03   Trombone solo with ostinato background

1:40   Soft and increasingly loud low brass punches; fading ostinato

2:07   Cymbal roll leading to rhythm section and brass in tempo with jazz phrasing and accents

2:36   Saxophone solo with very light rhythm; long tone chordal support in other instruments; muted trumpets

3:09   Strong brass chords

3:15   Trombone solo returns

3:22   Sax and brass ostinato returns

3:47   End

---

two separate but similar worlds, we find composers/performers, such as Anthony Braxton and George Lewis, that demonstrate the attributes and attitudes shared by the two traditions.

Although it is tempting to establish one of the traditions as the leader in this movement toward freedom, it is more likely that both musical traditions were responding to the general opening up of society that took place in the 1960s. Of interest to us in this chapter is the process used by the avant-garde jazz performers/composers as they pushed for more and more freedom in their work. As we have seen throughout this chapter, jazz has struck a careful balance between a compositional tradition and an oral performance tradition. The avant-garde school has within it a microcosm of that same balance.

Although the players/composers who have defined "free jazz" end up sharing the same aesthetic space, they came to it from both

## Charles Mingus

The range of Charles Mingus's musicianship was very apparent when he played bass as he included ostinato figures, pedal points, and double stops even while playing accompaniment for other players. When Mingus soloed, you were aware that he was also an outstanding contemporary composer. He explored myriad jazz styles and directions, everything from gospel-oriented music to free jazz. Charles Mingus approached his composition and performance with an intensity seldom matched in jazz. His emotional style spanned the gap between composition and improvisation. To maintain the intensity and accuracy of his ideas he would sometimes recite the compositions to the group rather than limit them by writing them down. Several times he would even stop performances to correct compositional ideas, or even scold the audience for not listening. His constant experimentation seldom placed him in the mainstream of jazz evolution, but it exerted a constant influence on it.

He attempted to channel the creative energies of the players into a unified statement. While he relied on the individual strengths of the players, he also expected them to work toward a common emotional statement during a performance. This approach differs from the traditional bop approach which encouraged players to seek very individual statements during their improvisations.

the oral and compositional traditions. By definition, avant-garde, means to stand against the norm. If we hold to this definition strictly, we will find two lines of players during this period, one that is clearly avant-garde and another whose natural development brought them to the arena of free jazz. The former group of players required a clear and conscious statement that new, nontraditional directions in jazz should be pursued, while the latter group of players unconsciously found themselves outside of normal practice because of their musical development.

Although their approaches are different, they share a common goal, a search for musical freedom. In general, those players that strike an avant-garde posture to jazz, such as Coleman, Taylor, and Braxton, tend to support their work with compositional arguments. Such players as Coltrane, Dolphy, and Cherry that grew into freer expressions tend to be more rooted in the oral tradition of jazz. Such a broad generalization breaks down quickly when the real personalities are discussed, because all players represent unique blends of both

By 1966, Mingus had established himself as one of the great soloists, leaders, and innovators of American music. He was in constant demand at all international festivals, although ill health greatly hampered his activities from the 1960s on. However, he did tour Europe in 1972 and 1975.

| | |
|---|---|
| *1922* | Mingus was born in Nogales, Arizona. |
| *1941–1943* | He played with Louis Armstrong. |
| *1946–1948* | He played with Lionel Hampton. |
| *1950–1951* | He played with the Red Norvo Trio. |
| *1952–1953* | He played with the Billy Taylor Trio. |
| *1952* | Mingus started his own record company called Debut. |
| *Mid 1950s* | He established himself as a prominent combo leader. |
| *1959–1960* | Mingus' "Jazz Workshop" appeared regularly in New York City. |
| *1960s* | He played at the Five Spot, Half Note, and other New York clubs. |
| *1964* | He toured Europe. |
| *1974* | He was presented at Carnegie Hall. |
| *1979* | Mingus died. |

compositional and oral approaches. However, this distinction helps us better understand the formative influence of these two traditions on each of the players.

## JOHN COLTRANE

Players that came to free jazz through the oral tradition of performance often began their work in more traditional settings and pushed the development of their styles until they strained the very descriptors of traditional jazz performance. Although Ornette Coleman is certainly the first free jazz figure to come to mind, it is John Coltrane that best demonstrates this slow transition to individual freedom. Rather than declare an independence from traditional form and harmonic practice as Coleman did, Coltrane extended the traditional harmonic chords until they no longer functioned tonally. The resulting atonal medium offered Coltrane a free environment to develop his melodic ideas.

*John Coltrane*

Michael Ochs Archives/
Venice, CA

# John Coltrane

**S**axophonist John Coltrane combined great emotion with excellent musicianship and discipline with freedom. Musicians disagree about other contemporary players, such as Ornette Coleman, but there were few disagreements about John Coltrane. He was a fine saxophone player (tenor and soprano) in every sense. He produced a large, dark, lush sound balanced with apparent drive. He advanced jazz improvisation harmonically through long excursions into the higher harmonics.

*1926*  Coltrane was born in Hamlet, North Carolina, on September 22.

*1955*  He joined the Miles Davis Quintet.

*1957*  He recorded *Blue Train* album.

*1959*  Coltrane recorded *Kind of Blue* album with Miles Davis.

*1959*  He recorded *Giant Steps* album.

*1963*  Coltrane's *Alabama* album is a reaction to tension in the South.

*1964*  He recorded *A Love Supreme.*

*1966*  He toured Japan to capacity crowds.

*1967*  Coltrane died of stomach ailments on July 17.

Coltrane used the modal jazz approach as a springboard for his characteristic melodic extensions. His melodies were often based on modes played over slow-moving harmonies. Rather than using the lower notes of a chord (i.e., root, third, or fifth), Coltrane centered his melodies on higher harmonics, such as the ninth, eleventh, and thirteenth. The result was a more complex harmonic sound that could, when pushed harder, develop into atonal passages characteristic of free form jazz. The slow-moving harmonies of modal jazz actually contained the seeds of atonality because they fostered a melodic approach to improvisation and allowed time for the player to explore more complex harmonic extensions. Coltrane uses this modal jazz approach on his recording of ''Alabama.'' Notice the relationship of his melody to the harmonic underpinning. He is able to consistently maintain an extended distance from the basic harmony. The opening and closing statements use only one chord over which Coltrane plays a modal melodic line. Coltrane completes his transition toward free

## John Coltrane
### ''A Love Supreme—Part I—Acknowledgement''
### Impulse Records A 77

John Coltrane, tenor sax; McCoy Tyner, piano; Jimmy Garrison, bass; Elvin Jones, drums.

:00  Saxophone fanfare with cymbal accompaniment

:30  Melody of four notes played by bass

:38  Drums start making time.

:46  Piano enters.

1:02  Sax enters with new melodic material (still motivic in nature); piano generally keeps two-note movement taken from opening bass motive as the comping pattern.

1:29  Example of ascending and descending chromatic chord patterns used by the piano; listen for constant motivic variation by the saxophonist.

2:01  Bass begins to move toward four-beat patterns instead of variations of the motive; loose references to the motive are maintained most of the time and passed between the various players.

3:08  Example of bass four-beat pattern that still reflects motive

4:05  Example of soloists using short fragmented statements of the motive

4:45  A return to the simple melodic motive, continually repeated

5:53  Players sing to motive, ''A Love Supreme.''

6:23  Motive moves down a step.

6:37  Saxophone drops out and ensemble begins to fade.

6:53  Piano drops out, only bass and drums remain.

7:07  Only bass remains, playing the motive.

7:32  End

form in such performances as ''Manifestations'' in which his later quartet operates in a very free interchange.[12] Even with the freedom allowed the players, Coltrane's guiding influence can be heard. The long but disjunct melodic lines, frozen harmonic centers, and emotional intensity characterize the later Coltrane performances.

ORNETTE
COLEMAN

Saxophonist Ornette Coleman represents a more dramatic break with jazz's traditional past. Both his rhetoric and his playing spoke of a new exploration of music free from the traditional strictures of jazz. He refused to comply with restrictions normally imposed by rhythm and meter, chord progressions, or melodic continuity as he searched for freedom to play any thought that occurs to him at any time, regardless of context.

In this regard, he paralleled those conceptual composers in the classical music tradition. His work, although supported by his ''harmolodic'' theory, is still strongly performance driven. Coleman is a hybrid between such traditionally-based avant-garde members as Coltrane and the later more classical and such theoretically-based performers as Anthony Braxton.

Even in the landmark recording of *Free Jazz* Coleman does not abandon all jazz trappings. The rhythmic underpinning is steady throughout the performance, and Coleman tends to preserve a certain allegiance to ''time'' in most of his performances. His innovations are more centered in melodic and harmonic directions. His rhythmic innovations result from the rhythmic excursions his melodic activity takes and how those excursions align with the underlying rhythmic setting.

SUN RA

Like most figures in free jazz, Sun Ra offered his own unique balance of tradition and avant-garde practice. He came out of Chicago, which is an ongoing center for avant-garde jazz. His background includes working as a pianist/arranger for the Fletcher Henderson band. Even at the end of his career his performances often began with arrangements written for that band.

While quite traditional in this respect, he also represented one of the most extreme avant-garde personalities in all of jazz. His own work began in 1953 when he assembled his own quartet, later expanded into a big band called Arkestra. His use of a large ensemble

---

[12]John Coltrane, *The Best of John Coltrane, His Greatest Years,* Impulse Records AS 9223 2.

### Ornette Coleman Trio
### "Faces and Places"
### Blue Note 84224 2

Ornette Coleman, alto saxophone; David Izenzon, bass; Charles Moffet, drums.

As you listen to the recording, notice the energy curve at work in this performance. Throughout the piece, the trio moves between very clear and hard driving sections, referred to as straight time. Contrasted with these sections are sections that have less metric focus. The bass generally maintains a straight four-beat pattern, but the drums use accents that sometimes conflict with the meter. As Coleman moves in and out of time in his solo, he is sometimes supported by a similar move in the drums and at other times is supported by a clear meter. Also listen for how Coleman's solo strikes varying amounts of independence from the harmonic areas implied by the bass. This performance shows the trio's ability to control both the traditional jazz language, as well as move "outside" that language as they shape their energy curve.

| | |
|---|---|
| :00 | Saxophone introduction with intermittent time in bass and drums |
| :18 | Short use of time in the drums but not yet in the bass |
| :26 | Time is established under saxophone solo. |
| :33 | Bass uses a repeating pattern establishing an "ostinato" feel with straight time in drums (with accents). |
| :47 | Bass walks. |
| 1:05 | Melodic variation shifts whole motive chromatically each statement |
| 1:32 | Drums fall into a straight time feeling with walking bass pattern. |
| 1:55 | Backup again moves away from straight time, creating a contrast for the harder swinging straight time areas. |
| 2:13 | Walking feeling as time returns |
| 2:31 | Drummer syncopates meter with cross accents. |
| 2:42 | Straight time returns. |
| 2:49 | Accents in drums |
| 3:13 | Straight time returns. |

*continued*

*continued*

| | |
|---|---|
| 3:30 | Cross accents in saxophone |
| 3:50 | Coleman uses more traditional melodic language here. |
| 4:01 | Coleman begins moving further from the harmonic area established by the bass. He also begins moving at an accelerated pace. His solo at this point has moved to a higher energy level which he began to set up during the first part of the solo. |
| 4:20 | Some vocalization? |
| 4:35 | Double-time saxophone solo leading to more fragmented solo lines |
| 5:10 | Listen for the exchange of rhythmic ideas between the saxophone and the drums. |
| 5:20 | Chromatically shifting lines which are more independent harmonically |
| 5:30 | Rhythmic and harmonic independence in the saxophone |
| 5:55 | Short double-time saxophone section |
| 6:10 | Motivic exchange between saxophone and drums |
| 6:40 | Rhythmic line passed from Coleman to drums, steady fast tempo maintained by drums (with accents) and bass |
| 6:55 | Rhythmic and metric cross accents to set up return to time |
| 7:05 | Straight time |
| 7:15 | Listen for rhythmic exchange between the saxophone and drums. |
| 7:35 | Cross accents in drums setting up drum solo and bringing the saxophone solo to a climax |
| 8:00 | Return to time and drum solo begins |
| 9:05 | Coleman enters with a double-time saxophone break followed by a fast metric support. Saxophone motivic lines even more independent of the harmonic area suggested by the bass. Drumming also gradually becomes more accented. |
| 9:48 | Double-time melodic lines |
| 10:01 | Half-time melody. Melodic lines become more chromatic and developmental. |
| 10:39 | Solo breaks with drum responses. Melodic material is the same as the beginning. |
| 11:08 | End |

## Ornette Coleman

**S**axophonist Ornette Coleman has been one of the most controversial free jazz players. Critics who have examined his work fall into two groups. One group is composed of staunch admirers, while the other group views his work as unworthy of any consideration. The adverse opinions were due to Coleman's apparent disregard for tradition. It has been said that he desires the freedom to play anything that occurs to him at any time. Regardless of this thinking, Coleman is very melody oriented, but he phrases with no obligation to pulse. In the late 1980s, Coleman continued to push into new theoretical and philosophical areas with his proposed "harmolodic-theory." His pursuit of such new ideas is a trademark of his continuing career.

*Ornette Coleman*
Michael Ochs Archives/
Venice, CA

*1930*    Coleman was born in Fort Worth, Texas.
*1958*    He recorded first album, *Tomorrow Is the Question* in Los Angeles.
*1959*    He came to New York City and performed at the Five Spot.
*1960*    He recorded the landmark album *Free Jazz* with double quartet.
*1966*    He recorded *At the Golden Circle*. He continued to perform in concert and record with groups under his leadership until the 1980s.
*1986*    He recorded *Song X* with Pat Metheny. This album was one of a series of collaborations with Pat Metheny and was a focal point for Coleman's "harmolodic-theory."
*1990s*    He continues to perform and record.

while maintaining an allegiance to collective improvisation required a type of musical coordination that has seldom been rivaled in jazz. His success here was based on the nature of his compositional process, a process that allowed the musical structure to emerge as a result of the extraordinary musical communication established among his players. Sun Ra struck an effective and unique balance between the preconceived compositional approach typical of notated western European music and the collective compositional practice typical of an oral tradition. Arrangements were not written but developed orally through careful rehearsal. The resulting performance was then free to move within the musical structure as the group improvisation demanded. One would surmise that the group rehearsed musical communication as much, if not more, than any specific arrangements. Large ensembles normally require fixed arrangements to coordinate all the players. However, the established communication process among the ''Arkestra'' players, fostered the emergence of complex compositional structures during the performance itself. Sun Ra's effectiveness as a compositional leader can be heard on *Heliocentric Worlds of Sun Ra,* (Vols. 1 and 2).[13]

## CECIL TAYLOR

Unlike Coleman, who had an extensive blues background, pianist Cecil Taylor came more directly to the free jazz arena with a compositional intent. He can be regarded as an avant-garde expression of third stream. He brings to jazz a conservatory background with an interest in compositional structures. Most of his music can be heard as either classical or jazz.

It may seem contradictory to say that a compositional intent is at work in a ''free'' medium like avant-garde jazz, especially after listening to the expansive improvisational flights of Taylor's recordings. However, compositional principles are clearly at work. The overall structure of a performance and the way it is related to the details of the performance are conceived compositionally. Taylor's large performance structures appear preconceived rather than self-generating. In a truly free improvisational performance, even the resulting musical form would be created during the performance. There may be little if any discussion about it before the performers begin playing. A more compositional approach would outline a musical structure that would house and influence the performance. The improvised detail would then work to support the overall structure.

By using a compositional approach, very long yet cohesive performances can be built, an approach characterized by Taylor. His music often requires stamina from both the listeners and players. His concerts are notorious for their long uninterrupted compositions. For example, *3 Phasis* is a single composition that spans two sides of a record and runs over fifty-seven minutes in length.[14] Even more amazing is the fact that this recording was the last of six efforts on one day. Holding together such long performances certainly requires compositional skills. The performers must then play with the

---

[13]*Heliocentric Worlds of Sun Ra,* Vol. 1, ESP 1014; Vol. 2, ESP 1017.
[14]Cecil Taylor, *3 Phasis,* New World Records NW 303.

compositional intent in mind so that the detail of their improvisations respect the compositional structure and help hold together the long performances.

Taylor has successfully carried the third stream tradition into the avant-garde arena. His music is recognized in both the jazz and the classical traditions and represents one of the most evenly balanced musical expressions between the oral and compositional forces always at work in jazz. The improvisational intensity of Taylor's ensembles is well grounded in the performance tradition of jazz, yet the musical materials are crafted with clear compositional intent.

## ASSOCIATION FOR THE ADVANCEMENT OF CREATIVE MUSIC

Throughout jazz history, musical styles have been associated with geographical locations, such as New Orleans and Chicago Dixieland, West Coast jazz, and East Coast hard bop. In the 1960s Chicago was again a center for a developing jazz style. A new, more world-based music was being explored by a group called the Association for the Advancement of Creative Music (AACM). The group was founded by composer/pianist/clarinetist Richard Abrams. His work focused largely on a group called the Experimental Band, which was made up of smaller units. This band had no permanent membership. It changed to meet whatever composition and performance demands were required for concerts and recordings. The personnel for the AACM included other prominent players of new music like trumpeter Leo Smith, saxophonist Anthony Braxton, and violinist Leroy Jenkins.

The work of AACM reflects a similar interest in musical exploration that could be found on major university campuses that were involved in ''new music.'' From the 1960s to the 1980s, avant-garde university music programs adopted some of the scientific method practices and language more typical of other more scientific disciplines and applied them to musical research. Many of the musical efforts were referred to as experiments and involved the deliberate exploration of all areas of musical practice. Although AACM is discussed most prominently in jazz history books, their work is quite similar if not indistinguishable from similar work in academic settings that view themselves as avant-garde expressions of classical music.

The similarity between these worlds leads to, even to the present, an exchange of personnel between the jazz and new music communities. George Lewis is an example of a musician who moves between the jazz and academic musical worlds. At one time he played in the Count Basie band and is still active in avant-garde jazz festivals. He also teaches at a university and works with computerized improvisational systems. As mentioned above, Cecil Taylor and Richard

Abrams also moved rather freely across the two worlds. Common to all such shared personalities is a respect for both the improvisational delivery of a music and its compositional premise.

## ART ENSEMBLE OF CHICAGO

Out of the Experimental Band came many important innovators of avant-garde jazz. Saxophonist Joseph Jarman developed into a leading composer for AACM and worked often in multimedia formats. Jarman came to the AACM from a rock and blues background. Woodwind player Roscoe Mitchell came to the AACM from a bop background by way of Ornette Coleman. Trumpeter Lester Bowie also worked in the Experimental Band before joining forces with Jarman, Mitchell, and bassist Malachi Favors in 1968 to form the Art Ensemble of Chicago. In 1969, the Art Ensemble moved to Paris and recorded some of their most notable albums.[15]

The work of the Art Ensemble, like that of AACM, is very difficult to describe in detail because of the variety of compositional and performance tactics they employed. The diversity of intent is perhaps their most defining trademark. There are, however, some general descriptors that apply to all their work:

1. Emphasis on collective interaction
2. Wide range of tone colors
3. Exploration of sound structures
4. Suspension of fixed rhythmic support (no drummer)

Like most of the music of the AACM, that of the Art Ensemble has a firm compositional base. The compositional detail does not describe the notes to be played but the way the performance is to proceed. While individual performances follow the charted composition, they also respond to the evolving collective improvisation. This balance between compositional intent and free improvisation is the foundation on which the AACM operates.

## ANTHONY BRAXTON

Much like Taylor, saxophonist Anthony Braxton strikes a balance between emotional and intellectual composition. It is really more a matter of degree. Braxton spent the mid-1960s in Chicago with the AACM and carried that group's compositional concerns into his own

---

[15]Art Ensemble of Chicago, *A Jackson in Your House,* Affinity Records AFF 9; Art Ensemble of Chicago, *People in Sorrow,* Nessa 3.

work. Braxton also works within the academic environment and considers himself more a classical than a jazz composer. His dazzling solo performances have established him as an important improviser, while he is also known for writing an opera involving improvisational elements. He has written a great deal about his aesthetic approach to music and, as a result, generated some controversy about his role as either a jazz or classical figure. Both Sun Ra and Braxton suffered criticism more from their writings than their music. While Sun Ra's writing carried a ''galactic'' tone, Braxton's is written in very convoluted and cognitive language. Sun Ra spoke of great universal truths that are practically independent of reasonable support. His language mirrored his very free and intuitive approach to performance. Braxton's writings also reflect his own musical approach, but differ from Sun Ra's in that they are very theoretical. Because both composers use extreme approaches in both their language and their music, they share a truly avant-garde status. Sun Ra is a satellite of the jazz community, while Braxton is caught between both worlds and is not a clear member of either.

## SUMMARY

We see in Braxton's work that the third stream legacy can result in an artistic dilemma. Even as the two art worlds of free jazz and new music align, their legacies continue to exert influence and center a performer in one world or the other. Avant-garde performers, by definition, take a stand against their own musical tradition. To be effective as potential transformers of that tradition, they must be respected by other members of the art form. As they deny some values of the tradition they also must uphold others or risk being totally rejected. Miles Davis offers a good example of transforming presence within a tradition. Anthony Braxton, on the other hand, holds a questionable membership in the jazz community because his work does not maintain a clear connection to jazz precepts. Although it contains an allegiance to improvisation, a tenet of the jazz tradition, his performance could just as easily be defined as an extension of the classical music world. His status is further confused by his own writings that adhere more closely to the academic music model.

It is clear that the classical and jazz traditions are different. Because they are different, the avant-garde of one is not reacting to the same traditional strictures as the avant-garde of the other. However, because both groups are reflecting an expanding openness and exploration in a society they share, they both push toward a shared arena of freedom. Although they both seek freedom from their respective traditions, they also carry inherited values from each. The new music world generally carries with it a strong interest in compositional thought and pushes toward freedom in performance. The free jazz players already carried an allegiance to improvisation but began to assimilate compositional approaches to explore new uncharted musical ground. The result was a new third stream intersection that was perhaps the most effective in the history of both traditions. It was effective yet risky. Both traditions eventually pulled back somewhat from their experiments but not before they had assimilated significant contributions from the other.

## SUGGESTED LISTENING

AACM. ''Steppin'.'' Smithsonian side J, band 3.

*Anthony Braxton, New York, Fall 1974.* Arista Records AL 4032.

Art Ensemble of Chicago. *A Jackson in Your House.* Affinity Records AFF 9.

Art Ensemble of Chicago. *People in Sorrow.* Nessa 3.

Art Ensemble of Chicago. *The Third Decade.* ECM/Warner Brothers Records 25014 1.

Coleman, Ornette. ''Faces and Places.'' *At the Golden Circle.* Blue Records 84224 2.

Coleman, Ornette. ''Free Jazz.'' Smithsonian J/2 (cd V/9).

Coltrane, John. ''Alabama.'' Smithsonian I/3 (cd V/6).

Coltrane, John. *The Best of John Coltrane, His Greatest Years.* Impulse Records AS 9223 2.

Coltrane, John. *A Love Supreme.* Impulse Records A 77.

Dave Brubeck Quartet. *Time Out.* Columbia Records CL 1397.

Davis, Miles. *Birth of the Cool.* Capitol Records N 16168.

Evans, Gil. *Out of the Cool.* Impulse Records A 4.

Evans, Gil, and Miles Davis. ''Summertime.'' *The Columbia Years 1955–1985.* Columbia Records C4K 45000, CK 45001.

Freedman, Robert. ''An Interlude.'' *Jazz in the Classroom.* Berklee Records BLPIA.

*The Futuristic Sounds of Sun Ra.* MG Records 12138.

Gershwin, George, and Paul Whiteman. ''Rhapsody in Blue.'' RCA Victor Records.

*Glenn Miller—A Memorial.* RCA Victor Records VPM 6019.

*Heliocentric Worlds of Sun Ra,* Vol. 1. ESP Records 1014; Vol. 2. ESP Records 1017.

The Jacques Loussier Trio. *Play Bach Jazz.* London Records 3289.

Joplin, Scott. ''Maple Leaf Rag.'' Smithsonian A/1 (cd I/1).

Laws, Hubert. ''Rite of Spring.'' CTI Records 6012.

Mangione, Chuck. *Land of Make Believe.* Mercury Records SRM 1 684.

Metropolitan Pops Choir with Robert Mandel. *More of the Greatest Hits of Bach.* Laurie Records LLP 2023.

The Modern Jazz Quartet. ''Django.'' Prestige Records OJCCD-057-2.

The Modern Jazz Quartet. ''Piazza Navonna.'' New World Records NW 216.

The Modern Jazz Quartet. *Third Stream Music.* Atlantic Records 1345.

Morton, Jelly Roll. ''Maple Leaf Rag.'' Smithsonian A/2 (cd I/2).

The New York Philharmonic Orchestra with the Dave Brubeck Quartet. Conducted by Leonard Bernstein. *Bernstein Plays Brubeck Plays Bernstein.* Columbia Records CL 1466.

Russo, William. ''Eldon Heath.'' New World Records NW 216.

Russo, William. ''Mirage.'' New World Records NW 216.

Schuller, Gunther. ''Transformation.'' *Modern Jazz Concert.* Columbia Records WL 127.

Shapero, Harold. ''On Green Mountain.'' *Modern Jazz Concert.* Columbia Records WL 127.

Simone, Nina. ''Love Me or Leave Me,'' ''Little Girl Blue.'' Bethlehem Records 6028.

Swingle Singers. *Bach's Greatest Hits.* Philips Records 200–097.

Taylor, Cecil. *3 Phasis.* New World Records NW 303.

Taylor, Cecil. *Silent Tongues.* Unit Care Records 30551.

Taylor, Cecil. *Unit Structures.* Unit Care Records 84237.

# CHAPTER 12

## *Fusion—An Art Form at Risk*

---

J azz has always been subject to fusion with other musical influences. In fact, jazz's very existence resulted from the fusion of many musical influences that converged in New Orleans. As we have seen in previous chapters, the two dominant influences were those contributed by the African Americans and the western Europeans. The music of the former slaves brought to the city already reflected a great deal of western Europe's harmonic language typical of the music of the Great Awakening.

At this seminal point in jazz's formation, there was certainly no thought of jazz as an art form. It was just beginning to form the distinguishing characteristics that would set it apart from the many other popular musical expressions at the turn of the twentieth century. We would have to wait until the late 1940s for those who followed jazz to begin talking of it as an art form.

Before it established a defined art tradition, jazz was particularly vulnerable to outside influences. It could move in any direction as it reflected and absorbed other musical styles. Jazz needed no protection from these influences because it had no tradition to preserve. It could borrow freely as it generated its historical front edge. Participants of jazz might prefer one style over another, a discussion we will encounter in chapter 13, but there was no established art form yet that could be challenged by other musical streams.

As jazz moved away from the dance floor during bop and away from popular fashion, it also began to claim an elite status among followers who began to search out the roots of its new tradition. This sense of retrospect began to help in the definition of future developments of jazz, essentially a standard by which new changes would be judged. This standard also offers a governing control over future fusions that the art form might encounter. If a fusion threatens to rob jazz of too much of its identity, then it might be judged inappropriate as a new jazz style. Such self-policing of a musical tradition is an important indicator of an art form's maturing.

Jazz remained relatively free from such worries until the bop period. It was on a slow fusion course that was still shaping its definition. The two dominant forces discussed throughout this text continually shifted in influence as stylistic periods came and went. The oral and compositional traditions played out a historical dance that set the jazz definition by which later jazz styles and their accompanying controversies would be judged. As that definition came into focus during the bop period, the mouth of the jazz mainstream was established. As that mainstream grew in strength, any new challengers to jazz's center stage could be more and more easily controlled as they sought to fuse.

## COOL FUSION

The first significant, or conscious, fusion with jazz since bop was the cool efforts typical of Miles Davis and Gil Evans. Although this musical crossover was identifiable enough to earn a label in jazz history, it really was not a new fusion at all. It proved to be more of a shift in balance between the already dominant forces in jazz's developing tradition.

The reaction to cool proved to be a first in jazz history, a clear, conscious, and relatively complete return to an earlier style. Surrounding this return was language by both players and critics that justified the return as a recapturing of the true jazz spirit. Although there were also some racial overtones that clouded the discussion, the arguments were a clear reaffirmation of an earlier tradition thought to be a more valid expression of jazz performance. Such a move works as a codifying force on the historical definition of jazz. Any new influence could potentially face the same reaction, and as we will see, several did.

The second conscious fusion with jazz proved to be the third stream efforts typical of Gunther Schuller and George Russell. Like cool, this movement was again more of a perceived imbalance in the shaping forces of jazz than a new full-scale fusion. However, it reflects an important precept of the jazz definition at work during the late 1950s that, of the two dominant influences in jazz, the oral tradition had preferred status. The performer rather than the composer has a prominent role in the history of jazz. To tip the scales too far in favor of the western European compositional approach is often considered risky. As we will see later, that concern relaxes somewhat during the neoclassical search for a jazz repertoire.

During the third stream period, the classical music tradition was a mature tradition capable of swallowing the relatively young jazz tradition. The new art form was at risk, a risk compounded by third stream's accommodation to western European analytical methods. This alignment with the western European literate tradition made it easy to teach and understand using standard musicological tools. As a result, for a relatively short historical period, third stream garnered a significant amount of coverage in many history books. An opposite response, premised perhaps on a fusion-as-risk argument, was also present. Some historians and critics merely ignored it, and in some cases, their history books do not even mention it.

**THIRD STREAM FUSION**

It was not until the late 1960s that jazz was to face its first real definition threatening challenge. Since bop had moved away from the popular listening market, jazz had retained a smaller more elite listening audience which supported the mainstream jazz tradition. Even with this smaller audience, jazz was viewed by much of the world population as America's indigenous music. During the Swing era, jazz had enjoyed a popularity that launched its status as an American art form. However, during the late 1950s, a new American music, rock and roll, was generating its own musical tradition. During the late 1960s, these two traditions faced off. In the resultant fusion, jazz played a reversed role from the one it played in the third stream fusion. It was now the more mature tradition being challenged by a younger and very popular musical force.

**ROCK FUSION**

By the late 1960s, rock had captured the attention of America's listeners. It was quickly becoming the most influential musical style in the United States, perhaps even the Western world. Jazz had passed

**JAZZ/ROCK FUSION**

the baton of popularity to rock and faced strong pressures to assimilate the new popular style. The fusion that resulted was most commonly called jazz/rock fusion and centered on the work of Miles Davis. Just as Davis's landmark recording, *Birth of the Cool,* had signaled the Cool era, his albums, *In a Silent Way* (1969) and particularly, *Bitches Brew* (1970) signaled a new fusion with rock that is still at work. Out of those recording sessions came a whole list of personnel who would help define the new fusion movement, players like Herbie Hancock, Chick Corea, Wayne Shorter, John McLaughlin, Joe Zawinul, Tony Williams, and Lenny White. Several of these players would go on to form the germinal fusion bands of the 1970s, Chick Corea with Return to Forever, Joe Zawinul and Wayne Shorter with Weather Report, and John McLaughlin with the Mahavishnu Orchestra.

The early use of electronic instruments can be heard in Miles Davis's *Bitches Brew.* The ensemble uses electric bass, piano, and guitar. Like rock groups, Davis gave the rhythm section a central role in the ensemble's activities. His use of such a large rhythm section offered soloists wide but active expanses for their solos. They sometimes held sustained lines in contrast to the rhythm section's activity, and at other times, they act as just another member of the rhythm section and add only punctuated statements.

---

ROCK'S
CHALLENGE TO
JAZZ

What was it in rock that challenged the definition of jazz? There are some significant distinctions between jazz and rock that may explain why rock is seen as such a challenge to jazz stylistically:

1. A straight metric approach versus a ''swung'' jazz style
2. Amplification and electronic instruments versus acoustic settings and instruments
3. Simple versus a more developed harmonic language
4. A vocal/song versus an instrumental/improvisationally-based music
5. A commercial versus art form status
6. A generational difference

The changes in the jazz/rock rhythm section are as definite as those made in the Bop era when the means of displaying the pulse was also revolutionized. In jazz/rock, the new feel is viewed as an importation from rock rather than just a new way to play jazz. To players, the rock feel is perhaps the most distinguishing feature between jazz and rock. The rock patterns make use of straight eighth

## Miles Davis

**P**erhaps no figure in jazz has influenced as many different styles over as long a time as did Miles Davis. His prominence in the jazz scene was not paralleled by the stereotypical attributes of poverty and prodigious talent. He was never a highly polished trumpet player in technical terms, but he had an aggressive nature that continually pushed him to the forefront of jazz developments. He reigned there despite dramatic musical changes inside and outside the jazz world.

| | |
|---|---|
| *1926* | Davis was born in Alton, Illinois, into a relatively affluent family on May 25. |
| *1944* | He sat in with the Earl Hines band. |
| *1945* | He attended Juliard Conservatory for a short period of time. |
| *1946* | Davis rejoined the Earl Hines band. |
| *1947–1949* | He played with Charlie Parker. |
| *1949–1950* | He recorded *Birth of the Cool* with members of the Claude Thornhill band and began his association with Gil Evans. |
| *1954* | Davis began playing more scale-oriented rather than chord-oriented improvisations. |
| *1958* | His important association with Gil Evans on recordings "Sketches of Spain," "Porgy and Bess," "Summertime," "Miles Ahead," etc. |
| *1958* | Davis developed the use of modal type solos with slow-moving harmonies. |
| *1969* | He recorded *Bitches Brew.* |
| *1985* | He recorded "You're Under Arrest," a blend of pop and jazz. |
| *1991* | Davis died in New York City of a stroke. |

*Miles Davis*

Michael Ochs Archives/
Venice, CA

# Miles Davis
*Bitches Brew*
## Columbia Records GP 26 CS 9995

Miles Davis, trumpet; Wayne Shorter, soprano sax; Lenny White, Jack DeJohnette, and Charles Alias, drums; Bennie Maupin, bass clarinet; Chick Corea and Joe Zawinul, electronic piano; Harvey Brooks (Fender) and Dave Holland, bass; John McLaughlin, electric guitar; Jim Riley, percussion.

| | |
|---|---|
| :00 | Bass solo |
| :07 | Keyboard striking a chordal cluster with percussion |
| :13 | Bass solo |
| :22 | Keyboard cluster with percussion |
| :28 | Guitar enters |
| :32 | Bass solo |
| :37 | Keyboard cluster with percussion |
| :40 | Trumpet enters (Miles Davis) with much reverberation. Section goes between trumpet entrances and keyboard clusters |
| 2:45 | Bass solo |
| 2:50 | Bass clarinet enters establishing its motive |
| 3:27 | Steady rhythm, bass clarinet and keyboard prominent, guitar playing punctuations |
| 3:46 | Trumpet solo fully integrated with the ensemble |
| 5:43 | Listen for chromatic comping patterns in keyboard behind soloist. |
| 6:10 | Trumpet gives way to keyboard and guitar, plenty of heavy rhythm on drums |
| 7:16 | Softens (Davis says, "Like that—nice.") |

 7:40  Keyboard, guitar, and drums building again, keyboard and drums very rhythmic

 8:20  Softens again, listen for such changes that define the ongoing energy curve.

 8:42  Trumpet enters

10:20  Rhythmic feel changed to suit Davis's new explorations

11:06  Trumpet out

11:18  Soprano sax solo backed by forceful rhythm

12:12  Soprano sax fades

12:15  Only rhythm with sparse keyboard interjections, but building from there

13:05  Everyone softens to build again, keyboard featured

14:17  Keyboard clusters and bass solo alternate several times as in the beginning of the selection

15:22  Trumpet again with lots of reverberation, alternating with the clusters as near the beginning of the selection

16:45  New subtle rhythmic feel to back bass solo

17:31  Add bass clarinet, intensity building again

18:37  Trumpet enters, driving forward

19:27  Trumpet exits, group softens only to rebuild

20:27  Trumpet enters rather subdued but quickly reaches out further

21:15  Bass alone—joined by drums, guitar, keyboard, soon an ensemble with these players and the bass clarinet—a long rhythmic interlude

23:15  Bass alone—alternating with keyboard clusters several times

23:52  Trumpet enters forcefully, as at the top of the selection, jabbing at openings

26:03  End

notes instead of the uneven eighth notes more typical of swing or bop. Fusion groups could make use of both rhythmic feels, many times simultaneously. The rhythm section would lay down a straight rock meter, while the soloist "swings" a boplike solo above it.

The use of new instruments is also viewed as an importation from rock. Jazz/rock players usually play electric basses instead of a traditional string bass. This allows them to play faster, invent more complex lines, and use electronic effects to alter their sound. The bass player also takes a more prominent position in the ensemble, often offering solo lines, as well as basic harmonic support. The rhythm guitar in most fusion groups plays chordal punctuations previously assigned to the piano, and the drums, like the bass, move to a more prominent position in the ensemble. In later fusion groups, the rhythm section is further expanded with multiple keyboards and electronic effects becoming common extensions for all the instruments. A commitment to a dominant rhythm section is a central feature of most jazz/rock groups.

The harmonies of jazz/rock reflected the slower moving harmonies of rock and contrast sharply with the quick moving harmonies typical of mainstream bop. The modal playing heard in such players as John Coltrane was very effective in the rock medium. A rhythmic groove with slow moving harmonies promoted long solos with very effective energy curves. The resulting intensity comes more from the rhythmic complexity than fast moving harmonies. Also, electronic instruments and effects offer performers effective tools for sustaining long harmonies and still have a great deal of variation, a process that would blur fast moving harmonies.

Along with the imported rock instrumentation came a new volume level, a trademark of rock. The rise of the adolescent class in America was accompanied by the emergence of a new music with which they associated. Loudness served as an adolescent banner that separated the music of the young generation of listeners from the music of their parents. That association clouds the musical issues that would normally arise when two musical traditions fuse. During the polarization of the 1960s, it became necessary for each generation of listeners to maintain distinct identities, and music was one of the distinguishing characteristics. Among those differing musical characteristics, loudness was clearly the most controversial.

The new jazz/rock fusion adopted the new loudness of rock but framed it in a relatively traditional jazz context. The rhythm section still worked to support improvisational flights and the role of the instrumentalist remained center stage. The change between the rhythm sections of bop and fusion (the term most commonly applied to the jazz/rock crossover) was no more striking than that between swing and bop. It was the social context of the later transition that set up the resistance to change.

Jazz was a more mature art form with a codified tradition. After that tradition is established, new fusions threaten to change the jazz canon itself. By the 1960s, jazz had established its new more elite audience. This audience expected a type of sophistication and traditional delivery from jazz, setting it apart from the more transient fashions of popular music. Art forms tend to change much more slowly than do their commercial counterparts. The flirtation with rock threatened to invalidate the new art status jazz had gained since bop by tying it to the fashionable whims of commercial music. Jazz/rock groups are still often accused of commercializing jazz, yet another indicator that jazz's art form status is firmly rooted.

The fusion between rock and jazz was not completely one-sided. Rock also borrowed from the jazz tradition, demonstrated in such groups as Blood, Sweat and Tears, Chicago, and later a group Sting formed with well-known jazz players, Branford Marsalis, Daryl Jones, Kenny Kirkland, and Omar Hakim. Although these groups still based their material around commercial song forms, jazz elements appeared in the instrumental solos.

---

## JAZZ/ROCK/POP

The fusion of jazz and rock took a new turn in the 1970s and 1980s as members of Miles Davis's *Bitches' Brew* ensemble formed their own groups. Although these new leaders are all associated with Davis, they did not receive their musical direction solely from his influence. Corea cites the formation of the Mahavishnu Orchestra and McLaughlin's use of the electric guitar as equally important to his own movement toward electric jazz fusion.[1]

These new groups were not characterized by the same modal harmonies and expansive solo areas characteristic of their work with Davis. They now showed a tighter compositional approach and a wholesale adoption of the new electronic technology. However, unlike some of the groups to follow, their performance was still based on a live ensemble interaction. The new stylistic shift common to these groups also stressed a virtuosic playing style. Much like bop, the fusion groups demonstrated a virtuosity that was accentuated by a new but characteristic melodic angularity. The virtuosity often permeated the entire ensemble and extended the performance expectations of all the instrumentalists in the group, including the rhythm section.

---

[1]Chick Corea, "Piano Dreams Come True," *Down Beat* 55, no. 9 (September 1988):16.

## JOHN MCLAUGHLIN, MAHAVISHNU ORCHESTRA

Guitarist John McLaughlin was perhaps most responsible for the sound of rock heard on the Miles Davis albums, *In a Silent Way* and *Bitches Brew*. McLaughlin played in British rock bands as he was growing up, and the sound appropriate in those early groups can be heard in his later ensembles. In 1969, he made his first appearance in the American musical arena with Tony Williamses' Lifetime. It was this same year that he also joined Miles Davis to record *In a Silent Way* and *Bitches Brew*. After his stay with Davis, he formed Mahavishnu Orchestra and recorded several high energy albums. The first few albums with this group, *Inner Mounting Flame, Birds of Fire,* and *Between Nothingness and Eternity,* clearly demonstrate the virtuosity and energetic sound associated with McLaughlin and his groups.[2]

After the second version of the Mahavishnu Orchestra disbanded, McLaughlin worked on some Indian flavored albums with the group Shakti. Particularly notable after his work with Shakti was a collaboration with two other virtuoso guitarists, Paco De Lucia and Al Di Meola, and their albums *Passion, Grace and Fire* and *Friday Night in San Francisco*.[3]

In addition to his formidable acoustic guitar playing, he has also embraced a newer synthesized guitar which is interfaced with the Synclavier Digital Music System. His work with this high-tech instrument can be heard on his 1985 album, *Mahavishnu,* a return to the earlier Mahavishnu format. When asked why he called this new group by the same name as his previous orchestra he said, ''personally, the kind of spirit that was established in my first ensemble with that name, something I love very much, is now present in the new band.''[4]

McLaughlin has always been a hallmark of virtuosic technique and high energy musical flights. He contributed the sound of rock to the jazz mainstream. He was among the first to adopt the volume and metallic tone color more typical of rock performers and place them in a more traditional jazz setting. He has influenced the current generation of guitar players, both jazz and rock, in much the same fashion Wes Montgomery did a generation earlier.

---

[2]Mahavishnu Orchestra, *Inner Mounting Flame,* Columbia Records 31067; *Birds of Fire,* Columbia Records 31996; *Between Nothingness and Eternity,* Columbia Records 32766.
[3]Mahavishnu Orchestra, *Passion, Grace and Fire,* Columbia Records 38645; Mahavishnu Orchestra, *Friday Night in San Francisco,* Columbia Records 37152.
[4]John McLaughlin, ''Spirit of the Sine Wave,'' *Down Beat* (March 1985):16.

## CHICK COREA, RETURN TO FOREVER, AND ELEKTRIC BAND

One of the most prominent and popular fusion groups of the 1970s and 1980s, Return to Forever was led by Chick Corea, formerly with Miles Davis. Corea, a well-schooled piano player, began to use the electronic piano while with Davis. After working with his own avant-garde group called Circle, he formed Return to Forever in 1970. His move to electronic piano soon led to a complete involvement with synthesizers of all kinds.

Corea's music demonstrates a virtuosic skill in both technique and ensemble. His themes are often quite angular and complex rhythmically yet quite accessible to the listener. Despite their complexity, his records are commercially successful. His music flows smoothly between up-tempo jazz, complex rock, and a more commercial rock style.

Return to Forever's 1977 album, *Musicmagic*, demonstrates Corea's ability to fuse many distinct musical styles into a single composition.[5] The title cut moves from a very smooth commercial sound through jazz interludes, to ''funky'' rock passages. The fusion trademark of an active rock rhythmic underpinning supporting a soloist with jazz phrasing above it appears throughout the cut. Corea opens and closes the arrangement with acoustic piano but uses an electronic piano and synthesizers throughout the body of the piece.

Chick Corea's later albums become more and more electronic as the instruments themselves become more accessible and more complex. With the advancing technology, outstanding keyboard players like Corea often experiment with much smaller groups, replacing the usual complement of musicians with sophisticated electronic instruments. Unlike the seven musicians who performed for *Musicmagic*, Corea used only two to three at one time for his 1986 album, *Elektric Band*.[6] The title is a play on words. On the surface, it is a reference to a poem called ''Elektric City,'' and secondarily it refers to the heavy use of electronic instruments. Even his drummer, Dave Weckl, uses an electronic drum set (Simmons) and drum synthesizer (Linn) on some of the cuts.

Corea wields this equipment quite effectively. His virtuosic keyboard technique and compositional skill showcase the potential for the new technology. His approach is still quite similar to that heard in the Return to Forever albums, rhythmically complex themes, tight

---

[5]Chick Corea and Return to Forever, *Musicmagic,* Columbia Records 34682.
[6]Chick Corea, *Elektric Band,* GRP Records GRP–D–9535.

# Chick Corea—Elektric Band
## "Stretch It, Part 1"
### GRP Records GRD 9601

Keyboards, Chick Corea; bass, John Patitucci; saxophone, Eric Marienthal; guitar, Frank Gambale; drums, Dave Weckl.

:00    Piano lead in joined later by the saxophone

:05    Irregular metric feel

:09    Return to opening motivic material

:22    Listen for the ensemble accents during this short contrast section.

:29    Return to irregular motivic material with drum fills between the disjunct melodic fragments

:39    Beginning of build up to final chords with irregular accents. Listen for how the melodic fragments are accented as a part of the active drumming.

:51    End of Part 1

ensemble, colorful orchestrations, and virtuosic display. His selection, "Got a Match," from the *Elektric Band* album offers an effective juxtaposition of jazz and rock phrasing. The solo areas again use the high energy rock backdrop with a more typically bop solo in the foreground.

On his next album, *Light Years*,[7] Corea had tried to make music that would fit into the radio format, i.e., four-minute songs with a consistent rhythm. This style is more characteristic of other more commercial groups like Spyro Gyra or the Yellowjackets. He moved away from that approach on his 1988 album, *Eye of the Beholder*,[8] and returned to a live recording process that allowed more room for performer interaction. Corea returned to his Elektric Band in 1990 after making an acoustic album, *Akoustic Band*.[9] On his later album, *Inside Out*,[10] he uses both acoustic piano and synthesizers. Some of

[7]Chick Corea, *Light Years,* GRP Records GRD 9546.
[8]Chick Corea, *Eye of the Beholder,* GRP Records GRD 9564.
[9]Chick Corea, *Akoustic Band,* GRP Records GRD 9582.
[10]Chick Corea, *Electric Band—Inside Out,* GRP Records GRD 9601.

the compositions are made up of several smaller parts, forming structures larger than are usually found in this style. The playing and melodic design continues in the complex, angular, and virtuoso style normally associated with fusion jazz. *Stretch It* or *Tale of Daring* from this album demonstrate the tight ensemble and virtuosic interplay increasingly associated with Corea compositions.

## JOE ZAWINUL, WAYNE SHORTER, WEATHER REPORT

Like Chick Corea, Joe Zawinul and Wayne Shorter worked with Miles Davis when *Bitches Brew* was recorded. Also like Corea, they formed one of the most commanding fusion bands of the 1970s and 1980s, Weather Report. A special chemistry existed between Zawinul and Shorter that gave their band a distinctive and popular sound. In an article by George Varga, Zawinul credits an even earlier Miles Davis recording with influencing his writing style, ''The record was 'Birth of the Cool,' and it had a great impact on me. I like to write in that sound-spectrum style.''[11] A majority of the writing during Weather Report's fifteen-year existence was done by Zawinul, and his respect for the composed approach to jazz typical on *Birth of the Cool* can be heard in his own compositions. Like Corea, Zawinul is an accomplished pianist who moved comfortably into the electronic medium of synthesizers.

Weather Report's 1980 album, *Night Passage,* offers several examples of fusion at different points along the jazz/rock line.[12] ''Rockin' in Rhythm'' is based on an Ellington tune and uses synthesizers to fill out a saxophone section sound under Shorter. The rhythm and style remain predominantly swing with very little borrowed from the rock idiom. ''Fast City'' offers the soloists an energetic arena for a type of virtuosity often associated with fusion groups. The thematic material is again rhythmically complex and punctuated with ensemble motives. Very often, even the bass player, Jaco Pastorius, joins the ensemble in the complex unison lines.

The song most associated with Weather Report is Zawinul's ''Birdland'' from the album *Heavy Weather.*[13] This composition is a beacon of 1970s fusion and reappeared later in settings by Manhattan Transfer and Quincy Jones.[14]

[11]George Varga, *The San Diego Union,* 9 March 1986.
[12]Weather Report, *Night Passage,* ARC Records CBS Inc. 36793.
[13]Weather Report, *Heavy Weather, 1977,* CBS Inc. Records, CK 34418.
[14]Manhattan Transfer, *Extensions,* Atlantic SD 19258; Quincy Jones, *Back on the Block,* Warner Brothers 9 26020 2.

## Joseph Zawinul and Weather Report
### "Birdland"
### 1977 Columbia 34418

Joseph Zawinul, Oberheim Polyphonic, Arp 2600, acoustic piano, vocal, and Melodica; Wayne Shorter, soprano, tenor saxophone; Jaco Pastorius, bass, mandocello, vocals; Alex Acuna, drums; Manolo Badrena, tambourine.

| | |
|---|---|
| :00 | Analog synthesizer bass line |
| :17 | Bass guitar with introductory motive |
| :41 | Synthesizer melodic riff-like motive with saxophone |
| :53 | Interlude, long low notes with a new riff-like motive above it |
| 1:00 | Short motive over low synthesizer notes—builds up energy |
| 1:27 | Saxophone enters with synthesizer to increase energy |
| 1:42 | Interlude to set up melody |
| 1:53 | Main melody enters with saxophone and synthesizer. Bass guitar plays fills in answer to melody. Repeat of melodic motive builds up energy. |
| 2:29 | Long-held note interlude with synthesizer line and some vocal sounds |
| 2:58 | Descending chords with saxophone solo over them to build energy |
| 3:25 | Return to opening bass guitar motive as synthesizer enters with opening synthesized bass line and some saxophone fills |
| 3:48 | Saxophone and synthesizer riff as in opening section |
| 4:02 | Interlude, long notes and riff motive |
| 4:13 | Melody returns to begin a build up. The melody repeats over and over with increasing interplay between players. |
| 5:38 | Fade out and end |

Zawinul and Shorter's last record together as Weather Report was *This Is This.* It was released in 1986 and showed another personnel shift.[15] Victor Bailey on bass and Mino Cinelu as percussionist-vocalist who had been playing with Weather Report, remained, but Peter Erskine returned on drums and John Scofield on guitar was a new addition.

Zawinul also came out with a solo album in 1986, *Dialects,* on which he uses four synthesizers and four drum machines.[16] The only other performers on the album are four vocalists, one of which is Bobby McFerrin. ''All the pieces are improvised,'' Zawinul told George Varga, ''each sound is a personality. It's like a conversation in which I'm the focus.''[17] Each piece on the album represents an exotic theme, such as ''6 A.M./Walking on the Nile'' and ''The Great Empire'' (Japan). Although there is often a rhythmic rock underpinning to the pieces, the musical idiom shifts sharply from piece to piece, reflecting the exotic themes. The compositions might better be thought of as jazz/rock tone poems similar in concept to classical overtures or music for film.

On his next recording, *Black Water,*[18] Zawinul returns to material more typical of his prefusion days. He continues to write music for a variety of media including film and classical ensembles. He also joined forces with Quincy Jones on his popular 1989 album, ''Back on the Block,'' with an arrangement of his already popular composition, ''Birdland.'' This composition was performed originally by Weather Report and later set to lyrics by Jon Hendricks and performed by Manhattan Transfer. Zawinul's success in diverse musical arenas allows him to say of himself, ''not jazz, not rock, just me. I am my own category.''[19]

---

These early fusion groups gained a new popularity that crossed over the generational lines that seem to delineate the jazz and rock communities. This popularity was not welcomed in the jazz community for reasons already discussed. If the popularity were complete, that is equal in magnitude to that of the Swing era, jazz could very well be redefined by the fusing elements, and the mainstream canon would be lost.

## MAINSTREAM/ FUSION

---

[15]Weather Report, *This Is This,* CBS Records CK 40280.
[16]Joe Zawinul, *Dialects,* FCT Records 40081.
[17]George Varga, *The San Diego Union,* 9 March 1986.
[18]Joseph Zawinul, *Black Water,* Columbia Records CK 44316.
[19]Leonard Feather, Los Angeles *Times, Calendar,* 18 Feb. 1990.

The controversy in the jazz world that surrounded the new jazz/ rock fusion was further aggravated by a new generation of players and groups who further embraced stylistic and sound ideals often found in the popular music of the 1980s. These new groups also gained a popularity not enjoyed by jazz musicians since the Swing era. This new interest in jazz does not necessarily spill over to the more traditional straight-ahead jazz groups. In fact, many listeners may have virtually no knowledge of the earlier jazz traditions from which these groups evolved. As a result, a new dichotomy has developed in the jazz community between those who hold a strong allegiance to the jazz tradition (embodied in performers like Wynton Marsalis) and those whose music is sometimes called jazz but may have roots more directly tied to the rock or pop tradition.

Many of the jazz/pop players sport backgrounds not necessarily rooted in jazz. Rather than jazz players importing rock attributes, we have for the first time in fusion, performers with backgrounds equally, if not predominantly, in rock. These players offer a viable connection between the mainstream jazz and the more current and popular rock styles.

## DAVID SANBORN

David Sanborn stylistically sits between these two emerging definitions of jazz. He is viewed by many as the new saxophone sound in jazz, importing strong R & B influences. Contrary to the opinion held by his followers, he continues to state, "Even when I do think in categories, I never think of myself as a jazz musician. I've never called myself a jazz musician in the public forum or privately."[20]

Despite this denial, he has figured prominently in the promotion of jazz's new popularity. He hosted a jazz radio program called *The Jazz Show* and a late night television show that featured leading jazz personalities. He also enjoys a popularity that extends beyond the traditional jazz community. His work with Bob James on *Double Vision*[21] demonstrates his improvisatory style in a more pop sounding environment. Sanborn's use of the very high range of the saxophone called the altissimo register is one of the trademarks of his sound. The use of this register, although not new to saxophone players, is now widely used by most players. Also on this album is a recording,

---

[20]David Sanborn, "R & B Altology," *Down Beat* (August 1986):16.
[21]David Sanborn and Bob James, *Double Vision,* Warner Brothers Records 25393 4.

"Since I Fell For You," with vocalist Al Jarreau, demonstrating the type of sound and style perhaps controversially called jazz by the newest listening audience of jazz/pop. This audience has only recently moved to jazz and carries with it a pop/rock background. David Sanborn, like other performers in this style, offers a stylistic bridge between the very commercial world of pop and the jazz tradition.

## MICHAEL BRECKER

Saxophonist Michael Brecker is certainly not new to the jazz/rock fusion scene. He and his brother Randy were at the forefront of the development with their first band, Dreams, in 1970. Like many of the players of fusion, Brecker's early musical experience included playing with rock bands. He later joined Steps Ahead, a group organized and led by vibist Michael Mainieri. It was not until 1987 that he stepped out to lead his own group with the album *Michael Brecker*.[22] It was at this same time that Brecker showed that the electronic wind instrument (EWI) could be a viable jazz instrument.

Brecker further established himself as a leader of a high energy jazz strongly influenced by blues and often a backbeat funk style on his next album, *Don't Try This at Home*.[23] His work with Michael Stern (previously with Miles Davis on *Tutu*) resulted in high energy virtuosic flights over driving rock, as well as up-tempo jazz backups.

Brecker makes a clear connection between the bop tradition, of which he is quite capable, and the fusion of the 1980s. His groups are characterized by the allegiance to soloistic flights founded in the Bop era. In fact, bop melodic idiom is dominant in his solos. It is the sound, and the feel, that is rock. He uses the volume and driving intensity of rock bands, as well as the slower moving harmonies. This apparent dichotomy between the mainstream jazz influences and a rock and roll format places Brecker in a controversial position. He is not necessarily supported by the mainstream jazz audience. Perhaps the fusion delivery interferes with such listeners' appreciation for the soloistic continuity Brecker offers the developing mainstream.

---

It helps to place both Brecker and Sanborn on a continuum of jazz to pop to see how they are viewed by the jazz community. On one end of the continuum might be Phil Woods who is the embodiment of

**THE JAZZ TO POP CONTINUUM**

---

[22]*Michael Brecker,* Impulse 5980.
[23]Michael Brecker, *Don't Try This at Home,* Impulse Records MCAD 42229.

# Michael Brecker
## "Itsbynne Reel"
## Impulse MCAD 42229

---

Michael Brecker, tenor saxophone and Akai EWI; Mike Stern, guitar; Don Grolnick, piano; Charlie Haden, acoustic bass; Jeff Andrews, fretless electric bass; Jack DeJohnette, drums; Mark O'Connor, violin.

| | |
|---|---|
| :00 | Melody on Akai EWI controller (A section of melody) |
| :08 | Violin enters and doubles the EWI |
| :15 | Piano enters |
| :31 | New middle B section |
| :38 | Repeat of B section |
| :46 | Return of A section |
| :54 | New melodic section with a development of previous melodic material with counterpoint between the violin and EWI. A sustained note creates a drone like the frozen harmonic areas to be used later. |
| 2:12 | Bass and drums enter with jazz/rock phrasing |
| 2:21 | Listen for synthesized brasslike punches on normally unaccented beats |
| 2:31 | Melody repeats |
| 2:47 | New ensemble-like section |
| 3:01 | More staccato and accented phrasing |
| 3:17 | Slow ascending bass and piano unison notes playing a cross rhythm |
| 3:48 | Ensemble material for transition to solo |
| 4:18 | Saxophone enters for a solo over the slow cross-rhythm notes in bass and piano |
| 4:47 | Saxophone line joins slow bass and piano notes for unison transition. Listen to rhythmic activity in the drums. |
| 5:00 | Solo breaks free over a frozen harmony (drone) |
| 5:21 | Harmony changes (first time since 5:00). Bass ascends and descends by step |
| 6:09 | Double-time melodic ideas move to climax |
| 6:17 | Return to original melodic idea with variations |
| 6:30 | Violin joins the saxophone in unison over the harmonic pedal (drone), very active drumming |
| 7:01 | The two soloists play independent lines in counterpoint |
| 7:40 | End |

mainstream jazz in many ways. Branford Marsalis also plays a main-stream role but has a clouded past due to his work with the rock band leader Sting. Brecker sits somewhere in the middle. His development as a player is rooted in the fusion tradition, while his recent playing can be heard as a fiery kind of bop. His rhythm section is most often characterized by a rock feel, although it works to support the soloists much like a bop rhythm section. Sanborn sits closer to the pop end of the spectrum. His R & B sound and simpler harmonic backup signal a music meant for a wider listening audience. To finish the line, one might place Kenny G on the end of the pop line. His music makes use of an instrumental and improvisational approach, yet it does not have the melodic and harmonic complexity typical of bop, the other extreme on the jazz to pop continuum.

To draw such a line is somewhat contrived, yet it offers us an insight into how fusions work. Players can settle at many different points along the continuum at different times in their careers. For example, Miles Davis worked at various points along that line in his later career. His album, *You're Under Arrest,* has a very pop sound and structure. He even played an arrangement of a song written and formally performed by Cindi Lauper, a prominent pop music star at the time. By the time Davis recorded this album, his place in jazz history had already been established, making such a flirtation with pop less risky than it is for such players as Sanborn or Brecker whose jazz credentials are still being confirmed.

## PAT METHENY

Guitarist Pat Metheny has gained a great deal of popularity because of his great proficiency on the instrument, as well as his blend of jazz, rock, and latin influences. His 1978 album, *The Pat Metheny Group,* gained him a wider audience than enjoyed by other otherwise successful jazz musicians. Unlike McLaughlin, Metheny's early background was primarily jazz based. His sound is, therefore, more in keeping with the more lyrical tradition established by Wes Montgomery.

In 1986, Metheny collaborated with Ornette Coleman to create an album, *Song X,*[24] that offers a blend of the two players' backgrounds. As the title suggests, the sounds of this album were to be songs that cannot be named, only experienced for their imagination and creativity. His collaboration with Coleman seemed like an unusual marriage between two distinct and different musical styles. Coleman, as the icon of free jazz, appeared to be an unlikely partner

[24]Pat Metheny and Ornette Coleman, *Song X,* Geffen Records 24096.

for the more jazz/pop style of Metheny. However, the album garnered a lot of attention in the jazz community.

Metheny's most recent albums include a Grammy Award winner, *Still Life (Talking)*,[25] released in 1987. It was followed by *Letter from Home*,[26] in which Metheny used sophisticated rhythmic settings showing strong Brazilian influences.

## SPYRO-GYRA, YELLOWJACKETS

Since the impact of Return to Forever and Weather Report, a second generation of groups has appeared that reflect many of the first generation's rhythmic and ensemble innovations. Most prominent of these groups are Spyro-Gyra and the Yellowjackets.

Spyro-Gyra, led by saxophonist Jay Beckenstein, offers a type of jazz/rock/latin fusion. Although pianist Jeremy Wall was later replaced by Tom Schuman, he continued as producer/composer/ arranger and studio pianist. Beckenstein and Wall together with guitarist Chet Catallo, bassist David Wolford, drummer Eli Konikoff, and percussionist Gerardo Velez created a sound that falls somewhere between the complexities of groups like Weather Report and a more pop style. They first became popular with their album *Morning Dance*.[27] A latin feel characterizes many of their performances, yet they are still effective at establishing their own type of jazz groove with a rock underpinning. "Swing Street" from their album, *Point of View*,[28] demonstrates a characteristic jazz/rock feel. Although the title implies a swing style, the meter has definite rock attributes. It begins with a straight-ahead feel but soon develops a half-time rock backbeat, leaving the swing feel to the smaller beat subdivisions. This rhythmic feel is characteristic of fusion groups. Over this backup, the soloists adopt a boplike melodic style as they improvise.

The Yellowjackets were started in 1980 and, like Spyro-Gyra, follow the legacy established by Weather Report. The four members of the group include Russell Ferrante, piano and synthesizers; Jimmy Haslip, bass; Marc Russo, saxophones; and William Kennedy, drums. They create complex and energetic arrangements that borrow from several previous jazz styles, as well as blend sounds more accessible to popular listening audiences.

The angularity of the melodic lines and the harmonic punches used by the Yellowjackets are reminiscent of Weather Report. The

[25]Pat Metheny, *Still Life (Talking)*, Geffen Records 24145.
[26]Pat Metheny, *Letter from Home*, Geffen Records 24245.
[27]Spyro-Gyra, *Morning Dance*, Infinity Records, INF 9004.
[28]Spyro-Gyra, "Swing Street," *Point of View*, MCAD 6309.

## Spyro-Gyra
### "Para Ti Latino"
### GRP Records GRD 9608

Jay Beckenstein, saxophones; Tom Schuman, keyboards; Dave Samuels, vibes, marimba and mallet-triggered synthesizers; Richie Morales, drums; Oscar Cartaya, bass; Jay Azzolina, guitar; Marc Quiñones, percussion.

:00   Syncopated harmonic punches, with drum fills. These angular rhythms are often used in later fusion bands.

:04   Unison theme in the horns. Listen for the harmonic activity in the rhythm section.

:12   Theme is repeated.

:19   Syncopated transition mirroring the introduction

:22   Guitar enters with the melody.

:32   Syncopated chords return.

:34   Guitar melody repeats.

:43   Harmonic chords set up the sax entrance.

:45   Guitar and sax play the melody in unison.

:57   Sax finishes the phrase alone.

1:01  Sax plays melody with the guitar playing a harmony part. Listen for the brass fills between phrases.

1:14  Sax again finishes the phrase alone.

1:21  Syncopated harmonic punches return but now the sax, instead of the drummer, plays the breaks.

1:27  Guitar returns with the melody.

1:38  Marimba solo. Listen for the underlying syncopated bass pattern.

2:10  Bass stops the syncopated pattern for the transition, setting up a contrast for the next section.

2:18  Very tight latin time pattern created under a sax solo. Listen to the funk bass pattern and how it works with the percussion cross rhythms.

*continued*

**continued**

2:48    Syncopated harmonic punches return as a transition.

2:52    Percussion solo over a keyboard ostinato

3:16    Syncopated harmonic chords over drum fills like the introduction

3:21    Guitar melody returns.

3:32    Sax enters and plays the melody with the guitar in unison.

3:48    Sax continues the melody as the guitar moves to a harmony part.

4:00    Sax continues with the last part of the melody as the bass moves back onto the beat.

4:08    Intro-like figure returns in anticipation of the ending. Notice that the sax fills are now played in unison with the bass player!

4:15    End

harmonic accents work in the same fashion that brass punches do in big band ensembles. "Out of Town" from their 1987 album, *Four Corners*,[29] exemplifies their use of synthesizers to give the impression of brass sections, and their use of bop solo lines over the intricate jazz/rock flavored backup (see Listening Guide in chapter 3). The Yellowjackets also blend latin influences into their music. The blend generally includes a rock feel.

On a later album, *The Spin*,[30] the Yellowjackets move in a more acoustic direction. This move brought them closer to the performance tradition common to earlier jazz ensembles. Their previous recordings took a studio approach. They used sequencers to lay down the first tracks and then built the song through successive overdubs. This album not only took an acoustic approach but used a sequencer on only one song. "The new album required more blowing, more of a band performance." Their effort on this album was consciously directed toward "trying to keep some sort of traditional direction alive."[31]

[29]Yellowjackets, "Out of Town," *Four Corners*, MCAD 5994.
[30]Yellowjackets, *The Spin*, MCAD 6304.
[31]Yellowjackets, "Yellowjacket's New Buzz," *Down Beat* 56, no. 11 (November 1989):28.

Even though the audience for these jazz/pop groups is much larger than that for traditional jazz, a move toward acoustic sounds is common among the jazz/rock/pop groups. For example, Corea has an Akoustic Band to balance his Elektric Band. Maintaining an acoustic expression, or trying to find one like the Yellowjackets, validates a group's membership in the jazz tradition.

---

Commercial music is the fastest changing of all music today. Because of the short life of so many of the emerging styles, their impact on jazz is difficult to immediately assess. At the height of disco's popularity, it was tempting to say that no music would be free from its influence, but several years after its decline, very little of its impact is being felt. It certainly strengthened the move toward a greater use of synthesizers and a refinement in studio techniques, but as a musical idiom it has almost entirely vanished.

Despite the unstable nature of commercial music, several notable jazz musicians have taken active roles in its creation. Their jazz heritage and fame often carry the jazz label into the new medium even when the music has very little recognizable jazz in it. Herbie Hancock and Quincy Jones are two such figures. Both composers have worked in the most diverse musical fields, from jazz to film scores, primarily in the rock idiom. Other players, such as Michael Franks, Ben Sidran, and Kenny G, have varying commercial jazz personas but have not been embraced by the jazz community itself. The most successful figures that work across the jazz/pop line are those who did their first important work within the jazz community and later moved out to the popular market, Quincy Jones and Herbie Hancock being prime examples.

## JAZZ AND COMMERCIAL MUSIC

---

On his 1989 album, *Back on the Block,*[32] Quincy Jones offers a very wide cross section of styles meant to represent the many diverse musical areas he has worked during his career. The album swings from rap to jazz fusion with singers, such as Ella Fitzgerald, Sarah Vaughan, Ray Charles, Take 6, Ice-T, Melle Mel, Dizzy Gillespie, Miles Davis, George Benson, Joseph Zawinul, and Herbie Hancock. The blend of individual and commercial styles is impressive and a tribute to his production skills. Particularly interesting is the arrangement of Zawinul's ''Birdland,'' which blends fusion and pop elements quite effectively. Miles Davis, Dizzy Gillespie, George

## QUINCY JONES

---

[32]Quincy Jones, *Back on the Block,* Warner Brothers Records 9 26020 2.

Benson, and James Moody are featured soloists. The underpinning rhythm arrangement, which contains electronic generated sequences as well as programmed drum parts, stays commercially consistent with the other cuts on the album.

## HERBIE HANCOCK

Herbie Hancock is particularly interesting because of his earlier association with the Miles Davis Quintet. While working on his many other projects, he has found time to reorganize this earlier group, with himself on piano, Ron Carter on bass, Tony Williams on drums, and Freddie Hubbard taking the place of Davis. The group called itself VSOP and featured mainstream jazz. VSOP 2 followed with the Marsalis brothers several years later.

While maintaining his jazz definition with excursions of this kind, Hancock is also producing albums with the Rockit band. Hancock says of these efforts, ''Most people who come from a jazz background and do anything in an area of electric or pop music still maintain a lot of the character of jazz in their pop stuff. So it's a true fusion kind of thing. I did that for a while, but I've been trying to take the pop stuff more into the pop area, and leave out the jazz. I think I've pretty much succeeded at that, because the last few records I don't consider jazz records at all.''[33]

What Hancock does carry to these later albums is the technical skill and approach more typical of an accomplished jazz player. The music of his album *Sound-System* falls more into the category of beat or breaker music, a specific type of music for break dancing.[34] Hancock may have accomplished in this album what he had intended, to leave the jazz out.

## SUMMARY

The list of musicians, all along the jazz/rock/pop line, is long and growing as fast as the music changes. To know which of these styles will leave legacies remains for time to decide. During the 1970s and 1980s, jazz began to import a great deal from the increasingly popular rock styles. This crossover generated some controversy in the jazz community. Was the jazz tradition being forsaken? Was this new music jazz at all?

By the 1980s, a new shift had taken place within this crossover group. A new popularity in jazz was developing. However, there were

[33]Herbie Hancock, *Down Beat* (July 1986).
[34]Herbie Hancock, *Sound-System,* Columbia Records 39478.

also some controversial aspects to this new popularity. Previously controversial groups, such as Weather Report and Return to Forever, had established themselves as jazz expressions, and the next generation of players was challenging the jazz definition. Because of the popularity that often accompanied these new groups, an accusation of commercial sellout was heard. Also, many of these new players are not proteges of the jazz art world. They often come out of the rock or pop styles. Although they may not have originally been a part of the jazz tradition, it is obvious they have a great respect for it as they offer to change it and perhaps earn a place in it.

---

*Blood, Sweat and Tears.* Columbia Records CS 9720.

Brecker, Michael. *Don't Try This at Home.* Impulse Records MCAD 42229.

*Chicago.* Columbia Records KGP 24.

Corea, Chick. *Akoustic Band.* GRP Records GRD 9582.

Corea, Chick. *Elektric Band.* GRP Records GRP-D-9535.

Corea, Chick. *Elektric Band—Inside Out.* "Stretch It, Part 1." GRP Records GRD 9601.

Corea, Chick. *Eye of the Beholder.* GRP Records GRD 9564.

Corea, Chick. *Light Years.* GRP Records GRD 9546.

Corea, Chick, and Return to Forever. *Musicmagic.* Columbia Records AL 34682.

Davis, Miles. *Bitches Brew.* Columbia Records GP 26 CS 9995.

Davis, Miles. *In a Silent Way.* Columbia Records PC 9875.

Davis, Miles, and Gil Evans. *Sketches of Spain.* Columbia Records PC 8271.

Davis, Miles, and Gil Evans. "Summertime." Smithsonian G/7 (cd IV/12).

Hancock, Herbie. *Sound-System.* Columbia Records 39478.

Jones, Quincy. *Back on the Block.* Warner Brothers 9 26020 2.

Mahavishnu Orchestra. *Between Nothingness and Eternity.* Columbia Records 32766.

Mahavishnu Orchestra. *Birds of Fire.* Columbia Records 31996.

Mahavishnu Orchestra. *Friday Night in San Francisco.* Columbia Records 37152.

Mahavishnu Orchestra. *Inner Mounting Flame.* Columbia Records 31067.

Mahavishnu Orchestra. *Passion, Grace and Fire.* Columbia Records 38645.

Manhattan Transfer. *Extensions.* Atlantic SD 19258.

Metheny, Pat. *Letter from Home.* Geffen Records 24245.

SUGGESTED
LISTENING

Metheny, Pat. *Still Life (Talking)*. Geffen Records 24145.
Metheny, Pat, and Ornette Coleman. *Song X*. Geffen
    Records 24096.
*Michael Brecker*. Impulse Records 5980.
Sanborn, David, and Bob James. *Double Vision*. Warner Brothers
    Records 25393 4.
Spyro-Gyra, *Morning Dance*. Infinity Records INF 9004.
Spyro-Gyra. ''Para Ti Latino.'' *Fast Forward*. GRP Records
    GRD 9608.
Spyro-Gyra. *Point of View*. MCAD 6309.
Sting. *The Dream of the Blue Turtles*. A&M Records.
Weather Report. *Heavy Weather, 1977*. CBS Inc. Records,
    CK 34418.
Weather Report. *Night Passage*. ARC Records/CBS Inc. 36793.
Weather Report. *This Is This*. CBS Records CK 40280.
Yellowjackets. *Four Corners*. MCAD Records 5994.
Yellowjackets. *The Spin*. MCAD Records 6304.
Zawinul, Joe. *Black Water*. Columbia Records CK 44316.
Zawinul, Joe. *Dialects*. FCT Records 40081.

# CHAPTER 13

## Controversy Among Stylistic Worlds

| | |
|---|---|
| *1890–1917* | Basic period for Early New Orleans Dixieland |
| *1917–1932* | Basic period for Chicago Style Dixieland |
| *1932–1942* | Swing bands predominate |
| *Early 1940s* | Dixieland revival |
| *1940–1950* | Bop emerges |
| *1949* | *Birth of the Cool* album recorded |
| *1949–1955* | Cool emerges |
| *1950s* | East Coast hard bop holding ground |

ur look at the many historical threads that define the jazz canon reveals a history that is much more continuous than is often suggested by period names like bop, cool and fusion. These threads connect the many otherwise unrelated events in jazz history and give it a continuity from which a tradition and an art form has emerged. The continuum of jazz styles was not always smooth, particularly at times of transition between the jazz periods. During these times, those who represent the older style find the tradition moving away from them. Some players, like Coleman Hawkins, attempted to move with the change. Others, like Miles Davis, took a lead in the change, while others were left behind. The instability caused by change is seldom a welcome byproduct of innovation. It is during these less stable times that the workings of jazz as a developing art form can be seen as old values are challenged and new replacements are found. What survives these transitions becomes the cornerstone precepts of the developed art form.

Most of the transitions from style to style were accompanied by some degree of controversy. What players and critics said then, and say now, about new styles is revealing. As an overview of the historical approach taken in this text, it is fitting that we follow one last thread that connects the controversies of jazz. Although the participants in the dialog change from period to period, the roles they play stay the same, i.e., protagonist and defender. In many cases, the protagonist of one period is the defender of the next.

If an art form is truly functional, it should work as an expression of contemporary culture, and jazz has served that function. Swing was popular before World War II when the public was celebrating an optimistic attitude; bop came along during the nervous time of the war; and relaxed comforting cool jazz soothed the public after the war was over. Music nostalgia is often a method for calling back the mood of previous periods. For example, swing nostalgia maps into good times. It creates a carefree atmosphere of dancing and a return to a time when jazz was more accessible and popular.

There have always been and always will be differences of opinion between advocates of the old and the new in the arts. On one side, we hear a call to traditionalism and on the other a call for innovation. At the same time, we hear accusations of bastardizing ''good'' music and accusations of commercialization. The response is usually couched in terms of progress and innovation. The term *unconventional* poses its own questions. Unconventional according to whom and what tradition? As compared to what other style? Such questions are especially troublesome when what was unconventional in one era later becomes the norm.

Players, listeners, and critics generally defend music in which they have invested. Players dedicate an enormous amount of energy and time to developing their skills. To find their skills outmoded and irrelevant is devastating. Listeners and critics often find comfort in familiar music. New styles require new understandings that may appear threatening. Critics might respond to such a dilemma by trying to decide issues of musical worth for the public and, in return, receive a validation of their own taste.

If jazz were always considered an art music, then the discomfort felt by many players and critics might be more easily resolved by applying principles of traditional practice to judge any new musical style that claims jazz status. However, such an approach is relatively new to jazz. Its short history allows us to see the popular roots of the now mature art form and weakens our defense of traditional jazz against contemporary popular and commercialized expressions. Jazz may still be too young to garner universal status as an art music of high esthetic value. Art music, in contrast to commercial music, is considered far away from the material world. Jazz still has a popular wing that works against this stereotypical criterion. How should records and other profits realized by leading jazz figures be considered within the jazz art world? Can traditionalists today hope to gain a lasting popularity? Wynton Marsalis seems to straddle this issue successfully. He is among the highest paid jazz figures but continues to preach traditional jazz values.

Stylistic controversy is not restricted to jazz. The classical music tradition, which is clearly secure in its art status, has suffered from the same transitional pressures. Wagner, Tchaikovsky, Mahler, Sibelius, and others pushed hard against the traditional classical music models of their day and created the late romantic styles they felt better expressed the emotions of the nineteenth century. A counterbalancing approach was taken in the impressionism of Ravel and Debussy. As striking as these new approaches were then, they now hold a firm place in the symphonic repertoire, while later twentieth century innovations have yet to gain significant concert programming.

The classical music model is not altogether encouraging as a model for a developing art form. Will jazz also fall further and further behind as a representative of contemporary cultural values? The twentieth century with its more complex lifestyles brought a definite break with the music of Schoenberg, Berg, Webern, Bartok, and Stravinsky. Even though these composers were responding to the values of their day, their contemporary listeners preferred music from earlier periods. One begins to question whether the very tradition that granted classical music an art status may interfere with the art form's interaction with contemporary culture. Mapping this into the jazz art world, we would find new jazz expressions without any considerable audience as the traditional audience continues to look back to traditional expressions rather than to contemporary ones.

## DIXIELAND TO SWING

Dixieland, because of its collective improvisation, might sound confused compared to a big band like Goodman's. The swing bands with their arrangements (homophonically in general) actually sound more traditional by academic standards. The more formalized arrangements grew out of the requirements big bands had to fill large ballrooms and theaters. Small bands like Dixieland, bop, or cool worked in smaller clubs. Dixieland players were generally concerned about future employment as the swing bands grew in popularity, and there were high salaries in some of the large bands. Many players hoped to get a job with a large band in order to survive. One of the problems was that more technical competence was demanded of the instrumentalists.

Either these players had to adopt the new tool kit of the big band player or try to continue their work as less popular Dixieland players. Although the change from Dixieland to swing appears historically smooth and free of controversy, the transition was not completely welcomed. The Dixieland revival was in some respects a call back to times when the small group format with improvisational arrangements was more popular and lucrative. The experimental work with the swing bands of Fletcher Henderson, Don Redman, et al., paved the way for a very profitable profession for those who could adopt the playing styles and skills needed in the sectionalized big band format.

## SWING TO BOP AND THE DIXIELAND REVIVAL

Dixieland stylization continued to be heard within the big band format but it usually appeared in the small groups that played the breaks of the big band. The popularity of the big bands appeared to be resistant to newcomers. However, the small group format was to reappear with a vengeance. Suddenly there was another great leap into complexity by the bop players. Like the many Dixieland players left out by the more technical big band requirements, many of the swing players found themselves unable to adopt the new complexity of bop.

> The health and vitality of swing during the early postwar years, perhaps generated by the enthusiasm of a successful war effort, gave it an impetus that carried it safely through the 40s and, with diminishing intensity, virtually to the end of the 1950s. Other styles began to develop, and they all coexisted with swing and the revived old-time jazz. Swing remained the most popular of all jazz styles, even though it was supplanted as the greatest influence in the jazz community.[1]

Tirro's mention of the revived old-time jazz refers to the fact that the Early New Orleans Dixieland style had an impressive revival in the early 1940s. Prominent in this movement was Lu Watters and his Yerba Buena Jazz Band based in Oakland, California. This band, like others in the movement, did everything possible to recreate King Oliver's style. The advocates of this style of jazz referred to their music as the ''real'' or ''pure'' jazz. This purist jazz school was intolerant, as jazz schools tend to be. With swing on the decline and another style (bop) moving in, there is no doubt that players of Dixieland saw an opportunity to gain status. They had a proven product

---

[1]Frank Tirro, *Jazz: A History* (New York: W. W. Norton & Co. Inc., 1977), 261.

(Dixieland) against an unestablished style that seemed to evoke strong opposition (bop), and Dixieland used small groups logical at this time of wartime drafts and transportation problems. However, even though Dixieland nor swing ever died out, bop became the next force in the changing music scene.

In the early 1940s, the big bands were going strong and the Dixieland revival was in full swing. The bop musicians were definitely not a part of the musical establishment. Nevertheless, the bebop (later simply bop) movement began to gain momentum in the mid-1940s.

The swing band pressures of accurately sight reading scores, traveling to one night stands, and feeling like a cog turned many players toward the new style. Bop was a revolt against the confines of the larger bands. The short, stylized solos typical of the large bands of the Swing era minimized the opportunity for exploratory expression. Soloists not only desired more freedom for experimentation, they also searched for a fresh and different approach to jazz. They felt that many musicians with little creativeness were earning more than their share of fame and wealth and that the time had come for many changes.

The shift to bop embraced the most radical changes in the development of jazz to this point. In the 1940s, jazz stopped being a music for dancing and became a music for listening. For greater freedom of expression, these players used extended harmonies in their improvised choruses. Harmonies were extended through the successive inclusion of higher harmonics of the overtone series. This resulted in an extensive use of ninth, eleventh, and thirteenth chords and beyond. Use of the flatted fifth became so ordinary that from this point on it was considered another ''blue note'' just as the third and seventh tones of the scale had been. Guitarist Eddie Condon, offering a Dixieland reaction, is reputed to have said, ''They flat their fifths, we drink ours.''

When large bands used bop harmonic and melodic developments, it was labeled ''progressive'' jazz. At first, the only contributions in this direction were solos in big bands by such musicians as Gillespie and Parker, but soon entire bands were dedicated to these new directions. The progressive band leaders included Stan Kenton (who even adopted the label ''progressive''), Woody Herman, Earl Hines, Billy Eckstine, Earl Spencer, Boyd Raeburn, and bands led by Dizzy Gillespie himself. The Boyd Raeburn band played music as far removed from earlier swing bands as could be envisioned.

Oddly enough, while one of the biggest complaints that the bop players registered about the swing bands was that there was not enough solo space, the Swing era fostered many of the greatest soloists jazz has known: Coleman Hawkins, Benny Goodman (with his big band), Lester Young (from the big Count Basie band), and Louis Armstrong who sounded superb in front of Louis Russell's big band.

Pianist Claude Thornhill, with arranger Gil Evans and a large band in 1947, recorded solos by Charlie Parker as he had played "Anthropology" and "Yardbird Suite," but large bands proved too unwieldy for bop.

In 1945, Dizzy Gillespie organized his first band. He preferred the larger band at a time when all other bop advocates were performing in combos. His big band, called Hep-Sations of 1945, was short-lived. The reactions to Gillespie's style of playing ranged all the way from unqualified enthusiasm to pure indignation. Today, such criticism is all but forgotten. Gillespie is highly regarded all over the world, and his contributions to modern trends are undisputed.

Bop would have seen earlier success had it not been for the musicians' union strike against the record companies. The strike resulted in a recording ban from 1942 to 1945. However, by the time Parker came on the scene, musicians and jazz fans alike had aligned themselves with either bop or prebop.

The lack of immediate acceptance and the flow of criticism caused each bop group to form cliques and adopt many nonmusical characteristics that set the bop players apart, such as language, behavior, goatees, berets, etc. The adage that creative musical adventurers are not appreciated during their time by the masses, critics, or musicians also proved true of the early boppers. Bop received harsh criticism even as late as 1959 with an article in the *New Yorker* saying,

> Of all the queer, uncommunicative, secret-society that jazz has associated itself with, few are lumpier or more misleading than "bebop." Originally a casual onomatopoeic word to describe the continually shifting accents of the early work of Charlie Parker, Dizzy Gillespie, Kenny Clarke, and Thelonious Monk (c. 1944), it soon became a free-floating, generic one as well, whose tight, rude sound implied something harsh, jerky, and unattractive.[2]

For all this criticism, bop is now established as the creative and artistic way to improvise jazz.

It is true that some musicians were attempting to create an exclusive and elite club; all who could not perform (compete) in their style were absolutely excluded. The musicians who played regularly at Minton's devised ways to discourage the unwanted from sitting in

---

[2]Whitney Balliett, *The New Yorker,* 7 November 1959, 158.

on the jam sessions. They would play tunes at such fast tempos and play (using substitute chords) what at the time were strange sounds that those musicians not really in the clique simply would leave the bandstand.

Retaliation went both ways: the unappreciative audience who did not understand bop shunned the new style as if it were truly a cult of some sort, and the disciples of bop in turn rejected the public and even the nonparticipating musicians. At first, this art that is now so well embraced was such a radical change that the bop players were disassociated from anyone, nonjazz public and/or nonbop musicians.

The goal of these musicians was truly a logical and perhaps even a noble one. They were enthusiastically attempting to raise the quality of jazz; whether they were consciously working to establish jazz as an art form is debatable. Evidently they have succeeded. The Dixieland revival had lost its impetus. The remaining swing bands were having survival crises. There was the progressive jazz of the big Stan Kenton orchestra and the more bop oriented big band of Woody Herman, both losing their grips on the huge swing audiences.

The bop players became the protagonists. They demonstrated a new playing style designed to establish a new elite in jazz. The speed of execution and angular melodic lines expected of new boppers was outside the normal performance skill of the average swing musician. The reaction to bop among swing players was strong but unsuccessful. However, the audience of the swing groups did not automatically follow the new direction bop took. Bop had essentially shed both players and audience as it began its ascendancy. As we will see later, this disassociation with the popular market eventually becomes the defense bop uses to maintain its place at the artistic center of jazz.

Cool players showed definite changes from bop, shifting away from virtuosic complexity to a more subtle delivery. Just as the bop style of jazz was a reaction against swing, the cool style of playing was a reaction against bop. In fact, one of cool's problems was that audiences react best to virtuosity and histrionics, whereas this music sacrificed excitement for subtlety, and the players underplayed their variations. Bop audiences did not always appreciate the subtle complexities of cool. Generally, cool phrasing did not permit the players to deviate far from the original line. Their opposition viewed this as backtracking rather than advancing. Their critics felt that cool lines usually lacked the boldness and richness of music of the Bop era. Critics overlooked the small but significant changes made in cool, for example, that drummer Chico Hamilton featured cellest Fred Katz or that Gerry Mulligan had a pianoless quartet.

## BOP TO COOL AND BACK AGAIN

The 1949 *Birth of the Cool* album with Miles Davis did not have the instrumental section typical of the swing bands, and it had too many melody instruments for bop. It was a group mainly from the Claude Thornhill band who wanted to test some Gil Evans and Gerry Mulligan arrangements. Other talented arrangers, such as John Lewis and John Carisi, also contributed. Retracters overlooked that the cool performers were seeking a more subtle means of jazz expression. After all, Lester Young, the model for cool tenor saxophonists, played softer than Coleman Hawkins (the swing standard bearer) and was more subtle and abstract. The cool players tended to group unlike instruments in search of a new ensemble sound.

Both cool and bop players could be found on both coasts. Their geographical locations were not as sharply drawn as marketing promotion of the day may have suggested. However, the West Coast did, undeniably, offer cool players a rich center for their exchange of ideas. The East Coast eventually did recapture the mainstream as the hard bop style emerged in response to the more intellectual cool style popular on the West Coast. The debate between the two styles was further fueled by the fact that the West Coast musicians were predominately white, while the East Coast hard boppers were mostly African Americans. The white players came most often out of the swing band tradition, while the African-American players usually were associated with the bop style.

Players and ensembles were not as easily categorized as the labels, cool and hard bop, might imply. Most musicians consider Stan Getz a cool tenor saxophone player even though bop comes through unmistakably on his records. Gerry Mulligan, a West Coast musician, also has shown his great talents in a variety of directions. Lester Young, the president of the Cool era, was weaned on the great swing sounds of the Count Basie band. Miles Davis was playing bop with that music's high priest, Charlie Parker. Hasn't George Shearing played many bop passages with a cool feeling? Bopper Dizzy Gillespie recorded with a large band of his own. The large bands of Kenton and Herman made bop sounds, while Thornhill's large band made cool sounds. Is the Herman recording of ''Four Brothers'' a swing band, a cool saxophone section, or a bop exhibition? These musicians, along with many others, have shown us that jazz does not stand still and is not confined to neat categories. They also show us that individual musicians need not remain in one groove and that many musicians have been constantly searching for, or are aware of, fresh new creative means to express their art.

Although the mainstream was not completely defined in the late 1950s and early 1960s, it faced its first real challenge by the avant-garde school during this period. The work of such players as Ornette Coleman threatened the continuity of the jazz tradition. Coleman's challenge was primarily a melodic and harmonic one. He does not threaten the basic rhythmic premise of the small-group ensemble in terms of the roles played by the performers. Although his rhythmic extensions explore heterophonic areas, his biggest challenge is in the areas of nonchord melodic activity and the dissolution of harmonic centers. The fact that he even worked without a piano player testified to his effort in this area.

What Coleman started was developed further by the Chicago school, which often exhibited even fewer of the traditional jazz attributes. The blur of activity with the classical music world's new music efforts further clouded these players' role in the development of a jazz tradition.

Just as the bop players had left one audience to find another, the avant-garde school abandoned the developing mainstream audience. The avant-garde audience was, at best, a small subset of the jazz community and depended as much on their academic audience as they did on their jazz supporters. As much as the experimental music of the 1960s reflected the scientific inquiry of the newly emerging technological society and the unrest it created, it was never well received by the mass jazz or classical audience who actually lived in that high-tech culture. Its very small audience created no real challenge to the more durable jazz expression established by mainstream players.

This does not mean there was no controversy, however. Dan Morgenstern expresses the dilemma the jazz community experienced as it tried to assimilate the innovative work of its avant-garde.

MAINSTREAM AND THE AVANT-GARDE

> But is it jazz? Some of the main elements are lacking. There is little of what we have come to know as "swing." There is often none of the formal organization found in most jazz—rhythm section and melody instruments, solo versus ensemble, strict time, etc. Yet, the sound and feeling is often of a kind peculiar to jazz as we have become accustomed to it, and it is certainly not "classical" music in any sense of that ill-defined word. Whatever it may be—and one often has the feeling that even the musicians don't quite know what they have hold of; it is a music in flux, if anything—it must not be burdened with comparisons that are unwarranted.

> To accuse a drummer of not swinging when he
> doesn't want to achieve swing in the sense that his critic
> has in mind is unfair and pointless. To demand
> adherence to formal patterns that the musicians are
> obviously rejecting is as foolish as taking a painter of
> geometric abstractions to task for being
> nonrepresentational.[3]

## MAINSTREAM AND FUSION

The established jazz mainstream met its first real challenge from the increasingly popular art world of rock music. Rock currently enjoys the same public favor that swing did in the 1930s and 1940s. Now the cry from the jazz traditionalists is that fusion with rock is a commercialization of the jazz art form. Wynton Marsalis' recording, ''Death of Jazz,'' expresses the neoclassical response to jazz's flirtation with the popular music culture.[4]

The jazz mainstream is founded on the bop expression, an expression that once acted as a protagonist in the developing jazz tradition, and now works to fend off new innovations or fusions that threaten its precepts. As we noted earlier, the loss of audience during the bop period helps substantiate that style as a musical art form worthy of an elite listening audience. By fusing with rock, jazz risks a popularity that seems to violate the definition of an elite jazz audience and, in turn, jeopardizes the art status of jazz.

## SUMMARY

There are many scenarios that can play themselves out as jazz matures as an art form. It may find, like classical music today, that it spends most of its time looking back as it searches for continued authentification. The fact that jazz is still a performer and improvisationally centered art form may prevent that from happening. We should remember that classical music also once had an exciting improvisational component but lost it to compositional intent. Jazz, as it looks for its own repertory, may suffer a similar loss. Also by looking back, jazz may respond more slowly to current cultural issues. For now, jazz still offers us a relatively quick response to social and cultural change. It still works as a mirror of the struggle for diversity prevalent in American culture and best reflects the dialectic posed when cultures merge. Most of all, jazz has offered us an example of how things that

---

[3]Dan Morgenstern, ''The October Revolution—Two Views of the Avant-Garde in Action,'' *Down Beat* 34, no. 30 (November 1964):33.
[4]Wynton Marsalis, ''Death of Jazz,'' *The Majesty of the Blues,* CBS CK 45091.

we value gain status in our society. The uniqueness of the jazz art form reflects the unique balance of influences at work in our culture as they are played out by the individual artists who have defined the jazz tradition.

---

Billy Eckstine Orchestra. *Big Band Jazz*. Smithsonian.

Blakey, Art, and The Jazz Messengers. *Album of the Year*. Timeless SJP 155.

Coleman, Ornette. ''Free Jazz.'' Smithsonian J/2 (cd V/9).

Davis, Miles. *The Birth of the Cool*. Capitol Records N 16168.

Gillespie, Dizzy, and Charlie Parker. ''Shaw 'Nuff.'' Smithsonian E/7 (cd III/11).

*The Great Benny Goodman*. Columbia Records CL 826.

Herman, Woody. *The Thundering Herds, Vol. 1*. Columbia Records C3L 25.

*The Kenton Era*. The Creative World of Stan Kenton ST 1030.

King Oliver's Creole Jazz Band. ''Dippermouth Blues.'' Smithsonian A/5 (cd I/5).

**SUGGESTED LISTENING**

# Epilogue: A Changing Historical Perspective

H istory is a collection of details related to us only through the present. The present status of jazz is the constantly moving window through which we struggle to see and understand its past. As the social and musical context of the present shifts under the influence of social, political, and cultural forces, so does our understanding of the events that have shaped the present context. In effect, our understanding of the past changes as the things we value change. It is possible for former heroes and heroines of the past to be forgotten or even vilified if the influence they exerted on history loses value in the eyes of future historians. The most prominent example is the historical role Columbus is believed to have played when he ''discovered'' America. From a New World perspective, he is a hero; from an indigenous rights perspective, he is a conqueror. As in this case, history is not static but constantly undergoing reevaluation.

Although it is the intent of historians to remain neutral in their interpretation of past events, the story they tell will always be presented through the filter of contemporary society and that society's values. For example, in the early days of jazz, it is unlikely that anyone questioned the fact that few women outside of vocalists took prominent jazz roles. Today, with our concern for gender equity, we are confronted by the glaring absence of women in jazz history. How we deal with this more recent revelation is then framed by our understanding of gender equity. Depending on individual interpretations of gender equity, we could paint figures from the past either as societally blind to the gender exclusion or as responsible for that exclusion.

Because of the controversy surrounding such a questioning of history, we tend to state only the details of history and hope they speak for themselves without risking the relevant connection to present values. The risk is intensified further by the fact that history is liquid. A relevant connection today may be a naive notion tomorrow. What may appear an obvious, relevant connection to our history now may prove controversial in the future.

Shifting historical understandings have often created controversy in our understanding of the developing jazz tradition. Because jazz is a uniquely American expression, it must emanate from uniquely American forces. In the case of jazz, those forces were the cultural crosscurrents of the western European historical context and the African-American performance practice. It is likely the players who found themselves at the center of the crosscurrents worked unconscious of any future controversy as they forged the expression we now call jazz. Our historical understanding of that effort surrounds it with some controversy as we try to recreate the context in which jazz grew to be an art form. What did each of the crosscurrents offer the jazz legacy? Which of the crosscurrents were dominant and might claim ownership? Unfortunately, a discussion of such questions can lead to heated debate rather than a better historical appreciation.

How might we investigate this exciting intersection of two global cultural crosscurrents in an objective and fair manner? As we have seen in earlier chapters, the larger evolutionary lines that sit above the historical data of jazz helped us see the crosscurrents more clearly. Understanding where we are today presents a much more difficult task. As a culture, we think differently and value different things than the early jazz figures. The fact that jazz was originally relegated to less respectful social areas and is now respected as an American art form certainly implies a shift in our historical understanding. It also presents more questions like those that introduced this text. If jazz is currently revered as an art form, when did the art tradition begin? Did it include the earliest players? Does it include the bebop players even if they were not seen as such during their own day? Does the art form work retroactively? Is it possible that the most popular players in the early tradition were actually lesser players in our current understanding of the jazz tradition?

Such questions lead us to an even larger evolutionary line that sits above those discussed in preceding chapters, an evolutionary line that serves as a musical analog for the interaction of these two cultural crosscurrents. It is at this larger level that we see the continually shifting balance between the two traditions. It is also at this level that we place our understanding of the jazz of the present in a more objective context.

## PREJAZZ

The influence each of the two crosscurrents of jazz exerted was not always constant. At times, one or the other dominated the expression or approach taken by the leading jazz figures. The interaction between the two currents began during the prejazz period in which the traditional song forms of the western European tradition met the expressive and spontaneous stylizations characteristic of the African Americans. The blending we see in New Orleans was not completely free from controversy. Although Jelly Roll Morton is considered one of the first African-American jazz figures, he adamantly associated himself with the Creole culture rather than that of the former African-American slave culture. The cross-cultural result is very interesting. Morton is respected for his early accomplishments in arranging for jazz ensembles. In effect, he placed the African-American stylizations on the western European construct of composition. It is ironic that Morton's first prominence was gained as a result of his compositional approach. He had essentially used a western European construct to offer the African-American expression a window to the American musical mainstream.

## DIXIELAND

The compositional glue weakened and the African-American voice found more prominence in the succeeding music of New Orleans Dixieland. The spontaneity and individual expression that characterized the music of the African American dominated the performance practice. As with the music of Morton, however, the shift in balance between the two cultural crosscurrents was not complete. New Orleans Dixieland often used as its musical substrate composed songs taken from the white musical mainstream. As Dixieland moved north, the balance shifted slightly as white players like Bix Beiderbecke and the Original Dixieland Band began to appear as main contributors to the developing genre.

## SWING

The next major shift occurred as Dixieland gave way to swing. Two paths were taken as the Big Band era came into full bloom. The East Coast expression kept the African-American stylization but moved toward a heavily composed platform. Henderson, Carter, and Redman all proved their arranging talent as they pulled the purse strings on the previously loose ensemble used in the Dixieland groups. Again the shift in balance was not complete. Although their work was noted, the arrangements left room for a wide range of stylization and individual contributions.

The second path to the big band expression was taken by Southwest bands like Basie. His approach at first followed the improvised compositional style typical of the Dixieland bands. The instrumental sections used riffing patterns to build spontaneous compositions that supported individual soloists. This approach relied heavily on the available soloists and proved too unstable for Basie to maintain. His later groups adopted the more composed approach and were characterized by an impressive ensemble accuracy that required a lockstep execution by all the players.

The compositional path launched the white bands commonly associated with the Big Band era. These bands often had arrangers who were as well known as many of the players in the bands. It was at this time that jazz became the world's music. Jazz had entered the American mainstream and America was playing out a major role on the world stage. At no other time would jazz be as popular as it was at this time. As we saw in chapter 8, these white bands were a critical factor in validating jazz as potential art form.

Perhaps the most balanced expression during this period was struck by Ellington, who placed jazz in a larger compositional construct but still maintained a compositional looseness that allowed his players to use their individual voices. During this time, African-American bands did not have the same access as white bands to the media and so were less known in the popular market than their white counterparts. As we will see later, our collective historical understanding of this period has addressed this disparity and shifted accordingly.

## BEBOP

The shift away from the swing bands to the smaller and more improvisational groups of bebop is perhaps one of the most dramatic in the evolution of jazz. As the musical style and intensity increased, its popular following decreased. The expression and the main players were predominantly African American. The individual became the focus and the musical composition secondary. The soloist's ability to speak spontaneously became a major criterion for success. This period has recently gained the most attention historically. It housed the players by which today's players are still judged. It is the manner in which they are judged that reveals the western European influence on our understanding of this period. Very often the long solos played during this period are analyzed for their compositional merit. Players who stand the tallest during this period were often the ones that crafted the most coherent solos, and coherency is often defined as compositional continuity. A comparison of the neoclassical jazz school, in many ways is a revisit of the bebop period, and bebop reflects some of this historical precept. Bebop of the 1950s and bebop of the 1990s, although quite similar on the surface, is somehow different. One is a mirror of the other but lost in the reflection is some of the fire and individuality that made the original what it was.

## COOL

In a very conscious way, cool was an attempt to take that fire out of the jazz expression and replace it with a very subtle and understated voice. The music itself was generated by a predominantly white group of musicians. Miles Davis was a central figure in the early stirrings of cool. Davis was the focus of and protagonist for the group. Again, as in the popular big band tradition, the personal expression of the individual voice was exchanged for a more defined ensemble sound. Rather than the sectionalized approach, which gave the big bands their big sound, the cool ensembles looked for subtle orchestrations that were new to the jazz medium. Although the pendulum had seemed to swing in the other direction as dramatically as bebop did from swing, it still left room for the individual voice within the compositional texture. Miles Davis' work with Gil Evans is a prime example. Cool reached the end of its swing in the West Coast style developed by many of the former players of Stan Kenton's band.

## HARD BOP

It was against the West Coast expression of cool that the hard bop group reacted. Unlike many of the former swings in style, this reaction may have carried conscious racial overtones. Some players were consciously trying to pull jazz back toward a more African-American expression. It was also at this time that jazz was developing a consciousness about its own tradition. At such times it is not surprising to have the participants of an emerging art form be concerned with its future direction.

Jazz was also facing one of its first big challenges as it again pulled away from the American musical mainstream. Because of the immense popularity of the big bands, jazz had earned a place in American culture that was originally tied to popular taste. In many ways, bebop went unnoticed by popular culture as listeners continued to listen to the music of the swing bands. The tug of war between bop and cool was not played out on the same popular music stage. Cool did work its way into movie and television more than bop did, but it still was not as popular as the sounds of the big bands. The big challenge to jazz came in the form of rock and roll. As we will see, the reaction to this outside influence left lasting marks.

## THIRD STREAM

As we saw in chapters 10 and 11, music of the third stream is perhaps the clearest example of the western European influence on the developing jazz tradition. Composers once again took the lead, this time to such an extent that they opened a relationship with the main participants of the classical school itself. Some very interesting hybrids began to appear that have not been fully claimed by either the jazz or classical traditions. Where do the works of Gershwin belong? They seem a little too popular to have claimed a place in the classical music canon, yet in both composition and performance, they are too similar to the classical music model to be considered a part of the third steam effort. Stravinisky and Milhaud, however, have earned such solid reputations in the classical music world that their jazz related works are embraced more by the classical music world.[1]

## FREE JAZZ

As we saw in chapter 11, there was more than one road to the free jazz expression. One grew out of the extended practice of jazz players like Coltrane, and the other developed out of a more compositional approach similar to that used in academia. As we relate these jazz periods to the interaction between the two dominant crosscurrents driving jazz, we find one of the most interesting balances in jazz. The main players in this medium, Coleman, Braxton, Taylor, Coltrane, and AACM clearly purport the African-American expression. At the same time, Academic classical music was experimenting with a free approach toward music composition and performance. In fact, the AACM grew out of an academic setting in Chicago. It is also at this intersection that players and composers are shared across the two art worlds, Braxton being the primary example.

---

[1]Stravinsky, "Ebony Concerto," Milhaud, "Le Boeuf sur le toit."

The first path to free jazz, that of extending the improvisational practice already at work in jazz until it becomes free, leads to an arena shared by those who took the other path of compositional reasoning. Depending on the context from which the result is viewed, free jazz could be seen as either the purest form of spontaneous and improvised music in step with the African-American tradition or as the ultimate in compositional abstraction, a western European historical value.

## FUSION, JAZZ, AND ROCK AND ROLL

Rock and roll grabbed the attention of youth in the 1950s the way swing had done for youth in the 1930s and 1940s. Jazz had several responses to this newcomer to the American music scene. On the one hand it flirted with fusion, and on the other hand, it attempted to shut it out. Early rock and roll's initial challenge to jazz as the popular American musical expression was not granted much credence, because by that time jazz had begun to define itself as more elite and not in need of a large popular audience. It was not until rock elements began to be imported by jazz practitioners that the challenge was taken seriously.

Rock, like jazz, grew out of the crosscurrents of western European and the African-American musical practice. This time the starting points were somewhat different, folk and country music on the one hand and rhythm and blues on the other hand. Also like jazz, rock is currently being defined by the two constantly blending but distinct cultural traditions.

As rock picked up the front edge of the two interacting currents, jazz was left to solidify its own identity and fortify it against possible absorption by the cresting rock popularity. It was during this period that the jazz participants first began to look back to their own tradition as a way to discover and maintain their own identity. As the jazz community looked back, disagreement arose about how the new rock influence was to be handled. One argument labeled rock a foreign influence that should be kept out of the jazz expression, while another touts it as the next step in jazz's development. This argument cooled as jazz retreated to a neoclassical model, leaving rock to address the more transient interplay between the two cultural crosscurrents.

The first efforts at fusing with rock took on a highly improvisatory nature in Davis's *Bitches Brew*. The later expressions took much the same path earlier forms did by formalizing it with compositional and ensemble performance requirements. The later fusion groups Return to Forever and Weather Report imposed ensemble virtuosity and angular composed lines over the imported rock rhythm section. There was still room for virtuosic solo flights but the overall structure had taken on a more controlled form.

A new hybrid of jazz and rock later appeared that softened the virtuosic display as it moved toward a more popular audience. The result was a pop/jazz/rock fusion that had a very short-lived stay in the jazz art world. It did not fade away. It only moved toward the popular mainstream and away from the center of the jazz community. It is ironic that this new popular form of jazz, although not embraced by the traditional jazz community, became the only jazz many young people knew. In fact, the response from the jazz community often expressed a frustration that this popular music should be called jazz when it seemed only loosely tied to the history they favored.

## *JAZZ HISTORY'S CENTER OF GRAVITY*

By the early 1990s the jazz community had found its center of gravity in the bebop period. This is particularly interesting because the music of that period was not the most popular at that time. In fact, it had a very small audience; the major jazz audience still listened to swing music. Why is it that bebop gained this eminence when other periods were so much more popular? It would seem that the Swing era would have garnered an equal if not greater respect because of its world-wide appeal.

At the same time that jazz's center moved towards bebop, there was also a subtle shifting of importance throughout our historical understanding of jazz. The white bands that were clearly the most popular during the Big Band era were losing pages in history books to their African-American contemporaries. The emergence of the neoclassical school of jazz, a historically conscious movement, traces its history exclusively through a line of African-American players. Although the details of history have not changed, certainly our changing understanding of it has caused us to reshape it.

Jazz has moved a long way from its earliest stirrings in the red-light districts of major urban areas to today's classrooms. Jazz as an art form was certainly not on the minds of the first jazz players, but it most certainly is on the minds of today's players and teachers. In fact, today's musicians carry the weight and responsibility of this new historical understanding. It is this historical framework that will continue to offer the criteria by which contemporary performance will be judged. Terms like *straight ahead* and *mainstream* jazz signal such an allegiance to the past. It is perhaps ironic that such a historical perspective is basically western European. Current consensus grants the ownership of jazz to the African-American crosscurrent, but at the same time, places it in a uniquely western European historical context, a context which is able to grant validity to jazz as an art form. This unique interplay of the two crosscurrents is embodied in the term *America's classical music.* This is further proof that the two crosscurrents remain both healthy and distinct.

## PROSPECTS FOR AN ART FORM

Jazz has ultimately followed a course similar to that of the classical music tradition, also defined by a particular center of gravity not on the front edge of its own development. The basic repertory of classical music comes from the tonal literature of the Baroque, Classical, and Romantic eras. Only a small portion of today's repertory is dedicated to the compositions from the last one hundred years. The basic repertory of jazz, as defined by the programming of the Lincoln Center's jazz series, also looks back more than ahead. The notion of repertory jazz is relatively new, a repertory that recognizes early jazz figures and charts a direct course to the leading figures of the Bebop era. Even after the controversial exchange with the rock musical stream, jazz remains a basically acoustic musical expression typical of the Bebop era. So solid and defined is the current jazz definition that even a logical derivative like the bebop laced rock fusion of Michael Brecker is not easily embraced by the established jazz community.

As this text began with questions, it ends with questions. If jazz continues to follow the same path as other art forms, such as classical music, will it also develop at a rate associated with larger and slower moving cultural shifts rather than the faster paced cultural fashions which guided it in its early years? Has jazz, like classical music, lost its front edge of discovery? What price has jazz paid for its ascendancy to art form status? Will jazz become a history in which the names of the players change but the music doesn't?

These questions like those that began this text lead us into areas of study that can only be understood within the context of our present values. Because those values are not stable, the historical truths that emanate from them are also not stable. The danger of dealing with the present is that we are too close to clearly see it. Only those who look back on us in the future will be able to place us in the greater historical perspective, and like us, their values will frame their understanding of us.

# *Appendix A*

## LISTENING GUIDES

# *Appendix B*

## DATELINE BIOGRAPHIES AND BOXES

# Glossary

**a cappella**
Vocal music without instrumental accompaniment.

**accent**
To stress a melodic note, rhythm, or harmony by playing it louder and with a sharper attack.

**accompaniment**
To perform with another performer or performers, usually in a less prominent role; for example, to play the piano accompaniment for a trombone soloist.

**amplification**
The process of electronically making a sound louder.

**analog**
The type of audio signal produced by early synthesizers. Voltage rather than numbers are used to describe the musical sounds.

**appoggiatura**
A musical ornament consisting of a single tone moving to an adjacent tone which is harmonized.

**arhythmic**
Seemingly without meter; music that lacks a definite beat.

**arpeggio**
The individual tones of a chord are not sounded simultaneously but performed like a melody (single tones), nearly always starting at the bottom or lowest tone.

**arrangement**
An adaptation of a musical composition (often called *charts* in musical slang). In a written arrangement, the musical arranger writes out the notes each performer is to play. In a head arrangement, the arrangement is made up out of someone's head, not written down.

**arranger**
One who writes musical compositions for particular groups of performers.

**atonal**
Lacking in tonal centers; free jazz often has atonal areas that avoid the chord and melodic relationships normally associated with the major-minor system.

**attack**
The manner in which the tone or tones are first sounded.

**avant-garde**
Composers and performers who break away from traditional practices and push for radical change; used primarily to describe postbop jazz.

**backbeat**
In a 4/4 measure, the second and fourth beats are sometimes called the backbeats; also, a song that has strong accents on those beats is said to have a backbeat.

**ballad**
A simple song, usually romantic in nature, which uses the same melody for each stanza.

**bar line**
A vertical line drawn down a music staff dividing it into bars or measures.

**bar of music**
A means of dividing music; also called a measure of music.

**bass (brass)**
The member of the brass family sounding the lowest tones; generally referred to as the *tuba.*

**bass (string)**
An instrument that looks like a very large violin; also called the *bass violin.* The string bass is played either by plucking the strings with the fingers (*pizzicato*) or by bowing (*arco*).

**beat or breaker music**
A musical style characterized by electronic drum machines and a heavy beat; designed for break dancing.

**block chords**
Usually chords with many notes that move in parallel motion.

**blue tonalities**
The alteration of the third and seventh tones of the major scale by a flatting inflection.

**bombs**
Spontaneous punctuations by the drummer.

**break**
A short interruption in the flow of the music; an interlude in which a solo player improvises or an accompanying group interpolates.

**bridge**
The name given to the third eight-bar section in the most common construction of a thirty-two bar chorus. In an AABA construction, the B is the bridge.

**call-and-response pattern**
A musical pattern common to much jazz and African music in which a "call," usually by a solo singer or instrumentalist, is followed by a "response" from one instrument, an ensemble, or the assembled participants in a ritual. In religious ceremonies, the congregation may respond to the "call" of the preacher.

**canon**
A form of contrapuntal writing in which the melody, announced by one voice, is imitated by an answering voice.

**canon, historical**
A historical description of the evolution of an art form which is supported by general consensus. This description identifies the historically important figures, events, and compositions most valued by contemporary listeners.

**chaconne**
Movement composed with a repeating bass line usually written in form of variations.

**chamber music**
Music intended for small groups performing in intimate surroundings, as distinct from large groups performing in concert halls, theaters, and the like.

**chance music**
Music based on chance or random relationships, such as the throwing of dice.

**Charleston**
A dance form extremely popular during the 1920s.

**chord**
The simultaneous sounding of three or more tones.

**chord changes**
A series of successive chords; also called *chord progression.*

**chorus**
The main body or refrain of a song as distinct from the verse, which comes first. Very often an arrangement contains many choruses played by individual instrumentalists.

**chromatic**
Refers to the scales or the alteration of scale tones by using half steps.

**collective improvisation**
A situation in which all members of a small group improvise simultaneously.

**combo**
A small instrumental group consisting of three to eight players.

**comp** or **comping**
The rhythmic pattern used by keyboard or guitar players as they accompany soloists. Comping generally makes use of short rhythmic statements of the harmony, leaving room for the soloist to be heard.

**compact disc**
A disc smaller than vinyl records which holds digital information that describes the musical sounds.

**concerto grosso**
A composition consisting of interplay between a large body of instruments (orchestra) and a small group of instrumentalists (combo).

**Congo Square**
A large field in New Orleans where slaves gathered to sing and dance.

**contrived**
Music that is planned beforehand.

**Creole**
A person with African and French or Spanish ancestry.

**crossover**
A style of music that appeals to more than one type of listener; usually refers to jazz/rock *fusion.*

**cross rhythm**
Two or more rhythmic patterns played simultaneously.

**cutting contest**
Individual musicians attempting to outplay one another, usually in a jam session type of situation.

**diatonic**
Pertains to the precise arrangement of tones as found in the major and minor scales.

**digital**
The use of numbers to describe a sound. The numbers can then be processed by computers or effects. The digital information is converted back to analog form for human hearing.

**digital recording**
Computer method of recording sound through the use of numbers.

**distortion**
The alteration of a sound, normally by overamplifying it, to create a rougher sound.

**Dorian mode**
The arrangement of tones found in the scale using only the white keys of the piano from D to D.

**double stop**
Two tones stopped by the fingers on a stringed instrument and sounded simultaneously.

**double time**
When the tempo of the music becomes twice as fast.

**drum machine**
An electronic device used to create drum patterns similar to those played by traditional set or trap drummers.

**editing**
Cutting or reassembling a recorded tape. Editing was originally done by actually cutting the tape. It can now be done electronically as the final mixdown is made.

**effects**
Electronic devices that alter electronic sounds (e.g., reverberation, delays, distortion).

**eleventh chord**
A chord consisting of six different tones, each separated by an interval of a third.

**embouchure**
Disposition of the lips and tongue in playing wind instruments.

**ensemble**
Usually a small group of performers, as distinct from an orchestra or choir.

**extended harmony**
Tones added to a chord.

**field hollers**
A secret means of communication among slaves while they worked in the fields; sometimes called *field cries.*

**fill-in**
Originally, a short interlude in a song (such as a blues song) played by an instrumentalist.

**flatted fifth**
Lowering by a half step the fifth degree of the scale or chord.

**flatted tone**
Used to lower the pitch one half step.

**flügelhorn**
A type of brass instrument with valves, similar to a trumpet.

**form**
Refers to the design of a composition, its repeated and contrasting parts.

**free form**
A term used to describe free jazz's lack of traditional restrictions in form and structure.

**free improvisation**
A descriptive term that stresses the complete improvisational nature of free jazz.

**front line**
Instrumentalists who are placed along the front of an ensemble.

**fugue**
A type of contrapuntal composition for a given number of parts. Each part is introduced individually, and successive parts are heard in imitation.

**fusion**
A style of music that appeals to more than one type of listener; usually refers to jazz/rock. See *crossover.*

**gospel song**
A song whose lyrics recount passages from scripture.

**guitorgan**
A guitarlike instrument with an organ sound.

**harmonics**
The frequencies that collectively create a single tone; also used to refer to the higher chord tones in an extended chord.

**harmonizer**
An electronic device that creates a parallel melodic line to accompany the original melody.

**harmony**
Simultaneous sounding of two or more tones.

**head voice**
Technique of singing in the high range (not falsetto).

**heterophonic**
A simultaneous performance of two or more musical lines that appear independent of one another in either time or harmony.

**higher harmonics**
See *extended harmony.*

**homophonic**
A single melody, usually in the highest voice part, with harmony in the lower voices acting as an accompaniment.

**horizontal texture**
Polyphonic texture; a simultaneous combination of melodies; the opposite of homophonic texture, which consists of a single melody with harmonic accompaniment.

**hymn**
A congregational song, with words not taken directly from the Bible, sung in praise of God.

**iambic pentameter**
A type of poetry consisting of an unaccented syllable followed by an accented one, with five of these combinations in each line of poetry.

**improvise**
To perform music that is made up (created) at the moment, not performed from memory or from written music; a manner of playing extemporaneously.

**instrumentation**
The different types of instruments making up an ensemble.

**jam session**
An informal gathering of musicians playing on their own time and improvising just for the fun of it.

**key**
A classification given to a particular arrangement of tones in a scale. The first degree of the scale is the tonal center or key name, and the necessary flats or sharps for a particular key form the key signature.

**liturgical**
Pertaining to the rites of a religious service.

**Mass**
The principal service of the Roman Catholic Church. The part that does not vary is called the Ordinary, or Common, of the Mass and consists of the Kyrie, the Gloria, the Credo, the Sanctus with Benedictus, and the Agnus Dei.

**master**
The name of the final recorded product used to make records.

**measure**
See *bar of music.*

**melisma**
A melodic ornamentation; one syllable sung on more than one tone of a song.

**melody**
A succession of single tones varying in pitch and rhythm and having a recognizable musical shape.

**meter**
The division of beats into accented and unaccented groupings of two, three, or more.

**middle register**
The middle part of the complete range of the voice or instrument.

**MIDI**
Musical Instrument Digital Interface. An established electronic standard used to carry musical information between synthesizers and computers.

**Mixolydian mode**
The arrangement of tones found in the scale using only the white keys of the piano from G to G.

**modal jazz**
A jazz style that typically has slow-moving harmonies and older modal scales. The chord relationships are not typical of the major-minor system.

**monophonic**
A single melody with neither accompanying melody nor harmony.

**mordent**
A rapid movement from one tone to an upper or lower scale tone and back again to the principal tone.

**motive** or **motivic**
Short melodic fragments used for developing a solo. Motives are often taken by soloists from the song's melody. Some entire pieces are built on short motives (e.g., *A Love Supreme* by Coltrane).

**multitracking**
The ability to record several different sounds on separate parts (tracks) of the recording tape. See *overdub.*

**Neoclassical jazz**
Jazz of the 1980s and 1990s that follows in the tradition of the bebop style.

**new thing**
An alternate name, used primarily by jazz players, for free jazz.

**ninth chord**
A chord consisting of five different tones, each separated by an interval of a third.

**obligato**
An accompanying or free melody played by a second instrument, less prominent and secondary to the main melody played by the lead instrument.

**offbeat**
Second or fourth beat in 4/4 meter.

**ostinato**
A clear melodic and/or rhythmic figure that is persistently repeated.

**overdub**
To record over existing recorded sound.

**overtone series**
Tones that are related to the first (fundamental) tone sounded. A series of higher tones, or upper partials, which make up a complex musical tone when the first or fundamental is sounded.

**pedal point**
A tone sustained below while harmonies change.

**pentatonic**
A scale consisting of only five tones as represented by the five black keys of the piano.

**phrase**
A small unit of a melody.

**pizzicato**
A manner of playing stringed instruments by plucking rather than by bowing.

**plagal cadence**
A specific chord progression, namely, the IV chord resolving to the I chord, for example, amen chords.

**polymeters**
Simultaneous use of several meters.

**polymodal**
The simultaneous sounding of several different modes.

**polyphonic**
The simultaneous sounding of two or more melodies of equal importance.

**polytonal**
The simultaneous sounding of tones in more than one key.

**portamento**
The movement from one tone to another higher or lower tone without a break in the sound.

**quadrille**
A square dance of five figures that was popular in the nineteenth century.

**raga**
A particular scale in Eastern music.

**real time**
Musical changes or events that are performed live rather than programmed earlier.

**reggae**
A Jamaican style of rhythm and blues.

**repetition**
Presentation of the same musical material in two or more parts of a composition.

**reverberation**
A series of rapid echoes that follow a sound.

**rhythm section**
The section of an instrumental ensemble that provides the most prominent rhythmic feel of the music, usually consisting of drums, piano, bass, and guitar.

**riff**
A short pattern of sounds repeated and played by a soloist or group.

**rim shots**
Produced by striking the edge or rim of the drum and drum head simultaneously.

**rondo**
A musical form in which one section of a composition recurs intermittently with contrasting sections coming between each repetition, for example, ABACADA.

**root tone**
The lowest note or tone of a chord when that chord is in its basic, or root, position.

**round**
A vocal canon for several voices.

**rubato**
A fluctuation in the tempo of the music for the purpose of giving music an additional element of expression.

**salsa**
A combination of jazz and Afro-Cuban rhythms.

**sample**
The individual number that describes the strength of a sound at any given moment. Samples can be taken of an analog sound up to approximately 40,000 times a second.

**sampler**
An electronic device that analyzes a sound and converts the analog voltage into a digital description that can be altered by a computer. The sampled sound then can be played back using a synthesizer keyboard.

**scale**
A precise progression of single tones upward or downward in steps. Chromatic scale: a twelve-tone scale with intervals of a half step. Diatonic scale: an eight-tone scale with a repetition of the eighth degree, pertaining to the major and minor scales. Pentatonic scale: consisting of five tones.

**scat singing**
The use of nonsense syllables while improvising vocally.

**Schoenberg's twelve-tone system**
A technique of composition in which all twelve half steps in an octave are treated as equal. A method used by Schoenberg in the form of a "tone row," in which all the twelve tones are placed in a particular order forming the basis of a musical composition. No tone is repeated within a row. The tone row becomes a "tonal reservoir" from which the composition is drawn.

**sequencer**
An electronic device that stores a musical series of notes to be played back later. Sequencers can be used to build up a performance by storing several musical sequences, one after another.

**sharped tone**
Raises the pitch one half step.

**sideman**
A player in the musical ensemble as differentiated from the leader.

**sonata allegro**
An instrumental composition with three large sections (ABA): exposition, development, and recapitulation.

**soulsa**
A combination of Latin jazz and soul.

**speakeasy**
A nightclub in the 1920s.

**spiritual**
A religious folk song of African Americans, usually of a solo-and-refrain design.

**standard tunes**
Familiar, well-established popular or jazz tunes. Copyright can be renewed for a certain number of years after the death of the composer.

**stock arrangement**
A published commercial arrangement, usually simplified and standardized.

**Storyville**
Red-light district in New Orleans where jazz originated.

**straight ahead**
A term used to describe jazz that falls squarely in the mainstream definition of jazz. This term usually refers to jazz associated with the bebop style.

**string bass**
A bass violin.

**substitute chords**
Chords used in place of the chords originally associated with a song. These chords are often more complex than the original ones.

**symmetrical**
Exhibiting a balance of parts.

**syncopation**
To accent a normally weak beat or weak part of a beat.

**tack piano**
A piano with thumbtacks on the felts of the piano hammers to make it sound older and more authentic for playing ragtime and similar music.

**tag**
A short addition to the end of a musical composition.

**tailgate trombone**
A name deriving from the practice of early trombone players sitting on the tailgate of a wagon so that their slides could operate freely out the rear. The phrase became associated with the trombone part in a Dixieland ensemble.

**tango**
A dance of Spanish-American origin commonly in 4/4 meter.

**tape loop**
A loop of magnetic recording tape used to repeat a sound. The speed of the tape determines how fast the repeats occur.

**tempo**
The speed of the underlying beat. The speed is determined by the number of beats counted over the span of sixty seconds.

**theme and variation**
A musical form in which the theme is introduced and successive repetitions of the theme, changed or altered in some manner, follow.

**third stream music**
A combination of classical music and jazz.

**thirteenth chord**
A chord consisting of seven different tones, each separated by an interval of a third.

**time, making time,** or **straight time**
Often after rhythmically contrasting interludes or a rhythmically complex "head," the rhythm section will fall into a very solid metric feel to launch a solo section. A straight time feel has very few unusual accents.

**time signature**
Sign at the beginning of a composition indicating the grouping of beats for each measure. The meter signature 3/4 means that there are three beats in a measure and that a quarter note gets one beat.

**Tin Pan Alley**
Refers to the industry centered in New York City that published popular music.

**tonal clash**
Tones played simultaneously that produce a discordant or clashing effect.

**tonal sonorities**
The overall effect of the juxtaposition of tonal sounds.

**trading fours**
Two solo instrumentalists alternating in playing four measures each.

**twelve-measure chorus** or **twelve-bar strain**
A composition or a part of a composition consisting of twelve measures.

**twelve-tone system**
A compositional system designed to avoid tonal centers, thereby creating a balanced atonal music.

**unison**
Two or more instruments or voices sounding on the same pitches (tones) or an octave apart.

**up-tempo**
Fast tempo.

**vamp**
A transitional chord or rhythmic progression of indefinite duration used as a filler until the soloist is ready to start or continue.

**verse**
The introductory section of a popular song as distinguished from the chorus. The latter consists commonly of thirty-two bars, while the verse may have an irregular number of bars and may be sung or played in a free tempo.

**vertical texture**
Block chords that accompany a melodic part; opposite of horizontal thinking.

**vibrato**
Refers to the pulsating effect produced by small and rapid variations in pitch. Most jazz uses vibrato for warmth and interpretation in imitation of the human voice.

**vocoder**
An electronic musical device that allows the player to choose the pitch of any syllable sung, and that can blend two sounds at will.

**walking bass**
The bass part that was originally introduced in boogie-woogie in ostinato form. It concisely spells out the notes in the chords being used and is usually played in eighth notes.

**well-tempered scale**
Refers to the tuning system found on a keyboard.

# Bibliography

Albertson, Chris. *Bessie.* New York: Stein & Day Publishers, 1972.

Allan, William Francis, Charles Pickard Ware, and Lucy McKim Garrison. *Slave Songs of the United States.* New York: Peter Smith, 1867.

Allen, Walter C. *Hendersonia: The Music of Fletcher Henderson and His Musicians, Jazz Monograph no. 4.* Highland Park, N.J.: Walter C. Allen, 1973.

Allen, Walter C., and Brian Rust. *King Joe Oliver.* London and New York: Sidgwick and Jackson, 1958.

Apel, Willi. *Harvard Dictionary of Music.* Cambridge, Mass.: Harvard University Press, 1955.

Armstrong, Louis. *Swing That Music.* New York: Longmans, Green & Co., 1936.

———. *My Life in New Orleans.* New York: Prentice-Hall, 1954.

———. *Louis Armstrong: A Self Portrait.* New York: Eakins Press, 1971.

Baird, David. *From Score to Tape.* Boston: Berklee Press Pub., 1973.

Balliett, Whitney. *The Sound of Surprise.* New York: E. P. Dutton & Co., 1959.

———. *Dinosaurs in the Morning.* Philadelphia: J. B. Lippincott Co., 1962.

———. *American Musicians.* New York: Oxford University Press, 1986.

Basie, Count. *Good Morning Blues: The Autobiography of Count Basie, As Told to Albert Murray.* New York: Random House, 1986.

Bechet, Sidney. *Treat It Gentle: An Autobiography.* New York: Hill & Wang, 1960.

Berendt, Joachim. *The New Jazz Book.* Translated by Dan Morgenstern. New York: Hill & Wang, 1962.

———. *Jazz Book: From New Orleans to Rock and Free Jazz.* New York: Lawrence Hill & Co., 1975.

Berger, Morroe, Edward Patrick, and James Patrick. *Benny Carter, A Life in American Music.* Metuchen, N.J.: Scarecrow Press, 1982.

Bernstein, Leonard. *The Joy of Music.* New York: Simon & Schuster, 1959.

Berton, Ralph. *Remembering Bix: A Memoir of the Jazz Age.* New York: Harper & Row, 1974.

Blancq, Charles. *Sonny Rollins, The Journey of a Jazzman.* Boston: G. K. Hall, 1983.

Blesh, Rudi. *Classic Piano Rags.* New York: Dover Publications, 1973.

Blesh, Rudi, and Harriet Janis. *Shining Trumpets—A History of Jazz.* New York: Alfred A. Knopf, 1946.

———. *They All Played Ragtime.* New York: Grove Press, 1959.

Bloom, Eric, ed. *Grove's Dictionary of Music and Musicians.* Nine vols. New York: St. Martin's Press, 1959.

Brask, Ole, and Dan Morgenstern. *Jazz People.* New York: Harry N. Abrams, Inc., 1976.

Brooks, Tilford. *America's Black Musical Heritage.* Englewood Cliffs, N.J.: Prentice-Hall, 1984.

Broonzy, William, and Yannick Bruynogle. *Big Bill Blues.* London: Cassell, 1955.

Brown, Charles T. *The Jazz Experience.* Dubuque, Iowa: Wm. C. Brown, 1989.

Budds, Michael J. *Jazz in the Sixties.* Iowa City, Iowa: University of Iowa Press, 1978.

Buerkle, Jack V., and Danny Barker. *Bourbon Street Black.* London: Oxford University Press, 1973.

Buszin, Walter E., ed. *Anniversary Collection of Bach Chorales.* Chicago: Hall McCreary, 1935.

Calloway, Cab, and Bryant Rollins. *Of Minnie the Moocher and Me.* New York: Crowell, 1976.

Carr, Ian. *Miles Davis.* New York: Williams Morrow, 1982.

Cerulli, Dom, Burt Korall, and Mort Nasatir. *The Jazz World.* New York: Ballantine Books, 1960.

Charles, Ray, and David Ritz. *Brother Ray.* New York: Dial Press, 1978.

Charters, Samuel B. *The Country Blues.* New York: Doubleday & Co., 1958.

———. *Jazz: New Orleans (1855–1963).* New York: Oak Publishers, 1964.

Charters, Samuel B., and Leonard Kunstadt. *Jazz: A History of The New York Scene.* New York: Doubleday & Co., 1962.

Chase, Gilbert. *America's Music from the Pilgrims to the Present.* New York: McGraw Hill Book Co., Inc., 1955.

Chilton, John. *Billie's Blues.* New York: Stein & Day Publishers, 1975.

———. *Who's Who of Jazz.* New York: Da Capo Press, 1985.

Cole, Bill. *John Coltrane.* New York: Schirmer, 1976.

———. *Miles Davis.* New York: William Morris and Co., 1976.

Collier, Graham. *Inside Jazz.* London: Quartet Books, 1973.

Collier, James Lincoln. *The Making of Jazz.* New York: Dell Publishing Co., Inc., 1978.

Coryell, Julie, and Laura Friedman. *Jazz-Rock Fusion.* New York: Delta Books, 1979.

Courlander, Harold. *Miles Davis: A Musical Biography.* New York: William Morrow, 1974.

Dahl, Linda. *Stormy Weather: The Music and Lives of a Century of Jazzwomen.* New York: Pantheon, 1984.

Dale, Rodney. *The World of Jazz.* Cambridge: Basinghall, 1980.

Dance, Stanley. *The World of Duke Ellington.* New York: Charles Scribner's Sons, 1970.

———. *The World of Earl Hines.* New York: Charles Scribner's Sons, 1974.

———. *The World of Swing.* New York: Charles Scribner's Sons, 1975.

———. *The World of Count Basie.* New York: Charles Scribner's Sons, 1980.

Dankworth, Avril. *Jazz: An Introduction to Its Musical Basis.* London: Oxford University Press, 1968.

Davis, Francis. *In the Moment: Jazz in the 1980s.* New York: Oxford University Press, 1986.

Davis, Miles, and Quincy Troupe. *Miles.* New York: Simon and Schuster, 1989.

Davis, Nathan. *Writings in Jazz.* 3rd ed. Scottsdale, Ariz.: Gorsuch Scarisbrick, 1985.

Dexter, Dave. *The Jazz Story: From the Nineties to the Sixties.* Englewood Cliffs, N.J.: Prentice-Hall, 1964.

Dineen, Janice D. *The Performing Women,* 26910 Grand View Ave., Hayward, Calif. 94542.

Drake, Russell, Ronald Herder, and Anne D. Modugno. *How to Make Electronic Music.* Pleasantville, N.Y.: EAV Inc., 1975.

Ellington, Duke. *Music Is My Mistress.* New York: Doubleday & Co., 1973.

Ellington, Mercer, and Stanley Dance. *Duke Ellington in Person: An Intimate Memoir.* New York: Houghton Mifflin, 1975.

Feather, Leonard. *Inside Jazz.* New York: J. J. Robbins & Sons, 1949.

———. *The New Edition of the Encyclopedia of Jazz.* New York: Horizon Press, 1960.

———. *The Book of Jazz: A Guide from Then till Now.* New York: Horizon Press, 1965.

———. *The Encyclopedia of Jazz in the Sixties.* New York: Horizon Press, 1966.

———. *From Satchmo to Miles.* New York: Stein & Day Publishers, 1974.

———. *The Encyclopedia of Jazz in the Seventies.* New York: Horizon Press, 1976.

———. *Pleasures of Jazz.* New York: Horizon Press, 1976.

————. *The Encyclopedia of Jazz.* New York: Da Capo Press, 1984.

————. *The Jazz Years: Earwitness to an Era.* New York: Da Capo Press, 1987.

Finkelstein, Sidney. *Jazz: A People's Music.* New York: Da Capo Press, 1975.

Flower, John. *Moonlight Serenade.* New Rochelle, N.Y.: Arlington House, 1972.

Francis, André. *Jazz.* Translated and revised by Martin Williams. New York: Grove Press, 1960.

Gammond, Peter, ed. *Scott Joplin and the Ragtime Era.* New York: St. Martin's Press, 1975.

————. *Duke Ellington: His Life and Music.* New York: Roy Publishers, 1977.

George, Don. *Sweet Man: The Real Duke Ellington.* New York: G. P. Putnam's Sons, 1981.

Giddons, Gary. *Satchmo.* New York: Doubleday, 1989.

Gillespie, Dizzy, and Al Fraser. *To Be, or Not . . . to Bop.* Garden City, N.Y.: Doubleday & Co., 1979.

Gitler, Ira. *Jazz Masters of the Forties.* New York: Macmillan Co., 1966.

————. *Swing To Bop.* New York: Oxford University Press, 1986.

Gleason, Ralph. *Celebrating the Duke.* New York: Dell Publishers, 1975.

Goddard, Chris. *Jazz Away from Home.* London: Paddington Press, 1979.

Goffin, Robert. *Jazz: From the Congo to the Metropolitan.* New York: Da Capo Press, 1975.

Gold, Robert S. *A Jazz Lexicon.* New York: Knopf, 1964.

Goldberg, Joe. *Jazz Masters of the Fifties.* New York: Macmillan Co., 1965.

Gridley, Mark C. *Jazz Styles.* 3rd ed. Englewood Cliffs, N.J.: Prentice-Hall, 1985.

Hadlock, Richard. *Jazz Masters of the Twenties.* New York: Macmillan Co., 1965.

Handy, W. C. *W. C. Handy: Father of the Blues.* New York: Collier Books, 1970.

Harris, Rex. *Jazz.* Baltimore: Penguin Books, 1956.

Harrison, Max. *Charlie Parker.* New York: A. S. Barnes & Co., 1961.

————. *A Jazz Retrospect.* Boston: Crescendo Publishing Co., 1976.

Haskins, Jim. *Black Music in America.* New York: Thomas Y. Crowell, 1987.

Hentoff, Nat. *Jazz Life.* New York: Da Capo Press, 1975.

————. *Jazz Is.* New York: Random House, 1976.

————. *Boston Boy.* New York: Alfred A. Knopf, 1986.

Hentoff, Nat, and Albert McCarthy. *Jazz: New Perspectives on the History of Jazz.* New York: Da Capo Press, 1975.

————, eds. *Jazz.* New York: Holt, Rinehart & Winston, Inc., 1959.

Hickok, Robert. *Exploring Music.* Dubuque, Iowa: Wm. C. Brown, 1989.

Hodeir, André. *Jazz: Its Evolution and Essence.* Translated by David Noakes. New York: Grove Press, 1956.

————. *Toward Jazz.* New York: Grove Press, 1962.

Holiday, Billie, and William Dufty. *Lady Sings the Blues.* New York: Doubleday & Co., 1965.

James, Michael. *Dizzy Gillespie.* New York: A. S. Barnes & Co., 1959.

Jewell, Derek. *Duke: A Portrait of Duke Ellington.* New York: W. W. Norton & Co., 1977.

Jones, LeRoi. *Blues People.* New York: William Morrow & Co., 1963.

————. *Black Music.* New York: William Morrow & Co., 1965.

Jones, Max. *Salute to Satchmo.* London: Longacre Press, 1970.

Jones, Max, and John Chilton. *Louis: The Louis Armstrong Story.* New York: Little, Brown & Co., 1971.

Jost, Ekkehard. *Free Jazz.* New York: Da Capo Press, 1981.

Kaminsky, Max. *My Life in Jazz.* New York: Harper and Row, 1963.

Kaufman, Frederick, and John P. Guckin. *The African Roots of Jazz.* Sherman Oaks, Calif.: Alfred Publishing Co., 1979.

Keepnews, Orrin, and Bill Grauer, Jr. *A Pictorial History of Jazz.* New York: Crown Publishers, 1955.

Keil, Charles. *Urban Blues.* Chicago: University of Chicago Press, 1966.

Kennington, Donald, and Denny L. Reed. *The Literature of Jazz.* 2nd ed. Chicago: American Library Association, 1980.

Kimball, Bob, and Bill Bolcum. *Reminiscing with Sissle and Blake.* New York: Viking Press, 1973.

Kinkle, Roger D. *The Complete Encyclopedia of Popular Music and Jazz.* New Rochelle, N.Y.: Arlington House, 1974.

Kirkeby, Ed. *Ain't Misbehavin': The Story of Fats Waller.* New York: Da Capo Press, 1975.

Lee, William F. *People in Jazz: Jazz Keyboard Improvisors of the 19th and 20th Centuries.* Hialeah, Fla.: Columbia Pictures Publications, 1984.

Leonard, Neil. *Jazz and the White Americans.* Chicago: University of Chicago Press, 1962.

———. *Jazz: Myth and Religion.* New York: Oxford University Press, 1987.

Levine, Lawrence W. *High Brow/Low Brow.* Cambridge, Mass.: Harvard University Press, 1988.

Litweiler, John. *The Freedom Principle of Jazz after 1958.* New York: William Morrow, 1984.

Lomax, Alan. *Mr. Jelly Roll.* New York: Grosset & Dunlap, Universal Library, 1950.

McCarthy, Albert. *Louis Armstrong.* New York: A. S. Barnes & Co., 1959.

———. *Big Band Jazz.* New York: G. P. Putnam's Sons, 1974.

Marquis, Donald. *In Search of Buddy Bolden: First Man of Jazz.* Baton Rouge, La.: Louisiana State University Press, 1979.

Martin, Henry. *Enjoying Jazz.* New York: Schirmer, 1986.

Martin, John H., and William F. Fritz. *Listening to Jazz.* Fresno, Calif.: University of California Press, 1969.

Meeker, David. *Jazz in the Movies: A Guide to Jazz Musicians, 1917–1977.* New Rochelle, N.Y.: Arlington House, 1978.

Megill, Donald D., and Richard S. Demory. *Introduction to Jazz History.* 2nd ed. Englewood Cliffs, N.J.: Prentice-Hall, 1989.

Mehegan, John. *Jazz Improvisation.* New York: Watson-Guptill Publications, 1959.

Miller, Hugh Milton. *History of Music.* New York: Barnes & Noble Books, 1957.

Mingus, Charles. *Beneath the Underdog.* New York: Alfred A. Knopf, 1971.

Morgenstern, Dan. *Jazz People.* New York: Abrams, 1976.

Muro, Don. *An Introduction to Electronic Music Synthesizers.* Melville, N.Y.: Belwin-Mills Publishing Corp., 1975.

Murray, Albert. *Stompin' the Blues.* New York: McGraw Hill, 1976.

Nanry, Charles. *The Jazz Text.* New York: D. Van Nostrand, 1979.

Ogren, Kathy J. *The Jazz Revolution.* New York: Oxford University Press, 1989.

Oliver, Paul. *The Meaning of the Blues.* New York: Macmillan Co., Collier Books, 1960.

———. *Bessie Smith.* New York: A. S. Barnes & Co., 1961.

———. *The Savannah Syncopators.* New York: Stein & Day Publishers, 1970.

Oliver, Paul, Max Harrison, and William Bolcom. *The New Grove Gospel, Blues and Jazz with Spirituals and Ragtime.* New York: W. W. Norton & Company, 1986.

Ostransky, Leroy. *The Anatomy of Jazz.* Seattle: University of Washington Press, 1960.

———. *Jazz City.* Englewood Cliffs, N.J.: Prentice-Hall, 1975.

———. *Understanding Jazz.* Englewood Cliffs, N.J.: Prentice-Hall, 1977.

Panassie, Hughes. *The Real Jazz.* Translated by Anne Sorrelle Williams. New York: A. S. Barnes & Co., 1960.

———. *Louis Armstrong.* New York: Charles Scribner's Sons, 1971.

Placksin, Sally. *American Women in Jazz.* Wideview Books, 1982.

Pleasants, Henry. *The Great American Popular Singers.* New York: Oxford University Press, 1959.

———. *Serious Music and All That Jazz.* New York: Simon & Schuster, 1969.

Porter, Lewis. *Lester Young.* Boston: Twayne Press, 1985.

Priestley, Brian. *Mingus: A Critical Biography.* New York: Da Capo Press, 1984.

Ramsey, Frederic, Jr., and Charles Edward Smith. *Jazzmen.* New York: Harcourt, Brace, Harvest, 1939.

Reisner, Robert G. *The Jazz Titans.* New York: Doubleday & Co., 1960.

————. *Bird: The Legend of Charlie Parker.* New York: Da Capo Press, 1975.

Roach, Hildred. *Black American Music: Past and Present.* Boston: Crescendo Publishing Co., 1973.

Roberts, John Storm. *Black Music of Two Worlds.* New York: William Morrow and Co., 1974.

Rose, Al. *Eubie Blake.* New York: Schirmer, 1979.

Russell, Ross. *Jazz Styles in Kansas City and the Southwest.* Berkeley: University of California Press, 1971.

————. *Bird Lives: The High Life and Hard Times of Charlie (Yardbird) Parker.* New York: Charterhouse Books, 1973.

Russell, Tony. *Blacks, Whites and the Blues.* New York: Stein & Day Publishers, 1970.

Sales, Grover. *Jazz, America's Classical Music.* Englewood Cliffs, N.J.: Prentice-Hall.

Sanders, Ruby W. *Jazz Ambassador Louis Armstrong.* Chicago: Childrens Press, 1973.

Sargeant, Winthrop. *Jazz, Hot and Hybred.* 3rd ed. New York: Da Capo Press, 1975.

Schafer, William J., et al. *The Art of Ragtime.* Baton Rouge, La.: Louisiana State University Press, 1973.

Schenkel, Steven M. *The Tools of Jazz.* Englewood Cliffs, N.J.: Prentice-Hall, 1983.

Schuller, Gunther. *Early Jazz: Its Roots and Musical Development.* London: Oxford University Press, 1968.

————. *The Swing Era: The Development of Jazz. 1930–1945.* London: Oxford University Press, 1989.

Scott, Allen. *Jazz Educated, Man.* Silver Springs, Md.: Institute of Modern Languages, 1973.

Shapiro, Nat, and Nat Hentoff, eds. *The Jazz Makers.* New York: Grove Press, 1957.

Simon, George T. *The Big Bands.* New York: Macmillan Co., 1967.

————. *Simon Says.* New Rochelle, N.Y.: Arlington House, 1971.

————. *Glenn Miller.* New York: Thomas Y. Crowell Co., 1974.

Simpkins, C. O. *Coltrane: A Biography.* New York: Herndon House, 1975.

Skowronski, Jo Ann. *Women in America: A Bibliography.* Metuchen, N.J., and London: Scarecrow Press, 1978.

Southern, Eileen. *Music of Black Americans.* New York: W. W. Norton & Co., 1971.

Spellman, A. B. *Black Music: Four Lives in the Bebop Business.* New York: Schocken, 1970.

Standifer, James A., and Barbara Reeder. *African and Afro-American Materials for Music Educators.* Washington, D.C.: Music Educators National Conference, 1972.

Starr, S. Frederick. *Red and Hot, the Fate of Jazz in the Soviet Union.* New York and Oxford: Oxford University Press, 1983.

Stearns, Marshall. *The Story of Jazz.* London: Oxford University Press, 1958.

Stewart, Rex. *Jazz Masters of the '30s.* New York: Macmillan Co., 1972.

Stewart-Baxter, Derrick. *Ma Rainey.* New York: Stein & Day Publishers, 1970.

Strange, Allen. *Electronic Music: Systems, Techniques, and Controls.* Dubuque, Iowa: Wm. C. Brown, 1972.

Sudhalter, M. Richard, and Philip R. Evans. *Bix: Man and Legend.* New York: Harper & Row, 1974.

Swenson, John. *The Rolling Stone Jazz Record Guide.* New York: Random House, 1985.

Tallmadge, William. *Afro-American Music.* Washington, D.C.: Music Educators National Conference, 1957.

Tanner, Paul O. W., David W. Megill, and Maurice Gerow. *Jazz.* Dubuque, Iowa: William C. Brown, 1992.

Taylor, Billy. *Jazz Piano: History and Development.* Dubuque, Iowa: Wm. C. Brown, 1982.

Thomas, J. C. *Chasin' the Trane.* New York: Doubleday & Co., 1975.

Tirro, Frank. *Jazz: A History.* New York: W. W. Norton & Co., 1977.

Ulanov, Barry. *Duke Ellington.* New York: Farrar, Strauss & Young, 1946.

————. *Handbook of Jazz.* New York: Viking Press, 1959.

Ulrich, Homer. *Music: A Design for Listening.* 2d ed. New York: Harcourt, Brace, & World, 1962.

Unterbrink, Mary. *Jazz Women at the Keyboard.* Jefferson, N.C.: McFarland, 1983.

Walker, Leo. *The Wonderful Era of the Great Dance Bands.* New York: Doubleday & Co., 1972.

Werner, Otto. *The Origin and Development of Jazz.* Dubuque, Iowa: Kendall/Hunt, 1984.

Williams, Martin T. *King Oliver.* New York: A. S. Barnes & Co., 1960.

————. *Jazz Masters of New Orleans.* New York: Macmillan Co., 1965.

————. *Jazz Masters in Transition (1957–69).* New York: Macmillan Co., 1970.

————. *The Jazz Tradition.* New York: Oxford University Press, 1983.

————. *Jazz Heritage.* New York: Oxford University Press, 1985.

————. ed. *The Art of Jazz.* London: Oxford University Press, 1959.

Wilson, John S. *The Collector's Jazz: Tradition and Swing.* Philadelphia: J. B. Lippincott Co., 1958.

————. *The Collector's Jazz: Modern.* Philadelphia: J. B. Lippincott Co., 1959.

————. *Jazz: The Transition Years, 1940–1960.* New York: Appleton-Century-Crofts, 1966.

# Discography

## Collections

*The Bass.* Impulse Records, 9284 (6 sides).

**Big Bands '80s Record Library**
(by mail only)
9288 Kinglet Drive
Los Angeles, CA 90069

**Big Band Jazz,** Smithsonian Collection of Recordings.

*Capital Jazz Classics.* Capitol Records.
Volume 1 *Miles Davis*
Volume 2 *Stan Kenton*
Volume 3 *Art Tatum*
Volume 4 *Gerry Mulligan*
Volume 5 *Coleman Hawkins*
Volume 6 *Various Artists: All Star Sessions*
Volume 7 *Serge Chaloff*
Volume 8 *Nat King Cole Trio*
Volume 9 *Woody Herman*
Volume 10 *Various Artists: Swing Exercise*

*Collector's History of Classic Jazz.* Murray Hill Records, 927942.

*The Definitive Jazz Scene,* vols. 1, 2, 3. Impulse Records, A 99, A 100, A 9101.

*The Drums.* Impulse Records 9272 (6 sides).

*Encyclopedia of Jazz on Records.* Decca Records, DXSF 7140 (8 sides).

*Folkways Jazz Series.* Folkways Records, FJ 2801–2811.
Volume 1 *The South*
Volume 2 *The Blues*
Volume 3 *New Orleans*
Volume 4 *Jazz Singers*
Volume 5 *Chicago No. 1*
Volume 6 *Chicago No. 2*
Volume 7 *New York (1922–34)*

Volume 8 *Big Bands*
Volume 9 *Piano*
Volume 10 *Boogie-Woogie*
Volume 11 *Addenda*

*Giants of Jazz.* Time/Life Records.

*History of Classic Jazz.* Riverside Records, SDP-11.
Volume 1 *Backgrounds*
Volume 2 *Ragtime*
Volume 3 *The Blues*
Volume 4 *New Orleans Style*
Volume 5 *Boogie-Woogie*
Volume 6 *South Side Chicago*
Volume 7 *Chicago Style*
Volume 8 *Harlem*
Volume 9 *New York Style*
Volume 10 *New Orleans Revival*

*Jazz Odyssey.* Columbia Records, C3L-30, 32, 33.
Volume 1 *The Sound of New Orleans (1917–47)*
Volume 2 *The Sound of Chicago (1923–40)*
Volume 3 *The Sound of Harlem*

*Jazz Piano Anthology.* Columbia Records, PG 32355 (4 sides).

*Jazz: The '60s,* vols. 1 & 2. Pacific Jazz Records, L893-H and L895-H.

*The Jazz Story.* Capitol Records, W2137–41.
Volume 1 *New Orleans*
Volume 2 *North to Chicago*
Volume 3 *The Swinging Years*
Volume 4 *The Big Bands*
Volume 5 *Modern and Free Form*

Miles Davis, *The Columbia Years 1955–1985* Columbia, C4K4500 CK45004.

New World Records (100 albums), suggested album numbers:

204 *Loxodonta Africana: The Jazz Sound of Ricky Ford*
210 *The Jazz of the Seventies*
216 *Mirage: Avant-Garde and Third Stream Jazz*
217 *Jammin' for the Jackpot: Big Bands and Territory Bands of the 30s*
235 *Maple Leaf Rag: Ragtime in Rural America*
240 *Where Have We Met Before? Forgotten Songs from B'way, Hollywood, & Tin Pan Alley*
242 *Nica's Dream: Small Jazz Groups of the 50s and Early 60s*
248 *The Music Goes Round and Around: The Golden Years of Tin Pan Alley 1930–39*
249 *Rock 'N' Roll*
250 *Little Club Jazz: Small Groups in the 30s*
252 *The Roots of the Blues*
256 *Sweet and Low Blues: Big Bands and Territory Bands of the 20s*
259 *Cuttin' the Boogie: Piano Blues and Boogie Woogie, 1926–1941*
261 *Straighten Up and Fly Right: Rhythm and Blues*
269 *Steppin' on the Gas: Rags to Jazz 1913–1927*
271 *Bebop*
274 *Jive at Five: The Style-Makers of Jazz (1920s–1940s)*
275 *Introspection: Neglected Jazz Figures of the 1950s and Early 1960s*
279 *Yes Sir, That's My Baby: The Golden Years of Tin Pan Alley 1920–1929*
284 *Jazz in Revolution: The Big Bands in the 1940s*
295 *When Malindy Sings: Jazz Vocalists 1938–1961*
303 *Cecil Taylor: 3 Phasis*

*The Saxophone.* Impulse Records 9253 (6 sides).
*Singers and Soloists of the Swing Bands.* Smithsonian Collection of Recordings.
*Smithsonian Collection of Classic Jazz* (by mail only).

Smithsonian Institute
Department 0006
Washington, D.C. 20073–0006
*Three Decades of Jazz.* Blue Note Records, LA 158–60.
1939–49
1949–59
1959–69

## Albums

*African Drums.* Folkways Records, FE 4502.
*Anatomy of Improvisation.* Verve Records, 8230.
*Art of Jazz Piano.* Epic Records, 3295.
*The Art Tatum Touch* (Paul Smith). Outstanding Records, vols. 1 and 2, 004 and 007.
*Basic Miles.* Columbia Records, C 32025.
*The Be-Bop Era.* RCA Victor Records, LPV 519.
*Benny Goodman Carnegie Concert.* Columbia Records, OSL 160.
*The Best of Dixieland.* RCA Victor Records, LSP 2982.
*Big Bands' Greatest Hits.* Columbia Records, CG 31212.
*Bix Beiderbecke and the Chicago Cornets.* Milestone Records, M 47019 (4 sides).
*The Blues in Modern Jazz.* Atlantic Records, 1337.
*The Blues Roll On.* Atlantic Records, 1352.
*Boogie-Woogie Rarities.* Milestone Records, MLP 2009.
*Bop Session.* Sonet Records, 692.
*Chicagoans (1928–30).* Decca Records, 79231.
*Chicago Jazz Album.* Decca Records, 8029.
*A Child's Introduction to Jazz.* Wonderland Records, 2435.
*Classic Jazz Piano Styles.* RCA Victor Records, LPV 543.
*Classic Piano Styles.* RCA Victor Records, LPV 546.
*Energy Essentials.* Impulse Records, ASD 9228 (6 sides).
*Fifty Years of Jazz Guitar.* Columbia Records, CG 44566.
*From Spirituals to Swing.* Vanguard Records, VRS 8523/4.
*The Golden Age of Ragtime.* Riverside Records, 12–110.
*The Great Band Era.* RCA Victor Records, RD4-25 (RRIS-5473).

*Great Blues Singers.* Riverside Records, 121.

*The Greatest Jazz Concert in the World.* Pablo Records, 2625704.

*The Greatest Names in Jazz.* Verve Records, PR 2–3.

*Guide to Jazz.* RCA Victor Records, LPM 1393.

*Introspection—Neglected Jazz Figures of the 1950s and Early 1960s.* New World Records NW 275.

*Jazz of the 1920s.* Merry Makers Records, 103.

*The Jazz Makers.* Columbia Records, CL 1036.

*Jazz at Preservation Hall.* Atlantic Records, S-1409, 1410.

*Jazz at the Santa Monica Civic '72.* Pablo Records, 2625701.

*The Jazz Scene.* Verve Records, 8060.

*Jazz Scene I.* Epic Records, LA-1600.

*Jive at Five—The Style-Makers of Jazz 1920s–1940s.* New World Records NW 274.

*Kansas City Jazz.* Decca Records, 8044.

*Mainstream Jazz.* Atlantic Records, 1303/S.

*A Musical History of Jazz.* Grand Awards Records, 33–322.

*Never Before . . . Never Again* (Joe Venuti/ Tony Romero). Dobre Records, DR 1066.

*New Orleans Jazz.* Decca Records, 8283.

*New Orleans: The Living Legends.* Riverside Records, 356–57 (s).

*The New Wave in Jazz.* Impulse Records, A 90.

*New York: Fall 1974* (Anthony Braxton). Arista Records, AL 4032.

*Piano Giants.* Prestige Records, 24052.

*Piano Roll Hall of Fame.* Sounds Records, LP 1202.

*Ragtime Piano Roll.* Riverside Records, 126.

*The Roots of American Music.* Arhoolie Records, 2001–2.

*Saxophone Revolt.* Riverside Records, 284.

*The Soul of Jazz.* Riverside Records, S-5.

*Steppin' on the Gas—Rags to Jazz 1913–1927.* New World Records NW 269.

*The Story of the Blues.* Columbia Records, G 30008.

*Thesaurus of Classic Jazz.* Columbia Records, C4L 18.

*This is Benny Goodman.* RCA Victor Records, VPM 6040.

# Index

Italic page numbers indicate a photograph.

# C

# K

# L